D1353996

The multi-professional handbook of child sexual abuse

Child sexual abuse is a minefield for all concerned – for the abused, the abusers, and the professsionals involved in treatment and care. It is a genuinely multidisciplinary problem, requiring the close co-operation of a wide range of professionals with different skills. Tilman Furniss, a leading figure in the treatment of child sexual abuse, has written a unique, practical handbook, designed for all professionals involved in the treatment and care of sexually abused children and their families. It will enable them to develop knowledge and skills to deal with their particular task, and at the same time help them to understand the effects of their actions on the work of others.

Focusing on child sexual abuse as a syndrome of secrecy and addiction, Furniss shows how practical steps in therapy and management directly influence each other. In the first part of the book he outlines the principle ways and basic concepts used in dealing with child sexual abuse. In the second part he deals with the many practical problems and countless obstacles that arise in day-to-day practice, jeopardising successful multi-professional management and therapy. Cross-referencing between the two parts allows the reader to concentrate on immediate and specific practical problems while never losing sight of the underlying issues involved.

Based on fifteen years innovative practical work by the author, the book will be essential reading for all professionals involved in the initial intervention and management of child sexual abuse: these include lawyers, the police, social workers, paediatricians and health visitors. It is equally intended for psychiatrists, psychologists, counsellors and therapists involved in the treatment of sexually abused children and their families, and for whom it will be of immense practical value.

The multi-professional handbook of child sexual abuse

Integrated management, therapy, and legal intervention

Tilman Furniss

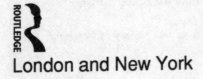

London and New York

First published 1991
by Routledge
11 New Fetter Lane, London EC4P 4EE

Simultaneously published in the USA and Canada
by Routledge
29 West 35th Street, New York, NY 10001

Reprinted 1992 (twice) and 1995

© 1991 Tilman Furniss

Typeset in Times by
LaserScript Limited, Mitcham, Surrey
Printed and bound in Great Britain by
Mackays of Chatham PLC, Chatham, Kent

British Library Cataloguing in Publication Data
A catalogue record for this book is available from the British Library

Library of Congress Cataloguing in Publication Data
A catalogue record for this book is available from the Library of Congress

ISBN 0-415-02832-9 (hbk)
ISBN 0-415-05563-6 (pbk)

To my parents

Contents

Figures

Preface

This book brings together the child abuse work I have done in Berlin, Amsterdam and London over the last 15 years. I saw my first sexually abused patient when I was working in paediatrics under Arend Koers in the Dutch confidential doctor system against child abuse and neglect. We were treating physically abused children and their parents. Child sexual abuse did not seem to exist and we did not look for it. It came to us first through the adults. A change in readiness to listen and to hear must have happened to the staff on the paediatric ward so that suddenly several young mothers who had brought their battered babies began to talk about their own long and often severe experience of child sexual abuse.

My work with child sexual abuse therefore began with the parent generation and I owe much of what I have learned about child sexual abuse to the trust of these young mothers, some of whom were still nearly children themselves. Their response to some changes in attitude on the ward, which had helped them to trust to disclose, and my own very personal response to their disclosure of sexual abuse taught me that dealing with child sexual abuse begins first and foremost with the professionals and with our very own personal attitude as people ourselves. I have learned that the crisis intervention in child sexual abuse begins with the crisis of the professionals.

Surviving child sexual abuse as an intact person may be as difficult for the professional as it is for the child and the family members. Just think how you would react if I were to meet you for the first time and ask you after two minutes 'Tell me all about the last sexual contact you had.' How would you take that? How would you feel about speaking to a stranger about your very intimate sex life? Would you have the language to talk about it in an open, but at the same time dignified, way? Only too often do we just talk about 'it'. Working with sexually abused children we soon understood the interactional nature of motivation between professionals and clients. We can either allow our clients and patients to come out with their experience of child sexual abuse or we can through subtle interactional communication stop them from doing so. (See The Interactional Nature of Motivation, Chapter 2.4.1.)

Thinking back of my own first case, how could I, as a man during a counselling session of a beautiful 18-year old mother who had been abused by her father for 10 years, get sexually aroused myself? Feeling confused, ashamed, in panic and an unbelievable male chauvinist pig I rushed to Arend Koers, my consultant and mentor in Amsterdam for supervision and survival. I will never forget his laughing response, which in its humour taught me all: 'Well done Tilman, that you got your erection. That is what Jane is doing to you. You got the message, that is fine. Just don't do it. When Jane was small and wanted cuddles from her father, she got sex. Now she brings sex to you but what she wants from you are cuddles.' The acceptance of my very own personal reaction and my supervisor's support helped me to regain my personal self-respect and my professional attitude. It allowed me to retain my openness to talk as a professional and as a man to Jane about her own experience of child sexual abuse. I was able to go back to her and was taught by her and soon by other mothers about the confusion between sexual abuse and emotional care.

I now have this little switch inside me when I deal with child sexual abuse. Whenever the message 'sex' comes in, the switch turns it round and the message 'cuddle' goes out. But personally and professionally we all have to dare to let the message 'sex' arrive first whatever it does to each of us. 'Cuddle' in child sexual abuse means cuddle with words and with behaviour, not physical cuddle, which can easily be experienced as renewed child sexual abuse. 'Cuddle' means emotional care. That was what Jane wanted but what I was only able to give after having dealt with my own personal panic and my own personal reaction to the sexual nature of child sexual abuse myself.

The process of discovery of different forms of child sexual abuse took a typical path. First we saw mothers, then adolescent daughters, then small children between 2 and 5 years. It was then that we also saw boys. In the last step we learned to listen to abusers and not only to condemn them. We began to understand the physical, emotional and sexual abuse of many sexual abusers.

After we had survived our own personal panic about child sexual abuse we needed to develop knowledge and skills to deal with it. It was to help me survive the complex, confusing and often overwhelming messages and the seemingly contradictory requirements for action which led to the development of the principle concepts in this book. These concepts formed the basis of my work in Amsterdam before I brought them over to London when I began to work at the Hospital for Sick Children, Great Ormond Street. Working with Arnon Bentovim, Marianne Tranter, Liza Bingley-Miller and Danya Glaser changed child sexual abuse from a previously never seen psycho-social diagnosis in the hospital to a daily clinical occurrence. Although the overwhelming complexity between legal and therapeutic problems seems to make the work at times depressing and hopeless, helping sexually abused children and their families has also been tremendously rewarding when the abuse has been the background for long and undiagnosed physical, psychosomatic and psychological suffering of children whom we did not understand before and whom we were unable to help. Our ignorance had often led to previously repeated treatment failure until we began to learn to read the signs.

This book is based on material from previously published papers, on unpublished papers given at different clinical and scientific meetings and conferences over recent years and on my current clinical work. A major part of the chapter on children's groups is based on the paper written in co-authorship with Liza Bingley-Miller and Annemarie Van Elburg in the *British Journal of Psychiatry*. My gratitude and my thanks belong to Arend Koers and Arnon Bentovim, first as my mentors and now as colleagues. They have enabled me to develop this work which has become the basis for many treatment projects in the UK and elsewhere. I also want to thank Marianne Tranter and Liza Bingley-Miller as colleagues who dared to join the work in London right from the beginning, both enduring the tremendous stress from the families and the professional network but also sharing the reward from the children. Finally I want to thank Liza, her husband Peter and little Sam as dear friends for the two months I was allowed to spend with them to write essential parts of this book.

Introduction

How to use this book

Child sexual abuse is as much a normative and political as a clinical issue. It has important sociological and anthropological aspects. As an issue of sex it is a sexist issue and a battleground for strong opinions. For practitioners, who have to deal with the aftermath, child sexual abuse is a nightmare, a minefield of complexity and confusion, personally and professionally, a threat to traditional professional roles, a challenge to traditional structures of co-operation and a constant danger zone for professional burn-out. This book is written for practitioners of all the different professions, from police to therapists, involved in daily practical work with sexually abused children.

Working with sexually abused children and their families is basically complicated by four factors. As a genuine and generic multi-disciplinary problem it requires the close co-operation of a wide range of different professionals with different tasks. As a legal and a therapeutic problem it requires from all professionals involved the knowledge of the criminal and child protective aspects, as well as the psychological aspects. It involves children as structurally dependent human beings who are persons in their own right, but who cannot exercise this right themselves and need protection and parental care. The specific nature of child sexual abuse as interlocking syndrome of secrecy for the child, the abuser and the family and as a sydrome of addiction for the abuser complicates both legal and child protective intervention, as well as therapy itself.

The disclosure of child sexual abuse leads to an immediate crisis in the families and in professional networks alike. An integrated family approach therefore needs to pay as much attention to processes in the professional network as to events in the family. In child sexual abuse as syndrome of secrecy only the very naming of the abuse creates the abuse as fact for the family. This often seems reflected in the professional network and in our own professional panic and crisis when we intervene blindly in a process we often do not understand. In a metasystemic family approach to intrafamiliar and extrafamiliar child sexual abuse the legal and linear effects of child sexual abuse as crime and the need for child protection need to be integrated with the circular psychological and relationship aspects of sexually abused children and their families.

Professionals on all sides need to learn that the context in which a certain specific professional act is performed can be as important, or even more important, in determining the overall outcome than the act itself. Notions of 'anti-therapeutic therapy', 'crime-promoting crime prevention' and 'abuse-promoting child protection' stress the need for professionals not only to understand what they themselves are doing but also what affects the action of one professional has on the work of other professionals and on the general direction of the complex overall intervention. Therapists and child mental health professionals must know as much about child protective aspects of child sexual abuse in order to remain therapeutic as policemen need to understand about the psychological effects of interviewing on sexually abused children if they want to perform their legal task. Professionals of all agencies need to recognise how their own task and action influence the task of fellow professionals and how in turn their own task is affected by the process in other parts of the professional network. Concepts of 'non-therapeutic therapy' and 'therapeutic non-therapy' illustrate the need for thinking in wider contexts. Dealing with child sexual abuse requires a re-examination of legal procedures, rapidly advances the areas of forensic child psychiatry, poses hitherto unknown problems of protection for child protective agencies, promotes and advances aspects of professionalisation in foster care and challenges therapists of all orientation and persuasion, to reconsider their tasks and to develop their techniques and approaches. In addition new professionals who had only marginal roles in physical abuse such as teachers and youth workers become central to the task and need to be fully integrated into the professional network.

This book is divided into two parts. The first part outlines the principle ways of conceptualisation and illustrates the basic approaches in dealing with sexually abused children and their families. This part of the book has been kept as brief as possible because it may make difficult and somewhat dry reading. More than 10 years of experience of working with child sexual abuse, however, has taught me that without exception all professionals involved need to know about the principle ways and basic concepts in dealing with child sexual abuse in order to fulfil successfully their own specific professional task as well as helping co-professionals of other agencies to be able to take their part and share in the overall responsibility of the intervention. Some of the conceptual notions may at first seem academic, but all without exception are described here because of their fundamental practical relevance. They should help to clarify areas of common and often disastrous confusions in professionals of all backgrounds.

The second part deals with some of the numerous practical problems which always ensure that the intervention never works as it should according to the clever theory of the first part. The second part addresses some of the countless obstacles for helping sexually abused children and their families which makes me jubilant if I do not get 9 out of 10 but only 8 out of 10 cases wrong.

To understand the complexity of the interlocking processes in child sexual abuse can often be tiring and offputting, especially to practitioners who just need assistance in an urgent specific practical problem. Readers who got into this book for this reason can turn to the second part first, beginning initially with the specific practical problem. The danger of inflicting secondary damage on sexually abused children and their families will however require the reader to turn back to the first part before acting. The reason for this lies in the fact that the task in child sexual abuse is larger than the task, the responsibility and the professional skill of any separate individual professional involved. This requires putting specific professional action into the wider overall context of child sexual abuse as a genuine, multi-professional and metasystemic problem. The danger of inflicting considerable secondary damage on the child leaves us with the responsibility to ask ourselves the following three questions at any stage of our intervention. What do I want to achieve? What am I doing to achieve it? What do I think I am achieving in the wider context of the wider multi-professional intervention when I act in a specific way in the context of my own narrow professional responsibility? We therefore need some ideas of how we can act in specific situations, but we also need to understand our own actions in the wider context of what other people do, both in the family and in the professional network. The first part of the book shows the way and the second part helps us to understand why it never works as it should and why we hardly ever get there.

In reading both parts of the book practitioners will quickly realise that it fails in both areas and on both accounts. It will soon become obvious that the conceptual part is much too crude and general and that the clinical part is lacking in completeness, specificity and differentiation, leaving out a huge number of conceptual issues and practical situations with which we are confronted in each new case. As well as giving some limited guidance, this book should therefore primarily assist colleagues of all different professions involved in work with child sexual abuse to develop these concepts further and to advance new clinical practice in the context of a multi-professional treatment approach.

For practical purposes cross-references are made within the book to link the 'principle ways' and 'practical problems' which should enable the reader to start at his or her own particular point of professional interest. Individual effects of child sexual abuse and the family pattern are described first in order to set the framework for the outline of the structure and organisation of the professional network and the interprofessional process in the intervention. Alternatively, the book could have described the professional process first in order to emphasise the influence the professional network has on the individual and the family.

'I see you have a rotten time, sit down and have a cigarette' was Henry Kempe's attitude to physically abusing parents in the 1960s, revolutionary at the time in the depths of the profound understanding that physically abused children and their abusing parents form an interlocking unit. We obviously need to learn more about sexually abused children, but we also need a similar revolution of our attitude and understanding towards the sexual abuser. The specific family process in child sexual abuse will only change in response to a basic shift in our understanding and in our approach to sexual abusers. This points at the interactional nature of motivation which influences sexual abusers to disclose and to find help or to keep the secret and to continue abusing. Over the last 10 years we have learnt something from the sexually abused child as the victim. We now need to learn from the sexual abuser, an even more emotionally difficult task.

At present the half-blind are talking to the blind. One of the major causes of secondary damage to sexually abused children and of burn-out of professionals is the immense pressure on professionals and the feeling that we have to pretend we can see fully and that we know well how to act. But none of us does yet. Learning to understand and to deal with child sexual abuse takes time. Children as structurally dependent people need parents and families. This book therefore describes a metasystemic family approach to dealing with intrafamilial and extrafamilial child sexual abuse. A metasystemic family approach is not a family therapy approach and must not be confused with it. As integrated treatment approach a family approach conceptualises interventions always in family terms, even in extrafamilial child sexual abuse. This is based on the fact that children need carers. The use of the term 'mother' or 'father' in this book does not therefore refer to any biological concept but stands for any female or male adult who is *in loco parentis* to the child. In terms of abusers that may include male friends, stepfathers, cohabitees, grandfathers, uncles and much older brothers. Similarily I do not refer to a specific legal status when I talk about 'husband' and 'wife'. These terms stand for any male and female partner who may or may not live together under one roof.

Part one

Principle ways

Chapter one

From mad to bad: multi-professional and metasystemic starting point

1.1 Legal abuse and psychological damage

The increasing awareness of child sexual abuse amongst professionals has its origin in two related but very different sources. The first is the growing children's rights movement which in the historic context of the human rights movement is following the women's rights movement. The second source is the increasing knowledge and concern about child health and child mental health. Child sexual abuse needs to be seen both as a children's-rights issue and as a health and mental health problem (Beezley Mrazek, 1981b). Child protective agencies and legal professionals intervene from a normative perspective to protect children from abuse and to punish perpetrators for the crime, whereas mental health workers set up treatment programmes to deal with the psychological sequelae of child sexual abuse. The reasons for intervening may therefore be purely legal or it may be purely therapeutic or a mixture of both, in which case it is absolutely essential to distinguish between the two aspects and clarify the relationship between them.

Traditionally, legal and normative interventions are regarded as being incompatible with therapeutic approaches. The seemingly irreconcilable principles and aims of legal and therapeutic approaches is reflected in a split between the professionals of these two domains. On the one hand we find qualified and competent professionals working in the legal field and in child protective services, who from a legal point of view are highly skilled in dealing with criminal issues and child protective aspects of child sexual abuse. At the same time these professionals are often unable to identify the psychological problems in child sexual abuse as an interlocking sydrome of secrecy and addiction. They are unable to use the therapeutic potential of the individual and family crisis they create when they intervene on the legal level. This does not only mean missing an opportunity of great therapeutic potential. The lack of psychological knowledge in the legal intervention itself may even defeat its own purpose resulting in 'crime-promoting crime prevention' or 'abuse-promoting child protection'. The legal intervention may therefore not only fail in its own aim but may inflict additional secondary psychological damage on the child. (See The interprofessional process in context, 5.2.)

On the other hand we find highly skilled therapists who deal with psychological damage to children and with dysfunctional family relationships. Mental health professionals, however, often do not know how to deal with normative aspects and with the linear and legal tasks of child protection and further crime prevention. Individual and family therapists are often negligent if not dismissive of legal and linear aspects. They positively refuse to treat patients and families when the law is involved because they see any legal involvement as incompatible with a therapeutic stance. If they get involved at all, they do not know how to deal therapeutically with the legal aspects. Usually they try to ignore the legal process.

The result of this dichotomy is that the two sides do not meet, do not understand each other and fail to co-operate. Therapists feel that police and judges 'put the boot in' whereas police and child protective services may regard therapists as 'softies who destroy evidence and fail to protect'. Where legal requirements force therapists to co-operate with statutory agencies this tends to be kept to a formal minimum and is not used to foster an integrated understanding of the overall process.

When professionals get involved in child sexual abuse normative and mental health aspects need to be integrated and differentiated in an overall approach in which therapists may have to rely on the support of legal agencies for their own therapy as much as legal professionals may need to understand the psychological dimension of child sexual abuse as syndrome of secrecy and addiction in order to do their own professional work. Both sides need to change their way of working and both sides need to give up cherished and basic notions of professional independence.

1.1.1 Legal aspects and linearity

On the legal level child sexual abuse is defined by implicit or explicit normative statements within the context of specific cultural, social and legal systems. Normative definitions relate to acceptable or unacceptable child rearing practices and to the position of children in different societies. They describe the norms, limits and boundaries of appropriate and acceptable behaviour of adults towards children. Schechter and Roberge (1976: 129) have given one of the best known and most helpful normative definitions: 'The sexual exploitation of children refers to the involvement of dependent developmentally immature children and adolescents in sexual activities that they do not fully comprehend, are unable to give informed consent to and that violates the social taboos of family roles.' I would add to this 'and which aim at the gratification of sexual demands and wishes of the abuser' in order to include the crucial intentional element of the abuser to abuse. This normative definition highlights the notion of structural dependence of children and the inability to give informed consent to sexual relationships. It points to children's right to grow up without sexual interference by adults for their own satisfaction. Underlying most normative definitions is the notion that sexual relationships between adults and children constitute child abuse because sexual relationships should only be formed with free will and out of free choice without coercion. In addition both sexual partners need to be able to give full and informed consent to any sexual act in which they get involved.

In differentiating between human rights aspects and mental health issues in child sexual abuse we cannot and must not make the equation that all sexually abused children are automatically psychiatrically disturbed, although all may be confused to some degree by the experience (Baker, 1983) (See Therapy and protection work, 7.2.2). We need to be extremely careful when we interpret figures of incidents and prevalance of child sexual abuse. When Russell (1983), in a study of sexual abuse in San Francisco, describes 38 per cent of women as being sexually abused at least once by the age of 18 then we have to be aware that this figure is formed on the basis of a normative and not a mental health definition. We therefore cannot draw the conclusion that 38 per cent of women in San Francisco are psychiatrically disturbed by their experience of child sexual abuse. But it also means that regardless of how many of the 38 per cent of women are psychologically damaged, the abuse is in normative terms still abuse and should not happen. We need to be very careful not to confuse the two different elements, judging the severity of the violation of legal norms through the outcome of physical or psychological damage. This would mean saying that sexual abuse is only abuse when we find psychological damage, as if bank robbery were only a crime when the bank manager gets a nervous breakdown. Conversely, it is quite inappropriate to use the fact that child sexual abuse in normative terms is so widespread to argue the case that we should not worry about the health or mental health effects of child sexual abuse because the experience is numerically nearly 'normal'.

The mental health and the legal arguments are related but they have nevertheless quite separate roots. The confusion in child sexual abuse between legal and health definitions arises from the difference in the social attitude in our society towards physical and sexual violation of children's integrity. In physical abuse 'a little bit of physical violence' is regarded as acceptable and only severe forms of physical punishment or violence are identified as abuse. The normative definition of physical abuse is therefore much more equated with an unacceptable degree of physical force or violence rather than with its presence in principle.

In contrast any sexual violation of the child's integrity is labelled as abuse and the normative definition is much narrower for sexual abuse than for physical abuse. While no parent will be taken to court and no child put into care when parents smack the child's bottom, a father may well end up in prison and the child may be taken into care for any slight rubbing of the child's genitals. Whereas 'a bit of violence' is acceptable, 'a bit of sex' is not. This relates to the fact that socially it is less tolerable to display open sexual behaviour than to act with physical violence. However the more narrow normative definition of child sexual abuse also has a rationale in terms of intervention. The specific problems in dealing with child sexual abuse as an interlocking syndrome of secrecy and addiction makes control, protective intervention and therapy much more difficult and complex than with physical abuse. (See The individual process, Chapter 2.)

The current legal and child protective problems in child sexual abuse are compounded by the fact that in the developing children's rights movement the child is increasingly becoming a subject before the law in his or her own right. The structural dependence of children as a result of the lack of biological maturation prevents children from exercising their right fully to take their position as independent subjects before the law, which at present is mainly geared to the provision of justice towards adults who are able to take full independent personal responsibility for their actions. The incompatible legal position of the child as a subject before the law without being able fully to realise this role is increasingly leading to changes in legal procedures which have to take the structural dependence of children into account.

The biological lack of maturation on emotional, social and cognitive levels results in a different quality of children's communications and their way of behaving, relating and thinking. Up to now the qualitative difference between adult and child communication is in the legal system taken as merely a quantitative difference, with the result that in cases of conflict 'children lie and adults speak the truth'. This basic and fundamental legal concept has to my knowledge never been proven by legal professionals. I as clinician do not see that the concept that adults speak the truth and children lie can be supported by any evidence. The existence of this precarious basic legal concept relies on the inappropriate reduction of the qualitative difference in the child's communication into a lesser quantitative version of mature adult communication. To refuse to acknowledge the different quality of children's communication would be like saying that a blind person cannot swear an oath because he or she cannot read a normal Bible.

Primary legal and child protective interventions in child sexual abuse are not related to psychological damage in the child. The legal process and the child protective intervention therefore proceed whether the child is psychologically affected by the abuse or not. Secondary psychological damage may then be easily inflicted in legal or child protective interventions because developmental psychological concepts are not genuinely part of the legal domain and are only taken into account by courts and other legal agencies as far as legal procedures admit.

1.1.2 Mental health and circularity

The second group of professionals which got involved in child sexual abuse are workers in the field of child health and child mental health. These professionals are not primarily interested in the notion of the child as a legal subject or in issues of children's rights. Health and mental health professionals try to identify and to deal with factors which lead to physical and psychological damage of the child.

Mental health definitions of child sexual abuse address themselves to psychological aspects and to developmental factors in the psycho-sexual development of the child. Anna Freud directs her definition of child sexual abuse to the description of factors in the child's psycho-social and psycho-sexual development which effect normal processes of maturation. She states that in child sexual abuse the child 'cannot avoid being physically aroused and this experience disastrously disrupts the normal sequence in his sex organisation. He is forced into premature phallic or genital development while legitimate developmental needs and accompanying mental expressions are by-passed and short-circuited' (Anna Freud, 1981, pp. 33–4). This quotation is part of a longer description. It is not important whether we agree with the content of this mental health definition or the content of the previous normative definition. The important practical difference is that normative definitions as part of the social, cultural and political domain can be defined unconditionally according to opinions and beliefs. Normative definitions can therefore change freely and rapidly through cultural and political changes which are represented in the law. Health and mental health definitions are part of the scientific domain which requires proof through physical and mental health examination. Mental health definitions must be operationalised and have to be supported by data.

Valid and reliable data are still very scarce in child sexual abuse. The work of others and ourselves, however, allows in a very careful and very preliminary conclusion, to state that psychological damage in child sexual abuse may be positively related to the following seven factors (Finkelhor, 1979, 1980; Baker, 1983; Baker and Duncan, 1985; Oppenheimer et al., 1985; Furniss, 1988):

1 The age at onset of the abuse.
2 The duration of the abuse.
3 The degree of violence or threat of violence.
4 The age difference between abuser and the abused child.
5 How closely abuser and child are related.
6 The absence of protective parental figures.
7 The degree of secrecy.

1.1.3 The interlocking process

We need to link the legal and the health and mental health domain. In a legal context the abused child may be removed from parents because a law has been broken and the child has the legal right to be protected from further abuse. In terms of mental health, however, this legal protection may be an extemely bad service to the child when the abuse in itself does not lead to significant psychological or developmental damage, while the lawful removal of the child and possible family breakdown as a consequence of the legal process precipitates secondary psychological trauma and psychiatric disturbance in the child. Conversely, in the early years I myself have been involved in preventing child protective services from intervening. I tried to resolve the therapeutic and child protective problem in child sexual abuse purely by traditional forms of individual therapy and family therapy. The metasystemic analysis of this therapy revealed that I as therapist had become part of the family's system of secrecy. Therapy became 'anti-therapeutic therapy' with the effect that the child remained unprotected. The abuse continued under increased threat to the child and under decreased risk of disclosure to the abuser and was worse and more damaging than before.

1.2 Responsibility, participation, guilt, power and blame

It has been most useful to examine the different concepts of responsibility, participation, guilt, power and blame in a metasystemic framework of linearity and circularity in order to help distinguish between child protective, legal and therapeutic aspects of child sexual abuse. A linear relationship is a relationship which is not open to any form of redefinition through any reinterpretation or punctuation of the interaction. Circularity defines interactional aspects of interpersonal relationships which can be equally attributed to both partners according to the context (Selvini-Palazzoli et al., 1978). The distinction between the linear and legal concept of responsibility and the circular and psychological concept of participation, and the legal and psychological aspects of the concept of guilt, are of great practical and therapeutic importance in child sexual abuse.

1.2.1 Structural dependence and responsibility

Biological factors of maturation determine the degree of structural dependence of children on parenting figures starting from total dependence in babyhood and leading to independence and full individual responsibility of adults. In terms of normal childhood development, the child ceases to be a child the moment his physical, cognitive, emotional and social development has reached the stage which allows the child to make independent decisions, take full responsibility for all activities and potentially care for himself, and support himself independently. The legal inequality between parents and children, in which parents are always, and children never, legally responsible for what happens within the interaction between them is based on the biological immaturity of children. Childhood can therefore in simple, but in operationally clear, terms be defined as 'structural dependence on an adult for physical, emotional, cognitive and social care and protection due to the lack of biological maturation'. Structural dependence of children means that children must be able to trust that whatever a parent does is on the whole good for the child and furthering the child's development.

1.2.2 Participation

Active participation in sexual abuse constitutes the circular and relationship element. The distinction between the legal concept of responsibility and the psychological concept of participation is often confused. The contention that all children are actively involved in the abuse is then wrongly attacked as implying that the child is in any way responsible for the abuse.

We need to distinguish between two forms of active participation. The vast majority of sexually abused children do not take any active role in initiating the sexual abuse, but all children are active participants in the abusive interaction even if forced against their will. It is important to understand that also a passive and non-initiating role of a victim in the parent–child interaction of child sexual abuse constitutes an activity of participation which is the basis for the child's experience of the abuse.

Just as the seeming non-communication of two people in a room is still a form of communication, so does passivity in the role of a victim still constitute, on the interactional level, active participation. This must not be confused with initiative or responsibility. For example, one sexually abused girl reported how her father used to order her to come over to his car workshop to bring him tea. She knew exactly what this really meant and that she would be sexually abused when she arrived at the workshop. She felt confused and did not want to go, but she still went every time and complied with the father's demand. Although no actual violence took place this child had no choice and was forced by threats into compliance. As a forced participant this girl was an active interactional partner in the abuse which took place over many years and constituted the most important and intensive, though also damaging, relationship experience in her life (see Child sexual abuse as syndrome of secrecy, 2.1).

The interactional aspect of participation relates to the psychological concept of feelings as evaluation of experience. They form the basis for psychological experience and account for the psychological fact that children *may feel responsible* for the abuse itself, although they can in fact *never be responsible*.

1.2.3 Guilt

Guilt contains a double concept with a legal and a psychological component. It reflects the combination of linear and circular elements in child sexual abuse (see Figure 1.1). The linear aspect of *being guilty* is directly related to the abuser's legal responsibility as parenting figure as a result of the structural dependence of the child on the abuse. When this responsibility is violated the parent can be found guilty by courts or statutory agencies. The psychological aspect of *feeling guilty* is linked to the relationship aspect of participation and results from the fact that the abuser and the child are in interactional terms equally involved in the abuse. The distinction between the legal and psychological aspects of guilt means that only the parent can be *found guilty*. But the abuser and the child can *feel equally guilty* as an expression of psychological events which are derived from the experience in the abusive interaction.

The child's experience as participant in the abuse explains how children who have suffered long-term abuse often express strong guilt feelings regardless of the degree of co-operation and willingness to participate in the abuse. The child's sense of guilt originates from her mistaken sense of responsibility which she derives from the fact that she has been a participant in the abuse. This confusion is often reinforced by threats of the abuser that the child will be held responsible for the consequences if she discloses the abuse. The persistent psychological experience of participation and guilt also accounts for the low self-esteem and later victim behaviour of adults who have been sexually abused as children.

1.2.4 Power

Political, sociological, interactional, psychological and physical concepts of power have often been confused in the discussion of child sexual abuse with the result that the use of the term is often really meaningless. The crucial distinction between actual and structural power is rarely made. Over-simplification and sometimes inflammatory statements about concepts of power are not helpful when dealing with clinical issues of child sexual abuse. This does not mean that the concept of power could not be used or that power issues are not involved. It does mean that the concept has to be clearly defined.

In child sexual abuse, power issues are involved on a structual and an interactional level. In our clinical work with sexually abused children and their families we can substitute the structural aspect of power through the concept of responsibility, disregarding the issue of power on the interactional level altogether. I want to illustrate this with an example from physical abuse: Who is more powerful, a four-week-old baby who screams continuously for several hours or her 20-year-old mother who tries in vain to calm the baby down, with the baby crying the more, the more the mother tries to help?

On the structural level the concept of power could be applied but does not quite fit because it is unclear what the word 'power' means within this context. It could refer to the difference in muscle power, in reasoning power, in emotional power and in social or legal power between the mother and the baby. All these different forms of 'power' do in fact refer to greater abilities the mother has due to maturation and advanced psycho-social development which has made it possible for her to assume a parental position towards the child. The greater abilities on all levels form the material basis for the fact of structural res-ponsibility of the mother towards the baby due to which we expect her to protect the child and to further his development.

On the interactional level the simplified concept of power is meaningless. Both the baby and the mother are equal participants in the interaction. The mother may feel as powerless and helpless to stop the screaming as the baby and she may get increasingly unhappy and desperate herself. The example shows that the concept of power does not make sense on the interactional relationship level. The mother's greater 'power' on the structural level, however, means that in contrast to the baby the mother has the structural ability to leave the vicious circle of events in which the child and she have become interlocked. She can leave the

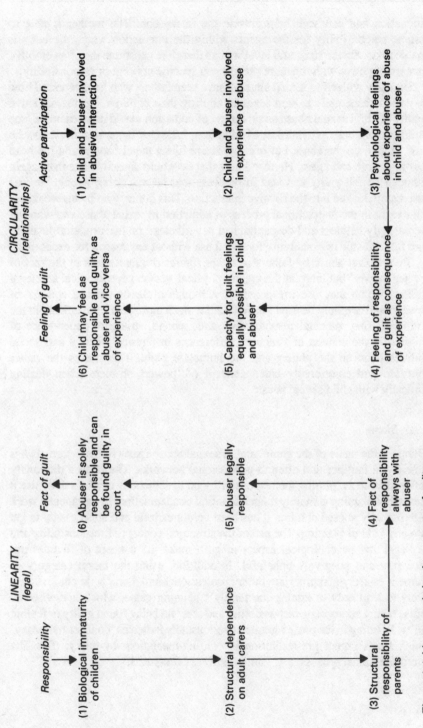

Figure 1.1 Linear and circular aspects of guilt

interaction and can seek help outside the interaction. The mother is able to assume responsibility for the events within the interaction which the baby is unable to do. On the structural level we can therefore substitute the often emotive concept of power with the more precise and specific concept of responsibility.

Similarly with child sexual abuse. I have seen fathers who have reported how they tried desperately to stop sexually abusing their children, but the addictive quality of child sexual abuse as syndrome of addiction would drive them on (see Child sexual abuse as syndrome of addiction, 2.2). One father described how he tried to give up the abuse but felt a pressure like a metal band round his head returning time and again. He then knew that he would abuse his daughter again although he felt guilty and was fully aware that he was doing wrong. He was desperately locked into the abusive interaction. This father, who by his weakness felt caught in the interactional process of addiction in sexual abuse and who felt increasingly helpless and desperate, had nevertheless, on the structural level, to take full and sole responsibility for the abuse without any reason for excuse.

Child sexual abuse by fathers or father figures originates less in the fact of greater 'power' but more in the greater physical, social, psychological and legal abilities which they use irresponsibly. Although a clearly defined concept of power could certainly be used I have found it much more helpful to talk about the notion of, first, parental responsibility and, second, structural dependence of children in the context of structural differences in physical, mental and social abilities between the abuser and the immature child. This makes the rather confused and emotionally laden concept of 'power' obsolete when dealing clinically with child sexual abuse.

1.2.5 Blame

'Blame is the name of the game' and in sexual abuse issues of blame are always close by in families and often in professional networks. The Oxford dictionary defines blame as 'putting the responsibility on to somebody else'. In daily use it seems that blaming is mainly related to moral condemnation. In therapeutic work with sexually abused children it has been very unhelpful and unnecessary to get into any kind of blaming. The use of the structural concept of responsibility and the legal and psychological aspect of guilt make the concept of 'blame' un-necessary and positively unhelpful. In addition, using the moral category of blame is entirely inappropriate in any professional and therapeutic context. It is likely to lead only to joining the family's blaming game, which is devised to refuse taking appropriate responsibility and to avoid being found guilty or feeling guilty. Blaming in the professional network usually indicates 'conflict-by-proxy' which needs urgent pre-resolution in conflict-resolutions-by-proxy. (See The interprofessional process, 5.1; Family process , Chapter 3.)

1.3 Implications for practice

1.3.1 Rejecting the experience, rejecting the child

Out of a well-meaning sense of protection for the abused child, adults and professionals often say or convey the message to the child 'it is all your father's fault, it has nothing to do with you'. They then try to talk as little about the abuse as possible with the hope of helping the child in this way to forget what has happened. This seemingly protective measure of not talking about the experience of sexual abuse in fact often conveys a very different message to the child.

The first part of the sentence 'it is all your father's fault' reflects the basic confusion of the concepts of responsibility, participation, guilt, power and blame. Professionals want to convey to the child that he or she is not responsible for the abuse and this part of the message means to address the legal aspect of the parental responsibility for what had happened. By adding 'this has nothing to do with you' the message includes the psychological and relationship aspect of the child's involvement and we take away the important fact of the child's experience and participation in the abuse. In doing so we deny the child's experience itself and by denying and rejecting the child's experience of sexual abuse we reject the child herself. What comes over to the child is that the adult does not want to listen to her experience in the same way as people had not wanted to believe the abuse or to know of it before.

Even if the abuse were very damaging the relationship with the abuser, the attachment to him and the interaction of sexual abuse may have been nevertheless the most intensive and important experience in the child's life. By rejecting for protective reasons to consider and to examine this experience, professionals precisely repeat the previous traumatic experience of child sexual abuse as syndrome of secrecy. (See Child sexual abuse as syndrome of secrecy, 2.1.)

What we want to say to the child is 'it is all your father's responsibility (legal aspect), but you have been involved, and tell me how was it (interactional aspect)?'. This differentiation has been most helpful to sexually abused children. It enables the breaking of the circle of secrecy and allows children to talk about their experience. They may talk about how they *feel* responsible or *feel* guilty. This gives us the opportunity to differentiate and to point out to the child that 'daddy's are not supposed to do those things' allocating the *fact* of responsibility and the *fact* of guilt squarely to the abuser or abusing parent, allowing the child at the same time to own her experience, which is the precondition for any therapeutic work.

1.3.2 The 'seductive child'

The stereotype of the 'seductive child' who entices her father and who enjoys the abuse has little to do with the reality of child sexual abuse. It has its origin mostly in adults' projections of their own adult sexual thinking on to the child. This leads to confusing the seemingly adult sexual experience of the abused child with the child's true level of psycho-sexual development, which is usually lacking underneath. Sexually abused children are often emotionally much more immature than their peers.

It is expected that fathers in their role as parents draw appropriate boundaries. This means that even if a child were to behave in an openly sexual way, behaviour we have increasingly learned to regard already as the result of previous sexual abuse rather than as the starting point, and even if children were openly seductive and were trying to initiate sexual abuse for example by going into the father's bedroom in a sexually inviting way, it would always be the father's parental responsibility to set limits. Not even the most extreme sexualised or seductive behaviour could ever make the child responsible for an adult response of sexual abuse in which the abuser satisfies his own sexual desire in response to the child's request for emotional care. At the same time we may not expect a father to be able to handle the situation on his own. As in physical abuse it would then be his responsibility to leave the situation and seek help.

1.3.3 Understanding the abuser

To express empathy and understanding for sexual abusers often provokes strong irrational and angry responses amongst the public and professionals alike. This response originates from a confusion in which people feel that understanding abusers and showing empathy means making apologies for them and blaming the child. The distinction between interactional and structural elements of responsibility, participation and guilt in child sexual abuse allows us to show empathy and to try to understand why fathers and stepfathers and others become sexual abusers. In the process we may learn about traumatic life events in the abuser's own history, including possible severe physical and sexual abuse in their own childhood. We may understand how the abuse came about and how further abuse may be prevented.

Showing empathy and understanding towards sexual abusers does not take away one iota from their full responsibility for the abuse they have committed. The legal and psychological distinction between responsibility and participation facilitates the move from a position of revenge and rejection of abusers towards a therapeutic mode of understanding and empathy with the abuser's own life experience, maintaining at the same time a clear notion of his sole responsibility for the abuse.

1.3.4 Losing the intergenerational perspective

The loss of the intergenerational perspective with the subsequent loss of the notion of structural dependence of children has led to some misguided and misinformed concepts of 'liberation' of children in some extreme feminist approaches and to some precarious notions supported by paedophiles.

Child sexual abuse is undoubtedly predominently a matter of male adults abusing both girls and boys. Although the presentation may still change, at present more than 90 per cent of sexual abusers are male. This has led to some feminist projects in which the shared victimization of women and girls has created a postulated identical position of children and women as victims of male aggression. Sexually abused women and women abused as children are seen in the same way as children who are abused by father figures.

Child sexual abuse is not only a problem between the sexes but also between parents and children. The loss of the important intergenerational perspective may not only conceal issues of maternal letdown and female rivalry in the mother–daughter relationship which any therapeutic approach needs to take into account. It also overlooks that 20–40 per cent of sexually abused children are boys (Baker and Duncan, 1985; Finkelhor, 1979; Furniss et al., 1984). The loss of the intergenerational perspective can also lead to very inappropriate demands of 'liberation' of children from abusing parents. Women can liberate themselves indeed, but children are structurally dependent and can never be 'liberated' from parental figures. They can only mature and grow out of their dependence over time. Or they can be transferred from not good enough parents to good enough parents.

The denial of the intergenerational issue in child sexual abuse often leads to equating child sexual abuse in the family with rape of women. Although there is an area of overlap in the social and psychological preconditions for both situations, with regards to management there are crucial differences which must not be blurred. Rape as sudden attack by an unknown man as well as the rape of women within the context of ongoing adult relationships have very different dynamics and require different forms of interventions compared with child sexual abuse in the family. The necessary differentiation between rape of women and long-term child sexual abuse in the family does not mean that one form is more or less damaging than the other.

Paedophiles in the past often tried to pretend that an intergenerational boundary with structural dependence of children and structural responsibility of adults does not exist. This leads to the bizarre extreme of the paedophile argument which states that genital sex in childhood is desirable for normal child development and that children today are deprived of the right of early genital sexual relationships. This line of reasoning has all to do with the projection of adult sexual wishes on to the child. It has nothing to do with the psycho-sexual stage and development of children. The loss of the intergenerational perspective also ignores the fact that pre-pubertal children can never give informed consent and that sexual activities with children are performed for the satisfaction of the adult's sexual wishes and not in response to the child's needs.

1.4 Primary and secondary damage

The disclosure of child sexual abuse usually leads to the involvement of a great number of different professionals and agencies. The evaluation of 64 clinical cases revealed that on average 8.2 different agencies with many more individual professionals had been involved (Furniss, 1988). The disclosure of sexual abuse often leads to a crisis in the professional network which can be greater and sometimes more complex and confusing than the family crisis. Uncoordinated approaches often lack problem solving capacity and result in conflicts-by-proxy and non-therapeutic action responses. Uncoordinated interventions can lead to greater damage and traumatisation of family relationships and individual children than the original abuse. (See The interprofessional process, 5.1.)

In child sexual abuse as interlocking syndrome of secrecy and addiction we need to distinguish more than in any other area of child and family work between primary damage through the abuse itself and secondary damage through the professional intervention. This notion takes account of the fact that in child sexual abuse as normative human rights problem, not all children are psychiatrically disturbed although all children are affected and confused through the effects of child sexual abuse as a syndrome of secrecy. This leads to the necessary differentiation between 'protection work' and 'therapy' (see Therapy and protection work, 7.2.2). In child sexual abuse any professional intervention must therefore primarily aim at avoiding secondary damage through the intervention before addressing the primary therapeutic task of treating the trauma of child sexual abuse itself.

Secondary damage and victimisation of sexually abused children happens on five levels.

1 Social stigmatisation Sexually abused children and their families can become socially stigmatised by the reaction of neighbours, schools and peers. The child is often further victimised by the consequences of family breakdown. Material and social hardship bring additional problems when abusers leave the family or are imprisoned.

2 Secondary traumatisation in the interprofessional process Sexually abused children can become disturbed through secondary victimisation when they get drawn into structural institutional conflicts and into conflicts-by-proxy in professional networks (see The interprofessional process, 5.1). Secondary traumatisation through structural institutional conflicts happens most often in conflicts between the legal system and the child's protective and psychological needs. This is based on the fact that the legal system has not yet adapted fully to the human rights aspect of the child as subject before the law who is nevertheless structurally dependent on adult care. Conflicts-by-proxy in professional networks occur on all levels and lead to non-therapeutic action responses resulting in anti-therapeutic therapy, abuse-promoting child protection and crime-promoting crime prevention which can all result in severe secondary trauma in the child. (See The interprofessional process in context, 5.2.)

3 Secondary traumatisation in the professional–family process. In the professional–family process secondary traumatisation happens as a result of the choice of the basic professional intervention and through changes of the basic form of the intervention by families and family members. Professionals can choose a Primary Punitive Intervention or a Primary Child Protective Intervention in the first place as much as families and family members may succeed in influencing the professional network in a way which changes a Primary Therapeutic Intervention into a Primary Punitive Intervention or a Primary Child Protective Intervention. Whether, in the interactional professional–family process, families or professionals prevent a Primary Therapeutic Intervention, similar secondary damage can be afflicted on the child in a Primary Punitive Intervention and a Primary Child Protective Intervention. (See Three basic types of intervention, 4.1.)

4 Secondary traumatisation in the family process. Non-believing of the child and denial by abusers and family members in unproven cases of child sexual abuse can lead to secondary damage to the child, as may scapegoating, punishing and blaming of the child by parents, siblings and other family members for all family problems as a result of disclosure.

5 Secondary traumatisation in the individual process. Sexually abused children can finally induce secondary traumatisation through their own behaviour. They often provoke rejection, punishment or re-abuse through sexualised behaviour or victim behaviour which makes them more vulnerable and unable to protect themselves from the consequences of their own sexualised communication and victim messages. This process can easily lead to the induction of entirely new cycles of secondary victimisation and abuse.

Highly competent professionals often intervene in the wrong context, inflicting secondary damage when they intervene prematurely and out of context. Fathers are arrested only to be released without taking the crime-promoting effect of such a crime-preventing intervention into account. Children are removed aimlessly with long-term results of abuse-promoting child protection when they are finally returned to the family without any fundamental protection work or treatment being done with the family. Families who have been subjected to uncoordinated and unsuccessful interventions close up again under the effects of child sexual abuse as interlocking syndrome of secrecy and addiction and the child can be subjected to further aggravated child sexual abuse.

Secondary damage is also often inflicted by non-intervention. This happens more often in medical and therapeutic situations where doctors or therapists either deny the obvious abuse or think they can deal with the issue without any statutory support. This often results in anti-therapeutic therapy. Child sexual abuse as interlocking syndrome of secrecy and addiction with interlocking human rights and health aspects always requires a genuinely multi-professional approach in which legal issues and treatment relate to each other in complex and new ways. The concept of primary and secondary damage is therefore a particularly important and poignant concept for all professional groups who work with child sexual abuse.

1.5 Acknowledgement and belief, admission and owning up

1.5.1 Proof, admission and owning up by abusers

Proof and admission are concepts in the legal domain whereas belief and owning up are psychological phenomena. It is important to keep the legal aspect of proof and admission separate and independent from the psychological events of believing and owning up. Admission of abusers in the legal domain is the precondition for a straightforward therapeutic approach. Abusers who do not admit even in the face of legal proof need to undergo denial work. (See Aims and steps in the primary therapeutic intervention, 6.2; Dealing with primary denial, 10.6.)

In child sexual abuse as syndrome of secrecy and addiction, legal admissions by abusers cannot be equated with owning up in the psychological domain. Having admitted legally and having broken the secrecy does not mean that the abuser is facing his responsibility and is owning up to what he has done to the child and other family members. Admissions in court and legal proof will support the treatment of abusers but the legal admission does not yet constitute the therapeutic step of owning up in psychological terms. (See Child sexual abuse as syndrome of secrecy, 2.1; Child sexual abuse as syndrome of addiction, 2.2; Working with sexual abusers, 7.4.)

Even when abusers admit their abuse in legal courts they can still do so in a mechanical way. The admission can become something alien and abusers are often able to disassociate themselves entirely from the psychological reality of the court proceedings around them. The assumption that in themselves admissions by abusers in courts already establish psychological reality is often thoroughly disproved when abusers have to go to prison. Prison compounds the reality avoidance and abusers often come out without having owned up psychologically. We also find secondary denial where the admission of child sexual abuse is taken back on the psychological level after initial legal admission. The occurrence of tertiary denial is the most dramatic manifestation of this process. (See Relapse into secrecy and secondary denial, 12.13; Tertiary Denial by Fathers, 12.14.)

Just as legal admissions cannot be seen automatically as responsibility taking on the interpersonal and psychological level, so it is equally inappropriate to assume that the denial of abusers makes treatment impossible. Admission in the legal domain is necessary for the subsequent process of protection. An abuser who does not admit to proven sexual abuse can never be protective, but he can be treated. The interactional nature of motivation must teach us that denial is often based on realistic fears or on unconscious anxieties which need to be addressed in denial work before the abuser can admit to the abuse. (See The interactional nature of motivation, 2.4.1; Dealing with primary denial, 10.6; Relapse into secrecy and secondary denial, 12.13; Tertiary denial by fathers, 12.14.)

Initial admissions by abusers that they have sexually abused must be taken as a first step but not as owning up, and the abuser can still not be trusted. The parallel to other forms of addiction is striking. The abuser needs to be treated like an alcoholic who admits for the first time to drinking and says that it will never happen again. Sexual abusers need to be believed that they may want to stop abusing and the initial admission is the precondition for therapy. But they must not yet be trusted that they will not relapse into abuse in the future until they have owned up in long-term therapy. Abusers remain even then at risk of relapse as in other forms of addiction if they do not avoid high-risk situations.

Initial admissions are sometimes put forcefully with the intention of doing just the opposite of owning up. Abusers hope that the quick superficial admission spares the long and difficult treatment process of owning up. This explains why many abusers who, in the beginning, admit readily to the abuse often become non-motivated after two or three sessions. They maintain that after the initial admission and some superficial work there is no risk that abuse could ever happen again and they become hostile to the suggestion of further treatment. When the process of psychological denial is pointed out these abusers can become very aggressive and often leave treatment if therapy is not supported by the legal process.

1.5.2 Proof, acknowledgement and belief by mothers

When non-abusing mothers and carers have not been directly involved in the disclosure interview, legal proof and reported admissions by abusers and disclosures by children are often not enough to make mothers believe that sexual abuse has really happened. They may acknowledge the abuse superficially and even legally, but when they are confronted by professionals with the child's disclosure it often still does not 'hit home'. The difference between external acknowledgment and psychological belief makes it so important that non-abusing mothers and carers are present at the disclosure interview either in the room or behind the screen or at the Handover Meeting immediately afterwards. Or that mothers hear in the first family meeting as responsibility meeting, from the abuser himself, that child sexual abuse has taken place. (See Aims and steps in the Primary Therapeutic Intervention, 6.2; Organising the disclosure interview, 9.3; Disclosure by mothers, 9.7; The first family meeting as reality-creating responsibility meeting, 9.11; The handover meeting, 9.14.)

Mothers who acknowledge the abuse but do not believe cannot be protective. Protection work and therapy are equally required. Denial work needs to be conducted with non-abusing mothers and carers who cannot acknowledge that any abuse has taken place. (See Helping protective mothers, 12.11; Mothers who do not believe, 12.12; and see Naming, creating and maintaining sexual abuse as reality, 2.4.3.)

Mothers who do not believe are often not only regarded as non-protective but they are also, and quite inappropriately, seen as non-treatable. This is not the fact and denial work needs to be done on the feared disasters behind the denial and on the interactional nature of motivation between the mother and the professional network. (See The interactional nature of motivation, 2.4.1; Dealing with primary denial, 10.6.)

It is important not to take the external acknowledgement of non-abusing mothers and carers as believing. One mother who had acknowledged that abuse had happened and who had been involved in treatment for over one year suddenly said one day, 'I have to tell you, if I'm honest, I still don't believe that abuse has happened'.

Psychological denial and the inability to believe can even go further. In several cases where abusers had confessed, the mother still maintained that nothing had happened. In one case the mother told the father to his face that he had lied. The mother in another family kept to the belief that the abuser who had pleaded guilty went to prison for false admissions. The mother was extremely hostile towards any mention of the abuse. She put the abused girl under such pressure that the child became increasingly disturbed. The mother only began to acknowledge, though not believe, that sexual abuse had happened when the professional team of therapists and child protection workers threatened to bring the mother to court for emotional abuse.

Figure 1.2 shows the different reactions of abusers and non-abusing carers after disclosure and the type of work which is possible and required for each of them. The intervention is divided into the three essential aspects of sexual abuse work: (1) denial work, (2) protection work, and (3) therapy.

1.5.3 Disclosure by children and the integration of the experience of abuse

As for abusers and non-abusing parents and carers, we need to distinguish between the initial and external disclosure of children and the deeper psychological aspects of integrating the experience of the abuse. In disturbed children this is often only achieved after intensive therapy. Absused children like abusers and carers may be so frightened of facing their abuse that they try to avoid therapeutic confrontation by maintaining that they have talked enough and that everything is fine with them. Cases of successfully concluded treatment must therefore be clearly distinguished from cases of secondary psychological denial after initial admissions.

Reaction after disclosure

Abuser (Denial / Admission / Owning up) — *Non-abusing parent or carer* (No acknowledgement / Acknowledgement / Belief)

Intervention	Denial — No acknowledgement	Denial — Acknowledgement	Denial — Belief	Admission — No acknowledgement	Admission — Acknowledgement	Admission — Belief	Owning up — No acknowledgement	Owning up — Acknowledgement	Owning up — Belief
Denial work	+	+ with abuser	+ with abuser	+ with carer	0	0	+ with carer	0	0
Protection work	−	+ with carer	− with abuser / 0 with carer	+ with abuser	+	+ with abuser / 0 with carer	+ with abuser	+	0
Therapy	−	+ with carer	+ with carer with abuser	+ with abuser	+	+	+ with abuser	+	+

+ Possible and indicated

− Impossible

0 Possible but not required

Figure 1.2 Acknowledgement and belief, admission and owning up after disclosure.

Chapter two

The individual process

2.1 Child sexual abuse as syndrome of secrecy for the child

The specific nature of child sexual abuse as syndrome of secrecy for the child and the family, and as syndrome of addiction for the abuser, highlights the difference between child sexual abuse and other forms of child abuse. These two inter-locking conditions in child sexual abuse make for a unique constellation. Child sexual abuse as syndrome of secrecy for the child is determined by external factors, by specific aspects of secrecy in the abusive interaction itself and by internal psychological factors.

2.1.1 External factors of secrecy

We find five main external factors which constitute the external aspect of child sexual abuse as syndrome of secrecy.

1 Forensic proof and medical evidence

Forensic proof and medical evidence is only available in a minority of cases. The present rate of proven cases with physical evidence will hopefully increase with skill (Hobbs and Wynne, 1987). Professionals will have to live with the fact that also in future the majority of cases will not yield conclusive medical evidence of sexual abuse. For example, severe long-term oral abuse may not be medically detectable at all. But even clear medical evidence of sexual abuse often still does not constitute forensic proof as to the person of the abuser. (See Forensic proof and medical examination, 9.5.)

2 Verbal accusations

The lack of medical evidence and forensic proof requires the verbal accusation of the child or of another person on the child's behalf and we need the admission of the abuser. Under the currently often still primarily punitive approaches against perpetrators, many abusers will not admit to sexual abuse. Threats against the child often lead to prolonged suffering of sexual abuse when the child does not dare to disclose. Out of fear for herself, for the family or for the abuser the child may still deny the abuse even when asked openly. (See Explicit therapeutic permission to disclose, 8.5; Legal interviewing of children, 9.2.)

The assumption that the non-abusing parent is the natural ally of the abused child leads to one of the most common forms of intervention failure when mothers, who have not been the person to raise the suspicion of sexual abuse, are approached separately and prior to the abuser with the question whether sexual abuse could have taken place. This often leads to a straight denial by the mother and to a premature disclosure of the suspicion towards the father. The result is certain denial of sexual abuse. (See Steps in the crisis intervention of disclosure 8.2).

3 Non-believing of the child's communication

I have not yet seen cases of long-term child sexual abuse within the family context where the child has not tried to communicate the abuse to someone within the family or outside. Time and again we find children reporting that they have tried to tell their mothers, other family members or outsiders, only not to be believed, to be called a liar and to be punished for the disclosure. In addition, outside agencies often do not believe the child's disclosure either.

A typical example of family members and outside agencies colluding in the denial is the case of a 14-year-old girl who had been sexually abused by her stepfather since the age of 7 years. Abuse had started when her mother was pregnant again. Although the girl had tried to tell her mother, her mother instead of believing her and confronting her husband, went to her General Practitioner for advice. The GP labelled the child as showing signs of jealousy in reaction to the mother's pregnancy. The mother still did not want to confront her husband with the child's disclosure. She merely reported the disclosure to him, linking it instantly to the GP's diagnosis of jealousy. The mother's avoidance of confronting her husband and her collusion with the GP's denial of sexual abuse allowed the father to scapegoat the girl and call her a liar. She was severely punished for her disclosure and was further abused under increased threats of violence. The child did not dare repeat the allegation of sexual abuse, which continued until she reached adolescence, when she tried to commit suicide.

The non-believing finally extends to the legal system. Entire legal codes are built on the hitherto unproven notion that children lie and adults speak the truth or that children's communications are less valid or reliable than the statements of adults. Sexually abused children's disclosures or communications are often not believed for legal reasons. As a result of the legal process sexually abused children are then forced to continue to live with the abuser and the abuse. (See From mad to bad, Chapter 1.)

4 Lying under threat

Abused children are often told not to disclose to anyone within the family or outside. The child, and especially young children, may be told that what happens during the abuse is a secret between the child and the abuser. Secrecy is usually reinforced by violence, threats of violence or punishment. Sometimes we find a mixture of threats and bribery where the secondary gain of bribes and of special treatment maintains the secrecy, which is nonetheless basically founded on threats.

As a result of threats of violence and threats of family disaster, children lie more often when they deny that sexual abuse has taken place than when they falsely accuse a family member of sexual abuse. Legal, child protective and health professionals need to face up to this crucial fact of child sexual abuse as syndrome of secrecy.

5 Anxieties about the consequences of disclosure

In many cases children have been threatened that they will be sent away, that the abuser may kill them or may kill himself, that the marriage of the parents will break up and that the disclosure will lead to family disintegration. These threats to the life and to the integrity of the child are implicitly, and often enough all too explicitly, linked to the attribution of guilt and full responsiblity for these events to the child. 'If you tell anyone, it is all your fault if daddy goes to prison' or 'It is all your fault if mummy gets upset, and you will have to be sent away' etc. The full range of threats from the warning that nobody will believe the child anyway to the threat of murder constitutes a strong external factor for the child not to disclose.

Finally, not least important and contrary to popular belief most sexually abused children do not want to lose their fathers through imprisonment or divorce. They do want a father, but a father who does not abuse. A primary punitive approach towards abusers is therefore a strong external factor for children to maintain secrecy and not to disclose.

2.1.2 Interactional aspects of secrecy: entrance and exit rituals

1 Lying and denial

The preoccupation with legal and child protective aspects of child sexual abuse has led to severe neglect of the psychological and interpersonal aspects of child sexual abuse. Psychological events of conscious lying and unconscious denial are often confused. In lying the child is fully aware of the facts. In denial the child is unaware of the unconscious communication of the abuse. Lying is based on the external elements of child sexual abuse as syndrome of secrecy, and the external and conscious form of denial as negation is in fact lying. It needs to be called so when we want to make the psychologically important distinction to unconscious denial and unawareness.

Children lie about child sexual abuse because they are frightened to be punished and not believed and protected. Psychologically and in terms of family relationships, child sexual abuse usually remains a family secret even after open disclosure and even when legal and statutory threats have long been removed. This is the result of denial, not of lying. Lying relates to the legal concept of proof, denial belongs to the psychological concept of belief and owning up as outlined in Chapter 1.

2 The undoing of the abuse in the abusive interaction itself

The sexual nature of sexual abuse and the entire experience is negated and undone on three contextual levels.

a. By the context in which the abuse takes place.
b. By the change of the abuser into 'the other person'.
c. By a further interactional layer of denial through entrance and exit rituals.

a. Context of abuse. The central characteristic of the sexual interaction between abuser and child is the attempt by the abuser to create a context which undoes the very external reality of the ongoing sexual abuse in the process of the abusive act itself. Children often describe how the abuse would take place in silence or without any eye contact or in total darkness and with drawn curtains, even if nobody would have been able to look in from outside.

The physical sensations of the abuse and the interactional context created by the abuser leads to an entirely conflicting and contradictory physiological, perceptual and emotional double experience. Intense skin contact and body stimulation during the sexual act create a state of most intense physical and physiological stimulation in the child whether in vaginal, anal or oral inter-course or in masturbation. The physical stimulation can induce extreme body sensations of pain and arousal. High anxiety levels can be further increased by the helplessness and the inability of the child to leave the scene.

The intense skin contact and the body stimulation constitute the sexual aspect of sexual abuse. The confusing sensory experience of the sexual act happens in a context in which the abuser tries to deny that the sexual abuse takes place at all. The sexual nature of sexual abuse is meant to be split off and undone by the abuser through minimising the input of other sensory modes which negate the ongoing abuse. This is achieved through silence, darkness, ritualised physical contact, avoidance of eye-contact and many ritualised aspects of the interaction. The undoing by splitting off is coupled and enhanced by usually highly rigid and ritualised forms of interactions which are maintained by brief and stereotyped verbal commands and threats.

b. Change of abuser to 'other person'. The second layer of undoing is the transformation of the abuser from the father figure into 'the other person' as pseudo-partner. Sexual abusers in states of sexual arousal often behave very differently from their usual self. This can be very frightening when fathers turn into 'the other person' with changed gestures, unusual speaking pattern, altered tone of voice and strange physical behaviour. Nearly all children have most vividly described changes in facial expressions.

The undoing through splitting off of ongoing external reality of the sexual abuse during the sexual act itself does not allow the child to perceive reality as reality and to name the experience of the abuse as abuse. It is as if the abuser were to say to the face of the child 'What do you mean, nothing is happening, is it?' whilst at the same time he is penetrating the child sexually down below. Abusers usually attempt to deny any real relationship aspect between them and the child during the abuse itself and they try to avoid any open recognition of what is happening. During the most intensive bodily and physical contact which is humanly possible they try totally to disconnect themselves from the child psychologically.

c. Entrance and exit rituals. Entrance and exit rituals are the third layer of undoing. They form a central part of the interactional aspect of child sexual abuse as syndrome of secrecy. The entrance ritual serves to transform an ordinary father–child interaction into the 'other person'–child interaction without naming this transition. In the exit ritual the equally unnamed reversed process of the transition from 'the other person' of the abuser into the father and trusted adult takes place. Entrance and exit rituals do not only further reinforce the undoing and negation of sexual abuse in its very process. They also reinforce the powerful splitting of the contradictory physiological sensory messages during the abuse itself.

Entrance and exit rituals extend the incongruent experience of external reality into the dimension of time. They create the consecutive time-split in the person of the abuser. The abuser may be a caring father before and after the abuse who changes into the different 'other person' during the abuse. The same human being can be a kind father person at one point in time and terrifying abuser during the abuse.

The entire time span between the very beginning of the entrance ritual and the very end of the exit ritual marks the time span of the sexual abuse. After the abuse the abuser and the child cut out the time span and experience between entrance and exit ritual from their mutually recognised reality as if it had never existed. They become the lost and split-off units of fifteen minutes in the child's life.

For example a father at home may greet a child who comes from school, saying 'hello, how was it at school?'. He may then initiate the entrance ritual and sexual abuse takes place ending in the exit ritual. The abuser may then turn to the child as if he had just said 'hello, how was it at school?', going on to say 'go now and do your homework', pretending to himself and to the child that in between

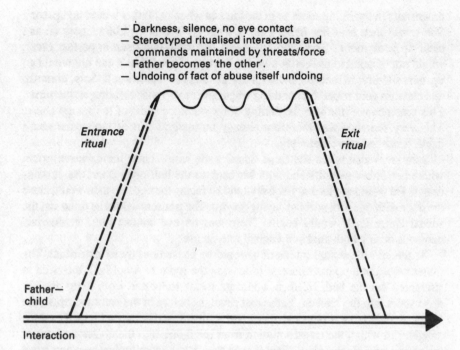

— Darkness, silence, no eye contact
— Stereotyped ritualised interactions and
   commands maintained by threats/force
— Father becomes 'the other'.
— Undoing of fact of abuse itself undoing

*Entrance
ritual*

*Exit
ritual*

Father—
child

Interaction

Figure 2.1 The abusive interaction in child sexual abuse as syndrome of secrecy

the first 'hello, how was it at school?' and the much later 'go now and do your homework' no time has elapsed and no sexual abuse has taken place. It is as if these two sentences followed each other directly with nothing in between, as illustrated in Figure 2.1.

The entrance and exit rituals always create a physical space and a time space between the abuser and the child in which the transformation from 'father' to 'abuser' takes place in the entrance ritual, and the reverse occurs in the exit ritual. This separation is vital to be able to maintain the splitting and undoing. I have never heard of a father who openly took his child by the hand, looked at her creating eye contact saying 'let's go to bed and have sex'. This acknowledgement of the reality of sex and of the relationship aspect which is the mark of open sexual relationships and lovemaking seems unthinkable in child sexual abuse.

Clinical examples

Sara had been sexually abused for 8 years before she disclosed. She told that the abuse happened at daytime when her mother was out at work. She used to be downstairs in the living room or in the kitchen when her father would go upstairs. She would then hear her father calling from her bedroom, 'Sara, come up and clear up your room'. Sara who knew that her room had been in perfect order, would not respond to the explicit verbal content of her father's call but would go upstairs silently. In fact she knew for certain that her father's call 'Sara, come up and clear up your room' had nothing whatsoever to do with clearing up her room. This sentence was the very beginning of the entrance ritual of the sexual abuse. This very sentence was therefore already an integral part of the sexual abuse itself. It needed no verbal reply.

Sara knew that when she came upstairs she would enter her darkened room where her father would stand with his back to the half-open door, the curtains drawn. He would not look at her but would be facing the bed. He then would close the door with one foot without saying a word. The trousers would be open and the sexual abuse itself would begin. There was no eye contact only stereotyped demands during both anal and vaginal intercourse.

At the end the sexual interaction would be phased out by an exit ritual. The father would pull up his trousers. In leaving the room he would tell the child to straighten out the bed. He then would go to the toilet and from there directly downstairs into the kitchen. In the exit ritual, as before in the entrance ritual, the father would create a physical space and a time-space between himself and his daughter in which the transformation from the father into the abuser and out of the abuser would take place. Sara would stay in her room on her own and some time would pass until the father would call 'Sara, you must be thirsty from school'. She would be expected to go downstairs and have a drink as if nothing had happened. Only the very sentence 'Sara, you must be thirsty from school' was the end of the exit ritual and the conclusion of the sexual abuse. The father had become the father again and both Sara and the father lived on as if no sexual abuse had ever happened in between.

2.1.3 Secrecy internalised: accommodation, concentration-camp syndrome and sexual arousal

Roland Summit (1983) in the 'Child sexual abuse accommodation syndrome' has described how the sexually abused child in secrecy, helplessness and entrapment begins psychologically to adapt to what is an unliveable situation over time. The abusive interaction which may continuously threaten the child's physical and psychological integrity and life is turned in the process of accommodation into a seemingly normal event. Basic psychological structures develop which allow psychic survival at the cost of severely distorted perception of external and emotional reality.

She may discover altered states of consciousness to shut off pain or to disassociate from her body as if looking on from a distance at the child suffering the abuse. The same mechanisms which allow psychic survival for the child become handicaps to effective psychological integration as an adult. If the child cannot create a psychic economy to reconcile the continuing outrage the intolerence of helplessness and the increasing feeling of rage will seek active expression. (Summit, 1983, p. 185)

Summit then continues by describing the great variety of self-punishing symptoms and expressions of long-term child sexual abuse.

Accommodation to the abuse and the creation of pseudo-normality is the result of the impossible psychological task of integrating the experience. Secrecy and helplessness and possible unpredictability and threat to life are constantly reinforced in renewed invasions into the child's physical and mental integrity and autonomy. Threats by the abuser and the structure of the reality-denying experience prevent the child from ever being able to call abuse abuse. The child is forced to live a seemingly normal life in which no abuse seems to exist. The process of accommodation happens through the internalisation of the inherently incongruent experience of the abusive interaction.

Children try to survive the abuse in different ways. Some pretend it is not they who are abused and try to look at the abuse from a distance as Summit has described. Others try to go into altered states of consciousness and try to pretend to sleep. Another way to normalise is to pretend during intercourse that the lower part of the body does not exist. These are only some of the extreme ways in which some children try to undo the abuse in the process itself, to split themselves off from the experience and to create a pseudo-normal state which allows them to survive the abuse. In trying to undo the ongoing experience they create a complementary fit to the abuser's wish to deny the ongoing abuse as unlawful interaction.

Accommodation creates a different psychic state from that of denial. The translation of the structural violation of the child's integrity into the pretence of normality seems in its long-term consequences very similar to processes described in the 'Concentration camp syndrome' (Bastiaans, 1957). The extreme survival mechanism of normalising which concentration camp survivors had developed during life in concentration camps later often led to a psychological state in which the concentration camp experience seemed to be psychologically completely wiped out. It only re-emerged when the coping mechanisms and the defences were shattered later in life by new stressful life events. When the experience re-emerged, however, it threatened in flashbacks to flood and to overwhelm entirely the coping mechanisms and defences of the survivor.

The internalised experience of long-term child sexual abuse can lead to similar difficulties in establishing child sexual abuse both as external fact and as internal, psychological and interpersonal reality. Child sexual abuse as syndrome of secrecy and the concentration camp syndrome can create similar personality problems of guilt and self-worth. The common guilt aspect does not relate to the specific survivor guilt in the concentration camp syndrome but to the forced living-together experience of perpetrator and victim over a long time and the complex developing psychological pattern of interdependence and attachment between the abuser or jailer and the victim. Problems of guilt and self-worth also relate to the incongruence of experience of secrecy under threat in which reality must never be named as such. Secrecy independent of threats forms an important disturbing factor, which blocks orientation and congruent experience. To a much lesser degree we see the same interactional psychological process in cases of long-term hostage taking.

The pseudo-normal interactional pattern between the victim and the perpetrator becomes further complicated by the fact that the abuser, the camp guard and the terrorist are not only people who threaten life and integrity. They are at the time the perverted provider of life, maintenance and external care, and even of positive emotional attention. This element is crucial in understanding the possibly bizarre attachments and loyalties between victim and perpetrator and the fact that the victim begins to speak the language of the jailer. Forms of loyalty and attachment can emerge which can be extremely difficult to understand and to accept. Dealing with these loyalties, attachments and guilt is a central element in the therapy of child sexual abuse.

2.1.4 Interlocking effects: dissociation and 'multiple personality'

The interactional and internal elements of child sexual abuse as reality anni-hilating syndrome of secrecy can create extreme forms of dissociations in the child and in the abuser. The splitting and undoing of reality through external secrecy, the change from the father into 'the other person', the creation of 'lost time' and the creation of physical space between the abuse and non-abusing interactions in the entrance and exit rituals create a syndrome of abuse in which the naming and creating of the external reality of the experience of sexual abuse becomes a central therapeutic challenge and task. This task is in its extreme manifested in the dissociative state of multiple personalities, the extreme form of inability to create an integrated reality of experience.

The undoing of reality on different interactional and internal levels and the external secrecy during the act of the abuse itself makes the non-experience an integral part of the experience of child sexual abuse. The non-experience as expression of the secrecy which surrounds the abuse creates the unique thera-peutic and child protective problem in child sexual abuse as syndrome of secrecy. This is confounded by aspects of addiction.

2.1.5 Sexualised attachments, habit formation and secondary gratification

Physiological arousal, secondary gratification and sexualised attachment contain elements of positive experience in sexual abuse. They contribute to the extremely loyal behaviour of some sexually abused children and adolescents.

Physiological arousal of the skin and especially the genital area in sexual abuse can be extremely painful and frightening and that is well accepted. It is

(1) Ordinary trauma

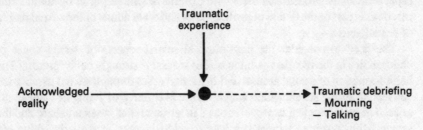

(2) Trauma in child sexual abuse

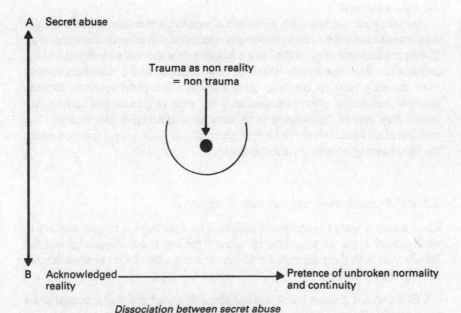

Dissociation between secret abuse
and acknowledged reality

Figure 2.2 The nature of trauma in child sexual abuse

more difficult for professionals to bear the thought that some children and adolescents feel generally sexually aroused. To allow children to talk about aspects of sexual arousal can meet with extreme hostile response by adults. This response is part of the denial of professionals and other adults of the sexual nature of sexual abuse.

The need to consider the physiological sexual aspects of sexual abuse in children lies in the fact that genuine sexual arousal is strongly habit forming. The habit formation of sexual arousal and in tension relief through sexual stimulation can lead to strong sexualisation which we see in children of young age and adults alike. The physiological aspect of arousal in tension relief in sexual abuse and the strong habit-forming element can lead to addictiveness in sexually acting-out behaviour which can be extremely difficult to treat.

Secondary gratification through bribes and rewards can have extremely corrupting effects. Sexually abused children who show devious behaviour have very often been in abusive relationships with abusers, which had been maintained by aspects of bribery and rewards. This includes material rewards which the child knows other children who are not abused do not get. It also relates to persuading children that they are nicer, better and more special than other significant people in their lives, such as their mothers, their siblings and other children. A perverted sense of specialness can result in an inflated sense of self which is phoney and false and not held by the appreciation of the child's true needs and of the care for the child's true self.

Sexual abuse can bring the child into a pseudo partner role which the child may want to maintain even at the cost of emotional disturbance and confusion. The strong attachment of victims to the abuser is in some cases a reflection of the fact that the abusive attention which the child gets can be the most important or even the only parental care and attention which the child receives. Despite possible detrimental effects children may not want to give up this relationship which they feel to be positive until they have alternative experiences. The strength of this attachment can be seen especially in single parent families where the father as single parent is also the abuser.

2.2 Child sexual abuse as syndrome of addiction

Child sexual abuse as syndrome of addiction for the abuser is complementary to child sexual abuse as syndrome of secrecy for the child, the abuser and the family. Although there are specific differences from other forms of addiction the similarities are striking.

1 Child sexual abusers know that the abuse is wrong and that it constitutes a crime.
2 The sexual abuser knows that the abuse is damaging to the child. Nevertheless the abuse takes place.

3 Sexual abuse, like other addictions, does not primarily create a pleasurable experience but serves tension relief.
4 The process is driven by repetition compulsion.
5 Guilt feelings and the knowledge of damaging the child may lead to attempts to stop the abuse.
6 The egosyntonic sexual aspect of sexual abuse gives the abuser the 'kick' which constitutes the central addictive element.
7 The sexual gratification of the sexual act serves reality avoidance and supports a low frustration tolerance, weak coping mechanisms and weak ego-functions.
8 The egosyntonic and sexually arousing aspects of child sexual abuse and the subsequent tension relief create psychological dependence.
9 The sexual abuser tends to deny the dependence towards himself and to the outside world independent of legal threats.
10 The attempt to stop abusing can lead to withdrawal symptoms such as anxiety, irritability, restlessness and other symptoms.

The important difference between physical and sexual abuse is the egosyntonic aspect of sexual abuse and the 'kick' the abuser gets from it. The knowledge that the abuse is wrong, the damage to the child, the tension relief, guilt feelings and repetition compulsion are common elements in physical and sexual abuse. Only in a very small minority of severe cases of physical abuse do we see open sadistic pleasure in the process of physically beating and abusing the child. In physical abuse addictive egosyntonic elements are usually absent. Child sexual abuse as syndrome of addiction does not mean that sexual abusers do not suffer or may not be in need of help. The difference lies in the sexual nature of sexual abuse. Arousal and subsequent sexual release creates psychological dependence and denial of dependence. It poses specific problems in the general management of child sexual abuse and in the therapy of perpetrators.

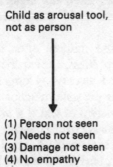

Child as arousal tool,
not as person

(1) Person not seen
(2) Needs not seen
(3) Damage not seen
(4) No empathy

Figure 2.3 The function of the child in sexual abuse

One father who had abused his daughter for 4 years described how he would feel a physical tension rising in his body when he was under stress. It would make him feel like bursting, and he knew that he would sexually abuse his daughter and he created the circumstances accordingly. He was tense and driven and felt as if in a cloud of mist around him. He then abused his daughter. Afterwards he felt guilty, but avoided facing what he had done by literally avoiding to face his daughter for a certain time. Once he had attempted to stop the abuse and told the girl not to come near him when they were on their own in the house . . . only to create a situation where the father and his daughter would be in the house on their own at a time when he took a bath, leaving the bathroom naked, seeing his daughter and starting to abuse her again. He then tried to blame her for it.

Again we need to differentiate between lying and denial. Sexual abuse can still be denied psychologically as expression of reality avoidance under the syndrome of secrecy and addiction even in cases in which the abuser has confessed openly in court. To own up fully to the sexual abuse as psychological reality can be extremely threatening and frightening for sexual abusers. The very weakness of ego-strength which has led to sexual abuse as a means of reality avoidance makes it very difficult for sexual abusers to face up to their responsibility for the abuse. One father who had admitted legally to the abuse and who had been in prison for 2 years reported after discharge that he did not know what had happened and that he wanted to find out. A stepfather in a similar situation maintained a psychological state of denial by saying he had only gone to prison in order to protect his stepdaughter from having to testify in court. Neither of the two men needed to lie for legal reasons. Neither of them had faced up psychologically to the abuse and for neither of them had the abuse become psychological fact and reality despite lengthy legal actions. Child sexual abuse as syndrome of addiction also means that sexual abusers are not 'cured' after successful treatment. In circumstances of stress and in situations which may give them the opportunity, sexual abusers can remain in danger of re-abusing again.

Aspects of addiction also occur frequently in victims of child sexual abuse. Amongst common addictive symptoms are drug addiction, solvent abuse, alcohol and nicotine abuse, dependency on minor tranquillisers and other tablets. The mechanism which leads to addiction in victims seems to be a combination of two main elements.

Long-term sexually abused children often develop maladaptive coping mechanisms for tension relief of stress. The experience of sexual abuse has taught them to deal with stress and anxiety by direct tension relief in addictive behaviour. The addiction has the same function as sexualised behaviour and compulsive masturbation of victims of sexual abuse.

The second element in the addictive behaviour is increased levels of anxiety as a consequence of the total experience of sexual abuse and its context. Inadequate coping mechanisms are met by increased anxiety from the abuse. The addiction creates tension relief and reality avoidance which helps the victim to avoid facing the reality of the abusive experience.

2.3 The interlocking process between secrecy and addiction

The syndromes of secrecy and addiction are interlocking syndromes. Child sexual abuse is an illegal interaction which is addictive for the abuser where the 'drug' is a structurally dependent child. In many cases the child relates to the abuser as parenting figure. The addiction to a 'drug' which is a structurally dependent child makes the effective discontinuation of the addiction both most difficult and of the utmost importance.

The aspect of secrecy and the aspect of addiction are both mechanisms of reality avoidance for the abuser in which the child is forced to join in under the syndrome of secrecy. The great difficulty in stopping child sexual abuse, in breaking the secrecy, in creating and maintaining reality and in dealing with the often extremely strong and destructive mutual attachments between abuser and child are specific effects of child sexual abuse as interlocking syndrome of secrecy and addiction.

Although the fully developed interlocking syndrome of secrecy and addiction is more important in long-term child sexual abuse within the family, we may find similar features in short-term abuse, especially with younger children and even in extrafamilial abuse. One case of extrafamilial abuse by a middle aged man in a small community which involved several children continued over a period of 2 years, showing all the crucial elements of child sexual abuse as interlocking syndrome of secrecy and addiction. (See Extrafamilial child sexual abuse, Chapter 13.)

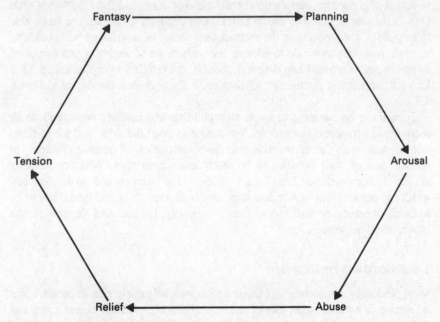

Figure 2.4 The addictive cycle in child sexual abuse

2.4 The individual process in context

2.4.1 The interaction nature of motivation

Motivation has traditionally been regarded as an internal psychological process of the individual which is owned by the client and patient. The decision about treatment and therapy was therefore assessed in terms of the presence or absense of motivation as individual property.

The move from 'mad' to 'bad', from psychological and relationship problems to legal and child protective issues in work with physical and sexual abuse, has taught us that in this context an intrinsic state of non-motivation does not exist. As there is no state of non-communication in a social context, there is equally no state of 'non-motivation' in the intervention of child sexual abuse. There is a motivation to be motivated or a motivation not to be motivated. In child sexual abuse as syndrome of secrecy and addiction, family members can be motivated to trust or they can be motivated not to trust, which is often falsely interpreted as being 'non-motivated'.

Whether sexually abused children or abusers are motivated to trust is the result not of an internal state but of an interactional process between professionals and the child, the abuser and the family. Whether the child or the family is motivated to trust or not depends therefore as much on the skills of professionals as on their own motivation. This interactional element of motivation is crucial in dealing with child sexual abuse. In child sexual abuse the denial of abuse and the refusal to accept help does not automatically mean that children and families do not want help. It may mean that they are frightened and that they do not trust us to be able to help them. Understanding the interactional nature of motivation will enable us to begin from our own side to address the wide range of anxieties and imagined or real disasters which keep children, abusers and families from disclosing. (See Explicit therapeutic permission to disclose, 8.5; Legal interviewing of children, 9.2.)

It needs to be our skill to know why children and families are unable to be motivated to trust and to disclose. We ourselves need the skills and the motivation to deal with the often understandable motivation of abused children, of abusers and of their families to be motivated not to trust. Whether sexually abused children and their families are 'motivated to be motivated' to disclose and to accept our services or whether they are 'motivated to be motivated not to be helped' depends on individual factors, family factors and factors in the professional network.

1 Individual and family factors

Most obviously, abusers are not motivated to seek help out of fear of prosecution. As strong or even stronger can be the fear of divorce or family breakdown and the fear of loss of economic and social status. The first interactional factor of motivation is therefore the degree of objective threats of punishment and the legal and social attitude towards sexual abusers. A punitive response increases the motivation for abusers to keep the abuse secret. The main obstacle in many countries to gain the trust of abusers is the lack of sufficient treatment facilities which can deal with the addiction. Problem-oriented professional help needs to be available before abusers will disclose and seek help. In the end any therapeutic approach to child sexual abuse is only as good as the treatment of abusers.

Children are often motivated not to seek help because they have not previously been believed. They have been punished, they have been scapegoated for attempts to disclose, they have been threatened by the abuser with disaster and they are frightened of the consequences of disclosure for themselves, for the abuser, whom they may still love, and for the family. Mothers may be motivated not to be motivated to try to find help because they fear the loss of their partner, family breakup and the loss of the breadwinner. They may be frightened of being reminded of sexual abuse in their own childhood. They may fear facing their own maternal role in maintaining the abuse. Often they fear that professionals will do more damage than good to them and their families.

It needs to be our professional skill to know why and when children, abusers and families are motivated not to be motivated to accept our help. We need to address the underlying fears and feared disasters which threaten the material and social existence of the family and its individual members. We can therefore change the state of motivation towards an increased motivation to trust and to want to find help. This way of putting the issue may look rather laborious. However, describing the interactional nature of motivation enables us to understand that the second interactional element is our own motivation as professionals.

2 Professional factors of motivation

The first direction of motivation is the family–professional direction. The second is the professional–family direction. It also holds for professionals that in the intervention of child sexual abuse there is no state of 'non-motivation'. Whether we as professionals are motivated to be motivated is determined by our ability to cope. The ability of professionals to cope depends on three basic factors:

a. The ability to cope personally with the issues of sexual abuse and to find personal and professional support.
b. If we are able to cope personally, we need professional knowledge and professional skills.
c. No personal ability to cope and no knowledge or skill will motivate professionals to help dealing with sexually abused children and their families without resources, structures and settings for services.

We need to take these three elements equally seriously to avoid inappropriate professional conduct and action and to avoid destructive personalising and blaming between professionals, which easily leads to structural institutional conflicts and conflicts-by-proxy. The huge new task of dealing with child sexual abuse cannot be undertaken without the careful examination of personal issues of identification, without considering professional training and structures of co-operation in a multi-professional metasystemic approach and without stating clearly the resource implications of our work.

We as professionals may under certain circumstances and for our own good reasons not be motivated to be motivated to deal with complex cases of child sexual abuse. I am not talking about any open refusal to fulfil our professional duties but about subtle interactional processes which may not even be conscious to the professional. Children and families invariably get the message not to disclose when we are for personal reasons, or due to lack of skill, support or resources, unable to deal with sexual abuse. Professionals who deal with complex cases of child sexual abuse are always vulnerable to burn out. Acknowledging the interactional nature of motivation requires us as professionals to be responsible and kind with ourselves. We need to know and observe the limits of our own abilities to cope and we need to be aware of our own needs for personal, professional and interagency support.

We must not confuse our own motivation as professionals towards the family with the family's motivation towards us as professionals when we consider the interactional nature of motivation. There are legitimate situations for professionals not be motivated to be motivated to intervene in child sexual abuse. This can be ethical and most responsible as long as we do not pretend we ourselves are motivated to help while labelling the children and families as 'unmotivated', as 'inadequate' or as 'untreatable' when in fact we are the ones who are not motivated because we cannot cope for our own good reasons.

The truly interactional nature of motivation becomes obvious when we understand that the child is only as motivated to disclose child sexual abuse as we are motivated to listen. That means being willing and being able to cope with the message. We constantly give very subtle messages to clients and families about what they can tell us and what not. I would even go so far as to say that the emergence of unconscious issues of which the client and patient is unaware is strongly influenced by our own motivation as professionals to bring these issues to light.

Sexually abused children have a very acute sense of the interactional nature of motivation. They primarily act on our cues, which are the starting point. What seems their beginning of opening up and of disclosing is usually in fact already a response to our own cues (see The use of the 'trusted person', 8.6). This element of the interactional nature of motivation is crucial because we need to become aware that disclosures which seem to be initiated and started by the child are in many cases in fact triggered by the professional. We can use the interactional nature of motivation to foster children's disclosure by the way we interact with them as much as we can avoid triggering a premature full disclosure at the wrong moment by withholding the explicit licence to communicate.

2.4.2 Giving explicit licence to communicate

Even in the face of obvious sexual abuse children often flatly deny that abuse has taken place. In child sexual abuse as syndrome of secrecy children need explicit permission and licence to communicate. This is necessary for legal and for therapeutic reasons.

The psychological process of giving explicit permission to communicate addresses itself to the external, the interactional and internal aspects of child sexual abuse as syndrome of secrecy. Children need to feel that they can trust to disclose sexual abuse without being rejected or punished by their family or by professionals. Giving children explicit licence to communicate about sexual abuse means addressing openly all the possible anxieties which may motivate the child not to disclose. We need to address:

1 The secrecy.
2 The fear of non-believing.
3 The fear about the threats not to disclose.
4 The anxieties about the consequences of disclosure for the child herself and for the family.
5 The fear of punishment and rejection by family members and professionals.
6 Finally we need to give explicit licence to communicate in sexual language by introducing sexual language ourselves.

In cases of suspicion or partial disclosure, giving explicit permission to communicate takes a very specific and indirect form. First we need to give the child the message that 'I know that sexual abuse takes place and that you are frightened to disclose'. This message addresses the syndrome of secrecy. The second step is a more complex indirect interactional process which aims at the message 'I know that you know that I know that you are frightened and why you are frightened'. If given over time the communication of secrecy will, it is to be hoped, induce trust in children that we understand their anxieties and predicaments. (See Explicit therapeutic permission to disclose, 8.5; Legal interviewing of children, 9.2.)

We need to find ways of giving the message of secrecy for legal and for therapeutic purposes. This can happen in the form of the use of the 'third person' or by telling 'the story of the other child' as described in Section 8.5. Or we can show prevention films and work with prevention material as a means of giving explicit licence to disclose already ongoing abuse (see The use of prevention films, 8.12; Dealing with primary denial, 10.6). Professionals often need to take the initiative to raise the issue first, starting to communicate explicitly about child sexual abuse, whether through films, through stories or through the use of the 'third person' as metaphor. Legal and statutory workers and mental health professionals often try anxiously to avoid 'giving explicit licence to communicate' out of fear of interfering with the legal process.

Professionals unfortunately often confuse the difference between legal interviewing of children in order to gain evidence and to validate legal facts and the very different though connected task of giving children licence to communicate in order to free the child psychologically. This severe misunderstanding of the psychological and interactional motivational processes in child sexual abuse as syndrome of secrecy for the child often prevents disclosure. To give children explicit psychological licence to communicate about sexual abuse is a necessary precondition for subsequent legal interviewing and disclosure. Giving explicit licence to communicate and legal interviewing are therefore complementary tasks. They are not mutually exclusive processes and must not be construed as such. Just as the use of prevention films does not put ideas into children's minds as long as professionals differentiate appropriately between what happens in the films and what might have happened to the child, so will the story of the 'third child' not manipulate the child as long as the professional clearly presents the 'story of the other child' as *his* story.

The 'story of the other child' and the use of the 'third person' makes therapeutic use of the interactional nature of motivation in the specific context of child sexual abuse as syndrome of secrecy. The very moment the child acknowledges that sexual abuse has taken place and begins to tell her own story, the rules of factual information gathering and of legal interviewing have to be applied instantly. The complementary relationship between the mental health process of giving explicit licence to communicate and the need for factual legal interviewing cannot be overemphasised. Giving explicit licence to communicate is as much furthering the legal process as legal interviewing may be therapeutic in establishing the facts of the abuse and the abuse as fact.

The child may also need explicit permission to acknowledge sexual abuse as psychological reality when the abuse has only been acknowledged legally without a responsibility session with the family (see Family-session-by-proxy, 9.13). The initial responsibility session with the family is a very effective way of giving children explicit permission to deal with the abuse (see Aims and steps in the Primary Therapeutic Intervention, 6.2). The open acknowledgement by the abuser or other family members of the abuse as fact and the clarification of responsibilities give the child explicit and open licence to communicate about the abuse, which is the precondition for the child's ability to make use of any subsequent therapy.

2.4.3 Naming, creating and maintaining child sexual abuse as reality

Even in legally proven cases, child sexual abuse usually remains a family secret in psychological and relationship terms. The three steps of (1) naming reality, (2) creating reality and (3) maintaining reality in child sexual abuse are often very difficult to achieve. In child sexual abuse as syndrome of secrecy and addiction the naming of sexual abuse as reality has specific meaning. The process of naming and the very words spoken aloud only create sexual abuse as psychological reality for the family and for family members. Without the openly and audible spoken words the abuse does not exist.

Naming the abuse aloud has for professionals the sometimes startling effect that the person who utters the words is seen as the person who creates the abuse. This process explains the extraordinary phenomenon that professionals who hold a first family meeting in legally well-established cases of child sexual abuse may face a family whose members continue fiercely to attempt to avoid using the words to name the abuse. The first person, and often it is the professional, who uses sexual language and names the abuse is then blamed for the family crisis and is scapegoated for it . . . as if the person who has broken the family secret were actually himself the abuser and responsible for the abuse.

Naming the facts of sexual abuse creates the abuse as family reality. It is important to use explicit sexual language like 'sexual relationship', 'sexual intercourse', and 'putting the penis up the bottom'. The process of reality creation is aided by talking explicitly about the context in which the abuse took place. At what time of the day did it happen, how often and where did it take place, who else was in the household and what happened just before the abuse and just afterwards, and for how long had it gone on? We see how much the legal and therapeutic aims of establishing the abuse as family reality are complementary in a metasystemic approach.

It is important for the child to hear in one or two family sessions from the abuser himself what had happened and that the abuser himself takes full responsibility for the abuse. It is most striking how even adults of 60 and 70 years have talked about the confusion of what really happened in the abuse, saying 'if only once in my life I could have told my father what he has done to me and if I only could have heard from him once why he did this to me', often adding the typical statement of the abused child 'and what was wrong with me that it had to happen to me?' The need for sexually abused children to establish once in their lifetime the facts of the abuse openly with the abuser himself and other family members relates to the problem of creating psychological reality in child sexual abuse as syndrome of secrecy.

Professionals often experience that family members individually make statements disclosing sexual abuse and admitting to it only to retract the statement again the next day. This could be attributed entirely to the legal threat when children, mothers and abusers realise the possible legal consequences of the disclosure. The interesting fact is that child sexual abuse as syndrome of secrecy and addiction is maintained as reality once the abuser, the child and the mother plus possible siblings have openly talked about the facts of the abuse in the presence of one outsider. Even in cases where the legal threat still exists, sexual abuse will remain reality. This seems to be based on the fact that the family meeting in the presence of one outsider as 'naming event' breaks through the secrecy and creates in itself a reality which every family member shares as the moment of creating the abuse as individual reality and as family fact. The 'naming event' serves as a lasting point of reference to maintain the abuse as reality when the family members feel drawn back into secrecy and denial during the following treatment.

The need for the child to create child sexual abuse as reality by naming the details of the abuse is very similar to the process of 'traumatic debriefing' of victims of sudden disasters. Although the abuse may have been happening for years, the same process of cognito-emotional incongruence and dissonance exists. In child sexual abuse the disaster is created by the process of naming the fact of abuse and not by the previous years of secret sexual abuse itself. The disclosure induces a crisis similar to that of other sudden disasters. The need to go step by step through the sequence of events in order to understand and relate specific emotions to specific cognitions in the sequence of the abuse constitutes a central therapeutic element in dealing with child sexual abuse in the same way as in the treatment of other sudden psychological traumata and disasters.

Naming, creating and maintaining reality is especially difficult in individual therapy. The external context of the one to one situation in individual therapy and the specific transference–countertransference interaction make it extremely difficult to establish the external reality of the abuse as a necessary basis for the related fantasy and feelings in the therapeutic process of individual therapy. This does not mean that naming, creating and maintaining reality of sexual abuse cannot be achieved in individual therapy. It only means that individual therapists need to be aware of the specific problems of child sexual abuse as interlocking syndrome of secrecy and addiction (see Individual counselling and therapy, 7.3).

2.4.4 The unconscious and secrecy

Child sexual abuse as a syndrome of secrecy can often be unwillingly maintained by professionals who confuse unconscious communication and secrecy. School children describe in essays, pre-school children in drawings and children in therapy in verbal or non-verbal hints, directly or indirectly, their experience of child sexual abuse. A child who writes in a school essay about 'a nightmare' and describes explicit sexual matters may be punished for exhibiting dirty fantasy. In individual therapy these communications may be interpreted as part of unconscious fantasies. What seems to be unconscious material or 'dirty fantasies' may in fact be the child's secret attempt to communicate about the reality of sexual abuse.

Unconscious and secret communications are of a fundamentally different nature and need to be followed up in very different ways. Unconscious communications in individual therapy need to be interpreted when the child is re-enacting traumatic events. The therapist's task is to interpret the unconscious re-enactment as part of the therapeutic process. The timing of the interpretation depends very much on the stage and the transference situation in therapy and it can be highly therapeutic not to interpret a certain unconscious communication immediately.

Professionals need to react very differently when a child tries secretly to communicate the facts of child sexual abuse. If there is any suspicion that the child may consciously indicate sexual abuse, this communication must never be interpreted. The child must be given the explicit therapeutic licence to communicate instead. The child may be very aware of what she is doing and will test secretly whether we take up the reality aspect of the hint about sexual abuse, whether we are able to see the reality in the child's communication and whether the child can trust us to help. Secret communications are part of the conscious aspect of the interactional nature of motivation.

The moment we think a child is communicating the reality of child sexual abuse we need to switch from an 'interpretative mode' into an 'investigative mode'. In the first process we tend to give meaning to events, in the latter we would want to gain factual information. The sexually abused child who communicates secrecy knows perfectly well what the secret communication means. We do not need to tell her. But the child does not trust us to understand the hidden facts. Children usually select one very specific person as 'Trusted Person' whom they trust to give these hints. Usually children do not dare to disclose when the indirect hints as cry for help have been dismissed or disgarded. Not taking up a secret communication about sexual abuse on the level of reality can therefore be extremely damaging. (See The use of the 'trusted person', 8.6.)

Unconscious	Secrecy
(1) Child is unaware of communication	(1) Child is aware of communication
(2) Communication of psychological experience	(2) Communication of external reality
(3) Re-enactment of traumatic event	(3) Child is testing whether reality aspect is understood
(4) Interpretation to change meaning of events	(4) Therapist needs to ask questions to herself or child to clarify external reality
INTERPRETATIVE MODE OF THERAPY	INVESTIGATIVE MODE OF DEALING WITH SECRECY

Figure 2.5 The unconscious and secrecy

Having made the categorical distinction between unconscious and secret communication I need to qualify this dichotomy. Young children who have not yet reached the developmental stage at which they can fully understand and operate the concept of secrecy often play and talk about sexual abuse in a way which blurs the boundaries between the unconscious and secrecy. However, even in these cases therapists need to respond in the same way. We must not interpret, but we need to switch to an investigative mode.

Asking questions about the possible reality of sexual abuse in the investigative mode does not mean immediately asking the child. The questioning begins with the therapist himself. The self-questioning can lead from a vague first-line suspicion to a well formed second-line suspicion, and an anonymous inter-professional diagnostic consultation may be involved. Only later, and sometimes after many weeks or months, may the therapist himself or somebody else need to ask the child openly in order to establish facts. (See Steps in the crisis inter-vention of disclosure, 8.2.)

Interpreting secret communications in child sexual abuse as fantasy becomes anti-therapeutic therapy with the result of a likely increased disturbance in the child. I myself had several referrals of young children who had been labelled as 'psychotic' by therapists. These children only tried to communicate the reality of ongoing sexual abuse which was dealt with as fantasy and which was interpreted accordingly. These interpretations induced increasing confusion and disturbance in children who were subsequently then regarded as psychotic. In the context of the specific problems of child sexual abuse as syndrome of secrecy, the com-munications of these children, which out of context seemed 'psychotic', made perfect sense within the context of sexual abuse.

Chapter three

The family process

3.1 Confusion on different levels of dependency

In families of child sexual abuse intergenerational boundaries have broken down in certain areas of family functioning and remain intact in others. The reversal of the family hierarchy between parents and child in some areas leads to incongruence between different levels of family functioning, which is disorienting and disturbing to the child. On the level of practical care, there seems to be no difference in the range of standards between families with sexual abuse and other families. On the sexual level the structural dependence of the daughter or son as a child clashes with their role as pseudo-equal partners in the inappropriate intergenerational sexual relationship with the abuser. In terms of emotional dependence, the father is on a similar level of immaturity as the child.

On the background of a wide range of different aetiological and precipitating individual factors which lead to sexual abuse, the central underlying process in relationship terms which creates a family pattern that can maintain long-term child sexual abuse is the hidden emotio-sexual conflicts between the parents, who are locked in an unequal emotional and sexual partnership. The term 'emotio-sexual conflict' sounds rather dreadful. Yet I could not find a more normal sounding term which describes precisely the point I want to make. The term 'emotio-sexual conflict' describes the confusion between conflicts on emotional and sexual levels. When a child comes for emotional care it gets a sexual response. Later on sexually abused children in their confusion between emotional care and sexual experience may bring sexualised behaviour when they in fact want emotional care. In the extreme boys may then grow up to become sexual abusers themselves and girls repeat the emotio-sexual confusion by becoming promiscuous and prostitutes. In marriage the sexual conflict is ignored and not dealt with. It is substituted with emotional care which enables the couple to ditch the issue of sexual conflict. The inability of the parents to deal with the specific confusion between their sexual and emotional problems and the introduction of a taboo against an acknowledgement of these tensions and conflicts in the family sets the scene which can maintain long-term child sexual abuse in the family once it has started.

In a secondary process which maintains the abuse, the child is locked into sexual abuse with the father on the basis of paternal threats, either physical or emotional, or both. Mutual guilt feelings and fear of punishment prevent disclosure by either of them. On the other hand, the development of trust and emotional closeness between mother and daughter is blocked by feelings of rejection or guilt, despite a possible pseudo-closeness between them. This hinders the open acknowledgement of sexual abuse and prevents the child from getting help from the mother as non-abuse parent. The secrecy is linked to the overall confusion of hierarchies within the different levels of practical care, emotional care and sexual partnership between the parents, and between each parent and the child. The systemic confusion of hierarchies on different functional levels in a system of secrecy, binds the family members into a collusive system in which sexual abuse can continue for many years (see Figure 3.1).

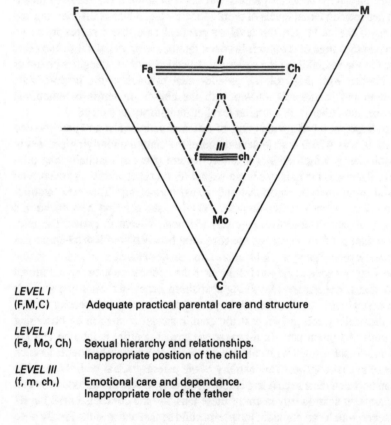

LEVEL I
(F,M,C)   Adequate practical parental care and structure

LEVEL II
(Fa, Mo, Ch)   Sexual hierarchy and relationships.
                      Inappropriate position of the child

LEVEL III
(f, m, ch,)   Emotional care and dependence.
                      Inappropriate role of the father

Figure 3.1 Confusion of different hierarchies between father, mother and child

3.2 Family pattern

We have found different patterns of relationships in families of child sexual
abuse. These patterns arose from the different responses of different families and
family members to the disclosure and subsequent treatment and we have identified different functions of sexual abuse which operate as conflict-avoiding or as
conflict-regulating mechanisms in these families (Furniss, 1984a).

Individual psychological and psychiatric factors obviously influence the interpersonal relationships within any family. A wide range of personality factors and
different previous individual life experiences of parents, and the great variety of
circumstances under which family units are established, act as aetiological and
precipitating factors in the formation of the common final relationship pattern of
child sexual abuse in the family. The individual reason for fathers to become
abusers, or for mothers not be able to be protective, can be very varied. Both may
themselves have been sexually or physically abused as children. The individual
life experience of the parents makes it often understandable why the parents react
in the way they do and why they choose each other as partners, often re-creating
the family pattern of their own family of origin.

The different family pattern and the difference in function of sexual abuse can
lead to very different reactions of families and family members during disclosure
and therapy. The description of the family pattern with the respective function of
child sexual abuse as 'conflict-avoiding' or 'conflict-regulating' mechanism is
primarily a tool for practitioners to understand the family process in the intervention. The question is not why and for what individual reason the present
relationship pattern arose but how it works. It is therefore not an aetiological
pattern but a maintaining pattern which sustains long-term child sexual abuse in
the family. They are the extremes of a continuum rather than distinct entities. In
the complexity of the organisation of families no typology could ever do justice
to the uniqueness of real families. However, the distinction between conflict
avoidance and conflict regulation in the organised and disorganised family has
important practical implications which have helped clinicians to orientate themselves in the complexities of intervening in families of child sexual abuse.

3.2.1 The organised family

3.2.1.1 Emotional dependence and immaturity of fathers

Family hierarchy, in terms of emotional dependence, does not necessarily correspond with family hierarchy on the level of observable family interaction (Glaser
et al., 1984). We know from clinical experience that the behaviour of an aggressive and authoritarian father towards a seemingly weak and silent mother in no
way automatically reflects the governing family structure and experience of
emotional dependence. Working on the underlying pattern of emotional depen-

dence can reveal a reversed constellation, with an emotionally weak father and a much more emotionally mature and independent mother.

The stereotype of the strong independent father, the 'gorilla' who does not only take his wife for sex but also his daughter, does not hold. Literally millions of sexually frustrated men separate, divorce or have extra-marital relationships. Everyone who works with couples knows that truly emotionally strong and independent men separate, divorce or have extra-marital adult relationships in situations of unresolved sexual partner conflict. Many men as well as women have sexual problems. Truly independent and autonomous men do not turn to children for sexual gratification but find other adult sexual partners. Fathers in families of long-term child sexual abuse often seem to be emotionally immature and heavily dependent on their wives for emotional care. Combined with emotional immaturity, the fathers make normal or excessive adult sexual demands or are perceived as doing so by their partners. This pattern is confirmed when therapists deal with aspects of separation, individuation, autonomy and emotional independence. The fathers in these families are typically less able to deal with these issues than their wives.

3.2.1.2 The mother's role as non-abusing parent

Mothers in families where child sexual abuse takes place usually have the role of non-abusing parent. In this role the protective function is crucial in long-term child sexual abuse. Despite the apparent dominance of fathers, mothers may determine the family culture in terms of the quality of emotional relationships in the family. This includes the way in which sexual and emotional matters are talked about in the family.

In strict and moralistic families mothers often compensate for a moralistic or punitive attitude towards sexuality by compulsive caretaking. On a practical level these mothers usually provide perfect care for their children and appear to be very close and caring. In many areas they are very competent and caring mothers indeed. The distance in the mother–child dyad emerges when it comes to issues of protection against sexual abuse. When children try to indicate openly that sexual abuse is taking place, the mothers either dismiss these claims or do not take their daughters and sons seriously, although they may take token steps to disprove the allegations.

In two cases, daughters had told their mothers about sexual abuse by their fathers several years before the final disclosure. The mothers, rather than trying to establish the situation with their husbands, took the girls to their family doctors. In one case the doctor labelled the girl 'jealous'; in the other, he declared the allegations to be 'fantasy'. In neither case did the mother confront the father. The visits to the doctors served in both cases to avoid clarifying the suspicion of sexual abuse within the family, seeking a professional ally outside the family to confirm the denial.

Child sexual abuse does indeed also happen in families with a close and protective mother–daughter relationship. However, in these cases the sexual abuse will not continue for years. These mothers are often mothers who themselves disclose the abuse. They pick up the signs of sexual abuse from the children who tell and who are believed. Or they recognise changes in the family process when husbands and children start to behave strangely. When they detect indicators for sexual abuse or find out *in flagrante* they take seriously what they see or hear and act accordingly. They usually take protective actions and induce a disclosure in order to protect the child.

3.2.1.3 The child's position

Children in families of long-term child sexual abuse do not feel emotionally understood or adequately cared for by either parent. Following paternal threats, sometimes of death, children comply with their fathers' inappropriate sexual demands because they are frightened to be punished by both parents if they try to disclose. They experience their mothers as either emotionally rigid or distant or they feel that they would not believe them or would not protect them from paternal abuse. Children have often tried to disclose and many have constantly but in vain appealed for the protection of the non-abusing parent. Some of the children had never felt close to their mothers, and had turned to their father for emotional care, who betrayed their trust when they were sexually abused in the process.

In sexually abused children feelings of being special, of rivalry and of triumph can stand next to extreme self-blame, feelings of total worthlessness and feelings of being dirty and unloved. Self-destructive punishment and acting out by repeating the abusive pattern in other relationships is often an expression of the continued strong and destructive attachment to the abuser. It is hard to understand and difficult to learn again what we have learnt in physical abuse: even extremely damaging relationships can be very strong and important relationships. The attachment to the abuser can, despite extreme sexual abuse, be the most important attachment in the child's life. 'Why was I so bad that my father had to beat and sexually abuse me as a child?' mirrors 'I hate my father but for once I wanted to be seen and appreciated by him' – both said by a woman in her late 50s.

The family taboo against talking about sexual abuse prevents children from being able to find any help from inside or outside the family. All children in therapy are at some stage angry with the abuser for the abuse as much as all blame their mothers at some stage in therapy for not having protected them from the abuse and from the helpless and desperate position they had to endure in the family without being able to talk to anybody about the sometimes extremely frightening or confusing experience of sexual abuse.

3.2.1.4 Clinical example: the M family

From early childhood until his mother's death 5 years previously, Peter, a

33-year-old ship's engineer, had tried to please his grossly overweight mother and strove to be a loving son to her. However, whatever he did was wrong in her eyes, and she would punish him at will, first by being silent and ignoring him and then by suddenly breaking into ferocious shouting and slapping. Although Peter never seemed to please his mother, she would not allow him to leave her to play freely with other children. She often kept him in the house, under her ever-frightening gaze. Nevertheless, he continued in vain to try to please her and to gain her recognition by being helpful, often making expensive presents. But the very fact of his presence or, at times, his absence could lead to a sudden fierce onslaught. In a constant state of fear and insecurity Peter also felt continuously guilty towards his mother.

Peter's father was a nice but very weak man. Peter reported: 'He was a pure slave of my mother and he had to do what she wanted. He was sent to wake us children from our sleep at night to punish us for what we had done to her during the day.' When he was 11 years old, Peter ran away for the first time. At 16, he became a seaman and escaped his family. 'At home, not once in my life did I get a glimpse of love and real affection from my mother.' As a seaman, he 'sowed his wild oats' in the ports of the world, but always went back to his mother, although these holidays were always disappointing. At 22, he met his wife, Anna, who, at that time had a 3-year-old boy and a baby girl.

Anna was 32 years old and came from a large, very religious family from a small rural village in the South. Her family was poor and Anna had been used to hard work since childhood. Her father was an alcoholic and ever since the age of 9, Anna had had to take over adult tasks in the family. Though her father was rough, she took his side, but overcompensated for her hatred of his violent alcoholism by adopting strict moral views for herself. At 17, she became engaged to a boy in the village. They had intercourse and Anna became pregnant, giving birth to a boy. The boyfriend broke off the engagement and left but returned 2 years later, again promising to marry her. They resumed intercourse and Anna became pregnant again. The relationship did not last and following the birth of the second child, Anna moved with her children to a large town and went to work as a kitchen help. There she met Peter and married him. After their wedding Peter went back to sea for 3 years and then settled ashore. Two boys were born in the marriage and the hard-working Anna ran the household in a strongly matriarchal way, caring well for her children and her husband. They were regarded in the neighbourhood as hard-working, upright people, good parents to their well-dressed and well-behaved children. Peter reported: 'Ever since I met Anna, I had a real family and I felt safe.'

Like his father who was 'a slave to his wife', Peter had been his mother's slave. When he met Anna, he found in her a strict, rigidly moral but caring mother figure as a wife, who looked after him and the children with the same motherly compulsion. Anna had always looked after people, especially her father, and Peter had looked for someone who would care for him. They formed quite a stable complementary pseudo-mother–son relationship. On the sexual level, they also had different needs. During therapy, Anna disclosed that she thought Peter had always been 'oversexed'.

The sexual abuse between Peter and his stepdaughter, Elizabeth, developed slowly. It began when Anna had sent Peter and the children, including the 8-year-old Elizabeth, to shower together. Father and stepdaughter soaped and washed each other, and these actions became progressively more sexualised by the father. By the time she was 9, Elizabeth had been subjected to full sexual intercourse.

Peter made several attempts to stop, but at the same time would arrange situations which led to the continuation of the abuse. Taking a bath he would leave the bathroom door open and was unable to withstand Elizabeth coming into the bathroom naked while he was bathing. As Elizabeth approached puberty, Peter became increasingly obsessed and sexually involved with her and used force on several occasions. The relationship became more tense when Elizabeth started going out with boys of her own age. The abuse ended when Elizabeth was nearly 14 years old and told a worker in a youth club about the abuse. The disclosure of the abuse threatened the survival of the family and the marriage. Anna, the mother, was extremely upset and claimed she knew nothing about the abuse.

3.2.1.5 Interlocking vicious circles in the M family

The confusion of intergenerational hierarchies and the relationship pattern in the M family led to the following circular process which maintained the ongoing abuse: (i) The more Mr M became involved in the sexual abuse with Elizabeth (ii) the more he felt guilty and became submissive to his wife. (iii) Mrs M, in turn, took a moralistic attitude towards her husband and cared compulsively for him, (iv) which then enabled her to reject his sexual demands. (v) Mr M in turn got more involved with his daughter.

The second vicious circle was interlocking with the first: (i) The more Elizabeth wanted to be understood by her mother, the more she felt rejected. (ii) She then moved closer to her father for emotional care (iii) who used his daughter's trust and wish for emotional care to abuse her and to satisfy his sexual demands. (iv) In the process Mr M became more closely bound to his daughter in a pseudo-partner system of secrecy (v) which increasingly alienated the daughter from her mother. (vi) This made Elizabeth feel more guilty towards her mother, (vii) but wanting to be closer to her she then tried to distance herself from her father but did not feel understood by her mother. A more detailed illustration of the abuse-maintaining circular process in the M family is given in Figure 3.2.

3.2.2 The disorganised family

The basic abuse maintaining family pattern in the disorganised family is similar to that of the organised family, but there are some important differences. Child

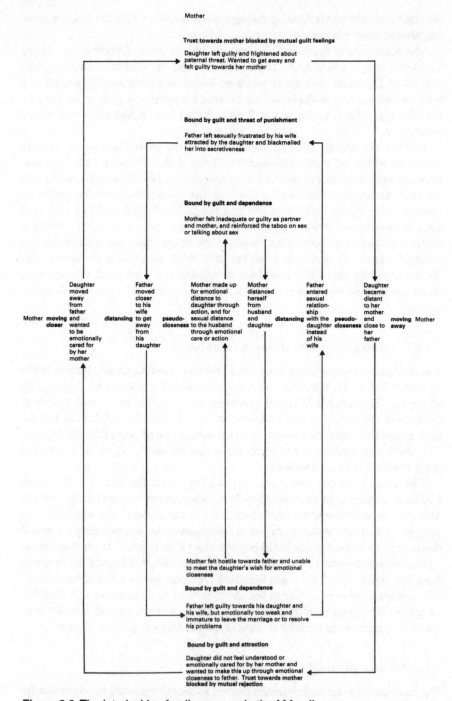

Figure 3.2 The interlocking family process in the M family

sexual abuse in the organised family is the expression of a very specific focalised problem in a family which otherwise shows satisfactory or good overall family functioning. The disorganised family has much poorer overall family functioning and parents and children seem to be on a pseudo-equal emotional level. Often one of the children takes the role of family organiser and emotional caretaker for the parents and siblings. As a consequence of both parents' own emotional deprivation and mutual dependency these families do not have any adequate emotional intergenerational boundaries. The father is more openly controlling and often physically violent. Illness, physical malformation or physical handicap make the father also more externally dependent on his wife as parental figure for practical care. Typically the mother is more permissive and less moralistic in her attitude. The abuse may be more or less known to other family members. The taboo to communicate the abuse takes the form more of a collusion of the entire family against the outside world.

The family is often known to educational services, to police or social services for other reasons and many other professionals may already be involved. The family is much more a multi-problem family with open marital conflict, and more than one child is often involved in the abuse. Boys and girls may be sexually abused simultaneously. There can even be an element of competition for attention between the different abused children. The father often starts abusing younger children once an older child has left home. This is contrary to the organised family where we find a highly special and emotionally laden relationship between the father and the abused child with a strong loss reaction when the abused child has left.

3.2.2.1 Clinical example: the Q family

When Ruth, aged 27, brought her 7-year-old son, Daniel, to the hospital a long history of minor illnesses since birth emerged. Ruth was accompanied by her own mother, who spoke for everyone and talked as if she herself were Daniel's mother. Mother and grandmother were competing with each other for the last word and soon both women talked about Ruth having been sexually abused by her father for 14 years. Sexual abuse had started when Ruth was 4 years old. Her father was blind, unemployed, and was always confined to the house. He was a very bitter, impatient and violent man. There was constant fighting and trouble at home, and Ruth became used to severe physical punishment. Following an early discovery of the abuse by the mother when Ruth was 5 years old, the mother had taken all three daughters with her whenever she had to leave the house. This lasted only a short while, and Ruth was soon left alone in the house with the father again. Later, in therapy, Ruth said, 'My mother knew about it, but she did not want to see it. I could never talk about it to her.' Ruth complained that her mother had never wanted to listen to her problems. When Ruth was 8, she bought her mother presents from her own money because she felt her mother needed her help: 'I am like my mother, always ready to care for others but never for myself.'

The sexual abuse took place at night. Ruth's father would come into her room when she was asleep and force her into intercourse. Often he had gagged her so that she could not cry out. When Ruth was older, she used to run away to stay with her maternal grandfather to whom she was very attached. She disclosed the sexual abuse but the grandfather did not believe her and always took her back home. When she was unable to get help from her brother either, she went to the police who returned her home, accepting the parent's collusive denial of Ruth's allegations. When Ruth was 9, she ran away several times. This time the police believed her and her father was sent to prison on a charge of sexual assault. After release Ruth's mother immediately took him back home. During the interview Ruth's mother explained: 'I had wanted a divorce for years. But I could not do it. He was blind wasn't he? I married him out of compassion and he needed me.'

Later, the father had intercourse with both of Ruth's younger sisters. Ruth reported bitterly that the youngest was father's favourite and enjoyed the abuse. There was a sense of rivalry and Ruth did not even have any secondary gains from the abusive relationship with her father. At 18, Ruth made a serious suicidal attempt and spent some days in hospital. Only then, after an incestuous relationship spanning 14 years, was her father sentenced to a longer term in prison, where he died soon afterwards. While still in hospital, Ruth met a man of her father's age. She married him within weeks so that she would not have to return home and live there again.

The couple lived in the same street as Ruth's mother, and their family life became completely dominated by her. Soon after giving birth to a baby boy and when she was pregnant again Ruth divorced her husband. She had numerous chaotic relationships with men, but her ex-husband remained a permanent husband–father-figure in the background. After the divorce, Ruth and her two children moved in with her maternal grandmother. The family pattern of total lack of individuation and the complete confusion of intergenerational boundaries was illustrated by the children who called both their mother and grandmother 'Mummy'.

3.3 Family function of child sexual abuse

3.3.1 Child sexual abuse as conflict avoidance

In conflict-avoiding families we find a huge discrepancy between the family's self-image and the reality of the quality of the actual family relationships. Conflict-avoiding families present themselves to the outside world as well-functioning, and are governed by strict moral family rules. Child sexual abuse serves as a means of denying any emotional and sexual imbalance and tension between the marital partners. To the outside world, all members of the family appear to agree with and conform to the family's strict moral code which may be reflected in active involvement in church activities. The family is often well-respected in the neighbourhood and successful in other areas of life. All family members enter into a collusion against any open acknowledgment of the abuse, which, as an open family reality, would be totally unacceptable to any family member.

The organised family	The disorganised family
General family functioning	
Satisfactory or good overall family functioning. Huge discrepancy between family self-image and reality of family relationships	Poor overall family functioning. Little discrepancy between family self-image and reality of family relationships
Marriage	
Marriage kept idealised	Open marital conflict, father kept in the family through sexual abuse
Secrecy	
Highly secretive incestuous relationship	More or less openly known. Incest sometimes acknowledged but then dismissed again and not talked about
Taboo	
Taboo on recognising sexual abuse or acknowledging any sexual problem	Taboo about revealing sexual abuse publicly
Collusion	
Parents against one child	Whole family against the child and outside world
Child's involvement	
Only one child, in highly special relationship. Only one gender involved	Several children often involved. Element of competition of siblings within abusive relationship. Girls and boys involved

Figure 3.3 Basic family patterns

The punitive and moralistic attitude towards sex and towards talking about sexual issues, and the simultaneous emotional dependence and sexual rejection between the marital partners, feeds the interlocking process of conflict avoidance. The sexually abusive relationship serves to uphold the split between the emotional and sexual aspects of the marital relationships, and between the emotional and practical caring aspects of the relationship between mother and child. The sexual abuse covers up the unequal balance of emotional dependence in the marriage and takes the pressure off the precarious sexual relationship between the parents.

The parents are unable to bear open marital and sexual conflict. Marital and family relationships are idealised which prevents adequate problem solving. Partner problems need to be denied to keep the pretence of problem-free marital harmony. The problem avoidance of any open sexual marital conflict leads to the triangulation of the child. The delegation of the sexual relationship puts the child into a pseudo-adult sexual alliance with her father and gives her the status of a pseudo-partner on the sexual level, from which the mother is excluded by secrecy. At the same time, the daughter retains a jointly agreed child status at the level of practical care. The secret, sexual pseudo-partner role of the child results in a disturbing victimisation. At the same time, it gives her a central position in the family, about which the family under high and rigid morality never communicates.

3.3.2 Child sexual abuse as a conflict regulator

In conflict-regulating families the marital and family conflict is openly visible and acknowledged and there is not much discrepancy between the families' self-image and the reality of the quality of their family relationships. In conflict-regulating families, we find open and aggressive family conflict. The sexually abusive relationship helps to decrease marital conflict which could lead to family breakup. The child is surrendered to the father with relatively more open knowledge. This does not mean that the abuse is ever talked about openly in the family. The whole family colludes in keeping the secret from outsiders. In addition to the immediate sexual function, the abuse provides an outlet for the father's aggression arising from his own personal problems.

In the conflict-regulating family, the sexual abuse itself does not pose the major threat to the family. Although the abuse may never be discussed openly both parents may covertly agree on the role of the sexually abused child or children in the family. The collusion between the parents increases the father's dependence on his wife, and she, in turn, tolerates or may even openly facilitate the abuse. This serves, despite all open and often violent conflicts, to keep the father emotionally dependent and firmly bound to the family. In the conflict-regulating family, the sexual abuse serves to level off the peaks of the often violent marital conflict which threatens the cohesion of the family.

3.3.3 Different reactions to disclosure and treatment

Public disclosure of child sexual abuse in the organised and conflict-avoiding family gives rise to immediate family disaster. The often huge and glaring discrepancy between the proclaimed family self-image of high moral standards of family relationships and the reality of the actual relationships creates a maximal crisis at the point of disclosure which threatens immediate family disintegration. Mothers usually see it as their duty instantly to file for divorce and father may threaten suicide. Unfortunately, I have been involved in two cases where fathers have, to the detriment of the abused children and the entire families, succeeded to take their own lives.

In organised conflict-avoiding families, drastic actions of violence, self-harm, running away or the development of psychosomatic symptoms by fathers at the initial disclosure are as much acting out in order to avoid facing the real issues as are immediate requests for divorce. Marital issues indeed need to be addressed and divorce may finally be the adequate solution. Instant requests for divorce at the moment of disclosure, however, are always reactions to the blow against the family's self-image after disclosure. Prompt legal actions by mothers have the function of relieving their acute sense of guilt and shock. After some weeks or months, however, we often find mothers who initiated instant divorce procedures linking up secretly with their husbands again. In view of the maximal initial family crisis, the moment of disclosure is not the time to talk about divorce. This should happen later in treatment (see Aims and steps in the Primary Therapeutic Intervention, 6.2). Following the initial crisis, organised and conflict-avoiding families are very often able to face the underlying family problem in therapy and to change family relationships.

In disorganised and conflict-regulating families the disclosure of child sexual abuse to the outside world does not lead to a crisis of the magnitude comparable to that in the organised and conflict-avoiding family. There is neither a great gap between the family's self-image and the reality of their actual family relationships nor the same degree of secrecy within the family. Not the disclosure of sexual abuse but the change of family relationships and the introduction of emotional and sexual intergenerational boundaries during the following treatment induces the family crisis and threatens the foundations on which the family is built.

Social services and other agencies have often already been involved in family problems and the new professional may add to an already existing large professional network. Disorganised and conflict-regulating families often integrate further professionals like 'uncles' and 'aunts' in an extended family network. These professionals are played off one against the other and meet each other at surprisingly large case conferences, often attended by 10–20 very qualified and highly experienced professionals. These case–conferences often mirror the family process of the disorganised and conflict-regulating family in which nobody is allowed to become effective nor has permission to leave either. Enormous amounts of coffee are consumed, usually at the expense of social services, but nothing changes in the family for months or years. These families are often world champions at getting large professional networks going without allowing them to have any effect on the family relationships and on the family functioning.

The major crisis in disorganised and conflict-regulating families is triggered when professional networks stop behaving like 'aunts' and 'uncles' in an extended family and when they cease to mirror the family process. When the professional network succeeds in drawing appropriate boundaries within the network and allows some colleagues to withdraw and others to take clear responsibility and to become effective, disorganised and conflict-regulating families react with maximum crisis. They try, often successfully, to break off therapy in order to avoid change at any cost.

The M family was a good example of an organised and conflict-avoiding family. The Q family, being a disorganised and conflict-regulating family, was not as moralistic, rigid and secretive as the M family. In contrast, they were more open and the father was more superficially exploitative: when Ruth was not available for sexual abuse, a sister soon had to take her place. In terms of long-term prognosis for therapy and change of family relationships, the organised and conflict-avoiding family would have a much better prognosis for rehabilitation than the disorganised and conflict-regulating family.

Sexual abuse as conflict avoidance	Sexual abuse as conflict regulation
Reaction to disclosure	
Threat of immediate family breakup and maximal family crisis due to destroyed idealised self-image of family relationships	Little immediate danger of family breakup. Tendency to re-establish previous family pattern immediately
Reaction to therapeutic intervention	
Initial dismissal of help due to discrepancy between family self-image and reality of relationships. After initial crisis, wish for change and intensive work possible	No rejection of therapy initially. Therapists welcome as 'uncle and aunts'. Break away when therapy starts to change family relationships
Critical points in the therapeutic process	
Revelation of huge discrepancy between family self-image and reality of family relationships at the moment of disclosure threatens the family	Concrete change of dysfunctional relationships in the course of treatment threatens to change the homeostasis which threatens the family unit

Figure 3.4 Family reactions to disclosure and treatment

Chapter four

The family and the professional network

The moment professionals intervene in a family of child sexual abuse the family ceases to be autonomous. Legal and child protective duties make outside agencies liable to intervene once child sexual abuse has been disclosed. A professional–family system is created. This results in changes in the family process and in the professional network involved. The abuse becomes both a family and a multi-professional problem. The structure of the intervention by professionals does not only influence family factors such as the place of stay of different family members and the degree of contact amongst them. The very external form of the intervention also directly influences the family relationships and the social and psychological situation of each individual family member involved.

Criminal, child protective and therapeutic aspects require multi-professional co-operation. Professionals from different disciplines and agencies form a professional network complementary to the family system. Very quickly different professionals become identified with different aspects of the family relationships, reflecting the different life situations of individual family members. For example, a social worker may identify with the mother, a teacher with the child and an adult psychiatrist with the father. There can also be identifications with different roles. The social worker may become identified with child protective aspects which may seem to clash with therapeutic aims represented by a child psychiatrist, which in turn may seem to be incompatible with criminal aspects of the case represented by the police. All these different aspects of the case may seem mutually exclusive and can lead to instant conflicts-by-proxy in the professional network. From the outset of the intervention the professional sub-system develops a dynamic of its own which is quite separate, though not independent, from the dynamic in the family sub-system. Both sub-systems immediately begin to interact and influence each other. The resulting interlocking process and the wider professional–family system determines what happens in the professional network and in the family.

4.1 Three basic types of intervention

Different basic forms of professional intervention lead to specific directions of change in the family relationships and to specific psychological changes in each family member. The type of the intervention influences whether family relationships revert to the original relationship pattern, whether the intervention leads to family breakdown or whether therapeutic changes might be achieved which enable the family to clarify their relationships and to live without sexual abuse.

We can distinguish three basic forms of professional interventions. Each type deals differently with the legal and relationship aspects of responsibility, participation and guilt described in Chapter 1. Each intervention has different aims and involves family members in very different ways. The three different types of intervention do not only reflect different organisational and external factors. The very external form and organisation of the intervention itself influences very differently the internal and psychological structure of each family member. The different interventions also influence differently the way in which everybody in the family interprets the meaning of the abuse. The very external form of the intervention can therefore be extremely therapeutic or very harmful respectively.

4.1.1 Primary Punitive Intervention (PPI)

The term 'Primary Punitive Intervention' (Figure 4.1) describes any intervention by any professional which has as its target the abuser with the aim of punishing him as perpetrator according to a monocausal explanation of sexual abuse. Terms such as 'perpetrator' model or 'victim' model might seem to be more specific in their immediate reference to the target in the family (Rosenfeld, 1979). Yet it attributes roles in the family as fixed properties of individuals rather than pointing at an interactional process. The term 'Primary Punitive Intervention' indicates the direction of an interactional process between the family and the professional network. The term 'primary' indicates the basic direction which guides the overall intervention.

Any criminal intervention by police and courts is by definition punitive when unlawful acts are involved. In child sexual abuse the Primary Punitive Intervention is directed against the abuser as perpetrator who is guilty of the assault. The PPI resolves child sexual abuse in the family by punishing the abuser, who is often put into prison. The lawful removal and conviction of the abuser is based on a monocausal attribution, not only of responsibility, but also of activity, guilt, blame and power, which is ascribed solely to the abuser.

The Primary Punitive Intervention does not only cover the pre-existing emotio-sexual conflicts between the parents (see The family process 3.1). It also makes it impossible for the child, the family and the professional network to deal with the positive aspects, and the often extremely strong attachment between the child and the abuser, which the child and the family are not allowed to recognise and to deal with. The Primary Punitive Intervention also enables mothers and children in a scapegoating process to mask their own guilt feelings and any mutual feelings of emotional or sexual competition for the father as partner. The child's accusation against her mother for not having protected her from the abuse are easily covered by reactive pseudo- overcloseness between mother and child. Denying the recognition of the fact of the child's active participation on interactional level and denying the conflicts and attachments involved allows professionals and the family, in a defensive moralistic response, to deny the sexual nature of sexual abuse and the importance of any positive and caring aspects in the relationship between the child and the abuser.

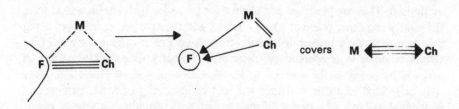

Monocausal model directed against father as the perpetrator.
Covers conflict between mother and child and child's feelings of
letdown. Covers aspects of child's positive attachment to abuser.

Figure 4.1 Primary Punitive Intervention

4.1.2 Primary Child Protective Intervention (PCI)

The Primary Child Protective Intervention includes all forms of interventions where the child is the target of direct action with the declared aim of protecting the physical, emotional and moral development and well-being of the child as the victim. The Primary Child Protective Intervention aims at the normative aspect of the abuse in which the structurally dependent child needs protection.

Social services, in their child protective role have like the police legal and statutory function. They employ their powers in order to act as 'better parents' for the child in competition with the actual parents as 'worse parents'. The PCI is directed against the parents in order to protect the child. The Primary Child Protective Intervention is based on the implicit or explicit attribution of failure to both parents in their parenting role and not only to the abuser as perpetrator. With the bicausal implication of child sexual abuse as parenting failure, the Primary Child Protective Intervention moves towards a family systems understanding of child sexual abuse.

Although in theory the Primary Child Protective Intervention aims to protect the child against parenting failure, it often leads to secondary victimisation of the child. The PCI threatens the child with removal from the family, and from important attachment figures with the separation from the mother, from siblings, friends, school and the wider social environment which the child in crisis, may need more than ever, as protective factors against secondary psychological trauma. For family members who remain at home, the removal of the child is easily interpreted as the expulsion of the core of moral evil from the family. The child is cut out of the family as 'sex-cancer' or scapegoated as a liar. Or, as one mother put it 'she has always been a sexy bitch'.

Children's removal from the family gives the parents the opportunity to cover up and deny their own emotio-sexual, marital problems. Children become doubly victimised. They are punished and blamed for the abuse by being separated from the family and other relevant social contacts and they are prevented from being able to resolve their primary confusion from the abuse through treatment in the family context. In residential or foster care, sexually abused children can in addition be suspiciously watched under the notion of special protection. They may be treated in a disciminatory way out of insecurity of foster parents and residential workers who find it difficult to deal with sometimes severe problems of sexualised acting out.

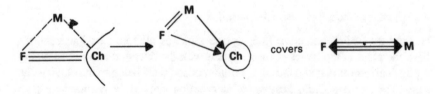

Bicausal model directed against both parents but hits daughter as the 'moral evil'. Covers marital conflict between parents.

Figure 4.2 Primary Child Protective Intervention

4.1.3 Primary Therapeutic Intervention (PTI)

The 'Primary Therapeutic Intervention' (Figure 4.3) includes all interventions which aim to treat individual psychological trauma and to change family relationships. The Primary Therapeutic Intervention therefore addresses primarily the circular and relationship aspects of child sexual abuse. The PTI aims at the underlying dynamics which led to and maintained the abuse. It is not directed in any statutory or legal way against any particular family member but towards changing family relationships.

Although the Primary Therapeutic Intervention has no legal or statutory remit it always needs to resort to legal backup due to the nature of child sexual abuse as an interlocking syndrome of secrecy and addiction. The PTI will need legal or statutory assistance when the crisis intervention makes temporary separation of family members necessary. The legal intervention often needs to assist the overall therapeutic process by helping to get children and abusers into therapy. (See Aims and steps in the Primary Therapeutic Intervention, 6.2; Court-ordered therapy, 12.16.)

No statutory and legal function. Directed towards family relationships.
Therapeutic use of statutory or legal intervention in metaystemic approach

Figure 4.3 Primary Therapeutic Intervention

In family-oriented treatment of child sexual abuse it may at first appear that only the father and the child are in need of therapy. From the outset the father's responsibility and the child's involvement are obvious. As the intervention proceeds the mother, initially regarded as the person least involved, often becomes central to the therapeutic process. Behind the evident father–child involvement and the father's sole responsibility for the abuse, three major and often unexpected problem areas in the relationship between mother, father and child appear during treatment. (1) The emotio-sexual and sexual marital conflict between the parents. (2) Maternal failure to prevent the abuse and to protect the child. (3) The competition between mother and child as an emotional partner for the father.

After the initial focus in therapy on the father and child the mother often finds herself in the most stressful position in the family, in which she needs a great deal of help and support. The Primary Therapeutic Intervention aims at problem solving and conflict resolution in the family according to operationalised and explicitly stated goals and aims of therapy. The aims and treatment steps of the Primary Therapeutic Intervention are described in Section 6.2.

4.2 Mutual influence and interlocking professional–family process

The linear nature of legal and child protective aspects in the intervention of child sexual abuse creates a hierarchy of sub-systems in which the family becomes structurally dependent on processes in the professional network. The hierarchy of sub-systems descends from the professional network to the family and from the family to the child. This hierarchy gives professional agencies the responsibility and the influence to decide on one of the three basic forms of intervention. The professional–family hierarchy does not exclude the fact that the family in turn influences the professional sub-system. Accordingly we find specific mutual interlocking processes between the family and the professional network.

4.2.1 The influence of the professional network on the therapeutic system

4.2.1.1 Decision on type of intervention

Deciding on a Primary Therapeutic Intervention does not mean excluding social services, police or courts from the process. On the contrary, if a Primary Therapeutic Intervention is to have any chance of success there needs to be agreement at the beginning of the intervention between legal and therapeutic agencies on the overall approach. The aims and means and the degree of involvement of each professional sub-group need to be clearly defined.

The nature of child sexual abuse as a 'syndrome of secrecy' for the family and as a 'syndrome of addiction' for the abuser usually makes it necessary to have legal support to protect the treatment and to serve as back-up at critical moments of therapy when family members try to opt out or try to create splits in the professionals network. The attempt to treat sexually abused children and their families without the involvement and to the exclusion of legal and statutory agencies can easily lead to anti-therapeutic therapy. In treatment without statutory and legal support the abuse can continue during treatment under heightened secrecy and increased threats to the child and the family by the abuser who is driven by the addiction and compulsion to abuse. (See Aims and steps in Primary Therapeutic Intervention, 6.2; The interprofessional process in context, 5.2.)

4.2.1.2 The need for consistency during the intervention

Changes of key professionals and referrals to new agencies during the initial crisis intervention often lead to strong reactions in the family and to changes in the direction of the overall intervention. Families are in danger of falling back into secrecy. Individual family members may withdraw initial disclosures and admissions of abuse, denying again that any abuse has taken place. Individual family members often try actively to change the basic form of the intervention. They can do this by activating other professionals outside the therapeutic setting when the professional network is not carefully co-ordinated during the crisis intervention. Abused children and mothers can finally involve new and uncoordinated legal agencies in order to change the basic direction of a Primary Therapeutic Intervention into a Primary Child Protective Intervention or a Primary Punitive Intervention.

It is important that professionals who are involved at the disclosure remain involved as 'Trusted Persons' throughout the acute crisis and during periods of acting out which often occur in early stages of treatment. Once treatment has broken down it can be very difficult to bring family members back into the framework of the original Primary Therapeutic Intervention. However, changes in professional networks are unavoidable and referrals to other professionals are often necessary. In these situations a 'handover meeting' is essential to safeguard the continuity of the treatment process. (See The use of the 'trusted person', 8.6; The handover meeting, 9.14.)

4.2.1.3 Interference by other professional sub-systems

There are two types of professional sub-system which can interfere in the treatment process. (1) Individual professionals can enter into an anti-therapeutic collusion with a family member against the aims of the Primary Therapeutic Intervention and against the specific professional network involved in the case. (2) Previously uninvolved professionals and agencies can intervene in an un-coordinated way and can try to take over.

Individual professionals from different agencies may, out of primary identification with the child, the mother or the abuser, collude with one family member and undermine therapy. I have seen police, courts or social workers support and foster a Primary Punitive Intervention by actively excluding fathers from treatment. Out of primary identification with the child as victim, I myself did succumb to the danger of wanting to rescue the child on my own. I conducted anti-therapeutic therapy when I prevented adequate protection for the child by colleagues from social services. On the way I undermined my social work colleagues and inadvertently introduced a Primary Child Protective Intervention through the back door. The child I wanted to rescue had to pay for it. I have seen probation officers and adult psychiatrists denying the severity of sexual abuse out of primary identification with the abuser. They belittled and undermined the efforts of their co-professionals in other agencies in their efforts to protect the child. Colleagues from all professions have fallen into this universal trap. (See The interprofessional process in context, 5.2.)

The typical example of outside agencies interfering in the overall process is the arrival of the police and of courts intervening in a therapeutic approach agreed by other professionals. A precondition for any successful therapeutic intervention is therefore the involvement and careful co-ordination and co-operation of all professionals who may be involved prior to the actual intervention. This includes not only the professionals involved at the moment of disclosure, but needs to integrate all professionals who may have to be involved at any stage in future in legal or statutory capacity. It is also important to reach potentially undermining professionals who may, in the developing process of therapy, identify with the resistance of one or the other family member. In collusion with this family member professional colleagues can actively help to undermine a Primary Therapeutic Intervention.

4.2.2 The influence of the family on the therapeutic system

4.2.2.1 Attempts to 'run away' from therapy

We need to anticipate that at some point in treatment family members will try to opt out of therapy. One of the most striking influences of the family on the professional network is the way in which family members and even fathers can attempt to turn a Primary Therapeutic Intervention into a Primary Child Protective Intervention or a Primary Punitive Intervention when therapy becomes emotionally unbearable. At this point the issue of punishment becomes relative.

Clinical experience shows that in established and proven cases of child sexual abuse, fathers can experience it as greater punishment to have to face in therapy the shame and the responsibility towards their wives and children than being punished in court. Abusers therefore often try and succeed in opting out of treatment if they have the freedom to do so. Legal support may be needed to keep them in therapy. I have seen abusers developing psychosomatic symptoms, attempting suicide or trying to blackmail other family members in their moves to avoid therapy. The ultimate form of opting out was paternal suicide which happened in two cases of father–stepdaughter abuse.

Mothers often want to avoid treatment by demanding instant divorce. I have also seen mothers becoming suicidal when they realised that they had lost their husbands as partners and when they felt overcome by guilt feelings of not having protected the child. Another reason for mothers to opt out of a Primary Therapeutic Intervention was increasing hostility towards the abused child who accused the mother of not having protected her from the abuse. Children often try to run away from home and from therapy because they feel too frightened to confront the abuser and do not trust that mothers or professionals will help and protect them. These are only some examples of ways in which different family members want to opt out at different stages of the Primary Therapeutic Intervention.

4.2.2.2 Attempts to change the nature of the intervention

The family for its part reacts actively to the way the professional network intervenes. Although the professional network as a higher sub-system initially decides on the basic form of the intervention, the family and family members can in turn influence how the professional network proceeds. Mothers and older children can refuse to participate in therapy when they want a Primary Punitive Intervention. Mothers and fathers often form alliances against the abused child, and try to introduce a Primary Child Protective Intervention. The child then becomes rejected, scapegoated and expelled from the family as a source of all moral evil. Adolescents themselves often trigger a PCI when they refuse to return home. They are then in danger of cutting themselves off from their mother, from siblings, peers and social support systems, and they can end up increasingly isolated, lonely and desperate.

Attempts to change the basic nature of the intervention often happen at moments when therapeutic changes challenge the established family pattern of relationships. Parents often try to introduce a Primary Child Protective Intervention at the point when the marital conflict becomes central to therapy. Mothers want to change a Primary Therapeutic Intervention when they feel blamed for the abuse.

4.2.3 Clinical example: the P family

The clinical example of the intervention is based on my work in paediatrics in Amsterdam. The crisis intervention on the paediatric ward was undertaken by a crisis team, consisting of two hospital paediatricians as confidential doctors, supported in their statutory child protective role by the social worker, the nursing staff, the playleader on the paediatric ward and a therapist for the parents and the girl. Therapeutic roles were taken by different professionals of the multi-professional team. The crisis team was supported by legal and statutory agencies.

The case demonstrates a far-from-perfect example of professional co-operation in a crisis intervention of a Primary Therapeutic type. Yet it seems to be typical in its pitfalls, and is, therefore, an excellent example to demonstrate the interlocking effects between professionals and family. The basic and principal problems in the structure of multi-professional co-operation are fully transferable to other settings and other countries with different specific structures of organisation and co-operation in professional networks.

Twenty-two professionals were directly involved. They came from seven different sub-systems of the professional network: (i) From medical insititutions, (ii) from therapeutic agencies, (iii) from special child care services, (iv) from general social services, (v) from school and educational services, (vi) from the police, and (vii) from legal agencies.

In a Primary Therapeutic Intervention the family has greater space to influence the professional network than in the other two basic forms of intervention. Three questions should serve to guide us through the process: (1) How does the professional system evolve as a counterpart to the family process? (2) How do the dynamic processes in the professional network influence the family process? (3) How does the family process influence the professional network? Each section of description of events is followed by comments on the development of the interlocking professional–family process.

Process I: preparation of the professional sub-system

1 First concern: The head of school phoned the confidential doctor (CD1). He reported that Louisa, a 14-year-old girl at his school, had told him in confidence that she had been sexually abused by her father. He was not sure how much to believe the girl. The games teacher later added that on several occasions she had seen weals on the girl's back, possibly as a result of physical abuse. The headmaster asked CD1 what should be done.

2 Interprofessional Diagnostic Consultation for Information Gathering: The social worker (SWCD) assisting CD1, contacted all professionals who might know the family. The school doctor confirmed the headmaster's report. SWCD then called a Pre-Intervention meeting.

3 Pre-Intervention Meeting for Planning of Action: The meeting was attended by CD1, SWCD, the school doctor and the headmaster. The questions were, who would take care of the family in the event of a full disclosure and where might the child stay if she either could not or did not want to return home? It was decided that Louisa could be admitted for the crisis intervention to the paediatric ward in the hospital. CD1 would co-ordinate the intervention and inform the public prosecutor. The social worker of the child protection team of the confidential doctor's office, as senior statutory key worker with the task of monitoring the overall intervention, would keep track of the professional–family process to prevent confusion about the tasks and roles in the professional network.

4 The Public Prosecutor gave the go-ahead to CD1 and CD2 to deal with the disclosure and the intervention as soon as the professional network was organised. Police and the Public Prosecutor was on stand-by if needed in the crisis intervention in order to give further legal backup.

Comments on process I

a. Preparations prior to the actual intervention are necessary in order to avoid a crisis arising within the professional network later in the intervention.

b. It is essential to gather as much information as possible at the stage of a vague first-line suspicion or of a partial disclosure in order to arrive at a well-founded second-line suspicion.

c. The second-line suspicion leads to the pre-intervention meeting which has the task of planning within the professional network the necessary action for full disclosure. The pre-intervention meeting also has to clarify the relationship between the family and the professional network when a full disclosure is underway. Agreement needs to be reached about who should initiate the full disclosure, where it should take place, and which legal and statutory issues are involved. When the intervention gets underway, the facts and the grounds for the intervention must be as clear as possible. All professionals involved need to agree that the stage of a well-founded second-line suspicion is reached before a full disclosure is induced. At that stage the main structure for co-operation between all professional sub-systems involved needs already to be established.

Process II: professional–family system: open disclosure of sexual abuse

1 Full Disclosure: The Headmaster phoned saying Louisa had told him that this morning for the first time her father had forced her to have sexual intercourse with him. She was scared and did not want to go home.

2 Activating and Co-ordinating the Professional Network: CD2, who had been informed by CD1, was on the ward and asked the headmaster to bring Louisa. CD1 and his office informed everyone involved in the case. The general practitioner who knew the family well was asked to contact the parents and to see them in his surgery together with the social worker. CD1 contacted the public prosecutor who assured him that he would exercise his discretion and not take direct action. He agreed to place the matter in the hands of CD1 and to give any emergency backup if the child was felt to be in danger of physical harm through paternal threat or action.

3 Handover Meeting at Admission: Louisa was brought by the headmaster to the hospital. She talked both in front of the headmaster and, helped by him, freely to the staff about the sexual intercourse with her father. It became clear that the abuse had in fact taken place for several years. Louisa wanted her father to go to prison and very much longed to see her mother.

4 Sense of Security: To give Louisa the maximum feeling of security the ward sister and a staff nurse met with Louisa to arrange who would be allowed to visit her and to discuss what she wanted to say on the ward about her being there. The staff provided a cover-story, and it was left to Louisa to tell as much or as little about the sexual abuse as she wished.

5 Special Person: Louisa had separated herself from her family. To prevent the unintentional introduction of a Primary Child Protective Intervention, and to avoid unnecessary loneliness, a special nurse was assigned and introduced to Louisa as a special person to whom she could talk. Unlike

CD1 and the sister, she would not be involved with any outside contacts.

6. Physical Examination and Pregnancy Prevention: With Louisa's consent a gynaecologist was consulted to examine her. He prescribed a drug to prevent pregnancy resulting from the intercourse that morning.

Comments on process II

a. The disclosure, rather than the fact of the long-term sexual abuse itself, provoked the acute crisis for the girl, making her too frightened to return home.

b. It is common that at disclosure it appears at first that intercourse has just occurred for the first time although it has often been happening for many months or years. The full disclosure of Louisa at this point clearly seems to be the result of the interactional nature of motivation (see The interactional nature of motivation, 2.4.1). As a result of the Anonymous Diagnostic Inter-professional Consultation the headmaster was able to listen to Louisa and to take her message seriously (see ADIC, 8.4). This in turn made Louisa motivated to make a full disclosure. She disclosed at this point because she had learned to see the headmaster as Trusted Person although the abuse had already happened for many years.

c. It is important that the first person to whom the child has disclosed is seen as the 'Trusted Person'. The Trusted Person is not automatically the child's mother. Only if she is the person who raises the first alarm can we take her as a Trusted Person right from the beginning. The Trusted Person should always be present at the 'Handover Meeting'. During the Handover Meeting the details of the initial story of the first disclosure should be retold by the child or the Trusted Person in the presence of the new carer. This has the effect of giving the child the explicit permission and licence to talk about the abuse to the incoming professional. Louisa's trust and the knowledge of the facts of the disclosure 'travelled' from the headmaster to the ward sister and CD1. This avoided splitting in the professional network and a relapse into secrecy. (See The use of the 'trusted person' 8.6; The handover meeting, 9.14.)

d. When the child rather than the abuser is separated from the family, specific arrangements need to be made to ensure that the child feels safe and contained. In order to avoid the dynamic of a Primary Child Protective Intervention Louisa was encouraged to see her relatives and friends. The child needs help not to feel pushed out of the family as punishment or attribution of responsibility for the sexual abuse.

e. The physical examination should take place after careful preparation of the child. Forcing a child to undergo a physical examination at the point of acute crisis and against her will might add to the traumatic experience in the opening crisis. It is important, on the other hand, to get medical evidence whenever possible. Undisputable medical evidence makes the situation considerably easier for the child and the treatment team. Clear forensic evidence is the most important support for verbal accusations. In cases where the abuser admits openly to sexual abuse, immediate physical examination might not be necessary, as long as legal procedures do not require any immediate forensic proof.

Process III: professional–family system: initial interference by a collusive sub-system

1 Collusion: The headmaster came to visit. He was extremely edgy and irritating, and became annoying to the staff. He wanted to leave the ward with Louisa to speak with her in secret. He told the ward sister that he felt guilty about the situation and talked about Louisa's father having to go to prison. Everything he said sounded very confused.
2 Attempt to Integrate all Professionals: CD2 and the sister asked the headmaster to co-operate and to tell the crisis team what he knew about the sexual abuse. The headmaster became very angry and agitated and departed, leaving the staff perplexed.
3 Consultation: CD1 and CD2 and the staff decided that only CD2 should deal with the headmaster to avoid the latter creating confusion in the crisis team.

Comments on process III
a. It is a common experience that professionals who are initially co-operative find themselves pulled into the family process, thus splitting the professional network and acting against the commonly agreed approach.
b. A collusive sub-system between a family member and a professional has to be explored and confronted in an attempt to reintegrate the professional into the treatment team. Otherwise the resulting conflict-by-proxy in the professional network will make a therapeutic solution to the underlying family problem impossible. (See The interprofessional process 5.1.)

Process IV: professional system: first review of shared tasks and responsibilities

1 Co-ordination Meeting: The distribution of tasks was reviewed, and it was decided that CD2 would keep in contact with the headmaster; CD1 kept in contact with the GP, public prosecutor and the police. The staff nurse remained the special contact person for Louisa. The exploration of a suitable long-term placement for Louisa would be undertaken by SWCD. The first meeting between Louisa and her parents would not just be a social meeting but a therapeutic session held in the presence of CD1 and the assigned therapist. This would, with Louisa's consent, take place as soon as the parents came to the ward.

Comments on process IV
In the ensuing turmoil of the initial stages of the crisis intervention, immediate feedback amongst the professionals about their position in the intervention is

necessary to protect the agreed approach and to help the members of the crisis team to adjust to the changes in the fast-moving process after disclosure.

Process V: family system: development of the family process during the opening intervention

1 Involving the Family: the GP phoned to say that the parents were with him. Confronted with the medical and the circumstantial evidence the father had admitted to sexual abuse and the GP thought that he was suicidal. The GP was encouraged to send the parents to the hospital immediately for an opening family meeting.

2 Meeting with Parents, CD1 and Therapist: The father talked of suicide. The mother was extremely upset. Louisa refused to see either of her parents when a meeting with them was suggested. Finally, the parents made two decisions: to stay together as parents for the time being and to tell the oldest son of 16 what had happened. The parents promised CD1 that they would return the next day.

3 Meeting with Parents, CD1 and Therapist the Following Day: Louisa still refused to see her mother because she was furious with her for staying with her father, whom she called 'the criminal'.

4 Parents' Reaction: Later, the father phoned, saying that his wife was suicidal after Louisa's refusal to see her. The therapist asked them to come and see him.

5 Session with Parents: The mother was in very low spirits; father became aggressive towards the therapist and demanded that Louisa should see them and should apologise to her mother.

6 Session with Louisa: Louisa agreed to see her mother the next day. She felt her mother should leave her father and stick with her against him. She had expected her father's instant imprisonment.

7 First Meeting between Mother and Daughter: The special nurse and the therapist were present. Louisa was very harsh and rejecting towards her mother, calling her and her father criminals.

8 Father's Attempted Boycott of the Treatment: Father phoned, cancelling the appointment with the therapist. He was activated by his wife's immense disappointment over Louisa's renewed rejection on the ward. The therapist stressed to the parents that whatever they decided he would expect to see them. They did turn up.

9 Session with Parents: Mr P felt responsible for his wife's misery and was livid with Louisa whom he blamed entirely for the present situation. He wanted to give himself up to the police and accused Louisa of destroying the family.

10 Louisa's Emotional Turmoil: The special nurse was worried about Louisa and raised her concern that the intervention was getting into the dynamic of

a Primary Child Protective Intervention. Despite rejecting her mother actively, Louisa appeared to feel excluded from her family and increasingly confused about her relationship with her parents and siblings. It was decided that as of the next day Louisa would start having some regular meetings with the individual therapist with a view to a family meeting as soon as possible.

11 Parents Struggle to Unite: The father was unable to bear Louisa's continued refusal to see her mother. He again decided to give himself up to the police, but Mrs P did not want him to go.

12 First Individual Session with Louisa: Louisa had cut herself off from the entire family. She suddenly was worried whether she would ever be allowed to go home again.

Comments on process V

a. The parents should be confronted by a professional who is well linked into the professional network and who is well informed about the evidence of the sexual abuse. Whether the primary contact person is a police officer, a child protection worker or another professional, he or she needs the full backing of the crisis team, particularly when the abuse is denied or when suicidal threats are made. The crisis team must be ready to link up with the family and should be prepared to join in.

b. After the first confrontation with the father as the sole responsible person for the abuse it is essential to ask both parents in their parenting role to attend the initial meeting together. The aim is to establish that as parents both are equally responsible for the parenting of the child. First, therapeutic boundaries are made, and family-oriented treatment begins.

c. To avoid forming secret alliances neither parent should be allowed to visit the daughter informally before the first therapeutic family meeting has taken place, in which the facts of the abuse and the abuse as family fact are established as the first therapeutic step in the Primary Therapeutic Intervention (see Section 6.2). In the example, the amount of contact between parents and daughter was largely determined by the daughter's initial refusal to see either parent.

d. A therapeutic plan which responds immediately and actively to the initial turmoil in the first days of the crisis after disclosure provides the basis for trust for the following long-term treatment.

e. Family members might want to induce a Primary Punitive Intervention or a Primary Child Protective Intervention rather than entering into therapy. In the clinical example, Louisa excluded her parents and wanted her father to be imprisoned. By attempting to turn the Primary Therapeutic Intervention into Primary Punitive Intervention, she got herself into the dynamic of a Primary Child Protective Intervention. The professional network had to counteract this process.

Process VI: professional–family system: second interference by the collusive system

1 The Headmaster Interferes Again: He appeared unexpectedly on the ward in a state of agitation, pretending that he had contacted CD1 about his coming. His behaviour became progressively mysterious and uncooperative. Louisa had often been on the phone to him.
2 Co-ordination Meeting: Since it did not appear possible to integrate the head-master into the agreed professional plan, it was decided that he would not be allowed to visit the ward without staff permission.
3 Session with Louisa: It became clear that there was a collusive alliance between Louisa and the headmaster. It seemed to have been he who gave Louisa the idea that her father would immediately go to prison.
4 Headmaster Continues to Interfere: The headmaster was seen at the entrance to the hospital wanting to speak to no one else but Louisa on her own.

Comments on process VI
The unresolved conflict-by-proxy and the resulting formation of the third collu-sive sub-system between the headmaster and Louisa as one professional collud-ing with one family member became the major interfering factor throughout the intervention. This collusive professional–family sub-system placed a direct block on the therapeutic process with the family and family members. Such a collusion between one professional and one family member is the expression of an intense conflict-by-proxy which inevitably blocks the therapeutic family process. In the case the girl appeared to be backed in her rejection of a Primary Therapeutic Intervention by the headmaster, who seemed to support Louisa against her parents and the crisis team in her pursuit of a Primary Punitive Intervention.

Process VII: professional system: alteration in the composition of the therapeutic team

1 Change in the Crisis Team: CD1 and the parents' therapist both had to leave for two days. No handover-meeting takes place.

Comments on process VII
Changes in the professional setting during the initial crisis can have major disruptive effects on the attempts to provide the family with clarity and continuity especially if no handover meeting takes place.

Process VIII: overall system in crisis

1 Louisa's 'Systems Runaway': Immediately after CD1 had left, Louisa phoned the headmaster. She was very silent and closed during her individual session. A friend and Louisa's brother visited her, and later Louisa and her

friend locked themselves in the bathroom. When the friend had left, Louisa had disappeared as well and could not be found.

2 Crisis in the Crisis Team: CD2 was informed and SWCD as key co-ordinator immediately called an emergency case conference. The decision was made that if Louisa had not returned in the evening, the parents, hospital administrator and public prosecutor would have to be informed. There was as yet no direct involvement of the police to search actively for Louisa.

3 Attempt by Crisis Team to Regain Control: The public prosecutor, the parents and the hospital administration were informed that Louisa had absconded.

4 Parents' Involvement: The parents rushed to the ward and met with CD2. They provided him with the address of a friend of Louisa's with whom she might be staying. There was no reply on the phone.

5 Involvement of New Outside Professional System: Louisa was still missing the following morning, and CD1 informed police to ask for their co-operation. This was met with a very uncooperative reaction from the duty officer in charge who felt that he should take the lead in any further action.

6 Crisis Feedback to Parents: CD2 phoned father informing him that the police had to be actively involved due to Louisa's disappearance. He told the father that the particular police officer in charge did not seem to be co-operative and might take action against him.

7 Take-over by New Outside System: In the evening two police officers arrived on the ward and enquired about Louisa. Her best friend's name and telephone number were familiar to them in connection with suspicion of prostitution and drug abuse.

8 Louisa's Open Attempt to Change the Nature of the Therapeutic Intervention: At 9 p.m. the police phoned informing the ward staff that Louisa was with them and that she had officially reported the sexual abuse and wanted prosecution. The police would now proceed against the father immediately.

9 Second Intervention by SWCD as Key Co-ordinator: The SWCD immediately went to see Louisa at the police station. When she arrived, the headmaster was already present. His motives remained unclear. Louisa did not want to return to the ward.

10 Co-ordination of the New Overall Professional System: A case conference took place with the police, public prosecutor and CD2. It was decided to ask Louisa to return to the ward on a short-term basis. It was agreed that the father would not be detained by the police.

11 Attempt to Re-establish the Therapeutic Setting: CD2 talked to Louisa who agreed to return to the ward for the time being.

12 Renewed Interference by an Outside Professional Sub-system: Against the decision of the case conference, the police arrested the father at 11 p.m., and took him into police custody.

13 Towards a Primary Punitive Intervention: In an uncoordinated move by the police, the father was taken into custody, and the therapeutic approach

collapsed. Mother visited the ward in a panic and stayed for three hours talking to the staff. She wanted to speak with Louisa, who refused to talk to her and avoided her. Mother made suicidal threats and needed to be comforted.

Comments on process VIII

a. Following the changes in the professional sub-system, Louisa reacted and took action to change the basic direction of the intervention from a Primary Therapeutic Intervention into a Primary Punitive Intervention. As result, the entire professional–family-system was thrown into confusion. In the overall crisis, the professional sub-system was split and lost its ability to act in a co-ordinated and goal-oriented fashion. The result was a non-therapeutic action response by the police.

b. It is essential to have a key co-ordinator or a consulting professional who is able to react immediately if the therapeutic system is to be re-established at the moment of a paralysing conflict-by-proxy between different professional sub-systems about the general direction of the intervention.

c. Professional sub-systems not directly involved in the case planning might take over the intervention as in this case when against prior agreement control was taken by the police as a new professional sub-group which remained un-coordinated. This changed the original Primary Therapeutic Intervention into a Primary Punitive Intervention, which left the crisis team unable to re-establish a therapeutic framework.

d. The crisis amongst the professionals as a result of the action of one family member in turn has an immediate effect on family relationships. The family began to shift towards the family dynamics of a Primary Punitive Intervention. When the father was removed as the guilty perpetrator, the mother instantly wanted to link up with Louisa. She reacted to the change towards the Primary Punitive Interaction with a move towards a coalition with her daughter against her husband.

Process IX: overall system: reorganisation of the therapeutic approach

1 Re-establishing the Original Crisis Team: CD1 and the parents' therapist returned. They immediately saw the family. The mother was still very upset.

2 Revised Professional Agreement about the Direction of the Intervention: CD1 contacted the public prosecutor with whom the original plan for the intervention had been agreed. They decided that the father should be released by the police as soon as possible.

3 Return to Therapeutic Intervention: Mr P was released from custody, conditional upon his 'obligatory report for co-operation and treatment under Dr X, Confidential Doctor on Child Abuse and Neglect'.

4 Therapeutic Intervention Continues: The parents continued to see the therapist, and Louisa took up her individual meetings again.

Comments on process IX

The re-establishment of the original crisis team enabled the therapeutic team to regain control over the intervention and over the processes in the professional–family system. When the police as interfering agency withdrew and assumed a clear back-up role again, the intervention reverted back to a Primary Therapeutic Intervention.

Process X: professional system: intermediate plans to safeguard the therapeutic process

1 Immediate Placement for Louisa: Louisa visited a friend in a children's home and wanted to stay there. The therapeutic team agreed to this placement.
2 Continuing Treatment: A case-conference was held at the office of the confidential doctor in order to arrive at a medium-term plan. It was decided that Louisa should, for the time being, remain at the Children's Home and that therapy with the father and the family should continue with the aim of reassessing the possibility of her returning home again.
3 Continued Co-ordination between Monitor Professional and the Professional Sub-systems: The SWCD remained the monitor person and she continued this task until the case was closed.

Comments on process X

After the acute crisis some members of the therapeutic team withdrew, the degree of involvement decreased and new agencies were drawn in by means of handover meetings. In this process, it was important that the Monitor Person who was initially involved followed the case to its conclusion to guarantee continuity and the completion of the agreed treatment plan.

4.2.3.1 The interlocking process in the P family

In the example of the P family the reactive mode of the professional sub-system as a response to the family's actions created a feedback spiral which, in the end, did not only change the external situation, but also affected profoundly the internal psychological state of each individual family member (Figure 4.4). It created a process where (1) the absence of two staff members and a change in the therapeutic team lead to (2) the removal of control from the crisis team. (3) Control was assumed by Louisa as the family member most resistant to the PTI who (4) actively transferred the initiative to the police, who (5) actively paralysed and changed the Primary Therapeutic Intervention when the father was taken into cutody. (6) The course of the intervention changed into a Primary Punitive Intervention, leading to (7) a change in the individual psychological state of different family members which left the mother desperate and on her own. (8) This in turn triggered changes in the family process and in family relationships when the mother moved closer to Louisa.

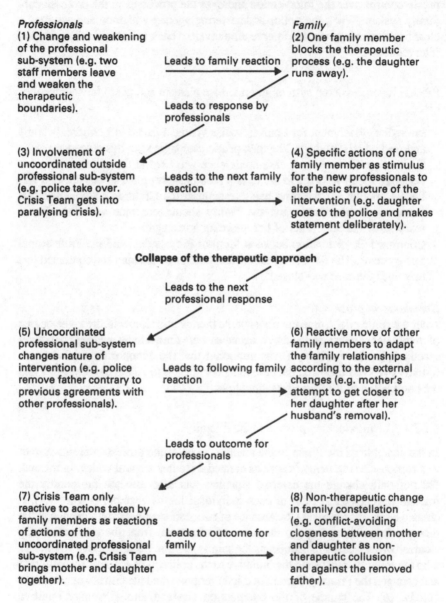

Figure 4.4 Action and reaction between the P family and the professional network

The complex process, which involved interlocking changes in the professional network, in the family and in the external and internal situation of each individual family member was initiated by one family member with the aim of changing the alliances within the family. In this process very external and organisational steps in the professional network were reactive steps which were triggered by Louisa. This process did not only threaten to change the external form of the overall intervention. It also began to change the basic family process and the psychological state of each family member involved and influenced the way how each family member interpreted issues of responsibility, participation, guilt, blame and power in relation to the sexual abuse.

4.2.3.2 Conflict-by-proxy and conflict-resolution-by-proxy in the P family

In the treatment of the P family, the professional network had been locked into the dynamics of the family system. Aspects of hatred and anger between daughter and father in their struggle for mother as an ally, which were part of the family conflict, became mirrored in the conflict between the police, the school and the crisis team. The developing conflict between the professionals was in fact a family conflict-by-proxy. First the headmaster and then the police acted on the daughter's behalf. The crisis team acted for the father and the mother was pushed and pulled in between. The conflict-by-proxy amongst the professionals had been triggered by Louisa's attempt to make a therapeutic resolution impossible. If the professionals cannot reach a consensus about the meaning of the conflict as a mirroring conflict-by-proxy, the therapeutic pre-resolutions in a conflict-resolution-by-proxy becomes impossible. (See The interprofessional process, 5.1.)

Unresolved conflicts-by-proxy in the professional network lead to Non- therapeutic Action Responses, in which professionals inevitably lose any goal-oriented and problem-solving perspective. They are only able to react bureaucratically and according to rules of formal competence and responsibilities of their profession and agency as it happened when the police intervened to detain the father. This was entirely out of context of the PTI, to which the entire professional network including the Public Prosecutor had agreed prior to the intervention. Therapeutic renegotiations of family relationships became completely blocked because the crisis team, the headmaster and the police were acting out between them a conflict which was in fact a family conflict between Louisa and her father. The eventual recognition of this process made it possible to arrive at a conflict-resolution-by-proxy amongst the professionals. The conflict- resolu- tion-by-proxy enabled the professional network to hand the conflict back to the family where it belonged. The professional network was then able to become problem oriented again, re-creating the multi-professional framework of a goal-oriented Primary Therapeutic Intervention.

Chapter five

The professional network

5.1 The interprofessional process

5.1.1 Mirroring processes and professional identification

Mirroring describes a process in which different members of a professional network take over roles in relationship to fellow professionals, complementary to roles different family members have in their family. The professional network enacts the family dynamics; for example showing splitting and fragmentation processes and reflecting in the professional network the way the family sees itself. Certain family members have specific roles attributed to them which, via identification, are mirrored in different members of the professional network. Complementary identifications of different professionals with different family members and aspects of family life can lead to a situation in which the relationship pattern between the professionals shows a mirroring pattern of the family relationships, with the result that the actions of the professionals become reactions to the family induced by the family process.

Anonymous and open diagnostic interprofessional consultations, pre-intervention meetings and case conferences are the most important and typical places in which mirroring of the family process is re-enacted visably in the professional network (see Anonymous Diagnostic Interprofessional Consultation, 8.4; The pre-intervention meeting, 8.7; Special issues in case conferences, 11.8). In pre-intervention meetings and case conferences we often find ourselves locked into mirroring the family's dysfunctional ways of relating and their inability at problem solving and conflict resolution. The family's unwillingness to believe sexually abused children, abusers' attempts to avoid taking responsibility for the abuse and the issue of shared responsibility for parenting is often mirrored in reactions of the members of large case conferences, some of them with up to 10 to 15 professionals. Nobody is allowed to take clear responsibility because everybody wants to have a say in the case, nor is anybody allowed to withdraw, because no one really wants to take effective responsibility allowing the other to leave either. The inability at problem solving and conflict resolution and inappropriate conflict avoidance or conflict regulation in families of child sexual abuse are often mirrored in professional networks of highly skilled and competent professionals. This is induced by the family process as a result of identifications of different professionals with different family members who are mirroring the family process in the professional network.

Mirroring does not happen because of incompetent professional conduct. Mirroring is the result of the striking influence families are able to exert even on very competent and highly professional networks. I discovered the process of conflict-by-proxy as mirroring the family process when I found myself undermining and mistrusting professional colleagues from other disciplines, whose professional attitude and competence I highly respected and admired. Nevertheless, I started to think of them as incompetent although I knew that this was not true. It was then that I realised that these events were induced by the family process.

The process of identification forms the underlying psychological mechanism by which professional networks mirror the family process and different aspects of the individual psychological life of family members. Different professionals identify with different family members and different aspects of the family process. In complex cases of severe child sexual abuse there is no way of not identifying differently because each professional is presented with different aspects of the family and of family members. There is only the way of denying the identification with the danger of acting out by proxy. The qualitative leap we need to make is explicitly to confess our inevitable identifications.

In a metasystemic approach we need to give ourselves the explicit licence and permission to assume a position which enables us as professionals to be allowed openly to acknowledge different identifications of different professionals with different family members and different aspects of family life and family conflicts as positive and important therapeutic tools. This step in the development of systems theory is historically analogous to the heretical step in psychoanalysis in the 1950s by Paula Heimann of declaring counter-transference, in distinction to Freud, as not only always present and as not necessarily the expression of the therapist's own problems, but as a crucial tool in the therapeutic process. Counter-transference changed from being regarded as the dysfunctional property of the individual therapist to a highly therapeutic concept of the interactional process between therapist and patient.

Similarly today the regard for identification. The admission of identification with psychological aspects of families' and clients' lives is at present considered either as individual property reflecting the individual problems of the professional concerned or it is seen as an expression of lack of professional experience in the beginner. My own reactions and co-operation with highly competent and experienced colleagues in difficult cases of child sexual abuse have taught me that identification takes place far beyond these negatively defined processes. It is a far more general interactional process which can be put to great therapeutic use when treated as an important positive professional interactional process and tool in the interprofessional process of complex professional networks.

5.1.2 Conflict-by-proxy

Conflicts-by-proxy are specific examples of mirroring processes. They are potentially the most damaging or most therapeutic aspects of mirroring respectively. In child sexual abuse we find, more than in any other field of family work, conflicts in the professional network which mirror the family conflict as the result of primary identification of professionals with different aspects of the family process. As mirroring conflicts they are not genuine conflicts between professionals; they are family conflicts-by-proxy. Conflicts-by-proxy in professional systems cannot be resolved therapeutically within the network because the conflict belongs to the family. Conflicts-by-proxy in professional networks are always an expression of the inability at problem solving or conflict resolution in the family. They need to be recognised as such.

If a relationship pattern of unrecognised identifications in the professional network shows a mirroring pattern of family relationships we often see the danger that the actions of professionals become primarily reactions to the actions of the family, induced by the family process. An unrecognised conflict-by-proxy amongst professionals makes any problem-oriented co-operation between professionals and any therapeutic resolution for the child and the family impossible. This becomes especially poignant when professionals begin to act out family conflicts amongst themselves with different professionals struggling against other professionals, whilst family members continue actively to uphold the conflict between the professionals in order to avoid bringing the conflict back into the family. The professionals become bound in a non-therapeutic conflict-by-proxy which they are fighting as stand-ins for different family members. A conflict-by-proxy can be most harmful to the family, becomes most harassing to the professionals involved and is by definition unresolvable.

In cases of child sexual abuse different professionals often identify with either child protection or treatment. If we fail to take each professional's identification as mirroring different but equally important parts of the overall problem of a specific case of child sexual abuse and if we create seemingly contradictory alternatives of, for example, immediate disclosure versus joining the secrecy or of protection versus therapy between different professionals or agencies, a conflict by proxy in the professional network is created.

One of the characteristics of conflicts-by-proxy is the fact that issues which need complementary and differentiated exploration about their mutual interdependence and about how they relate to each other seem to be put in a contradictory and mutually exclusive, antagonistic framework of 'either–or'. The question is then 'Do you want to protect this child, yes or no?', which is followed by a non-therapeutic action response as result of our own identifications as professionals and out of our own professional crisis. It becomes impossible to ask the necessary problem-oriented questions 'How can protection and therapy *relate* to each other? How can protection be done in a therapeutic way and how can therapy contribute to protection?'

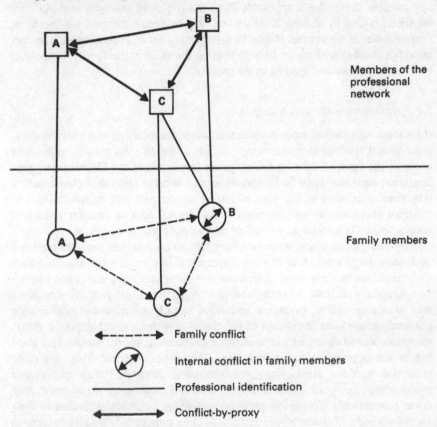

Figure 5.1 Professional identification and conflicts-by-proxy

The process is further complicated by the fact that the primary identification of different professionals, with different aspects of family life, makes us as professionals feel very good when we fight for the cause with which we identify. Professionals who fight conflicts-by- proxy feel subjectively right and at one with their crusade. They fight this conflict because they identify with their course of action and believe in it. For example, fighting for rescuing children and for the punishment and exclusion of abusers out of my own rescue fantasies and out of my own identification with the child as victim can make me as child psychiatrist feel very good when I take issue with probation officers or adult psychiatrists, who in turn may fight the battle for the father when they ally with his denial or his minimising of the danger for the child. Out of their respective own identification with the father they may feel equally good about their own course of action. The subjective and honest feeling of rightness in professionals does however not change the fact that these conflicts as conflicts-by-proxy amongst professionals are fought out of our own primary identifications and not as part of any sensible professional approach. If we make family conflicts into our own conflicts, failing to identify them as conflicts-by-proxy, the problem becomes unresolvable. If we act out of conflicts-by-proxy, we as professionals may feel good but this has nothing to do with helping the child or the family. They both become victimised and get lost in the process.

5.1.3 Non-therapeutic action response

If professionals cannot reach a consensus about the meaning of a specific inter-professional conflict as a mirroring conflict-by-proxy then pseudo-resolutions occur in the form of direct actions against family members. Decisions by professionals can then only be bureaucratic and become 'non-therapeutic action responses' according to the rules of formal competence and responsibilities of different professionals and agencies. These formal actions are expressions of uncoordinated behaviour as a result of unresolved conflict-by-proxy.

Non-therapeutic action responses have lost all capacity for goal-oriented and problem-solving work. Any Primary Therapeutic Intervention becomes blocked. Child psychiatrists may want to do therapy regardless of the context and without co-operating with child protection services or police. Child protective workers may take care action, or police and legal institutions intervene and initiate criminal proceedings regardless of the overall context. Non-therapeutic action responses according to formal competence and bureaucratic responsibilities often led to the opposite of their intention. Therapists treat and keep out child protective agencies conducting 'anti-therapeutic therapy'. Police take proper professional action according to formal laws and embark on 'crime-promoting crime prevention'. Workers in child protective agencies act according to their guidelines and still create 'abuse-promoting child protection'. We all intervene to the detriment of the child, blindly and in a formalistic ways in an overall process we do not understand. Each of us may have intervened in good faith and according to the very proper conduct of our own profession and the result is still a disaster for the child and the family. (See Clinical example: the P family, 4.2.3.)

5.1.4 Conflict-resolution-by-proxy

Conflict-resolutions-by-proxy are the opposite of fighting conflicts-by-proxy. Mirroring the family process and mirroring conflicts in professional networks can be most therapeutic when mirroring conflicts between professionals are recognised as conflicts-by-proxy which originate in the family. Once a mirroring conflict-by-proxy is identified by the professionals a conflict-resolution-by-proxy becomes possible. Primary identifications of professionals with different aspects of the family process and family life can then be fostered openly and can become one of the most therapeutic tools.

To identify conflicts-by-proxy and to come to a conflict-resolution-by-proxy does not mean ditching the interprofessional conflict but using it. I would, for example, positively encourage a colleague who identifies with the child's despair and the need for protection and who wants instant action to rescue the child to express his identification openly. I would encourage this colleague to find at least ten reasons why we should intervene immediately and instantly. If I or another colleague who is involved in therapy were identified with the child's therapeutic needs I would encourage myself or the colleague to think about at least ten other reasons why any instant removal at this moment would be damaging to the child and would lead to increased psychological disturbance. When we argue the case not as our own interprofessional conflict, but as conflict-by-proxy, we will begin to think in complementary terms of relating protection to therapy.

If we put the two sides of the argument openly we will slowly understand how protection may relate to therapy and vice versa. My ten reasons for not yet intervening out of my own identification with the child's therapeutic needs in relation to the colleague's ten reasons why we should intervene instantly to protect will result in a differentiation which allows us to understand under which conditions an instant intervention would be therapeutic and under which conditions it would lead to secondary psychological trauma. In the context of the argument for instant protection we can also think in a differentiated way about the question whether continued therapy prior to any open disclosure would still remain therapeutic therapy and at which point it would become anti-therapeutic therapy.

The more openly conflicts-by-proxy between professionals are acknowledged and fostered and the more we attempt to arrive at conflict-resolutions-by-proxy the more we will understand about the specific family process and the specific needs of the child, the abuser and other family members. We will move towards an understanding of possible ways of intervening in a Primary Therapeutic Intervention in which the different aspects of the problem are seen in a wider complementary and truly multi-professional and metasystemic context.

The openly argued conflict-resolution-by-proxy yields a wealth of information about the needs of individual family members and about the family process and its dysfunction. The conflict-resolution-by-proxy leads to a therapeutic pre-resolution of the family conflict in the professional network. When we deal with the conflict-by-proxy between the professionals as 'therapy-by-proxy' a great deal of individual and family treatment can already be achieved. The process of conflict-resolution-by-proxy guides the professional network out of an often extremely destructive process with severe problems of co-operation, into a positive, creative and problem-solving mode. The therapeutic process of conflict-resolution-by-proxy informs professionals about the family process and assists in thinking about problem-oriented help.

The process of conflict-resolution-by-proxy in legal or statutory interventions in child sexual abuse needs to take into account that the professional network is in hierarchical terms the higher sub-system in relation to the family. The professional network as higher sub-system needs to have an idea about possible resolutions of a specific family problem before the family, as the hierarchically lower sub-system, can find its own therapeutic answer to the family problems.

The pre-resolution-by-proxy does not have to be the particular solution which the family needs to find for itself. It is not the specific content of the pre-resolution-by-proxy that matters but the structural capacity of the professional network for problem solving and the capacity for conflict resolution. The problem-solving ability and the capacity for conflict resolution which the professional network develops in the process of the pre-resolution of the family's conflict are the structural elements and the crucial pre-conditions which facilitate the family's ability to find their own solution to their specific and unique problem for themselves. The structural capacity of the professional network for a conceptual pre-resolution of the family's problems achieved in a conflict-resolution-by-proxy enables professionals to provide a secure therapeutic environment for individual family members and for the family. The conceptual pre-resolution in the professional network is a therapeutic pre-resolution. It is already an integral part of the therapeutic process for individuals and families.

The process of conflict-resolution-by-proxy in professional networks can be compared to the need of parental agreement and conceptual pre-resolution of a child's problems which facilitates the child's ability to find her or his own solution to an emotional or behavioural problem within the family context. It is impossible for the child to find his own solution until the parents are able to agree on any possible solution which indicates that they agree in principle about the basic problem. The therapeutic pre-resolution by the parents is a prerequisite for the ability to evaluate and to accept any of the child's own solutions. Without parental capacity for agreement the child will be drawn into loyalty conflicts and into unresolvable intergenerational alliances with one parent against the other. We find a similar relationship between families and professional networks with statutory responsibilities.

The ability to identity conflicts in the professional networks as mirroring family conflicts and the capacity for conflict-resolution-by-proxy amongst professionals transform a potentially very destructive and divisive situation between professionals into a highly creative and unifying interprofessional process which facilitates therapeutic change in the family. Equally or even more important it allows professionals to maintain their respect for their colleagues and to learn from each other.

Conflict-resolution-by-proxy in professional networks can only occur if we respect unreservedly the formal professional position of our colleagues in other professions and agencies. Only then can we avoid real conflicts of formal competence and of professional responsibilities and can use the emerging conflicts amongst professionals creatively. The process of conflict-resolution-by-proxy can even be fun. It is certainly one of the most important processes for preventing professional burn-out in working with child sexual abuse.

5.1.5 Structural institutional conflict and institutionalised conflict-by-proxy

Conflicts in professional networks have predominantly three origins. They are:

1 Conflicts-by-proxy.
2 Institutionalised conflicts-by-proxy.
3 Structural institutional conflicts.

Structural institutional conflicts

Structural institutional conflicts include conflicts which derive from mutually exclusive institutional and professional requirements which are structurally fixed by laws and regulations.

At present the most important examples of structural institutional conflicts are conflicts between child health and child mental health institutions and the legal system. Legal institutions have not yet fully adapted to the children's rights movement and to the fact that children as biologically immature people are not little adults but human beings with qualitatively different structures of communication which require different legal parameters and procedures. Legal institutions have also not yet fully understood the specific problems of dealing with child sexual abuse as interlocking syndrome of secrecy and addiction.

Child health professionals in turn have not yet provided the legal profession with sufficient valid and reliable data and with the necessary tools to communicate with children, which in turn is essential for the changes required in the legal system. If structural institutional conflicts in specific areas of co-operation are recognised, inappropriate personalised conflicts can be avoided. Changes in different institutions through mutual learning on the basis of mutual understanding and respect for each other's position and professional task become possible. Multi-professional working parties which address the different aspects of management of child sexual abuse and changes in the legal, political and social domain are the adequate context for solving structural institutional problems in dealing with child sexual abuse.

Institutionalised conflicts-by-proxy

I have described conflicts-by-proxy in professional networks and their origin in the personal primary identifications of professionals with aspects of the individual or the family process. Conflicts-by-proxy in specific cases which are not acknowledged as such can over time lead to conflicts between institutions which appear to be structural institutional conflicts, but which are in fact solidified conflicts-by-proxy. If for example members of a particular child psychiatric clinic and social workers from a particular child protective team have had one case of child sexual abuse in which an unrecognised and unresolved conflict-by-proxy has led to intervention failure leaving mutual bad feelings and mutual bad professional opinion of each other's work, this will lead to some apprehension of working together again on the next case. The unoutspoken judgement of 'they are useless and incompetent', which may have been formulated mutually at the first unresolved conflict-by-proxy, becomes a certain 'they are useless and incompetent *anyway*' on both sides after the third case of unrecognised conflict-by-proxy. The interprofessional conflict starts out as unrecognised conflict-by-proxy which has nothing whatsoever to do with incompetant work of the professionals of either team of the two institutions. Repeated unrecognised conflicts-by-proxy between professionals turn into institutionalised conficts-by-proxy between professionals and institutions which the professionals mistakenly believe to be structural institutional conflicts.

It is most important to distinguish between 'institutionalised conflicts-by-proxy' and 'structural institutional conflicts' because they need to be dealt with differently. Structural institutional conflicts need changes on the level of basic structural professional co-operation and procedures. This may include necessary changes in the law. The appropriate framework for solutions are multi-professional working parties and social and political change.

Solidified working practices often make institutionalised conflicts-by-proxy look like structural institutional conflicts. Institutionalised conflicts-by-proxy do not require changes in basic rules and structures of co-operation. They require the recognition of the underlying solidified conflict-by-proxy. Subsequently they need an interactional change in the dysfunctional co-operation which is governed by symmetrical and antagonistic professional practice. Institutionalised conflicts-by-proxy demand a change to complementary and differentiated ways of interprofessional co-operation within the existing adequate structural framework for professional collaboration. The appropriate means of resolving institutionalised conflicts-by-proxy is inter-agency consultation with the aim of reaching a conflict-resolution-by-proxy.

5.1.6 Clinical example: the G family

The example describes the professional–family process and the inter-professional process of the first and fifth consultation with a family of four adolescents in which the father had sexually abused his eldest daughter for about 10 years.

After 2 years' custody and 4 weeks prior to his discharge the father came straight from prison to the first professional–family meeting. Just before the conjoint session I had brief separate meetings with him and with the other family sub-groups. The professionals involved had asked me to assess this family with the question of the possibility of the father's rehabilitation. All children were in care in a children's home.

In a meeting of the professional network some days prior to the first professional–family consultation it was agreed that the session would be attended by all
members of the family, by the statutory social worker for the children, by the
local probation officer, who would be responsible for the father after his release
on parole and by the team leader who was responsible for the residential care of
the children and who was politically responsible for the overall intervention,
which included the agreed aim of the father's rehabilitation. The statutory professionals wanted to transform the Primary Punitive Intervention into a problem-
oriented Primary Therapeutic Intervention. The father's initial imprisonment in
the context of a Primary Punitive Intervention was redefined as the first step of
the Primary Therapeutic Intervention with the other aims and steps still to be
worked on in order to achieve a therapeutic resolution (see Aims and steps in the
Primary Therapeutic Intervention, 6.2.)

In the first professional–family meeting immediate conflict-by-proxy between
the oldest son and oldest daughter developed, mirroring the original marital
conflict of the parents. The sexually abused daughter was sitting next to her
mother. She was entirely 'mother's daughter' who took it up for her mother. The
oldest son was entirely identified with his father and fought his father's battle
against the women in the family. The conflict-by-proxy then shifted to a conflict
between the parentified son and myself as the professional who was due to break
the sexual abuse as family secret. From there it was taken up again by the siblings
and later moved on to a conflict-by-proxy between the parents and the professionals. It finally arrived at the original marital conflict about the circumstances
of the abuse between a very angry and much stronger mother, supported by the
abused daughter, and a very weak, pathetic father.

During the session it emerged that the abused 16-year-old daughter was still
frightened of her father. She said that she would under no circumstances live with
her father again. She was very angry and wanted him to stay in prison for the full
length of his sentence. The girl was supported by her mother who did not want
the initial Primary Punitive Intervention transformed into a Primary Therapeutic
Intervention. The father was fiercely and furiously defended by his oldest son,
who started to blame his sister for the abuse. When maternal threats of murder
against father were uttered the probation officer got very frightened and tried to
intervene to calm the situation. After an initial assessment of the relationship
pattern in the family, the session concentrated on establishing the facts of the
abuse and the responsibility for it as the second and third steps in the Primary
Therapeutic Intervention. The session ended in a much more calm and relaxed
atmosphere.

The fifth session took place some 4 months later. The father had been discharged from prison and had returned to live with his elderly aunt just three roads
away from home. Steady improvement had been achieved in therapy which
included family sessions, separate group work for the abused girl and the father
and individual therapy for a sister who had not been abused herself, but who had
known about the abuse and who was as severely affected as the abused girl

herself. The inappropriate alliances of male family members against female family members had weakened and the children were less parentified and got on better with each other. The idealisation of the mother by the daughters and of the father by the sons had ceased and both sides saw their parents more realistically. Supervised access between the children and the father was going well and changes had taken place in the relationship between all family members involved.

The self-esteem of the abused girl and the father's self-confidence had improved. Father had bought a motorbike and rode proudly around in town. He became more actively involved with his children and was ready to resume a more important and central father role again. The children were still living on a care order, and the responsibility for the care and safety of the children still lay with the social worker, the housefather of the children's home and the team leader for the residential care. The 4–6 weekly family meetings, the weekly group sessions and the individual therapy had continued and the residential professionals and the statutory social worker had gone on working intensively with the children.

I had always left it to the professionals with statutory responsibility to bring the family and to use the sessions for consultation according to their needs. Earlier in the day of the fifth meeting a secretary had taken a telephone message which I had not quite understood but it was too late to phone back. At the time of the session, none of the family had arrived. Instead four professionals had turned up and were waiting in the waiting room: the team leader for residential care, the area social worker, the probation officer and the housefather of the children's home in which all four children were placed.

When I started the meeting I had no idea what it meant that no family member had turned up and why the professionals had come instead. As it turned out the family had not refused to come. Instead the situation was triggered by a disagreement between the four team members, who were very experienced and highly competent professionals. I had great respect for them as colleagues and for their excellent therapeutic work with this family. Initially the conflict seemed to be about who should attend this meeting and what the task of it was. It was implied that I was responsible for giving unclear messages. The probation officer was angry with me, accusing me of harsh and insensitive treatment of the children, saying that they did not want to come any more. His anger with me was a conflict-by-proxy which stood for a conflict between him and the statutory social worker. This became clear when the social worker became angry with the probation officer for interfering with issues concerning the children's therapy. Suddenly the notion of the 'children's camp' arose. It turned out that the 'children's camp' included the house father and the residential workers, the team leader and the statutory social worker. They had regular professional meetings about the family from which the probation officer felt excluded and to which he did not feel welcome.

The interprofessional process in the meeting revealed that the professional sub-system had become locked into the dynamics of the family system, mirroring the family process. This was expressed in the conflict-by-proxy between the professionals of the 'children's camp' and the probation officer. The probation officer felt excluded from the professional network of the 'children's camp' and from the decision-making process about the children which affected his work with the father. He in turn had commented negatively on the treatment of the children which was not his responsibility, but the responsibility of the 'children's camp'. The result was a threatening conflict of formal competence and of bureaucratic responsibility between the social worker with statutory responsibility for the children and the probation officer, who had statutory involvement with the father.

Until 2 weeks before this meeting the professional network had co-operated very well. Now the 'children's camp' threatened to exclude the probation officer. The conflict-by-proxy at this particular point in time in the professional network was mirroring the family conflict about the question of whether the father should or should not become more central to the family again. The children had been in care for 2 years and they and the professionals of their 'children's camp' had settled in nicely. The progress in therapy made the issue of father's final rehabilitation and his active paternal reintegration increasingly acute.

The ambivalence of the children in the family to let father back into the family was mirrored in the ambivalence of the 'children's camp' to let the probation officer in. Allowing the probation officer, as the professional who identified with the father, to enter fully the professional scene of the 'children's camp' and encouraging him to became fully integrated into the professional network would have meant the professionals of the 'children's camp' having to think seriously about the access of the father to the children and about his full rehabilitation into the family. This was what all professionals had planned and hoped for at the beginning. Now that therapy had progressed and this step was due to be taken it seemed that the social worker who stood for the protection of the children was not sure to what extent the children were safe and ready to have free access to their father; it was she who was responsible for their safety. The residential team leader was responsible for the overall approach and the doubt arose whether rehabilitation was 'in the best interests of the children'. The housefather was identified with the parental aspect of emotional care. He stood in direct competition to the real father and was in danger of losing his job as father figure in this family in which he had invested a great deal over nearly 2 years. The result was that the ambivalence of the professionals of the 'children's camp' was mirroring the children's ambivalence about their father's return, which blocked his reintegration into the family. In the conflict-by-proxy this was expressed in the exclusion of the probation officer from the professional meetings of the 'children's camp'. The probation officer's frustration was the result of his own identification with the father who wanted to be reintegrated back into the family and who felt excluded for too long.

A conflict-resolution-by-proxy became possible when the different identifications of the professionals were made explicit and were used openly and positively to demonstrate the conflict amongst family members in the mirroring conflict-by-proxy amongst the probation officer and the 'children's camp'. The conflict-resolution-by-proxy in the session did not only lead to the subsequent full inclusion of the probation officer into the professional network, it also yielded invaluable information about the present issues in the family. It was recognised that the ambivalence and the undermining behaviour of the professionals of the 'children's camp' towards the probation officer was in fact a reflection of the children's fear of how it would be if father were to return home again. It was recognised that the frustration and the anger of the probation officer was in fact not a personal issue but was induced by the father's frustration about his still isolated position.

The conflict-resolution-by-proxy therefore did not only help to gain a much deeper understanding of the problems in the family. The conflict-resolution-by-proxy and the integration of the probation officer into the professional network also enabled the professionals to find a problem-oriented and therapeutic pre-resolution for the present family problem. This meant thinking about the dangers and the advantages of father's full return to the family. The dangers were represented by the 'children's camp', the advantages of reintegration by the probation officer.

The conflict-resolution-by-proxy avoided non-therapeutic action responses by the social worker and the probation officer according to the respective formal responsibilities of their different statutory involvement. The recognition of the increasing conflict between the professionals as conflict-by-proxy and the positive and explicit use of the concept of conflict-resolution-by-proxy as therapeutic tool led to the integration of the probation officer into the professional network and to a successful conclusion of the case. This difficult case of child sexual abuse in the family had been handled most competently by excellent and very experienced colleagues, who, nevertheless, had been drawn into conflicts-by-proxy which threatened the intervention.

The professional network had been able to identify the conflict-by-proxy and to turn a potentially most destructive and exasperating process into a highly therapeutic and problem-solving endeavour which led to a successful conflict-resolution-by-proxy. Had they been unable to name and to use to conflict-resolution-by-proxy a problem-oriented solution of the case would have become impossible. The treatment for the children, for the father and the family would have inevitably failed. In addition there would have been the danger of an institutionalised conflict-by-proxy between the local social services team and probation services in future child abuse cases requiring multi-professional co-operation.

5.2 The interprofessional process in context

5.2.1 Management and therapy

Working with the complex interactional effects between the family and the professional network has taught me that the structure of the intervening professional network as a context for therapy has as much, and often even greater, therapeutic impact than therapy proper itself. Whether our help is effective or not does not only depend on the quality of the intervention itself, but on the organisation and the structure of the context in which help is given. Conducting individual, group or family therapy in the wrong context can lead to great harm. Some seemingly very simple external moves usually labelled as 'management' delivered by legal or statutory workers can, on the other hand, have highly therapeutic effects.

Traditionally we find ourselves in a position where therapy proper often seems to be in conflict with statutory or legal involvement when legal actions interfere and disrupt the therapeutic process. Yet in the problem-oriented context of a Primary Therapeutic Intervention a seemingly punitive measure can be as therapeutic as a seemingly proper therapeutic step can add secondary psychological damage to the child. It is not the intervention in itself that is therapeutic or non-therapeutic but the intervention in context. Some management moves may be highly therapeutic whilst others are not. Likewise, some therapy proper is very therapeutic although other highly skilled therapy can be very damaging if conducted in an inappropriate context.

We need to examine four specific contextual forms of intervention related to therapy and child protection:

1 Therapeutic therapy.
2 Anti-therapeutic therapy.
3 Therapeutic non-therapy.
4 Non-therapeutic non-therapy.

We do not need to consider for long the first and the last combination. Therapeutic therapy is the more rare situation in child sexual abuse when we conduct qualified therapy in the appropriate context of the Primary Therapeutic Intervention. Non-therapeutic non-therapy is the rather more common situation of bad external case management in a non- therapeutic context. The case is dealt with by non-therapeutic action responses according to formal responsibilities of the workers and agencies involved.

5.2.1.1 Anti-therapeutic therapy

Highly qualified therapy can be very anti-therapeutic and psychologically damaging when the therapy is conducted without considering the wider context. The description of the Primary Therapeutic Intervention illustrates the potentially disastrous effect that individual therapy or family therapy can have when we fail to consider the issue of child protection in child sexual abuse as syndrome of secrecy and addiction (see Aims and steps in the Primary Therapeutic Intervention, 6.2). What I as a therapist have done myself and what other individual and family therapists may consider doing is to conduct therapy without protection in the hope of dealing with the linear and legal issues of protection by dealing with the circular and interpersonal relationship aspects which are addressed in therapy. Therapists hope to achieve protection in family therapy by changing dysfunctional family relationships which should stop the abuse. Individual therapists hope that psychological changes make children strong enough to resist further sexual abuse.

In a family therapy approach to child sexual abuse, in contrast to a family approach, families may attend therapy in which abusers promise not to abuse again, in which all family members seem to co-operate and proclaim that sexual abuse has stopped and that relationships are improving. In child sexual abuse as syndrome of secrecy and addiction those statements may not be true. Sexual abuse may nonetheless continue under increased threat of severe punishment to the child if she discloses (see Syndrome of secrecy, and of addiction, 2.1, 2.2, 2.3). Ongoing family therapy can result in the paradoxical process that the better the therapy and the more qualified the therapist, the more disasterous may be the outcome for the child. The therapy is in fact anti-therapeutic therapy under the conditions of ongoing sexual abuse.

In a wider metasystemic context therapy of child sexual abuse which is not supported by statutory child protection serves the abuser as official permission for further abuse. Paradoxically the psychological damage can increase with the quality of the therapy when the discrepancy grows between the reality in which the child has to live under the secrecy and forced silence of ongoing sexual abuse and the child's inability to name the reality of the abuse in therapy.

The confusing aspects of the experience of child sexual abuse can be made worse in a 'therapy of secrecy'. In child sexual abuse, therapy without protection can easily become 'therapy of secrecy'. The therapist becomes part of the system of secrecy which leads to the increased confusion of the child. It is anti-therapeutic when ongoing sexual abuse increases the child's confusion about what is reality and what are feelings and fantasies about this reality – a confusion which brings sexually abused children into therapy in the first place. (See Naming, creating and maintaining sexual abuse as reality, 2.4.3; From secrecy to privacy, 6.4; Individual counselling and therapy, 7.3.)

Another area of confusion for therapists is the distinction between confidentiality and secrecy. Therapists are bound to confidentiality as part of the therapeutic contract. Therapists who do not take into account the legal aspect of child protection in child sexual abuse as syndrome of secrecy may expose the child to ongoing sexual abuse which as an ongoing crime is not covered by therapeutic confidentiality. Therapists who out of a misunderstood therapeutic paradigm of confidentiality want to safeguard confidentiality for the child and the family realise often and only too late that they have joined the family system of secrecy which leaves the child unprotected.

A common and even more damaging strategy to deal with this dilemma is to add a new dilemma for the child when therapists decide to solve this problem by colluding with the denial that sexual abuse has taken place at all. Adult patients have described this final trap. Some reported under greatest distress and despair how they had tried in years of psychiatric help and therapy as children and adolescents to talk about their abuse. General practitioners, psychiatrists, counsellors and therapists had never listened to their attempts to reveal sexual abuse. They certainly had never asked about the facts the patients tried to communicate in order to get help. The patients felt that the professionals had only glossed it over and had driven them into more despair and increased confusion in the process.

To avoid anti-therapeutic therapy in child sexual abuse as syndrome of secrecy and addiction requires child protective action independent of therapy and complementary to it. Addiction and secrecy in child sexual abuse means that protection of children cannot not be achieved by therapy on its own.

5.2.1.2 Therapeutic non-therapy

Management in its form and structure can be therapeutic whether therapy proper takes place or not. Therapeutic non-therapy can include statutory involvement by child protective services and legal actions by courts or the police. Therapeutic non-therapy as an external context and form of intervention is not so much a specific activity as a frame of mind which organises the entire intervention in the form of a Primary Therapeutic Intervention (see Aims and steps in the Primary Therapeutic Intervention, 6.2). This includes activities traditionally labelled as therapy as well as activities usually seen as management, or even activities traditionally seen as interfering with therapy when police and courts intervene.

The legal process   It is not necessarily anti-therapeutic or psychologically damaging when sexual abusers are brought to court and when they are sentenced, as long as legal procedures are part of a goal-oriented Primary Therapeutic Intervention. On the contrary, in child sexual abuse as syndrome of secrecy for the family and as syndrome of addiction for the abuser, the legal process can be highly therapeutic in several ways.

1 The addictive nature of child sexual abuse often makes legal responsibility-taking by the abuser for the abuse the most effective and at times the only way in which the abuser can face the abuse as fact and in which he can begin to own up psychologically for it at all. We need to remind ourselves of the primary difficulty of creating and maintaining reality and of the problem of responsibility-taking and owning up in child sexual abuse as syndrome of secrecy and

addiction. (See Proof and belief, admission and owning up, 1.5; Syndrome of secrecy, and of addiction, 2.1, 2.2, 2.3.)

2 Legal responsibility taken by the abuser conveys to him and to the professional network that he is not either 'bad' or 'mad'. It establishes the fact that the abuser is fully responsible for the abuse. He may have psychological problems as well and he may need therapy.

Stressing the relationship between linear and circular issues of 'bad' and 'mad' instead of creating false alternatives highlights the fact that abusers who are fully responsible for sexual abuse can nevertheless have psychological and relationship problems. Conversely, the existence of psychological problems in the abuser does not take anything away from the abuser's responsibility for the abuse. Abusers are usually not either 'mad' or 'bad'. They are both, they have been irresponsible and they have psychological problems and both need to be addressed equally.

3 Sexual abuse often ceases to be a family secret only after the abuser has taken legal responsibility which establishes the facts of the abuse and the abuse as external and acknowledged fact for the child, the abuser and the family. One of the most therapeutic moments in the entire intervention can therefore take place in a busy police station during a first family meeting which is quickly gathered in the acute crisis of disclosure after the admission by the abuser. The abuser does not need to do more than repeat or read aloud with the help of the investigating officer the statement he has just made to the police in which the facts of the abuse are openly established. An early family meeting does not interfere with the course of justice if sharing the abuser's statement is the only aim of the meeting. On the contrary, it will further the course of justice. Once the statement is shared in the presence of all family members and including one outsider, the abuser will usually not retract his admission, nor will the child or the mother withdraw back into secrecy and denial.

Reading out the statement is of highest therapeutic value because it breaks the secrecy for the family, the abuser and the child. For the abuser the detailed admission of the facts is the first step in the treatment of sexual abuse as syndrome of addiction. Hearing the abuser's admission aloud gives the child the explicit licence to communicate about the abuse and serves as implicit or explicit permission to make use of subsequent therapy.

Most important of all, hearing the statement and hearing the facts of the abuse read out loudly and in all reality may for the first time in the child's life allow the child to establish a most intensive and traumatic experience as reality and to call it such. You can see how a meeting in a police station, at the moment of the crisis of disclosure, which has nothing whatsoever to do with traditional therapy, can have greatest therapeutic effect, if handled in the right way and if used to its full potential.

4 The involvement of the legal process as a contextual support for therapy is often necessary for abusers as addicts, whose drug is the child. The legal

process can protect the treatment and can be used effectively to help evaluate true therapeutic change. (See Court-ordered therapy, 12.16.)

Child protective measures   In child sexual abuse as syndrome of secrecy child protective measures are often necessary to safeguard therapy.

1 When children go into therapy, changes in the child and emerging conflicts can provoke great anxieties and strong rejections in mothers, fathers and other family members. Parents are often tempted to discontinue therapy for the child and families close up again under the renewed cover of secrecy and denial. Without child protective action the child will be both without therapy and without protection from further abuse.
2 Unfortunately mothers are not always the child's natural ally. Mothers do not always safeguard necessary treatment for the child. They often choose for the abuser if forced to decide. Children easily remain unprotected and may even become scapegoated and rejected by mothers. Child protective measures are then necessary to safeguard the child's safety and mental health.
3 The intervention can be anti-therapeutic for the child when court actions against sexual abusers are designed as Primary Punitive Interventions in which legal measures are taken only to satisfy formal notions of punishment or revenge. Children often feel responsible for the family break-up and are frequently blamed for the father's imprisonment. A combination of legal and child protective measures can safeguard the therapeutic process of individual, group and family therapy. It is important to keep in mind that the vast majority of sexually abused children do not want their fathers to be imprisoned. They want the abuse to stop, they want to be protected and they want a father, but one who does not abuse.

5.2.2   Crime-promoting crime prevention and abuse-promoting child protection

Police, legal agencies and child protective services intervene in child sexual abuse in a Primary Punitive Intervention in order to prevent crime and to protect children in the belief that their action does just that. If we look at these actions in the wider contect we can see that the crime preventing actions undertaken out of context often led to 'crime-promoting crime prevention'. Child protective measures taken out of context often end up in 'abuse-promoting child protection'. This happens when the specific context of child sexual abuse as syndrome of secrecy for the child and the family and as syndrome of addiction for the abuser has not been taken into account.

5.2.2.1 Crime-promoting crime prevention

A highly professional and competent intervention by the police can turn into crime-promoting crime prevention when premature and uncoordinated actions are taken by the police which are based only on a vague first-line suspicion without well-founded evidence and without prior co-ordination of the entire professional network as a precondition for a Primary Therapeutic Intervention. (See First-line suspicion, second-line suspicion and partial disclosure, 8.3; Steps in the crisis intervention of disclosure, 8.2.)

Each member of the police force needs to be aware that any unsuccessful intervention by the police into a family of child sexual abuse with the aim of stopping and preventing further crime often results in exactly the opposite of its intention, facilitating and enabling further and often more aggravated crime of sexual abuse. Police officers need to know that in child sexual abuse as syndrome of secrecy and addiction any unsuccessful intervention in which they have to withdraw for legal reasons can be taken by the abuser as explicit and implicit permission to continue abusing. When the police have intervened unsuccessfully and have had to withdraw the abuser can take the police intervention as licence to continue the crime of sexual abuse under increased secrecy and decreased risk of disclosure.

The abuser has the official external legal confirmation that no sexual abuse is taking place even if this is not how the law would see it. Within the family the abuser can say to the child 'You see nobody will believe you, you are just a liar'. Sexually abused children become trapped and can be exposed to further aggravated sexual abuse with little chance of being believed and finding help as a direct result of police action. This holds true especially for small children.

Police interventions with crime-preventing intentions may have been conducted in a highly professional manner and according to the rules of police procedures. In the wrong context they can nevertheless become highly crime-promoting events. The example shows that child sexual abuse is a bigger problem than the task, the skills and the responsibilities of any single profession can cover. It is a truly multi-professional and metasystemic issue. Children have described how they were exposed to prolonged and aggravated sexual abuse after aborted and inconclusive investigations by the police. They reported how the abusers had used the withdrawal of the police against them. How sexual abusers forced them into compliance with more severe and prolonged sexual abuse, referring to the fact that nobody out there in the world would believe them because the police and courts had concluded that there was no evidence of sexual abuse.

Professionals often collude with the confusion between legal proof and factual reality. The fact that evidence in the legal domain is not sufficient to prosecute or to convict is easily taken as proof that child sexual abuse cannot be an ongoing family reality. In one case a girl had made accusations at the age of 6 years and police had intervened unsuccessfully. After the police withdrew, the father started beating up his daughter, calling her a 'bloody damm liar', and sexually abused her even more frequently for more than 5 years until she tried to kill herself. Then she was finally believed.

In child sexual abuse as interlocking syndrome of secrecy and addiction the police need to take full responsibility not only for their own professional actions, but also for the later consequences of their actions, for further crimes, psychological damage and secondary victimisation of the child, when the intervention is not part of a multi-professional Primary Therapeutic Intervention. Another important aspect of secondary damage through premature and uncoordinated interventions by the police and legal agencies is the social stigma and the secondary trauma to the child and the family in cases of false first-line suspicions in families where no sexual abuse has occurred.

Crime-promoting crime prevention can also be the outcome of criminal court proceedings when judges do not understand the specific implications of child sexual abuse as interlocking syndrome of secrecy and addiction. A criminal acquittal only means that there is no proof beyond reasonable doubt in the legal domain. It does not mean that abuse has not occurred. Addiction and reinforced secrecy can then lead to further crime of abuse if the abuser is acquitted. As in an unsuccessful police intervention, abusers take acquittal in court as official permission to continue the crime of sexual abuse. Crime preventing legal actions can become equally crime-promoting when in civil proceedings sexually abusing parents who are separated or divorced get free and unsupervised access or care and control of their children when legal grounds for a conviction of child sexual abuse are insufficient.

Police, judges and magistrates need to fulfil their duties within their own specific framework of the legal system. No other professional can tell the police, public prosecutors or courts how to deal legally with cases of child sexual abuse. And nobody but the legal profession and the police can take and exercise responsibility for legal procedures. The specific nature of child sexual abuse as syndrome of secrecy and addiction, however, makes it imperative that police and courts do not only consider how to intervene from their own perspective.

Any police officer, any public prosecutor and any magistrate or judge must also consider the consequence for other professionals if they have to withdraw at the legal level for established and highly professional legal reasons when in reality child sexual abuse is still an ongoing reality in the family. No other professional is able to prevent further sexual abuse nor to conduct therapy and no other professional can avoid subsequent secondary damage when the legal system as the highest linear system in the professional network has embarked on a narrow mono-professional approach according to the rules of law with the consequence of crime-promoting crime prevention in clinically ongoing cases of child sexual abuse. When police, public prosecution and courts intervene in an uncoordinated way and take unilateral action independent of the other professionals involved, they also have to take full and sole responsibility for possible further crime and for secondary psychiatric damage. In child sexual abuse as syndrome of secrecy and addiction no child protective agency can do abuse-preventing child protection and no therapist can conduct therapeutic therapy after a failed legal intervention.

5.2.2.2 Abuse-promoting child protection

Abuse-promoting child protection often happens when child protective workers intervene prematurely out of primary identification with the child or when they act according to guidelines which force social workers to intervene prematurely in a Primary Child Protective Intervention at the inappropriate stage of a vague first-line suspicion (see First-line suspicion, second-line suspicion and partial disclosure, 8.3). Unfortunately many guidelines and legal procedures are the solidified and formalised results of the professional's own crisis. Child protective workers fail to make the vital distinction between the crisis of the professionals and the family crisis in the overall crisis of disclosure and act out of their own panic and crisis (see Crisis of disclosure – crisis of professionals and family crisis, 8.1). Usually the child is swiftly taken into temporary care. When suspected abusers deny the abuse it often turns out in hindsight and too late that there was not yet enough evidence for long-term child protective measures which could support a Primary Therapeutic Intervention. The child returns home into an unchanged environment and is exposed to further abuse in the family as a consequence of abuse-promoting child protection.

If a care order is granted children are usually kept in care out of ongoing concern for their safety and well-being. In the ensuing long-term stalemate of allegations and denial between the professional network and the family, professionals slowly get worn out. The very same members of the case conference, who initially had swiftly agreed to remove the child in a Primary Child Protective Intervention, often find themselves several months or a year later feeling exhausted and helpless in a situation where the case has seemingly evaporated. The same members of the case conference then suddenly support the decision that the child should have access to the family or should return home, hiding the fact or trying to argue away that not a single family factor which had led to the child's removal might have changed. The child is then sent back into an unchanged environment in which the abuser can take the collapsed Primary Child Protective Intervention as permission for further abuse.

Describing the process of abuse-promoting child protection in no way implies any criticism of professional colleagues in the field of child protection. As in anti-therapeutic therapy and in crime-promoting crime prevention it only draws attention to the fact that a professional intervention in child sexual abuse, which in the narrow frame of reference of child protective services may be regarded as appropriate, can in a wider metasystemic context lead to exactly the opposite of what is intended. It can facilitate further sexual abuse as a direct consequence of child protective action. Child protective action in child sexual abuse must therefore be taken only on the level of a well-founded second-line suspicion and after the full co-ordination and co-operation of the entire professional network in the context of a Primary Therapeutic Intervention. Guidelines which instruct professionals to act on first-line suspicions without having turned a vague first-line suspicion into a well-founded second-line suspicion trigger cases of abuse-promoting child protection with severe secondary damage to children and families. Again we need to acknowledge that the multi-professional task in child sexual abuse is larger than the perspective, the tasks, skills and responsibilities of any single professional or agency involved can cover.

5.3 Changing interprofessional and institutional co-operation

5.3.1 Professional and institutional responsibility

Unresolved structural institutional conflicts and institutionalised conflicts-by-proxy often prevent a problem-oriented solution in child sexual abuse. The ensuing conflict-by-proxy amongst the agencies leads to a non-therapeutic action response. Professionals try to avoid taking responsibility at all or they take inappropriate responsibility for decisions for which they do not have the institutional responsibility and the professional skills. This is accompanied by sometimes fierce blaming and we see a full-blown conflict-by-proxy mirroring the family process. Professionals get drawn into a futile and exhausting process which is positively unhelpful and harmful to the child, the family and to the professionals themselves.

The specific professional problem in mirroring conflicts-by-proxy lies in the fact that professionals, like family members, begin to violate boundaries and professional responsibilities. As mental health professional I had to learn through my own mistakes not to try to be a better child protection worker than the members of a child protection team, or to be a better judge than the judge in court. Many times, I have tried to tell social services with statutory responsibility, what they should do about child protection and have attempted to tell judges how they should go about their legal business. This was usually the result of my being a typical 'kids' doctor' acting out my own rescue fantasies and my own personal identification with aspects of the structural dependence and helplessness of children. In my own identification with the child or sometimes with a parent, I tried to be a child rescuer or parent saviour.

I induced the confict-by-proxy becoming 'the good professional' fighting 'the bad professionals' who dared to interfere with my mission. My active attempts as therapist led to actions in which I tried to interfere in the responsibilities of colleagues in the field of child protection and in the legal domain. Child protection and the law are not the professional domains in which I am trained. Nor do I have the formal professional position in which I could take any formal responsibility in these areas. My fight as 'a professional who knew' against the 'professionals who didn't have a clue' when they took care orders or convicted abusers resulted in the logical request by social services or courts to guarantee through my therapy that sexual abuse would not happen again.

The conflict-by-proxy often led to a situation where the response of the professional network to my impossible child protective therapy as 'anti-therapeutic therapy' was to increase the likelihood of abuse in order to show me that they were right and I was wrong: a typical constellation we find in all conflicts-by-proxy in professional networks. I fought for therapy and against social workers, child protective agencies and the police. When I seemed to have won the battle as the 'good professional' the result was a rather Pyrrhic victory. The withdrawal of the child protective support made the child more vulnerable to abuse than ever when parents and families failed to attend therapy or broke off the therapeutic contact altogether. This happened in situations where I had implicitly given the assurance that my therapy would protect the child, which could only work as long as the parents wanted it to work. Therapy became anti-therapeutic because I had treated therapy and child protection as mutually exclusive alternatives. I had tried to take on a child protective role when in fact I did not have any child protective authority and was not in a professional position to take and to exercise any child protective responsibilities.

I realised that I myself was continuously and structurally violating professional boundaries of responsibility of fellow professionals, of other professionals and agencies. I also saw that colleagues from other professions did the same and it became obvious that this process was one of the essential ingredients for maintaining structural institutional conflicts and institutionalised conflicts-by-proxy between agencies. We cannot change colleagues from other professions or other agencies by trying to tell them what to do or by trying to do their job. Changes between agencies in professional networks can only happen if we fully respect the institutional task of colleagues in other agencies and the professional stance of the colleagues who do the work.

But all professionals are entitled and qualified to identify and to define the context in which fellow professionals perform their respective tasks. Instead of fighting the issue of either therapy or protection or either therapy or prosecution, I began to relate the outcome of child protective and legal actions to my own task and my own work as a mental health professional. This led to an integrated and differentiated metasystemic understanding of the relationships between the different specific professional actions and the importance of the context of these actions.

The understanding of this relationship allowed me to define the Primary Therapeutic Intervention and enabled me to identify anti-therapeutic therapy, crime-promoting crime prevention and abuse-promoting child protection. It also led to the development of the concept of 'prediction of bad outcome' and 'prediction of good outcome' as tool to deal with unresolvable conflicts-by-proxy, with persistent institutionalised conflicts-by-proxy and with structural insti- tutional conflicts.

5.3.2 'Prediction of bad outcome' and 'prediction of good outcome'

Trying to tell other agencies what they should do within the framework of their own professional responsibilities or taking inappropriate responsibilities which we in our own professional positions cannot reinforce are ways of attempting to change other institutions by undermining and by symmetrical conflicts where one agency is right and the other wrong, one the winner and the other the loser. The fairly predictable outcome is usually a hardening of interprofessional conflicts. Each side will dig in its heels and the child and the family are lost and forgotten in the process. It has been helpful to observe the following seven steps when we need to deal with unresolvable conflicts-by-proxy and with persistent institutionalised conflicts-by-proxy and when we want to change structures of co-operation between institutions and professionals in structural institutional conflicts.

1 Analysing formal responsibilities

First we need to identify within a given professional network the formal responsibilities and tasks of each professional and each agency involved. We can then analyse the specific formal tasks and responsibilities of statutory agencies who are paid for child protection, of police who are paid for crime detection and crime prevention, and of child mental health workers who are paid for improving children's mental health. On this basis we can establish the areas and domains of formal institutional responsibilities of all agencies and professionals involved in the case.

2 Define success and failure of specific different goal-oriented tasks

The analysis of the formal responsibilities and tasks of an institution allows us to define success and failure from within the narrow framework of each individual agency and profession. In a statutory intervention nobody else but a statutory child-care worker can hold and exercise the responsibility for formal protection of children. Nobody else but police and courts can ever have the responsibility for success or failure of formal crime prevention as result of legal actions. No-one other than child mental health workers can have the formal professional responsibility if patients' mental health improves or deteriorates as result of therapy.

3 Examining the effects of specific goal-oriented tasks in the wider context

In a third step we need to relate the proclaimed specific aims and the related actions of each agency to the wider context of multi-professional intervention. For example, we need to ask whether the decision of a child protective agency to take child-care action will in the wider context of the multi-professional intervention make it likely that this particular decision will in fact lead to real child protection and not to abuse-promoting child protection.

4 'Predictions of bad outcome' in terms of specific responsibilities

When we have linked the specific goal-oriented actions of all agencies into the wider context of the multi-professional intervention and have found in the analysis that the outcome of a specific action of one agency will in the wider context most likely result in exactly the opposite of the intended outcome we can make the 'prediction of bad outcome' in terms of the agencies' or the professionals' own stated aims and responsibilities. We may be able to point out to mental health professionals that trying to do highly qualified and competent therapy in child sexual abuse without protection may become anti-therapeutic therapy when therapists conduct therapy in the context of possibly ongoing abuse and secrecy. We may be able to point out to courts that a certain court decision as an expression of well established legal procedures which aim to prevent further crime will very likely lead exactly to the opposite outcome and to an increased likelihood of more crime and to crime-promoting crime prevention.

5 Respecting boundaries of professional tasks and responsibilities

We need to respect fully the actions of fellow professionals in their domain even if the analysis of the action or planned action of other professionals and agencies shows that the final outcome in the wider multi-professional context will most likely result in exactly the opposite of the planned and required result. We must not try to take over even if our analysis indicates that the action of the colleague will most likely end in intervention failure and secondary damage to the child and the family. It would be a certain recipe for long term institutionalised conflicts-by-proxy and for unresolvable structural institutional conflicts if we entered a symmetrical conflict in which we transgress the interprofessional boundaries of co-operation and tried to tell a fellow professional what to do in his or her own professional domain which is not our area of expertise or responsibility.

Neither must we suspend our own professional judgement that the intervention may end in disaster. In a three-step process I would (1) take the analysis of the planned inappropriate action as basis for the 'prediction of bad outcome'. (2) I would then state my explicit respect for the co-professional's professional stance and responsibility. (3) Finally I would point out the additional responsibility for the way in which the intervention will affect other professionals' freedom to act. I would for example say to a colleague from the police, 'Sure you may want to or may have to go into this family instantly. However, from what I know about this case the father will most likely express denial. For reasons A and B you will then have to withdraw and for reasons C and D we will most likely not have enough evidence for a full care order and the child will most likely stay at home. Your failed intervention which sets out to stop and to prevent crime will be taken by the father as permission to continue abusing. Most likely you will therefore conduct "crime-promoting crime prevention". But you may feel you have to do it for your own professional reason. This is OK with me. Only you will need to take not only full responsibility for your own professional intervention, you will also have to take full responsibility for the future consequences of your intervention when the child is further and more severely sexually abused.

Nevertheless you may want to proceed on your own and you may have to do it. That is fine – but it also means that you will need to take full responsibility for the most likely continuing crime of child sexual abuse and for possible resulting psychiatric disturbance.'

6 Examining the effects on the task and responsibilities of other professionals and agencies

We finally need to examine the effects of the specific actions of one agency on the work of the other professionals and on our own genuine professional tasks and responsibilities within the multi-professional intervention. A child protective worker can say to a therapist 'if you do therapy with a child who may currently be sexually abused without giving me the name and if you refuse to co-operate with child protection, you yourself will conduct anti-therapeutic-therapy, and that is your responsibility and your responsibility alone. But in addition you will also make it impossible for me in my specific responsibility for child protection to be able to fulfil my own genuine task to protect this particular child.' We need to add the sentence 'I obviously cannot interfere with your professional responsibility for therapy and with the need for confidentiality.' However you do not only have the responsibility for the therapy itself and for possible anti-therapeutic therapy. You also have the full responsibility for the future consequences of your actions and their effects on the tasks of other professionals in the wider context of the multi-professional intervention. If you think you do not need to co-operate with child protection you also have to take the sole professional responsibility for possible ongoing and aggravated sexual abuse because I cannot fulfil my own specific professional task of protection if you do not co-operate.

Attempting to take over or to interfere with the work of another colleague or agency usually only splits the professional network. It instantly creates inter-professional conflicts between 'the good professional' and the 'good agency' against 'the bad professional' and the 'bad agency'. I would respect other colleagues' and agencies' own specific professional stance and policy and their own professional responsibility, but I would always add that they need to take full responsibility for the influence which their specific professional action has on the way other professionals can perform their own tasks and responsibilities in the context of the multi-professional intervention.

In court, for example, I would need to demonstrate how a narrowly defined legal ruling in the wider multi-professional context of child sexual abuse as syndrome of secrecy and addiction can lead to further crime in crime-promoting crime prevention and how it can in my own domain of mental health result in secondary psychological damage and how it affects my own genuine task in a way which can make any therapy anti-therapeutic therapy. The judge would need to take full responsibility for these consequences in his own legal domain and in its effects on the work of other professionals when his correct legal ruling means to send a child home into a clinical context of ongoing sexual abuse. As a consequence of the narrowly defined legal ruling no child protection worker will be able to undertake child protection, nor is a therapist able to conduct therapeutic therapy.

It is crucial and of utmost importance that child protection workers, therapists and other professionals refuse to take responsibility in their own professional domain when the narrowly defined action of another professional group has made it impossible in the wider context of the multi-professional intervention to pursue one's own genuine professional and institutional task. I would for example point out how a narrowly defined legal outcome which may be entirely proper and professional in the mono dimensional legal domain would influence the area of mental health and what effect it may have on my ability to conduct therapy. I would also analyse how the mono dimensional legal outcome could lead to secondary psychological damage, how it may increase psychiatric disturbance and under which circumstances it would condemn me to undertake anti-therapeutic therapy or to withdraw altogether.

7 Making 'predictions of good outcome'

In the last step we need to open up the positive alternative. We should outline how the other agencies' action could in an interlocking multi-professional process positively support our task and how in turn we may be able to assist other professionals on their level of responsibility through complementary actions in our own professional and institutional domain. The 'prediction of bad outcome' therefore needs to include the specific analysis of the complementary 'prediction of good outcome'.

I can outline to other professionals under which framework and conditions of the overall intervention in child sexual abuse as syndrome of secrecy and addiction I will be able to carry out my own genuine task complementary to their task, which will inevitably be different. I, as a child mental health professional, for example, need to state to a court, to a child protective agency, to an education authority or to a children's home, 'If you take action "A" you will most likely create a context of crime-promoting crime prevention, abuse-promoting child protection, of denial-inducing abuse disclosure, etc. in which any therapy I could do would turn into anti-therapeutic therapy. But if you take action "B" I may be able to fit in doing therapeutic therapy.' I have to make a very well founded case from a mental health perspective, explaining why in the context of 'B', therapy would be most likely therapeutic therapy and why therapy under the context 'A' would be anti-therapeutic therapy. I would need to identify whether I need legal or statutory support to conduct therapeutic therapy and what form it should take, to positively support the aims and goals of a Primary Therapeutic Intervention.

Each professional needs to make the same 'prediction of good outcome' from her own specific point of professional expertise and institutional responsibility within the multi-dimensional orbit and context of the total intervention. It cannot be a surprise that professionals of different disciplines will discover that anti-therapeutic therapy usually also leads to abuse-promoting child protection and crime-promoting crime prevention or that crime-promoting crime prevention leads to abuse-promoting child protection and anti-therapeutic therapy. This process is the most convincing expression of child sexual abuse as a truly multi-professional and metasystemic problem.

In child sexual abuse as a genuine multi-professional and metasystemic problem the 'prediction of bad outcome' and the complementary 'prediction of good outcome' links a specific action of one agency into the overall context of the multi-professional intervention. Paradoxically the process of making a 'prediction of bad outcome' for the action of another professional has always helped me to respect this professional even more because it shows that in child sexual abuse even a highly professional action according to the narrow standard of each single profession and agency can create exactly the opposite of the intended outcome. The bad outcome is therefore usually not an expression of individual incompetence. The 'prediction of bad outcome' enables us to recognise this fact and to maintain our professional regard for other professionals in the network.

Respecting other professionals' competence and responsibility in the 'prediction of bad outcome' creates a complementary web of mutually influencing sub-units in the professional network. The 'prediction of bad outcome' and the 'prediction of good outcome' provide a metasystemic differentiation instead of distancing. They respect other agencies' different goal orientations, tasks and skills, and respect the personal stance of colleagues of these agencies. Most importantly they enable learning by helping to crystallise the interlocking effects of specific professional actions on the task of other agencies as well as analysing the likely effect a specific action has on the context of the overall intervention. The 'prediction of bad outcome' and the complementary 'prediction of good outcome' therefore create the positive environment for a truly multi-professional approach of a Primary Therapeutic Intervention which has metasystemic requirements which are different from the specific tasks and skills required in each separate specific and more narrow professional domain. Not least, the 'prediction of bad outcome' prevents professional burn-out because it avoids accusations on the personal and individual levels against colleagues who are in fact highly competent and professional in their work.

In child sexual abuse as a multi-professional problem the task is bigger than the perspective, the skills, tasks and responsibilities of any single professional group can cover. The 'prediction of bad outcome' puts pressure on all professionals and on all agencies to change. Under the 'prediction of bad outcome' no mental health worker would like to embark on or to continue with therapy when it has been pointed out to him that his therapy will most likely lead to greater psychiatric disturbance. Similarly, other agencies and professionals will begin to differentiate when they understand that their narrowly defined action will lead to precisely the opposite of the institutional responsibility of their agencies or to the opposite of their professional task for which they are paid. They will also be more careful when it is pointed out to them that they do not only have to take full responsibility for their own professional decisions but also for the consequences of their action and the way in which other professionals and agencies are able to conduct their work.

5.3.2.1 Clinical example: Jonathan O

A 17-year-old sexual abuser was already in treatment when the case came to court. The court was reluctant to convict the adolescent even after repeated sexual abuse because the abuser was still a minor and was in psychiatric treatment. The paradoxical situation arose that I was pushing for conviction of the boy while courts wanted psychological treatment only. I tried to tell the court what it should do and the court tried to tell me what I as a mental health worker should do. I solved this oppositional stance of either conviction or therapy by analysing the overall process and by making a 'prediction of bad outcome' to the court. In my court report I stated that the court would obviously have to make its decision according to legal procedures. If the court decided to convict the abuser and would give him a fine I could continue to conduct therapeutic therapy. The conviction would help to make clear to the boy that he was neither 'bad' nor 'mad', that he was neither irresponsible nor had psychological problems but that he was irresponsible *and* had psychological problems. He needed to take full responsibility for the abuse on the level of his psycho-social development and in addition he needed treatment for psychological problems.

In the metasystemic intervention the responsibility taking in court was already an important act of 'non-therapeutic therapy'. When the court decided not to convict the boy but to send him to me for further treatment, I wrote back to the court saying that the decision of not convicting the adolescent abuser would most likely be crime-promoting crime prevention. I predicted that the court's decision would in the particular case soon lead to renewed crime as I had stated already in my initial court report.

The court's decision meant in the wider context that the boy was now legally labelled as 'totally mad'. The court did not take the boy seriously as somebody who was capable of being responsible and who had been irresponsible when he abused. The problem of responsibility taking was one of the main problems of this boy and his family. His parents treated him like a baby and he had become increasingly devious and anti-social. Therapy needed to concentrate on the issue that this adolescent boy supported by family members avoided taking adequate responsibility for anything in his life. The therapy now became anti-therapeutic therapy because the abuser had the official certificate from the court that he was unable to take appropriate responsibility. The non-conviction by the court was taken by the boy and the family as official permission for the boy to continue behaving irresponsibly and madly.

As predicted re-abuse occurred. The accurate 'prediction of bad outcome' helped the court to come to a differentiated relationship between the legal process and therapy and the boy was convicted and fined. This need to take responsibility in court was very important and highly therapeutic for the boy. The conviction and the fine transformed the overall intervention into a differentiated and problem-oriented Primary Therapeutic Intervention.

5.3.3 Trusting one's own expertise

The use of the 'prediction of bad outcome' and the 'prediction of good outcome' will help many competent professionals who work with sexually abused children to maintain or to regain their own professional self-respect and sense of professional competence in their respective fields.

In child sexual abuse the basic process of undermining each other's professional competence is based on the confusion of the different levels of professional responsibilities and domains. The confusion of levels of reasoning only too often leads to inappropriate dismissal of particular arguments of one professional on one level by another professional on his or her level. Courts for instance may dismiss reports of mental health workers and child protective agencies for their very own legal reasons. This legal argument, however, can in no way devalue the mental health report or the child protection report as long as mental health professionals or child protection workers comment on the level of their expertise and responsibility in their own domain and as long as they do not attempt to be better police than the police or better judges than the judge. For example, it can never be the mental health workers' nor the child protective workers' task, skill or responsibility to prove a case of child sexual abuse on legal level in court.

Only too often do clinicians or child protective workers feel defensive in courts about their own reports when their arguments are challenged with legal lines of reasoning. If a clinical report were rejected on legal level, I would always bow to the lawyer or the judge, saying 'I am only a clinician and your legal reasons are certainly valid in the *legal* domain and in the line of *legal* reasoning on which I am not qualified to comment. However for me as mental health professional this does not change anything in my *clinical* judgement about this case'. When a case in which I as clinician have clear clinical indications of child sexual abuse is dismissed for legal reasons in court I must not allow my clinical judgement to be devalued by the legal dismissal. A young child who in my clinical judgement has been clearly sexually abused does not become less sexually abused in my clinical judgement if for particular *legal* reasons of evidence or procedure the court may not wish or may not be able to accept my clinical judgements on the legal level. Sticking to my own *clinical* judgement in this case does on the other hand in no way imply any criticism of the court.

The confusion of levels of reasoning is often enhanced by attempts of non-legal professionals to try to argue in the legal domain. It serves me right as mental health professional to be disqualified on the legal level if I try to argue in the legal domain. As a mental health professional I must limit myself to reasoning in the domain of child development, child health and mental health. There, however, I do need to be competent. In multi-professional interventions in child sexual abuse the confusion of levels of reasoning in different domains leads to most inappropriate and unprofessional personal denegrations of professional colleagues. This does not only hold when non-legal professionals enter the terrain of legal courts. It holds for any conflict between any combination of professionals in the professional network where one professional finds his line of reasoning which is based on his own professional expertise judged on a different level of a different professional domain. In doing this we are not only unfair to each other, we also fail to understand the truly multi-professional task.

In dealing with child sexual abuse all professionals invariably make mistakes because the problem is bigger than each of our individual professional skills, tasks and responsibilities. In sexual abuse work even the most qualified and experienced professional cannot avoid making mistakes. This is the invariable and direct result of the metasystemic nature of child sexual abuse as interlocking syndrome of secrecy and addiction which requires basic changes in the structures and understanding of multi-professional co-operation. This does not mean that we should feel deskilled and incompetent. We will only be able to face the multi-professional challenge of child sexual abuse if we maintain our respect for our own specific professional skills and trust our own professional expertise.

5.4 Therapy and consultation

Cases of suspicion or denial in child sexual abuse are often referred for therapy. Many of these referrals have in fact a double agenda. The child and the family are not referred for therapeutic change but as a result of the fact that the referring professional and the network do not know what to do with the case. Often professionals want help for themselves. They want the therapist to find out whether sexual abuse has taken place or not. This is common in three situations:

1 In cases of denial where professionals enter symmetrical and antagonistic conflicts with the family or where they feel that they want to give up exhausting attempts to get to the facts (See Dealing with primary denial, 10.6).
2 Children and families are referred when police or courts have withdrawn in a failed legal or child protective intervention and when child protective agencies are stuck in possible abuse-promoting child protection.
3 Cases are passed on when professionals get into unrecognised conflicts-by-proxy and when networks have been paralysed in their decision-making process.

Conflicts-by-proxy, denial and the inability to decide and to act on the legal or child protective level are often dealt with by the pseudo-resolution of a referral for 'therapy' to mental-health professionals when in fact interprofessional consultation is required. When legal and statutory agencies have investigated unsuccessfully and are unable to achieve positive results, statutory social workers are often still saddled with the responsibility of child protection in cases where they might only be able to do 'abuse-promoting child protection' (See The interprofessional process in context, 5.2). They refer the child for 'therapy' when in fact they want the mental health professional to be a better policeman than the police and to be a better child protector than the child protection worker. All these referrals are legitimate referrals indeed. But they are not referrals for therapy. They are referrals for consultation.

Consultation is a very different process from therapy even if in family work it may at first sight look the same. The basic differences between therapy and consultation are well known but they take specific form in the context of child sexual abuse.

1 Therapy is directed towards the family whereas consultation is directed towards the professional network and not towards the family.
2 Therapy aims at changes in clients and families where the task of consultation is to aid professionals in decision-making processes.
3 Therapy is therefore concerned with internal and external psychological and interpersonal boundaries of clients and families whereas consultation has the task of assisting professionals and agencies to clarify the functions and tasks of their work.
4 Therapy aims to help solve individual psychological and interpersonal relationship problems whereas consultation needs to address conflicts-by-proxy in the professional network with the objective of assisting the professionals to find conflict-resolutions-by-proxy. A referral for 'therapy' by an agency involved with statutory responsibility for a child or an abuser can only be consultation even if we do therapeutic work with individuals and families in the process of the consultation.

Therapy	Consultation
Intervention directed towards	
(1) Family	Professionals
(2) Relationships	Decision making
(3) Boundaries	Functions
(4) Family conflicts	Conflict-by-proxy
(5) Therapist free agent towards family (independent professional responsibility towards family)	Therapist is consultant in the service of other professionals and agencies (responsibility towards hierarchy of consulting institution)

Figure 5.2 Therapy and consultation

5 In therapy the therapist is a free agent towards the family and the family can accept therapy or can leave it. In consultation on child sexual abuse the professional is not a free agent towards the child and the family even if he does the same therapeutic work as a therapist because statutory issues are involved.

6 In therapy confidentiality is of paramount importance and needs to be observed closely. In consultation it is impossible to maintain confidentiality for the family towards the consulting professional.

In referrals for 'therapy' by statutory or legal agencies, professionals need to make decisions according to the responsibility of their agency as child protective or legal institutions. In these referrals my client can never be the abuser, the child or the family: it is always the professional and his agency. It is therefore of paramount importance to avoid turning to family members and asking them what they want to get out of therapy. We need to turn to the agency and to the professional to whom we consult, asking 'What question do you need answered in order to clarify your task and your responsibilities in this case?' or 'What question do you need answered in order to be able to make decisions according to your legal and child protective responsibilities?'

In openly acknowledged cases of child sexual abuse with legal or statutory involvement all therapy needs to be taken in the legal and statutory context of consultation. The child and the family do not come as free agents but as a result of statutory and legal involvement. For example, if a child protection worker refers a case, all 'therapy' needs to help the social worker to make decisions about the family which no therapist has the responsibility to make nor the means to enforce. If mental-health workers accept referrals for 'therapy' from statutory agencies as therapy cases instead of treating them as consultation to the professional colleague, they themselves accept or create a double agenda pretending that the family or the child is the client when in fact the professional colleagues ask for assistance in the decision-making process of the case.

Consultation requires close co-operation between all professionals. Therapists can conduct consultations over many months. The consultation can then look like therapy proper when we see individuals or families for many sessions in which we try to achieve therapeutic change. Nevertheless consulting therapists must not withdraw behind closed doors. In the context of consultation, therapy can only be therapeutic therapy when the therapist co-operates closely with the statutory agency. He needs to give open feedback about the process in treatment and needs to respond to requests by the professional colleagues from statutory or legal agencies to assess specific psychological and interpersonal change. One of the crucial differences between consultation and therapy is therefore the handling of confidentiality within the professional network.

The difference between therapy and consultation must also be understood by the family. The family needs to know that important issues will be shared, discussed and assessed within the entire professional network. This clarification helps professionals to avoid undermining other colleagues and minimises the dangers of conflicts-by-proxy between statutory workers and therapists. Even by conducting what looks like proper individual therapy or family therapy the therapeutic professional will always remain a consulting professional to fellow professionals who may not even be present.

It is impossible to see whether somebody is doing consultation or therapy without the knowledge of the context, just as we can see little from the outside as to whether somebody is doing individual therapy or family therapy merely by the fact that one or several family members are entering the consulting room. We need to know the context, the task and the frame of mind of the professional who conducts the session.

Conducting 'therapy' or 'consultation' does not mean that one situation is more therapeutic than the other. As much as individual, group or family therapy are still consultation in the context of legal and statutory involvement so consultation to the professional network can be extremely therapeutic when it leads to conflict-resolutions-by-proxy or to the resolution of structural institutional conflicts.

The clear distinction between therapy and consultation finally helps to avoid the very damaging process of splitting in the professional network which can easily be induced by the family, and which many professionals tune in to only too easily. If we take on a case for therapy which is in fact consultation we as professionals have immediately created a split between 'the good therapist' versus 'the bad social worker' or the bad police officer or judge. This conflict reflects the metasystemic problem in child sexual abuse that one professional needs to take legal and linear responsibility for the protective aspects of the abuse whereas the other professional takes on the interactional therapeutic task. Both are in danger of undermining each other.

It is very important that the consultant to the professional–family system conveys clearly to the family and to the professional network that he is not a free agent towards the family but that he is at the service of the professional colleague from the agency who has given him a specific task in relation to the overall intervention. This explicit clarification often frees the statutory social worker from the role of the scapegoat in the professional network. It enables the statutory worker to gain the required assistance in the decision-making process without becoming the 'bad professional' who is undermined by the therapist as the 'good professional'. Sometimes the therapist herself becomes scapegoated when she takes on a case for 'therapy' instead of consultation when the statutory and legal system expects her to take decisions about child protection which a therapist can never make. (See Practical problems in consultations, 11.5).

Consultation can be given by any professional who is not part of the specific professional–family system of a particular case. For example, if one social worker and her hierarchy are involved in a specific case of child sexual abuse a fellow social worker from another team or another agency could well be the consultant to this case. The excluding criterion for consultation is that the consultant is not part of the specific professional–family system in which decisions need to be made. The professional–family system also includes the entire social services hierarchy of this particular case and this needs always to be kept in mind.

Chapter six

The primary therapeutic intervention

6.1 Family therapy and family approach

Family therapists who regard child sexual abuse as a symptom of family dysfunction have increasingly taken on the task of treating sexually abused children and their families (Lustig et al. (1966), Eist and Mandel (1968), Gutheil and Avery (1977), Rosenfeld (1979), Furniss (1984a). They have described approaches and techniques of conjoint family therapy as therapy of choice in child sexual abuse (Machotka et al., (1967), Alexander 1985). The worrying aspect of most family therapy approaches to child sexual abuse is the neglect and the lack of appreciation of the linear, legal and child protective aspects of the problem. Family therapists are in danger of conducting 'anti-therapeutic therapy', joining the family system of secrecy against any statutory intervention when they address only the interactional elements of the family dysfunction in child sexual abuse as syndrome of secrecy and addiction.

When I first treated sexually abused children and their families I myself tried to be clever by avoiding co-operating with legal and statutory agencies, when I set out to treat these cases in a traditional family therapy mode. I believed that the families' attendance at therapy and their co-operation were an indication that sexual abuse had stopped. It was a disturbing and shameful experience to have to discover later that sexual abuse had been continuing during therapy with greater severity and under increased threat to the children, who kept the secret because the abusers had threatened to punish them if they disclosed. This taught me that a family therapy approach which only addressed interactional relationship aspects in the family was much too narrow a framework. I as therapist had become part of the families' system of secrecy under which the child remained unprotected from further abuse. In a wider systems context my family therapy was anti-therapeutic therapy providing in fact contextually the implicit permission for the father to continue the sexual abuse under increased damage to the child and under reduced risk of disclosure for himself.

Child sexual abuse in the family is on the interactional level a symptom of family dysfunction. On the legal level it is a crime which activates the legal system against the abuser and child protective services towards the child. A family therapy approach can only address the relationship aspects of child sexual abuse. A family approach needs to integrate linear aspects of legal proceedings and child protection and circular aspects of family relationships in a meta-systemic Primary Therapeutic Intervention. The Primary Therapeutic Intervention is based on the following six suppositions:

1 Children are structurally dependent on parental figures in their original family or in substitute families. Children cannot stand on their own. A family-oriented approach to child sexual abuse takes account of childrens' actual attachments to abusing and non-abusing parents and other family members. It addresses the children's need for carers.

2 In a multi-professional family approach to child sexual abuse conjoint family therapy on its own is only addressing the circular aspects of the dysfunctional family relationships. Family therapists can never take responsibility for legal and child protective issues. They are unable to guarantee protection from further sexual abuse for the abused child without legal and statutory assistance.

   In child sexual abuse as interlocking syndrome of secrecy and addiction family therapists become ineffective in their proper therapeutic task to enable changes in family relationships when they join the collusive family system of secrecy against other colleagues in the professional network. We need close and integrated co-operation between legal agencies, child protective services and therapists in which protective and therapeutic workers relate comple-mentarily to each other instead of perceiving their task as antagonistic and mutually exclusive.

3 A metasystemic family approach conceptualises the dysfunctional elements in child sexual abuse on a family level and in the context of family relationships. Using a family perspective serves to keep the vital family process in mind at any point during the intervention. On the treatment side conjoint family therapy is only one amongst other concurrent forms of therapy in a wider context of an integrated legal, statutory and therapeutic framework. Family therapy on its own will invariably create splitting in the professional network and induce conflicts-by-proxy inviting legal, statutory and other non-involved professional systems to interfere in symmetrical and antagonistic ways. A metasystemic approach allows differentiation instead. Guided by clearly defined goals in the overall Primary Therapeutic Intervention the work of legal and statutory agencies can be as crucial for therapeutic success as therapy proper.

4 A metasystemic approach makes a clear distinction between the concep-tualisation of child sexual abuse as a symptom which is maintained by family dysfunction and the intervention which employs different concurrent forms of therapy. In contrast to many family therapy approaches we clearly distinguish

conceptually between the task of family assessment which leads to explicitly stated criteria for improvement and therapy which can involve a wide range of different family therapy techniques and contexts according to the families' needs and the therapist's skills and orientation (Furniss et al., 1983; Glaser et al., 1984). The important notion that any family assessment is also family therapy and that any therapy needs to be continuous reassessment is thereby fully maintained.

The overall assessment and the goal-oriented way of working allow us to recognise when family therapy in the wrong context becomes damaging anti-therapeutic therapy, as much as it enables us to see that a linear legal and statutory action in the appropriate context constitutes highly therapeutic non-therapy (See The interprofessional process in context, 5.2).

5 The specific problems of child sexual abuse as syndrome of secrecy and addiction require the concurrent use of different modes of therapy including family therapy, group therapy and individual therapy. Whether the concurrent treatment modes are therapeutic or non-therapeutic and whether they succeed or lead to drop out and treatment failure is not primarily a function of the family or the nature of the different forms of therapy. Successful outcome or failure of concurrent forms of different treatment modes depends primarily on the quality of the co-operation between the different therapists who only too often in mutual disregard try to undermine each other as much as possible. We need different forms of therapy used concurrently in order to achieve the explicit and operationalised aims and steps of the Primary Therapeutic Intervention. Conjoint family therapy, the work with family sub-groups, group work and individual therapy are used as complementary forms of therapy within the overall metasystemic framework.

6 A family approach towards sexual abuse also takes into account that many elements in the family process during the treatment of extrafamilial abuse are often similar to intrafamilial abuse (See extrafamilial child sexual abuse, Chapter 13).

The failure to distinguish between a family therapy approach and a meta-systemic family approach can lead to severe problems of co-operation between family therapists and other professionals. I myself have repeatedly made two cardinal mistakes which I still see happening constantly. Family therapists who see families in the presence of statutory or legal professionals often conduct the meetings as if they were doing family therapy instead of consultation. Conducting family therapy in the presence of professional colleagues repeats on a higher level the common mistake of the beginnings of family therapy, when family therapists did not recognise the qualitative differences between individual and family therapy and often conducted individual therapy in the presence of the family. Consultation in the presence of fellow professionals which fully uses the professional–family process creates a new dimension of systems work which needs new concepts and new ways of working. To address and to use the genuine professional process in consultation is as different from family therapy as family therapy is different from individual work (See The interprofessional process, 5.1; Therapy and consultation, 5.4).

The second basic fault family therapists commit too easily is treating professional colleagues in consultation like patients or clients. This quite inappropriate and unprofessional conduct is usually not the result of malicious intent. It is based on the confusion between the two important different aspects which are represented in the professionals who are involved with the family. First, they represent the mirroring family process and the resulting conflicts-by-proxy in which they have taken aspects of the family process on board. In that respect they do represent the family and the family process. However the professionals are not the family even if they represent the family process. Professional colleagues are professional colleagues are professional colleagues. This fact must never be forgotten, and not only because we need to maintain a respectful attitude to fellow professionals. We also need a thorough understanding of the genuine interprofessional process in order to achieve conflict-resolutions-by-proxy and therapeutic pre-resolutions of the family dysfunction in the professional network.

6.2 Aims and steps in the primary therapeutic intervention

The Primary Therapeutic Intervention has the aim of changing family relationships and not of punishing abusers or removing children as isolated measures in their own right (see Three basic types of intervention, 4.1). Conversely the Primary Therapeutic Intervention does not exclude the involvement of child protective services and legal agencies. On the contrary the following treatment steps will often only be achieved if the therapeutic process and the therapeutic setting is supported and protected by legal and statutory measures.

It is necessary to identify the basic aims and steps in the Primary Therapeutic Intervention in order to facilitate therapeutic change in family relationships in families of child sexual abuse. The actions of all agencies involved from police to therapists need to relate to these overall aims and steps of a family-oriented treatment approach. The family process and the family perspective should always be maintained although the means, the setting, the context and the techniques may change according to the difference of each specific case and its contents.

The basic aims and steps of the Primary Therapeutic Intervention will remain very similar for all families of child sexual abuse but the sequence in achieving particular aims and practical steps can differ considerably according to the particular and unique situation of each different family. Earlier steps may be taken later and vice versa. The following seven aims and treatment steps form the basis of the Primary Therapeutic Intervention.

1 Blocking further sexual abuse

The first step in therapy must be to block further sexual abuse. In child sexual abuse as interlocking syndrome of secrecy and addiction this usually requires an initial and temporary separation of abuser and child during the crisis intervention. It is desirable for the father or other abusers, as the adults who are responsible for the abuse, to leave the family and for the child to stay at home. Already at this point therapeutic and legal agencies may need to co-operate to achieve this first treatment step. A legal injunction against the abuser to leave home temporarily may be required as part of the therapeutic process in order to prevent further abuse and anti-therapeutic therapy when the child and the abuser remain together at home during the initial phases of therapy.

Although the removal of the abuser should always be considered first, it may not be necessary when older children disclose sexual abuse and do not want to return home, or when rejection and scapegoating of the abused child by the mother or the entire family make it safer during the crisis intervention to place the child in care. I have seen several cases where the conflict between mother and child was so intense that the child had to leave the family. Nevertheless we should always try to work towards approaches where the abuser should leave the family and not the child.

Removing the child in the initial disclosure bears the serious risk of inducing the dynamics of a Primary Child Protective Intervention with the danger of secondary psychological damage to the child when the child's placement is not firmly based in a Primary Therapeutic Intervention (See Three basic types of intervention, 4.1).

A Primary Child Protective Intervention means punishment on top of the abuse for the child. If the child is removed careful steps need to be taken to guarantee continuous and free access to the mother, to siblings and to other important attachment figures in the child's life. The social network can at times of crisis provide an important part of the protective environment against secondary psychological damage, especially for older children and adolescents. This can especially include peers and teachers at school. (See Crisis of disclosure – crisis of professionals and family crisis, 8.1; Sections on placement away from home, 10.2, 10.3, 10.4.)

2 *Establishing the facts of abuse and the abuse as shared family reality*

The second step in the treatment of child sexual abuse as interlocking syndrome of secrecy and addiction needs to establish the facts of the abuse in order to establish the abuse as psychological fact and family reality. We need to help the child and the family to find explicit sexual language. Children, parents and families of child sexual abuse need to use explicit sexual language which they may have never used. They may have to describe events for which they may not have the words and the language to communicate. It is therefore important to give the family explicit licence to communicate about the abuse. By introducing explicit sexual language ourselves, professionals give the message to the family that they know how to talk about this most difficult topic. Giving explicit permission to communicate about sexual abuse demands that professionals be able to talk openly and appropriately about explicit sexual acts in front of the family (see Introduction).

3 Paternal responsibility taking for the abuse

As the basis for any further therapy the abuser needs to take full and sole responsibility for the sexual abuse in the initial stages of therapy. This does not mean that the abuser is the only active participant and that the child is entirely passive in the abuse, or that the mother may not have known about it. All abused children are participants in the abuse and in some cases of long-term sexual abuse, children may at some stage even play an activating role. But whatever the child does in the abusive interaction and whatever the mother knows, the responsiblity for the sexual abuse itself can never rest with either the child or the mother. It always and under all circumstances lies solely with the abuser. (See Responsibility, participation, guilt, blame and power, 1.2.)

The moment the abuser accepts sole responsibility for the sexual abuse, he becomes, as a father, a true parent to his child. By accepting sole responsibility for the abuse the abuser moves into a paternal position. The child in turn returns back into the position of being a child. The change in the abuser's position from a pseudo-partner to one of a parent helps to relieve the child of her sense of responsibility for the abuse and constitutes the abuser as responsible carer in a parenting role. The 'responsibility session' with the abuser should also take place if the abuser is not the father and if possible even in extrafamilial abuse. (See The Hansel-and-Gretel Syndrome and Sexual Abuse by Brothers, 14.2; Extrafamilial child sexual abuse, Chapter 13.)

4 Parental responsibility for general care

It is important that both parents are present at the first family meeting in which the abuse is discussed. Although the abuser is solely responsible for the abuse, non-abusing parents and abusers have to take equal responsibility as parenting couple for the general care and well-being of their children. Establishing the fact of their responsibility as parents towards their children does not confirm them as marital partners. This step follows later. Initial work needs to concentrate on the inter- generational boundaries and on the parenting functions, not on the parents' marital relationship. (See Different reactions to disclosure and treatment, 3.3.3.)

The differentiation between the parental and the marital couple is of paramount importance. The parents can stop being partners. They will always remain parents even if they are inactive parents in families of separation and divorce. In therapy it is for practical purposes often vital to keep these two distinct adult functions very separate. Parents in conflict often use partner arguments to avoid issues of parental responsibility as much as they use parental conflict in order to avoid facing partner problems when marital issues are addressed.

At an early stage of therapy we need to acknowledge to the parents that partner issues will indeed have to be dealt with, especially the question of separation and divorce, but that this will happen later. At this point in therapy the issue is whether both parents want to remain involved as parents and whether they want to take responsibility for the parental care of their children irrespective of their present or future partner position. One of the most paternal acts can then be for the father to leave the family home for the duration of the crisis intervention and not to take part in the daily care, but to give the child the chance to stay at home and feel safe. Correspondingly one of the most maternal reactions can be not to pursue instant divorce proceedings even if from a partner point of view the mother may want to do so. This can give the child the space to deal with the abuse and the disclosure without additional confusing and traumatising divorce procedures at an early stage.

5 Work on the mother–child dyad

After the sexual abuse between father and child has been blocked and both parents have taken equal parenting responsibility, therapy needs to focus on the relationship between mother and child. The work on the mother–child relationship is both therapeutic and preventive. It aims at making the mother a more emotionally central and protective person whom the child can trust to be believed and not to be rejected when she tries to find protection in case of renewed and further abuse.

In the process of working on the mother–child dyad, two central issues often emerge. The first is the mother's guilt feelings that she has failed to protect the child from the abuse and the child's need to be able to trust that the mother will be able to listen to what has happened to the child and to protect the child in the future. Only very few mothers are actively involved as sexual abusers themselves and not many know consciously about the abuse and allow it to continue openly. However, many mothers in long-term sexual abuse in the family have at some stage been told by the child, or have known in other ways about the abuse. The child's previous attempts to disclose usually emerge in therapy when issues of maternal care and letdown are dealt with in family sessions or in dyadic sessions with the mother and the child. Mothers needs to learn to identify and to appreciate the child's emotional and protective needs in general and in relation to the abuse.

The second issue is the at times strong rivalry between mother and child. This does not only happen between mothers and adolescent girls. Mothers can also have strong rivalrous feelings towards very young children. One mother of a 3-year-old girl who had been sexually abused by her father for more than one year, put it in a typical way: 'I am really angry with her. She is so precocious. She did not come to me and I just blame her.' She then talked about how she could understand intellectually how inappropriate her reaction was, but that she nevertheless was very angry, and felt very rivalrous towards her 3-year-old daughter. Strong reactions of mothers also towards sexually abused boys show that the rivalry has much deeper emotional components in the loss of important emotional attachments and relationships.

Once a 14-year-old girl pulled out letters from her father saying triumphantly 'whom does he love, she or me?'. Another 15-year-old girl in a session suddenly said 'and who has the nicer breasts, mum or I?'. These moments, and moments when mothers are accused by children for not having protected them from the abuse, are situations where mothers can get very angry and rejecting or depressed and suicidal. At this stage in therapy mothers often need intensive help and support as people in their own right.

6 Work with the parents as partners

Once parenting issues have been dealt with separately first, partner problems can be addressed. During partner therapy, the split between the couple's emotional and sexual expectations of each other forms the main focus of the work.

In order to avoid the conflicts about sexual and emotional partner problems both parents may join together in attempts to scapegoat the child as morally bad. Parents often try to induce a primary child protective intervention in which they deny all marital problems and blame everything on the child. This avoids having to face unbearable and threatening marital conflict in conflict-avoiding families. Alternatively, it blocks change in relationships in families where child sexual abuse serves to regulate marital conflict. (See Family pattern, 3.2; The family and the professional network, Chapter 4.)

It is important to keep in mind that in the initial crisis of the disclosure, mothers in their own confusion between parenting role and partner role tend to decide that they have to go for instant divorce, reacting to their own moralistic expectations or to the expectations from professionals. As parent they then demand instant divorce, whereas as partner they may be as intensely attached and married to the abuser as ever. Due to the confusion in professionals and in families about the separate aspects of the parenting role and the role as partner, instant requests for divorce are often welcomed by all sides.

Mothers often realise their continuing attachment to the abuser when the initial shock of disclosure has diminished again. Under moral pressure and under the influence of professionals they often feel unable to admit openly to understandable feelings of loneliness and that they miss the abuser as partner, as co-parent and as material provider for the family. Professionals may therefore need to check their own moral attitude. They may find it difficult to fulfil the important task of pointing out to mothers that the initial rejection of their husband may be very helpful to protect the child and to promote their protective role as mothers. But it is also important to allow mothers to miss the abuser as partner, even if she rejects any thought of missing him in the initial crisis of disclosure. Otherwise we risk the very common situation that the parents collude under renewed secrecy against the professional network, often successfully jeopardising a Primary Therapeutic Intervention. To allow mothers to miss the abuser as partner is completely separate from the final outcome of therapy which may well conclude appropriately in a therapeutic divorce of the parents as partners. (See Mothers who want instant divorce, 10.5).

The main issue for abusers is to face up fully to their sole responsibility of sexual abuse towards their wives. Abusers may initially say that they are sorry for what they have done. The initial responsibility taking is often followed by minimising what they have done to their wives or even by accusations against their partners. Truly to face up as husbands to their wives as partners is a long process which abusers often try to avoid. They employ strategies of appealing, seduction, accusation, minimisation and other defensive moves which show that psychologically they are still denying the sexual abuse and their own role in it even long after the initial admissions of responsibility for what they have done. (See Working with sexual abusers, 7.4)

7 Work on the father–child dyad

Once the basic problems in the mother–child dyad and the mother–father dyad have been dealt with, it is easier to return to the father–child dyad. Having opened up the secrecy and having addressed aspects of the syndrome of addiction for the abuser in concurrent forms of therapy including family sessions, group sessions and if necessary individual therapy, the renegotiation of the abusive relationship between the father and the child is a far less complicated issue (See Concurrent forms of therapy, 7.1).

Following disclosure the child may go through an initial phase of hate and rejection against the abuser. The degree of attachment of the abused child to the father can nevertheless be very strong, especially in cases of long-term child sexual abuse. Intensive and psychologically damaging attachments are nevertheless still extremely strong attachments. Positive aspects in the abuser–child relationship are often very difficult to handle for therapists. If the child is treated therapeutically and does not become a ready object for professionals' own personal projections, prejudices and moral judgement, positive aspects in the attachment between abuser and child need to be allowed and fostered equally.

It is essential for the normal emotional development of sexually abused children to be allowed to deal with their disappointed expectations of a good and emotionally caring relationship towards father figures. It is therefore crucial for any sexually abused child to be able to build or rebuild emotionally trusting relationships to the father and to father figures which do not end up in sexual abuse. The experience of trusting emotional relationships with men, which do not violate the intergenerational boundaries, is as important for the child's ability to develop trusting relationships in adulthood to men, as is the development of trust in the child towards emotional care and protection by maternal figures for the development of open and trusting adult relationships to women.

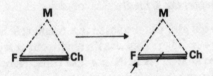

(1) Blocking the actual sexual abuse

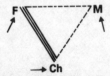

(2) Establishing facts of sexual abuse and sexual abuse as shared family reality

(3) Father taking sole responsibility for the sexual abuse. Move into parenting position

(4) Both parents taking equal parenting responsibility for the care of the child. Intergenerational boundaries

(5) Work on the mother—child relationship. Issues: emotional support by mother; child's disappointment; rivalry

(6) Work on the emotional-sexual marital conflict. Issues: sexual conflict confused with emotional immaturity and dependence

(7) Work on the relationship between father and child. Issues: child's feelings of hate and love; fathers jealousy of child's friends; paternal emotional care

Figure 6.1 Aims and steps in the primary therapeutic interventions

6.2.1 Clinical example: the K family

Barbara, a 14-year-old girl, had disclosed to a friend at school that she had been sexually abused by her father. This was first indirectly relayed to the teacher and the school head who thought about the possible consequences of a full disclosure and immediately phoned the social worker, who in turn contacted a residential unit in case the girl's admission was needed. When Barbara fully disclosed she was indeed too frightened to go home.

1 Blocking the abuse

Barbara was brought direct from school to the residential unit, with the assurance that her father would not be allowed to see her without prior preparation and without her consent.

2 Establishing the father's responsibility for the abuse

The police, after linking up with school and social services in a pre-intervention meeting at school, saw both parents and confronted the father with the allegations of sexual abuse. Mr K admitted to vaginal intercourse and took responsibility for it. He was released on bail. An injunction was served that he was not allowed to have free access to his daughter without professional supervision. The social worker saw Mrs K at home. She was shattered, saying that she had been totally unaware of the abuse. In the acute crisis of the disclosure the father felt extremely guilty and expressed suicidal intent as a reaction to disclosure. The reaction of both parents was typical of the reaction of parents in conflict-avoiding families. The social worker sent the couple to the crisis unit to talk to members of the treatment team. At this point, Barbara was told by staff that her father had admitted to the abuse.

3 Parents taking responsibility as parents

During the first interview the parents discussed whether or not to stay together. Mrs K's first reaction was to want to leave her husband immediately, and to file for divorce. However after making the distinction between their marital role and their parental role the parents agreed to stay together for the time being as a parenting couple for the sake of their children. The mother excluded any marital partnership with her husband, and therapy focused on the parenting function.

4 Immediate homeostatic move in the marital dyad

When Mr K took responsibility for the abuse he moved, as a parent, on to the same parenting level as his wife. However this move simultaneously unbalanced the established pattern of their marital relationship. Within hours of the disclosure of the abuse, Mr K became suicidal. This was an attempt on his part to underline his dependency on his wife and to appeal to her as a protective mother figure. Mrs K responded by becoming more compulsively caring towards her husband. The couple were then able to deny any marital problems.

At this point in therapy, we did not challenge the homeostatic re-establishment of the dysfunctional and rigid marital relationship. We allowed it to continue in order to avoid an immediate collapse of the marriage. It would have been impossible to work on both the parenting and the marital aspects at the same time, and any attempt to do so would have risked a complete breakup of the family and treatment failure. At this point the most important task was to deal with the parenting issues in order to help Barbara. Addressing the couple as parents was at that moment also less threatening than dealing with the underlying marital conflict and the dysfunctional interlocking individual emotional needs as partners.

5 Mother's and daughter's attempts to get closer to each other

After Barbara had arrived at the Crisis Unit, she wanted to see her mother. Mrs K reacted positively and visited her daughter. Barbara had hoped she could stay with her mother and that her mother would divorce her father. When she learnt of her mother's decision not to take divorce action immediately she was very disappointed and reacted hostilely towards her mother.

6 Competing for mother as an ally

Barbara began to feel excluded from the family. She felt her father had won the competition for her mother as ally. His initial suicidal threats had had greater impact on Mrs K than Barbara's accusations against him.

7 Barbara's rejection of both parents

Mrs K became increasingly distressed and disappointed about Barbara's rejection. She felt she had been a good mother and that she did not deserve her rejection. Although the father had taken full responsibility for the abuse both parents had assumed equal parental responsibility and had countered Barbara's wish to split them in their parenting role. Barbara interpreted her mother's acceptance of shared parental responsibility and her admission that she had failed to prevent the abuse as an admission of responsibility for the sexual abuse itself. Barbara felt both parents had let her down and both were equally to blame for the abuse, and she rejected them both.

8 The family's attempt to change the basic direction of the intervention

(a) *Mother's threat to opt out.* Mrs K's feeling of being rejected as a good mother made her feel very depressed and suicidal. This was an appeal to Barbara to accept her as a caring mother. Mrs K's suicidal wishes also activated her husband to back her up against Barbara's accusation of being a bad mother. In a move to distract from his own responsibility for the abuse and from his own parental failure Mr K turned his initial guilt feelings into open aggression towards his daughter, siding with his wife against her.

(b) Father's threat to opt out.   Mrs K's suicidal threat frightened Mr K. When he came to the next session he aggressively demanded that Barbara should apologise to her mother for her behaviour at once. He became very agitated and wanted the therapist to take action stating aggressively 'now my wife has become the victim'.

Barbara's attack on her mother had again unbalanced the established relationship pattern between the parents as partners. Mr K found it intolerable to see his wife suffer and he could not bear having to face his own responsibility in producing that pain. Instead, he threatened action against his daughter or against himself. He declared that going to prison would be a lesser punishment than seeing his wife suffering. He then blamed the therapist of stirring up the problems instead of helping the family.

(c) Parents' attempted coalition to expel Barbara as a scapegoat.   Barbara's parents joined forces and turned against her. They began to collude in an attempted solution which would exclude her in a Primary Child Protective Intervention from the family. She became scapegoated and was blamed for the abuse and all the present family problems. Mrs K shifted the blame from Mr K by saying that Barbara had seduced her father and that she had enjoyed the sex, choosing not to tell her mother about it. Mr K protected his wife from her feelings of failure when he declared that Barbara was an ungrateful daughter.

9 Accepting therapy

Each member of the triad had, in turn acted out in an attempt to avoid facing the sexual abuse and the underlying problems as family reality in therapy. The members of the crisis team had been able to deal with the family's aggression, hostility and threats of suicide, so far, without themselves being paralysed, split or drawn into the crisis. This had been possible by means of the close co-operation of all professionals involved. The close co-operation in the professional network led to a conflict-resolution-by-proxy and after some preparation the family met for a responsibility session, and then settled into therapy. (See The family and the professional network, Chapter 4; The interprofessional process, 5.1.)

10 Maternal failure to protect

Mrs K's allegation about her daughter's responsibility for the abuse stopped during therapy. Mrs K realised that Barbara had in fact tried at the beginning of the abuse to communicate that sexual abuse was happening. Mrs K had called her daughter a liar and had not taken her seriously. Now she herself began feeling responsible for the abuse. At this point Mrs K became very depressed and needed great help and support to realise that whatever she had done or omitted to do to protect Barbara from sexual abuse, she could under no circumstances ever be responsible or be to blame for the abuse itself. This responsibility lay firmly and solely with her husband as the abuser. The work on the mother–daughter dyad revealed that Barbara felt desperately unhappy, not understood and let down by her mother. Mrs K felt guilty and depressed in turn about having failed to protect Barbara from the abuse.

11 Open rivalry between mother and daughter.

Feelings of letdown and loneliness in Barbara which had come out in the work on the mother–daughter dyad could not be sustained. Barbara found it easier to introduce an area of conflict on the level of female rivalry rather than facing the issue of maternal letdown.

The female rivalry between Barbara as an adolescent daughter and her mother as a middle-aged woman had initially been camouflaged by the conflict about maternal care and protection. Rivalry between Mrs K and Barbara for Mr K as emotional partner emerged when Barbara refuted her mother's allegation that she had enjoyed the sex with her father. The conflict between mother and daughter became a conflict of two female rivals. It was a matter of open triumph of Barbara over her mother when, in an individual session, Barbara said provocatively, 'Whom does he want more, her or me!'

Mrs K acknowledged her own feelings of rivalry against her daughter and became very bitter and rejecting. She reached the point where, in a state of fury and tears, she said, 'If I did commit suicide, I know my husband would get together with Barbara again and they would start where they left it. I know they both enjoyed it, and, after all, Barbara did not tell me'.

12 Open marital conflict

The open rivalry between Barbara and her mother made it increasingly difficult for the parents to continue to avoid facing their partner conflict under the protection of their unity as a parenting couple. Mrs K reported that, 'Ever since things went wrong with Barbara, it hasn't been right between my husband and myself. We can hardly speak to each other any more and we are both very tense in each other's presence.' At the advanced stage in therapy it became possible to deal with the partner problems. They could now be addressed without interference from the initial acting out which followed the first shock of disclosure and without confusing the parental problems which involved issues of care and responsibility for Barbara with the partner conflict which had nothing to do with her.

During this next stage in therapy, Mr K reported that he had strange physical sensations in his head and felt phobic in the consulting room. He explained that he had had similar feelings when he had sexually abused Barbara, and also at certain times when he was young. He became increasingly phobic and frightened of the consulting room. After a dramatic event at home where Mr K thought he would die he was admitted to hospital for 3 days with the diagnosis of a suspected but unconfirmed heart attack. The development of these psychosomatic symptoms indicated the high level of stress and anxiety in Mr K about the marital conflict and some related earlier life events in his childhood which Mr K found extremely difficult to face.

After his discharge from hospital the marital sessions resumed. The partner conflict became central and Mrs K wanted to go for divorce. Her relationship with Barbara was improving and she felt it would be better for her if she were to live on her own with the children. Mrs K said that she was not interested in sex and accused her husband of being oversexed. She described how she used to lie frozen next to him in bed at night, while he masturbated himself. She had felt revolted by it but had never mentioned it to him.

Mr K was frightened of divorce. He saw his wife as a very good but strict mother figure and a woman of principle and he wanted to save the marriage. He saw himself as a weak man who could play strong but felt very insecure underneath. He was able to admit that he had failed his wife. He described how he had felt driven to the abuse by uncontrollable internal tensions and how he had been unable to resist abusing although he knew it was wrong.

Once the partner conflicts were largely dealt with, Mrs K wanted some time on her own to decide about the marriage. She left and stayed for 3 weeks with a sister to think about her own future. At this point Mr K became panicky because he was very frightened of losing his wife. Three weeks later on return Mrs K decided that she wanted to stay with her husband and the partner therapy continued.

13 Readjustment of the father–daughter dyad

Once the dysfunction in the mother–father and mother–daughter dyads had been addressed, it became possible to work directly on the relationship between Barbara and her father. In the process of therapy, Barbara had gained an emotionally closer and more understanding mother. This cleared the way for Mr K and Barbara to work on a more appropriate emotional and non-abusing father–daughter relationship.

The sexual abuse had not only been deeply frightening to Barbara. She had at times also been intensely aroused and confused. A lot of anger and bitterness on Barbara's side was followed by her wish to be seen and to be acknowleged by her father as a person in her own right. It was extremely difficult for Mr K to listen to his daughter without either interrupting her or defending himself. When he talked to Barbara about his own relationship with his own parents a real change in quality occurred. Mr K became a much more caring adult to his daughter. Towards the end of therapy, Barbara felt more safe with her father. She began to trust him and was able to have an emotional relationship with him without being frightened of becoming sexually abused again.

When Barbara returned home she and her parents made an agreement that Mr K would initially not stay alone with Barbara in the house. Both Barbara and her father were worried about their reaction towards each other and they felt unsafe to be on their own without a third person. However Barbara's relationship with her mother was much closer and her relationships to her peers had improved, and when she got a boyfriend this precaution finally became redundant.

6.3 Basic mechanisms in the therapeutic process

6.3.1 Therapeutic momentum in the work with dyads

During therapy of families of child sexual abuse each dyad of the parent–child triad often passes through phases of intense aggression which may be directed inwardly as depression and suicidal attempts or expressed outwardly as open hostility towards other family members.

In the mother–child dyad, which may initially seem to be the least problematic relationship, the most profound, hidden and quite unexpected negative dynamic can develop. In the crisis of disclosure mother and daughter often attempt to get closer. Later, severe hidden conflicts between them are often revealed. The mutual hostility can persist until the issues of the child's disappointment in her mother for not having protected her and issues of emotional and sometimes sexual rivalry are therapeutically resolved (see Figure 6.2).

The collusive secrecy between father and child during the abuse can at some stage in therapy reverse into open hostility of the child against the abuser. The child is then likely to distance herself from the father until a therapeutic resolution of the conflict between them is achieved and issues of non-sexual emotional care and trust have been addressed (see Figure 6.2).

We find two different patterns of reaction in the treatment of the marital dyad. The mother may immediately turn against the child and join her husband in order to avoid family breakup and partner conflict will only emerge later in therapy. Alternatively, the mother may instantly reject her husband and threaten to divorce. Only as result of therapy may the couple come together again or achieve a therapeutic divorce. The first pattern is more likely to occur in families where sexual abuse serves to regulate marital conflict, the second where it has the function of conflict avoidance (see The family process, Chapter 3).

Therapeutic progress is achieved in a continuous dialectic process in which dyads of family members distance themselves from each other in conflict and come closer again on different levels. The attempts of two family members to get closer on one level often produce conflict and distancing in another dyad at a different level. For example, when the child attacks the mother as a bad mother for not preventing the abuse the father may ally with the mother to protect her as a good parent. When, in the continuing process of therapy, the conflict between the child and the parents becomes less intense, the parents may no longer be able to maintain their seemingly harmonious collusive parenting alliance, and open partner conflict may emerge between them. The attempt at *parental harmony* then results in an accelerated appearance of *marital conflict*. It is the nature of this momentum, gathering behind the developing therapeutic family process, which soon takes the treatment focus away from the sexual abuse itself to the underlying, individual problems and the interlocking family process as described and illustrated in the K Family.

6.3.2 Dyadic collusion against the third member of the abusive triad

Attempts to undermine a Primary Therapeutic Intervention can be expressed in different dyadic collusions in the parent–child triad against the third member as scapegoat. Either the mother colludes with the father to expel the child as a 'sexy bitch' and as the source of all moral evil in the family, or the mother colludes with the child against the father who is seen as the 'criminal' and monster. I have even seen the child and the father trying to get together again against the mother. If the first collusion proves successful, the Primary Therapeutic Intervention will be turned into a Primary Child Protective Intervention which leads to the removal of the child from the family. If the second collusion is successful, it will precipitate a Primary Punitive Intervention in which the father is removed from the therapeutic system. Both collusions can be used by family members to jeopardise a Primary Therapeutic Intervention (see Figure 6.2).

6.3.3 Family members' attempts to break off therapy

The often extreme emotional stress and conflicts in families of child sexual abuse inevitably lead to repeated and frequent attempts by different family members to break off therapy. In an effort to change the direction of the intervention this can take the form of a family member literally running away, attempting suicide, developing physical symptoms, trying to blackmail or seduce the therapist or flatly refusing to attend therapy. It is vital to be prepared in advance that this will happen. Other professionals need to know and need to be prepared to provide backup which can deal with these attempts of families in crisis to run away from therapy in order to avoid professionals going into conflicts-by-proxy in the professional network. (See The family and the professional network, Chapter 4; The interprofessional process, 5.1; The interactional nature of motivation, 2.4.1.)

Parents tend to react differently. Fathers often react to disclosure with instant denial, violence or running away from taking responsibility. During therapy they may develop psychosomatic symptoms and opt out into physical illness. It is important to be aware that at times it seems easier for fathers, especially in conflict-avoiding families, to opt out immediately after disclosure in extreme ways which can go as far as to commit suicide. Mothers often initially reject any thought of therapy which would involve the abuser. In later stages the therapist needs to be prepared for maternal depression, suicidal thoughts and the mothers wish to break off all therapy including any help for the child when issues of maternal protection and marital conflict become central in therapy.

Children often come into severe loyalty conflicts towards their parents. When the child's own personal changes in therapy are not accompanied by changes in the family the child can threaten the established dysfunctional family pattern and it can become too frightening for the child to continue therapy. The child may then feel that rejoining the family system of secrecy and denial at the cost of the self-sacrifice to perceive the reality of sexual abuse as such is easier than working on her own problem in therapy at the cost of being scapegoated and losing the family.

In adolescence we often find extreme acting out throughout therapy. Adolescents act out sexually, they take overdoses, run away, cut their wrists and display the entire spectrum of psychosomatic and functional psychiatric and behavioural symptoms. Conversely they may attempt to convince themselves and everybody else that nothing had happened at all and that the allegation of sexual abuse was based on pure fantasy. It is then crucial to be able to return to previously established external points of reference such as the responsibility session or the responsibility session-by-proxy which have established the facts of sexual abuse and the sexual abuse as external fact and reality. (See The first family meeting as reality-creating responsibility meeting, 9.11; Family and responsibility-session-by-proxy, 9.13.)

6.3.4 Family collusion against treatment

After the initial crisis of disclosure the whole family often colludes against the professional network in order to avoid any change in family relationships. This does not necessarily mean that the family would deny that sexual abuse has happened. Therapy is rejected with the argument that all the problems have now been resolved and that the family feels happy together. This reaction is more likely in families where sexual abuse serves conflict regulation. At this point the support and the authority of outside legal and statutory agencies is often needed to back up the Primary Therapeutic Intervention and to bring the parents, especially abusers, but also often mothers, back into therapy.

6.4 From secrecy to privacy

The transformation from secrecy to privacy is one of the essential therapeutic aims in child sexual abuse as syndrome of secrecy and addiction (see Syndrome of secrecy, 2.1; Syndrome of addiction, 2.2; The individual process in context, 2.4). For the child to be allowed and to be able to name the sexual abuse as reality is the necessary precondition for concurrent forms of therapy which re-evaluate

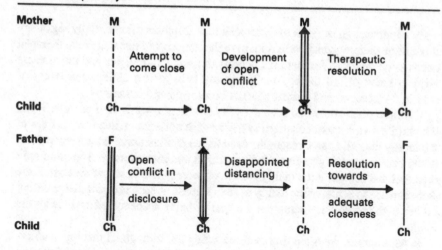

(a) Process of distancing and getting close during therapy

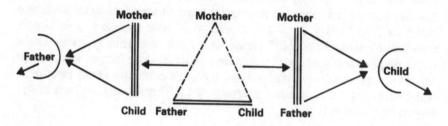

(b) Dyadic collusion against the third member in the family tryad

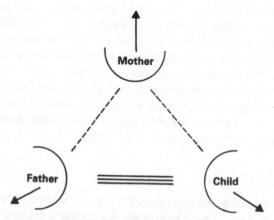

(c) Attempts to run away from the therapeutic process

Figure 6.2 Basic mechanisms in the therapeutic process in families of child sexual abuse

the experience, the confusion, the feelings and fantasies about the abuse. The transformation from secrecy to privacy poses different problems on different levels.

6.4.1 The social and legal domain

It is important to protect the child's right to privacy when the secret of child sexual abuse is disclosed legally and in the social domain. The need for the protection of privacy of children is well accepted in legal courts but is often very difficult to achieve in the social context. It can be impossible to protect a child's privacy when the family stays in the same house or in the same neighbourhood where the abuse has been disclosed. Police interventions or sensational reporting by the local press often make it impossible to keep the child's identity protected in the neighbourhood. It is equally important to think extremely carefully about the child's privacy when sexually abused children are placed in children's homes or in foster care. (See Placement in childrens homes, 10.2; Working with foster parents, 12.17.)

6.4.2 The interprofessional process

The right of privacy needs to be protected in the professional network as long as no well-founded second-line suspicion requires the planning of the intervention in the pre-intervention meeting. On the level of first-line suspicions an Anonymous Diagnostic Interprofessional Consultation (ADIC) may be necessary in order to protect the child's privacy from premature and overhasty interventions (see First-line suspicion, second-line suspicion and partial disclosure, 8.3; The pre-intervention meeting, 8.7; Preparing fellow professionals for impending disclosure, 8.13; Anonymous Diagnostic Interprofessional Consultation, 8.4). In the interprofessional process the child's right to privacy is reflected in the professional's obligation to confidentiality. The right to confidentiality towards fellow professionals has a two fold effect on the professional network. It protects the child's and the family's privacy from inappropriate and premature interventions. On the stage of early first-line suspicions it often increases the motivation and willingness of health professionals, educational staff and therapists to co-operate in a multi-professional approach to child sexual abuse.

The fear of therapists, of doctors, nurses and of educational staff that confidentiality will be broken prematurely often leads to collusions and non-disclosure by these professionals. Many professionals quite rightly are very frightened that at the very moment they break the confidentiality towards other professionals the entire control over the situation is taken away. They fear that their information will be used for inappropriate, premature and harmful non-therapeutic action responses which can lead to abuse-promoting child protection and crime-promoting crime prevention. (See The interprofessional process in context, 5.2.)

Medical, therapeutic and educational professionals also fear that parental responses to premature disclosure may lead to legal actions against the disclosing professional. Many professionals will become more motivated once the child's right to privacy expressed in the right of the professionals to an Anonymous Diagnostic Interprofessional Consultation is maintained until all professionals have agreed that a well-founded second-line suspicion makes it necessary to intervene. (See Crisis of disclosure – Crisis of professionals and family crisis, 8.1; Steps in the crisis intervention of disclosure, 8.2; Three basic types of intervention, 4.1.)

6.4.3 The family process

The key for the child's individual ability to deal with the violation of the privacy of body and mind lies in the disclosure of the secret in the family context. In the Primary Therapeutic Intervention concurrent forms of therapy are designed to avoid secrecy within the family. The Primary Therapeutic Intervention aims to give time and space for the development of adequate privacy for the abused child and the parents. The open communication between all therapists involved serves to avoid secrecy as a result of the universal process of splitting and dissociation in child sexual abuse. The agreed confidentiality towards family members in different concurrent forms of therapy maintains the confidentiality which safe-guards the therapeutic process in group sessions and in individual therapy without secrecy as a result of splitting. (See Concurrent forms of therapy, 7.1; From secrecy to privacy, 6.4.)

6.4.4 The individual process

In the transformation from secrecy to privacy the child who is linked in the secrecy of sexual abuse to the abuser can begin to develop personal autonomy and a sense of self. The external space to think and to relate in therapy creates the internal psychological space to develop the privacy of self as a reflection of integration and individuation in the therapeutic process from the dysfunctional over-involvement and fusion between child and abuser in child sexual abuse as syndrome of secrecy and addiction. (See Child sexual abuse as syndrome of secrecy, and of addiction, 2.1, 2.2; Group work with children, 7.2; Individual counselling and therapy, 7.3.)

The transformation from secrecy to privacy usually needs to be supported by external changes which often require the creation of time and space in the intermediate separation of abuser and child after disclosure. The external space and time of privacy provide the structure for the development of self in con-current forms of therapy in the Primary Therapeutic Intervention. (See Family therapy and family approach, 6.1; Aims and steps in the Primary Therapeutic Intervention, 6.2; Concurrent Forms of therapy, 7.1).

Chapter seven

Different modes of therapy in the primary therapeutic intervention

7.1 Concurrent forms of therapy

In child sexual abuse we need to use different forms of therapy concurrently if we want to achieve the goals and aims of the Primary Therapeutic Intervention. Combining several different forms of therapy seems to break all established rules of therapy. The concurrent use of different forms of therapy does not mean that the different therapies compete and undermine each other. Each therapy has specific different tasks representing different aspects of the overall process, all contributing to the overall goals and aims of the Primary Therapeutic Intervention. The metasystemic nature of the relationship between the different forms of therapy is based on the specific therapeutic problems of child sexual abuse as a legal and mental health issue and as interlocking syndrome of secrecy and addiction.

7.1.1 Functional differentiation

In the Primary Therapeutic Intervention each of the different modes of therapy addresses different areas of connectedness, interrelating, privacy, intimacy, autonomy and individuation of different family members; areas which are structurally violated in families of child sexual abuse. Family therapy is directed towards more appropriate connectedness and interrelating within the family. It deals with problem solving and conflict resolution at the level of family relationships. Concurrent group treatment and individual therapy highlight the structural need of different family members for privacy, autonomy, intimacy and individuation. In the context of an integrated family approach, individual therapy or group therapy concurrent with family sessions can be seen as a structural space for the central therapeutic task of transforming secrecy into privacy.

Concurrent family therapy sessions are necessary to open up child sexual abuse as a family secret and to give the child explicit licence and permission to change in therapy. Without concurrent family therapy, parents will withdraw their children from treatment. Individual therapy or group therapy for the child will most likely break down because parents feel too threatened by the child's treatment and by the changes in the child.

Severely sexually abused children may need the space in concurrent group treatment and in individual therapy to gain independently from the family sessions and probably for the first time in their life, a sense of privacy, autonomy and individuality which gives them control over basic aspects of their own body, mind and actions. Sexual abusers and parents can deal in individual and group therapy with aspects of their own personal life experience and with partner issues as part of the Primary Therapeutic Intervention. The structural violation of boundaries in child sexual abuse makes it quite inappropriate to deal with explicit marital and adult sexual problems in family therapy although the general confusion between emotional care and sexual relating needs to be addressed in conjoint family sessions as well. Sexual matters relating to parenting in which the child has been triangulated must not be confused with sexual issues in the partner relationship as outlined in the fourth and sixth steps of the Primary Therapeutic Intervention (see 6.2). In addition child sexual abuse as syndrome of addiction for the abuser poses specific therapeutic problems which need to be addressed in the framework of individual work or group work for abusers only and in partner groups. All concurrent use of different forms of therapy can be therapeutic as long as they are employed to achieve differentiated treatment aims in the context of a Primary Therapeutic Intervention.

7.1.2 The need for co-operation between different therapists

The basic rule that different forms of therapy should not be mixed concurrently has very little to do with an intrinsic incompatibility of different concurrent forms of therapy. The splitting and undermining which leads to breakdown of therapy is usually not the result of psychological events or family dynamics. The fact that different concurrent forms of therapy lead to splitting and non-therapeutic therapy is all to do with therapists themselves. The splitting between therapists of different persuasions who try to undermine each other as much as possible leads to treatment failure. If close co-operation and communication between the different therapists is guaranteed the differentiated use of different concurrent forms of therapy can be highly therapeutic and can accelerate the treatment process in a mutually informing way. This approach only works if therapists of different orientations give up ideological distancing and righteousness and see the use of concurrent forms of therapy as part of a goal-oriented and differentiated therapeutic process.

When we use concurrent forms of therapy the principle needs to be observed that absolute confidentiality has to be guaranteed in the different therapy settings between the different family members whereas only complete openness and close co-operation amongst all therapists involved can lead to a successful treatment outcome. The intensity of feelings and conflicts in the family process in the therapy often requires special meetings of all therapeutic staff involved. In these meetings all information from the different therapeutic settings needs to be shared. In addition different therapists' identifications with different family members and different aspects of the family process need to be openly declared so that the mirroring processes of conflicts in the therapeutic team can emerge, can unfold and can develop between the different therapists. This process then enables the identification of conflicts-by-proxy with the possibility of a therapeutic pre-resolution in the conflict-resolution-by-proxy. Without meetings with the openly stated agenda of dealing with arising conflicts-by-proxy, a meta-systemic treatment approach, with different concurrent forms of therapy and different therapists involved, will always be in danger of failing. Therapy teams in child sexual abuse can consist as much of social workers, probation officers and others who deal with children and parents in a therapeutic way as of professionals primarily employed as therapists.

7.1.3 The therapist: different positions in different settings

It can be very therapeutic if the group therapist or individual therapist for the child also takes part in the family sessions or if the family therapist is also the group therapist for the child. The presence of the group or individual therapist in family sessions provides a form of differentiated continuity and consistency in the treatment of child sexual abuse as syndrome of secrecy which can be crucial for the abused child.

It is possible for the therapist to attend different forms of therapy sessions as long as the therapist himself is able to distinguish clearly between the different positions and functions he has in the different settings. Therapists need to be aware that in individual and group therapy they are more in a parental position in reality, in symbolic ways and in the transference, than they are in family sessions. Family therapy uses the different family members' mutual projections on to each other. In a family therapy session the therapist is symbolically in a grandparental role and in a more indirect position to the child, which is mediated through the presence of the parents. The child who also sees the therapist in individual or group sessions can easily experience the more mediated contact in the family sessions as symbolic and transferential parental letdown. This experience of letdown in the family session is not hindering the therapeutic process as long as we are aware of it and assess carefully the limits the individual child can bear. The letdown can be taken up with great therapeutic benefit in the subsequent individual or group sessions.

The important therapeutic effect of the presence of the group therapist or individual therapist in the family sessions lies in the fact that the presence of the same therapist in both forms of sessions helps the sexually abused child to maintain the continuity of experience. It avoids the reintroduction of secrecy and splitting which can be most anti-therapeutic and damaging to the child. The presence of the same therapist in both kinds of sessions helps to keep the therapeutic process in the therapeutic domain of privacy in the individual and group work and in the domain of sharing and connectedness in the family sessions without relapse into secrecy.

7.1.4 Rituals of differentiation

Families and family members need help to link, and at the same time to separate and differentiate, therapeutic events when the same therapist conducts group or individual therapy and family sessions concurrently. We need 'rituals of differentiation'. For example an important, simple and effective device can be used to link group therapy and family sessions. As group or individual therapists, I would meet the child briefly before each family session in a separate room individually on her own and would ask two questions: 'Do you want any specific help in the family session today to bring up any specific issue?' and 'Is there anything you do not want to be discussed and brought up under any circumstances?' This kind of simple and brief ritual of differentiation is crucial in the overall metasystemic framework for the following five reasons.

1 The ritual links the two different forms of therapy in which the group or individual therapy is seen as the space in which explicit licence is given to develop privacy. This needs to be respected by the group or individual therapist in the family session. The 'ritual of differentiation' reaffirms for the child the boundary of privacy of the group therapy or the individual therapy towards the family.
2 The 'ritual of differentiation' gives the clear message to the child and to the family that the therapist who is family therapist during the family session is also the child's or the parents' therapist in another context.
3 The presence of the therapist in both group or individual therapy and family therapy avoids non-therapeutic processes of splitting and secrecy. The 'ritual of diffentiation' allows the therapist to support the differentiating process of individuation and connectedness in the different therapeutic events.
4 The 'ritual of differentiation' is an interactional process which not only affects family members. It is as important to the therapist. The ritual of differentiation enables the therapist to differentiate her own role between the two different therapeutic settings. It gives the therapist licence to move place and function between the different forms of therapy in the multi-dimensional orbit of the professional–family system in the Primary Therapeutic Intervention.
5 Finally the 'ritual of differentiation' is the commonly agreed and shared moment of functional transition from individual or group therapist to family therapist in the relationship between therapist and child.

'Rituals of differentiation' are only necessary in the direction from individual therapy to group therapy to family therapy, the direction of increased mediated and indirect work on relationships and decreased work in the direct and symbolic parent–child transference–counter-transference interaction between therapist and child.

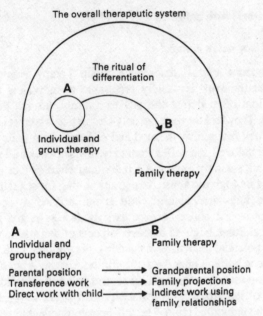

Figure 7.1 Rituals of differentiation in concurrent forms of therapy

7.1.5 The treatment contract with the family

At the beginning of therapy we need to state clearly to the family that confidentiality will be kept towards different family members attending different forms of therapy concurrently, but that the therapists who conduct the different therapies will co-operate closely with each other. Close co-operation between therapists may well mean that the individual therapist will keep certain issues from the individual sessions confidential towards the other therapists. The confidentiality 'as therapeutic collusion' remains therapeutic as long as it stays within the context of the pre-arranged therapeutic space for individual privacy of family members which has been agreed to by all members of the therapeutic team.

The 'therapeutic collusion' with the child or other family members in individual and group sessions only becomes anti-therapeutic when the therapist is drawn into collusions of secrecy towards other therapists. This will inevitably lead to conflicts-by-proxy in the therapeutic team. The constant differentiation between the therapeutic domain of privacy, and the anti-therapeutic domain of secrecy, is crucial for a successful Primary Therapeutic Intervention.

In order to avoid any danger of an overall systemic collusion of secrecy of the therapists–family system it must be agreed amongst all professionals, and it needs to be clarified with the family at the very beginning of therapy, that any sign of relapse into sexual abuse may mean that the confidentiality of the overall therapeutic process may have to be broken.

7.2 Group work with children

7.2.1 Being 'normal in context'

In pre-adolescence and in adolescence, group therapy which needs to be supported by family work is usually preferable to individual therapy. Sexually abused children often define themselves entirely through their experience of sexual abuse. They feel they are the only children to whom sexual abuse has ever happened. They feel guilty, isolated and different from their peers. They often feel dirty and unloved and suffer from very low self-esteem. In a situation where all children are sexually abused the individual child cannot continue to define herself solely through the abuse. In a group setting for sexually abused children in which the individual abused child is not defined as special through the experience of sexual abuse because everybody else in the group has similar experiences, children begin to discover aspects of their personality and areas of strength and potential in themselves and in other children in the group which had previously been buried under the self-definition arising from the abuse.

Within group sessions for sexually abused children all children are 'normal in the context' of the group. This makes it much easier to break the secrecy and isolation of the individual child. The self-help component in groups also counteracts the common feeling of uniqueness of their experience in the isolation of the sexual abuse of the individual child.

7.2.2 Therapy and protection work with children

The important differentiation between therapy and protection work with sexually abused children is usually not made. This distinction reflects the important difference between child sexual abuse as human rights issue and as child mental health problem. These two domains, although related, are quite separate in origin and in their requirement for response. (see Legal abuse and psychological damage, 1.1).

All sexually abused children need some protection work but not all sexually abused children need therapy. All sexually abused children are to some degree confused about their experience as a result of the secrecy. Sexually abused children need explicit licence and encouragement to talk about their sexual experience and they need some work which helps to prevent further abuse. All sexually abused children need some relief from their confusion and all children need prevention work. But not all sexually abused children are psychologically disturbed to a degree which requires therapy.

7.2.3 Protection groups

Protection work and protection groups relate to the legal aspects of child protection and the need to prevent further abuse. Protection groups can be much shorter than therapy groups. They can be more structured and directly educational in teaching children social skills and dealing with the external aspects of secrecy (see Syndrome of secrecy, 2.1). Although not all children are psychologically disturbed, all children are psychologically affected by the abusive experience. It is therefore paramount that sexually abused children are carefully assessed for psychiatric disturbance. Children who have been victims of less severe forms of abuse may need only short-term and structured prevention work. Other children may need intensive and long-term therapy.

Protection groups need to address the following seven areas in relation to secrecy and child protection.

1 Children need explicit licence and permission to break the secrecy and to communicate and talk openly about the abuse.
2 Children need help to find explicit sexual language to talk about an experience about which families do not communicate and for which children may not have a language so to do.
3 Children need to talk openly about the facts of their abuse and about their experience in order to prevent psychological disturbance as a consequence of the confusion about the abusive experience.
4 Children need to learn early enough to recognise different forms of approaches by adults which may indicate an intent of sexual abuse.
5 Children need to learn that it is important to find somebody who listens to them when they want to disclose further sexual abuse.
6 Children need to acquire the necessary skills to find the Trusted Person who will believe them if they feel threatened by renewed child sexual abuse.
7 Finally children need to be able to refuse inappropriate sexual, physical contact. They have to learn to say 'No' if somebody tries to touch them in a sexualised and frightening way and they need to know what to do in this situation.

The work on 'good touch' and 'bad touch' and on the children's 'own body' relates to this area. Protection work should teach children to become able to talk openly about sexual abuse and should show them how they can protect themselves from further abuse and how they can find other people who will help them so to do. Structured weekly groups of 3–4 months can often cover the seven areas of protection work in 8–12 relatively structured sessions. Protection groups can be closed groups with a relatively fixed programme and duration. Groups for protection work should become an integral part of the basic work of any child protective agency involved in statutory work with child sexual abuse.

Protection groups are also therapeutic when they help children to open up the secrecy and to talk about their experience. Conversely, all therapy groups need to cover the seven areas of protection work. Therapy and protection are not mutually exclusive or oppositional. They are complementary aspects of dealing with the consequences of child sexual abuse as legal and health problem and as syndrome of secrecy and addiction.

Therapy groups for children who have not only become confused but who are psychiatrically disturbed and traumatised by severe or long-term sexual abuse must focus beyond the child protective aspects and beyond the aspects of confusion through secrecy, on more fundamental aspects of child mental health. Therapy groups may need to start with structured sessions. They need to be followed by more open sessions addressing specific psychotherapeutic needs of the children involved. Therapeutic methods of change will have to be employed and therapy groups will need to run for much longer periods than protection groups.

Structured short-term protection groups are the group work of choice for young children who are not mature enough for the more complex processes of longer-term therapy groups which fully use group therapeutic processes. In older children protection work and fully developed group therapy can be used according to the child's needs. All children can start in protection groups. Older children who need more can then join therapy groups. With young children individual work or work with the mother–child dyad is more appropriate.

The clear distinction between protection work and therapy is based on differences in the children's needs, on differences in aims and goals and on differences in techniques and skills required. The clear distinction is necessary not least because of the growing number of sexually abused children and the very different resource implications for short-term protection groups and longer-term therapy.

Protection work as much as therapy needs to be conducted in the context of the 'Primary Therapeutic Intervention'. Prevention work needs to address all the stated aims and steps of the Primary Therapeutic Intervention when certain areas of family dysfunction undermine successful protection work. Without family work the work with children in prevention groups can easily be sabotaged by other family members. It can break down in the same way as therapy without minimal family work breaks down for children in therapy groups.

7.2.4 Group structure of therapy groups

Therapy groups can be closed groups or slow open groups. In slow open groups the membership can build up over time and new children join in during ongoing therapy. Slow open groups have the advantage that they are easier to start because they need fewer referrals initially. It is quite possible that a proper group process can be initiated in a group with three children. In slow open groups long-standing group members can help newcomers very effectively to break the secrecy and to talk about the abuse. Slow open groups can also more easily cater for the different time span which different children need in therapy. The disadvantage of slow open groups lies in the frequent interruption of the ongoing therapeutic process through the arrival of newcomers and when other children leave the group.

The advantage of closed groups lies in the shared starting and ending point which makes the therapeutic process much more homogeneous and coherent. The disadvantage lies in the need for sufficient numbers of referrals of children at about the same time who are about the same age and at about the same stage of psycho-social development. In addition closed groups cannot cater for divergent needs in the length of therapy. In closed groups children who need longer therapy may have to join new groups.

The goal-oriented nature of the groups makes only sexually abused children eligible. This can sometimes pose problems when siblings, who themselves have not been sexually abused, are nevertheless disturbed by their experience of the sexual abuse of a sibling. The disruption and the distortion of the specific group process through the inclusion of children who have not been sexually abused themelves should make the direct experience of child sexual abuse the precondition for group membership. It is advisable to provide disturbed children who have been affected by the sexual abuse of a sibling but who have not been sexually abused themselves with a combination of individual and family therapy instead of allowing them to join the group. However there may be exceptions where a sexually abused child and a non-abused sibling who has known about the abuse and who has been severely affected may both join the same group. This can especially be the case when non-abused older siblings are over-involved with the sexually abused child and have known or seen the abuse and feel entirely responsible for not having prevented the abuse and for not having protected the sibling.

In the combination of group therapy and family therapy mixed-sex groups and single-sex groups have been shown to be helpful. Specific sex-related experiences and psychological processes can be more easily dealt with when boys and girls have separate groups. This may not be so relevant in groups for younger children, but it certainly holds for adolescent groups where issues of full sexual maturation pose very gender-specific problems. Although it is helpful if all children in the group are of comparable age and stage of psycho-social and psycho-sexual development, mental state and the degree of disburbance should only be limiting factors in extreme cases when the group process is too disrupted in the presence of the excluded child.

Groups of five to eight children seem to be the optimal size. With less than five children, the group process can become too diluted. If only one or two children are absent or are in a withdrawn state the other children and the therapists have to work very hard to maintain the group process. The complex life situation of many sexually abused children after disclosure often leads to failure to attend sessions. Stressful periods in the family process when parents are less co-operative and when children are less willing to attend, and problems in the professional network for children in care, can prevent attendance of the group. A group number larger than eight makes it difficult to give each child appropriate time, space and attention during the group session. We need to make sure that individual children in the group have enough time and space to deal promptly with crisis issues whenever they arise, keeping in mind that sexually abused children often experience many environmentally and family induced crises during therapy.

Working with children in weekly sessions of one hour duration seems to be optimal. Longer sessions often overstretch children's attention span and can be psychologically too heavy for children and therapists. In addition it is always more easy and not harmful to the group process to negotiate longer sessions than to struggle with over-exhausting lengthy meetings or cutting down the duration.

It can be of great advantage to have a therapeutic couple of a female and a male therapist who can represent the respective female and male gender aspects and who can model important functions of co-operation and mutual support in the parenting couple. The disadvantage of a couple lies in the increased danger of splitting of the therapist couple by the children. Splitting of the therapist couple is an important problem in any group therapy. The danger of splitting is vastly increased in group work in child sexual abuse resulting from the specific gender issues for the therapists and from the enhanced ability of sexually abused children to split adult couples who have parenting functions.

The contentious issue of the gender of the therapist in groups run by a single therapist requires differentiation and not distancing. Male therapists can, as much as female therapists, run both boys' groups and girls' groups. It is important that male and female therapists be aware of different gender-specific advantages and disadvantages for both sexes.

The success of therapy in groups with single therapists depends above all on the female or male therapist's awareness of these gender issues and on her or his own personal ability to deal with the specific problems of child sexual abuse as a person himself or herself. The very personal attitude of the therapists and their skill determines whether they are able to use fully the advantages and to minimise the disadvantages of their gender in relation to the specific gender-related problems in the therapy of sexually abused children. I have seen some children refuse to see a male therapist out of fear of repetition of the abusive situation. I have equally seen children who were too frightened to be treated by a female therapist as a result of their experience of maternal rejection, non- believing, letdown or blaming for the abuse. Again ideology must take second place to problem-oriented professional differentiation. (See Does the gender of the therapist matter?, 12.15.)

7.2.5 Aims and goals in therapy groups

The basic aims and goals in group therapy for sexually abused children are directed at the children as individuals, as family members and as members of the peer group. The aims need to be adapted to specific group processes and communication structures according to the age and stage of maturation of the children in the group.

We have four main aims which are directed at the child as individual:

1 We try to help the children find a language to communicate about the abuse.
2 We teach sexually abused children about normal sexual development in the light of their often unexpected ignorance about basic sexual facts.

3 We try to help the rebuilding of their self-esteem.
4 Finally, we help children to develop a sense of choice about their lives, thus countering the sense of helplessness and victimisation they have experienced during the abuse.

We have three main goals in relation to parents and families:

1 Therapists working in couples need to reintroduce appropriate inter-generational boundaries. Male therapists can aim to give the children direct experience of non-abusing, non-secretive and non-threatening male adults. Female therapists can provide the experience of a reliable and trustworthy, though firm, female figure. Single therapists working on their own will aim at the same goals, trying to represent both sides.
2 It is important to offer a different parenting model from the one the children know from their families and to provide the experience of two united therapists who work together and who do not allow themselves to be divided.
3 It is crucial to help the children distinguish between the reality of the abusing parent's responsibility for the abuse and the consequences of disclosure, and their own feelings of responsibility, guilt, shame and self-blame.

In relation to the children's peer group sexually abused children need to work on three essential areas:

1 They need help to overcome the fear of isolation and to learn to talk openly about the abuse in front of their peers who had similar experiences.
2 Sexually abused children first need to build or rebuild normal adolescent or pre-adolescent peer group relationships within the group before they can develop normal peer group relationships outside.
3 Any sexualised behaviour must be addressed. Children need to become aware of unconscious sexualised messages they may give to others. They have to learn to desexualise interpersonal relationships with other group members and with the therapists. It is crucial, therapeutically and in protective terms, that sexually abused children become able to relate in non-sexualising ways.

7.2.6 Methods and techniques in therapy groups

In therapy groups for sexually abused children we need to employ some specific methods and techniques which relate to specific aspects of child sexual abuse as syndrome of secrecy in addition to those used in general group therapy. It is important for the individual child and for the other group members that each child at the beginning of the group tries to tell once openly what has happened to her in front of other group members and to hear from the other children themselves what has happened to them. It is also vital to deal with reality issues of sexual anatomy and explicit sex education. It is necessary to ensure that sexually abused children can name their anatomy and feel that they have an explicit licence to do so. Especially girls feel often physically damaged. If children complain about pains we need to be absolutely certain that they are not physically injured in reality before we deal with the many and frequent fantasies about internal damage. This is especially important for older girls who often fear that they will never be able to have children as punishment for the abuse. The differentiated use of the following six techniques according to specific areas of work has been very helpful.

1 Interpretation.   Interpretations should centre on the immediate process within the group and between the girls and the therapist.

2 Direct teaching.   Teaching methods can provide important factual information about issues of sexual anatomy and sexual development and may need to include such topics as pregnancy prevention in groups for older adolescent girls and boys.

3 Anxiety-reducing group games.   Anxiety-reducing forms of group games may be used to find the appropriate sexual language in the initial period of therapy and to address group issues which are otherwise too frightening. In order to find explicit sexual language in the first sessions, children can secretly write down on a piece of paper different names for different sex organs. These are then put into a box. The box is then emptied on the table and the members of the group and the therapist will read out the names aloud. This little game deals with an area which is loaded with shame, embarrassment and anxiety in a way which quickly engages all group members in an often very relaxed and non-threatening way.

When children in the group are too frightened the therapist may need to be the first person who starts reading out the names giving the children in the group explicit licence to use open sexual language themselves. It also conveys the message to the group that the therapists can cope with explicit sexual communication in an appropriate way.

4 Active physical intervention.   Therapists must be prepared to intervene actively and physically to contain children in situations of potentially dangerous acting out. Physical contact, especially by male therapists, is a very difficult aspect in treating sexually abused children and needs to be thought about extremely carefully. Appropriately used physical boundary setting, however, can be experienced as very anxiety relieving in self-destructive acting out in the group. The problem of physical contact and the protection or violation of physical integrity and boundaries can subsequently be verbalised as a central theme in the therapeutic process.

5 Addressing non-verbal communication.   Drawing materials, plasticine and other materials should be provided to help the children to express themselves non-verbally when verbal communication is not yet available or proves too problematic. Putting things on paper can sometimes be very helpful to enhance the children's sense of reality about issues of sexual abuse which have often been secret and hidden from open acknowledgement for many months and years.

6 Role play and video feedback. Role play and, where available, video feedback are helpful tools to increase social skills and self-assertiveness as therapeutic and directly protective elements in therapy.

7.2.7 Clinical example: the therapeutic process

The clinical example shows the treatment process in a slow open therapy group for sexually abused adolescent girls. Ten girls between 12 and 15 years attended the group during the 2 years of its existence. The age at onset of sexual abuse had varied from 3 to 13 years with a duration of sexual abuse between 1 and 10 years. One girl was abused by her 8-years-older brother. All other abusers were fathers or stepfathers. Eight of the ten girls had been subjected to full sexual intercourse. The children's experience of child sexual abuse as syndrome of secrecy led to specific characteristics in the developing group process. Although this clinical example only describes the process in girls' groups, the basic issues in boys' groups are very similar. Differences are described in Section 7.2.8.

1 Finding the language. The group started with the therapists actively helping the girls to find explicit sexual language to talk about the abuse by introducing and using explicit sexual terms themselves. This gave the girls licence to use sexual language themselves and carried the message that the therapists were able to handle open sexual communication. To establish the membership of the group, each girl was initially asked to give an account of her specific experience of sexual abuse. Girls who joined later were helped in this task by more long-standing group members who often retold their own story. The children were enormously relieved by being able to break the secrecy and talk openly about the abuse as they had felt different, unique and isolated both at home and at school.

2 Testing. Having settled in the group, the girls began to test the capacity of the therapists to maintain the confidentiality towards other family members whom one of the therapists met in concurrent family sessions. For example, the girls revealed ordinary family secrets and then checked out the reliability of the therapists in keeping them, often accusing them of telling other family members.

3 Group identity. A strong group identity and sense of belonging developed which seemed to be important to all group members. The common experience of child sexual abuse made the girls 'normal in the context' of the group and this strengthened their sense of belonging. Group members soon exchanged addresses in order not to lose contact. Although this is normal behaviour in adolescent groups, it was done with a sense of urgency which expressed the girls' fear of being thrown back into the previous experience of threatening secrecy and isolation. Non-attendance of members at the group met with apprehension, disappointment, anger and pressure to attend by those who were present.

4 The therapist couple. The girls attempted to split the therapist couple and to ally with one therapist against the other. They either wanted to seduce the male therapist, ignoring or denigrating the female therapist, or alternatively, they were hostile and aggressive towards him, trying to ally with the female therapist as a protective figure. At moments of extreme provocative and testing behaviour it was difficult for the therapists to remain united and to work together in setting boundaries. Several times the girls attempted to destroy the furniture and pictures in the room. On such occasions the two therapists had to communicate very quickly and unambiguously about the interaction required. While one of them intervened, the other had to support this action through verbal and non-verbal communications. When the therapists succeeded, the girls would show obvious relief or indicate their appreciation in typical adolescent mocking comments or mock provocativeness.

5 Sex differentiation of the therapists. The girls reacted differently to the male and female therapist as individuals. Initially they were often frightened of the male therapist and this fear was sometimes expressed by leaving the room briefly, coming back once they felt safer. A central feature was their sexually provocative and seductive behaviour. For example, one girl who had attended the group in a mini-skirt which hardly covered her pants complained about men passing comments in the street and accused the male therapist of being sexually seductive. A strong element of rivalry between the girls became apparent when they ostentatiously applied their make-up during the session.

Often the girls were angry with the male therapist and expressed suspicion about his motives in running the group. When extreme acting out required physical limit setting by the male therapist the issue of sexual or non-sexual physical contact was instantly and visibly brought into the centre of therapy. Some girls oscillated in extremes between very sexualised behaviour and phobic fear of physical closeness.

The group process quickly differentiated into two distinguishable levels. At one level the male therapist became the 'bloke' which was a metaphor for being a sexually threatening and abusing male. A second level slowly developed where the male therapist was seen as a caring and non-threatening parental figure.

When the female therapist joined the group she was initially regarded as an intruder and was ignored or denigrated by the girls. The girls tried to stop her from working with the male therapist. They attempted to get her to side with them when they were angry with the male therapist or tried to provoke him. Alternatively, the girls exclusively addressed the female therapist, totally ignoring the male therapist. Initially, the girls had little confidence in the female therapist's capacity to protect them from the male therapist when they were frightened of him. At other times, they were protective towards her, stopping new girls who had joined later from being rude to her and ensuring that the male therapist checked out her point of view. There was a slow change from rejecting the female therapist as a rival towards the wish for maternal care and attention.

6 *Individuation within the group.* Associated with the development of group identity and openness was the girls' capacity to be more forthcoming about their particular problems. Most girls who had felt desperate when they joined the group became able to talk about having never felt wanted by anyone. It was striking that each of the girls at some point confessed to suicidal feelings or intent. This feature and the girls tendency to resort to para-suicidal acts or self-destructive and self-mutilating behaviour did put the girls at particular risk. In one session, a previously suicidal girl had to be stopped physically by the male therapist, supported by the female therapist, from climbing out of the window on the second floor. Both the girl herself and the other group members were clearly relieved by the therapists setting firm protective limits on her self-destructive behaviour.

The self-help component of the group allowed the girls to discuss ordinary aspects of their lives which were not affected by the abuse. This helped them to discover positive aspects about themselves and their own individual strengths and enhanced their capacity to individuate within the group.

7 *Sexual experience and levels of psycho-sexual development.* It was most interesting to see how the girls, who had extensive premature sexual experience, gradually began to talk about their relationships with boys with the same apprehension and indecisiveness as other adolescents. In one session one girl who had been subjected to sexual intercourse with her father for several years asked the other group members to help her write a love letter to her boyfriend. The girls agonised at length about whether she should use the words 'kiss' and 'love', illustrating that their sexual experience was in no way matched by their level of psycho-sexual development and emotional maturity.

8 *Relationship to the family.* The group helped the girls to be more self-assertive. Having explored their fathers' responsibility for the abuse in the group first, some girls were then able to confront them with their anger in family sessions. One of the girls, who previously had been very anxious and frightened, dared to say in the first family meeting after the father's release from prison that he should have been punished by longer imprisonment for what he had done to her. Another girl, having dealt with her own sense of responsibility for the abuse, was able to go home and openly ask her mother to choose for her by divorcing her father. Having shared in the group a sense of letdown by her mother, one girl ran away from home in order to test out whether her mother still wanted her. In the next family session, this girl bitterly accused her mother of not protecting her from the abuse and of not caring for her as a daughter.

9 *Relationship to peers outside the group.*   The experience of talking as peers in the group about normal adolescent issues considerably eased the social isolation of these girls outside the group. The girls in particular valued discussing how to deal with any gossip about the abuse at school and amongst peers. Increased self-esteem gained in the group was gradually reflected in the girls' changed relationships with both male and female peers in their wider social context.

7.2.8 *Special issues in groups for boys*

In groups for young children boys and girls can be mixed. In late pre-puberty and in puberty, gender issues and issues of sexual identity become important and adolescent girls and boys need to be seen in separate groups. The basic principles of group work outlined earlier in this chapter also apply to boys. We need to keep in mind that the common issues of victimisation through sexual abuse are much more fundamental than gender-specific differences. However, we need to keep the following nine gender specific points in mind when we deal with sexually abused boys:

1 Boys tend to find it very difficult to open up in groups and to talk about psychological problems. They can be very embarrassed towards women as a result of homosexual abuse.
2 Sexually abused boys may have experienced that male abusers have made repeatedly derogoratory remarks about their mothers and about women in general. The abuser might have instilled feelings of hostility and denigration towards the mother and towards other women which can be reinforced by the boy's disappointment of not having been protected from the abuse.
3 In later adolescence boys may feel that they are expected to cope without help. Like male rape victims they might feel that their request for help is seen as a sign of personal weakness. Male stereotypes still play an important role, not only in relationship to abusing but also in relation to victimisation.
4 Homosexually abused adolescent boys are in a different position towards their mother as the non-abusing parent compared with girls. In gender identification adolescent girls can turn to their mothers for help and support. Adolescent boys usually find it impossible to turn to their mothers as the non-abusing parent to talk about issues of sexuality and even less about homosexual abuse. The confusion about sexuality and sexual identity which is normal in adolescence is already confounded through the abuse. Sexually abused boys need to find a non-abusing male confidant to whom they can talk about the sexual aspects of the sexual abuse and about their gender-specific relationships to men and women. If such a therapeutic and protective paternal figure cannot be found the role of peer group relationships within the group becomes even more important.
5 Sexually abused boys are nearly always to some degree confused about their sexual identity. Fears of being homosexual are generally strong. Mixtures of

pleasurable experiences and frightening abuse in the abusive interaction can add to the confusion. Some boys who had very frightening experiences feared that they had lost all masculinity. Boys who have been aroused during homosexual abuse need to deal with the real and at times strong aspects of homosexual tendencies which are induced through the abuse.

6 In addition to the topic of homosexuality, issues of sex drive need to be addressed. Some boys fear total loss of sex drive and feel emasculated. Other boys may have learnt to find tension relief in compulsive masturbation. The abuse has taught them to find instant tension relief in sexualisation of any form of anxiety and stress. This tendency can lead to the imagined or well-founded fear of boys that they may become sexual abusers themselves.

7 Many sexually abused boys are frightened of becoming abusers themselves. It is essential to address this fear because a substantial number of sexually abused boys do become sexual abusers later in life with the abusive activity often starting already in puberty. In fact, it is vital to keep in mind that adolescent boys might have already become abusers themselves. This risk is especially high when other children in the family have been abused as well. Alternatively sexually abused boys may also assume victim roles which is most strongly expressed by their becoming male prostitutes.

A circular and self-reinforcing process leads to a real danger of becoming an active abuser. Homosexual abuse by father figures prevents the boy from making normal adolescent relationships with girls in which he can re-evaluate his relationship to the opposite sex. The lack of normal adolescent experimenting leads to increased difficulty in developing open and positive relationships with girls. The more intense the sexualisation in the sexual abusive relationship and the less clarified the relationship with girls and women, the greater is the danger for the boy of finding tension relief in sexual activities and in compulsive masturbation. The sexualisation of anxiety and frustration in the context of increasingly estranged or hostile relationships with girls and women leads to the danger of sexually abused boys becoming sexual abusers themselves.

8 In cases where boys are more vulnerable through absent fathers the abuser has often become a 'good uncle' figure. The attachment of boys to abusers can be very strong and they may feel that they are disloyal towards the abuser when they talk in the group about the abuse.

9 At the other end of the spectrum abused boys can become very aggressive towards the abuser. They often wish to harm him and are frightened of losing control in violent outbursts.

Therapists in boys' groups need to address the following eight aims and goals:

1 Adolescent boys need specific help to open up in the group, especially in the presence of women.

2 Sexually abused adolescent boys need to overcome gender stereotypes and need to allow themselves to ask for help in the group.

3 The group needs to address fears and tendencies of homosexuality as a result of homosexual abuse.

4 The group needs to address possible ongoing sexual abuse by the boys themselves and they need to address the fears of becoming abusers later in life.

5 The boys need to be able to talk openly about issues of tension relief. It is crucial to deal with any sexualisation of tension relief.

6 The boys should be encouraged to talk in the group about their sexual fantasies and their masturbation fantasies in order to evaluate abusive tendencies. As in the process of opening up other difficult areas of sexual abuse, therapists will need to give the boys explicit permission to communicate about their sexual fantasies by introducing the subject themselves in a normalising and anxiety-reducing way. It can be very helpful if the therapist opens up the topic by saying that all men masturbate and that everybody has sexual fantasies and that they might be very strange at times. It is very important that the therapist then gives an explicit example in as neutral a way as possible.

7 The group needs to address the relationship and attitudes towards sisters, mothers and women in general. The ability to relate emotionally in a non-sexual way to girls and women is crucial for therapy and for prevention.

8 The group needs to help each boy to think about finding a non-abusing father figure to whom they can relate, to whom they might be able to talk about the abuse and with whom they can identify as boys and young men. It is often very difficult to find a trusting male figure for the boys and the group and the therapists might need to fulfil this role as successfully as possible.

Other aims and goals in boys' groups must be seen in the context of the general aims, goals and treatment process which is outlined earlier in this chapter. In some cases sexually abused boys will have already become adolescent sex offenders. The nature of sexual abuse as syndrome of secrecy and addiction requires that the boys take responsibility for abusing before their own victimisation and abuse can be addressed. Otherwise the experience of being abused will be used by the adolescent abusers to avoid facing the responsibility for their own abusive behaviour. (See Child sexual abuse as syndrome of addiction, 2.2; Working with sexual abusers, 7.4; Child and adolescent sex offenders who are sexually abused themselves, 14.3.)

7.3 Individual counselling and therapy

7.3.1 Individual therapy and family-therapy-by-proxy with children on their own

The fact that counsellors and therapists see sexually abused children individually does not automatically constitute individual counselling or therapy. Professionals often see sexually abused children on their own because the children are in care or because the family is unavailable or unwilling to co-operate. Seeing children in such a situation individually for counselling and therapy no more constitutes individual counselling and therapy as seeing several family members together automatically constitutes family therapy. Individual therapy and family therapy are defined by the way of working and by the frame of mind of the therapist according to the tasks of the sessions in the overall context of the Primary Therapeutic Intervention. The mode of therapy is not determined by the number of family members present.

When in the beginning we see sexually abused children individually because other family members are not available, we should usually not see them for individual counselling and therapy but for initial family-meetings-by-proxy. We start to work on relationship aspects using family therapy techniques with the aim of creating a framework of family-therapy-by-proxy before we embark on concurrent individual therapy. The distinction between concurrent forms of therapy does therefore even hold when sexually abused children are seen entirely on their own. We may have one meeting with the child on her own as family-session-by-proxy and a concurrent meeting as individual work. The fact that only the child is available for treatment can never be a reason in itself for automatically conducting individual counselling or therapy. The differentiation to family-work-by-proxy needs to be made. (See Family and responsibility-session-by-proxy, 9.13; The use of different family therapy techniques, 12.10.)

The specific nature of child sexual abuse as syndrome of secrecy gives individual counselling and therapy second place behind group treatment in which the children are 'normal in the context' of the groups. The fact that individual psychotherapy can pose specific difficulties does not mean that individual therapy cannot take place in the context of a metasystemic approach. The disadvantages of individual counselling and therapy can become distinct advantages with powerful therapeutic effects when individual therapists are aware of the disadvantages and are able to deal with the additional structural and technical problems involved.

Individual therapy which is conducted concurrently with family work in the Primary Therapeutic Intervention is indicated when group work is not sufficient or not available. It is also indicated for small children who are too young for group therapy when mother–child therapy is not possible. Individual therapy needs to remain firmly bound into the context of the metasystemic approach in which the therapist and the entire process of individual therapy is related to child protection, to the family process and to the integrated multi-professional intervention. Individual therapy will otherwise lead to anti-therapeutic therapy, to conflicts-by-proxy in the professional network and to treatment failure.

7.3.2 Structural problems in individual counselling and therapy

7.3.2.1 Problems of the setting

General individual psychotherapy aims to give the child full and undivided attention in the privacy of the one to one situation in a highly confidential setting behind closed doors. This unique and special experience which in general individual psychotherapy provides the desired therapeutic context easily re-creates structurally in the individual therapy of sexually abused children the very context of the original traumatic experience of child sexual abuse as syndrome of secrecy. For the child the confidentiality of the one to one situation can turn into a re-created structure of helpless isolation. Privacy turns into secrecy and the undivided individual attention can be experienced as the overwhelming closeness of sexual abuse.

The ritualised beginnings and endings of individual counselling and therapy sessions easily assume the meaning of the entrance and exit rituals of the abusive interaction. Ritualised beginnings and endings of sessions can repeat for the child the basic confusion between secrecy and reality that the child has experienced in the abusive interaction. The very contrast between the reality before and after the session and the privacy of the session itself can induce a state of altered psychic awareness in the child during the session which is analogous to the undoing of the abusive reality in the interactional process of the abusive experience itself (see Child sexual abuse as syndrome of secrecy, 2.1).

The very basic external structure and organisation of the therapy session can therefore transform the psychotherapy session in the child's mind into a sexual abuse session. We need to be aware that the one to one situation in individual therapy can be too frighteningly close to the experience of the one to one situation in the isolation of sexual abuse. Children can become phobic, frozen, sleepy or seemingly normal in extreme psychic splitting as psychological survival mechanisms in the re-enactment of the original abusive interaction. They may withdraw into passivity and victim behaviour and may break off therapy altogether.

7.3.2.2 Dealing with the unconscious and secrecy

Unconscious communication in individual counselling and psychotherapy requires interpretation whereas secret communication as testing behaviour needs to be taken up at the level of reality and must not be interpreted (see The unconscious and secrecy, 2.4.4).

The structural repetition of the abusive setting in the setting of individual psychotherapy and counselling can make it very difficult for therapists to distinguish between secrecy and the unconscious. They are always in danger of misinterpreting secret communication as unconscious communication. If secrecy is dealt with by interpretation and not in a reality-oriented investigative mode, the process and the external structure of individual psychotherapy exactly repeat the traumatic process of child sexual abuse. When the child communicates in the domain of secrecy in which she re-enacts the traumatic experience of the sexual interaction of the abuse where the reality of sexual abuse had been undone in the process itself, the interpreting therapist becomes the non-abusing parent who does not want to know what really happened repeating the psychic process of child sexual abuse in which external reality cannot be named as such.

Dealing with secret communications requires giving the child explicit licence to communicate. Therapists may need to ask questions in order to establish and clarify elements of external reality before the feelings and the fantasies about these realities can therapeutically unfold. Psychotherapists may feel that they are abandoning their psychotherapeutic stance and may ignore the secret communication. Therapy in the mode of secrecy can increase the emotional confusion and disturbance in the child when psychotherapy becomes the ongoing symbolic repetition of the abusive reality which has as core psychopathogenic element the taboo to perceive external reality as such. (See The individual process in context, 2.4.)

7.3.2.3 Naming, creating and maintaining reality in psychotherapy

Once sexual abuse has been established as external reality in psychotherapy and counselling, the very setting as an approximation to the abusive context can make it very difficult to maintain the once established external reality of child sexual abuse. Disassociations and strong forms of splitting tend to drive the reality aspect of child sexual abuse back into secrecy and denial. This threatens a maintained sense of the reality of the abuse as the central traumatic event which needs to be available for therapeutic interpretation. (See Naming, creating and maintaining child sexual abuse as reality, 2.4.3.)

The process of undoing and splitting in child sexual abuse is quite different from the unavailability of other traumatic life events which have been defensively repressed and denied. The unavailability of sexual abuse as fact is not only a defensive move. The unavailability contains the core of the traumatic experience itself, which the child may openly and undefendedly re-enact in individual therapy. It may nevertheless appear as if the child had repressed the experience although she may be re-enacting the undoing which can remain unrecognised by the therapist. The very experience of child sexual abuse contains the 'non-experience' of the experience as an integral part because the original experience has not only psychologically but also physiologically and perceptually been undone in its very process. (See Syndrome of secrecy, 2.1.)

7.3.3 The therapeutic dilemma

In long-term child sexual abuse which often starts in early childhood the basic primary trauma lies in an early dyadic failure. The child has turned to the parent for emotional care, which has been answered by sexual abuse. The specific abusive experience binds the fragmented part objects of the self in a psychic fusion as non-self parts to the abuser.

The therapeutic transformation in individual therapy from secrecy into

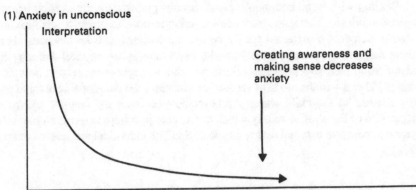

(1) Anxiety in unconscious

Interpretation

Creating awareness and
making sense decreases
anxiety

Whether patient 'ready' for interpretation is issue of timing

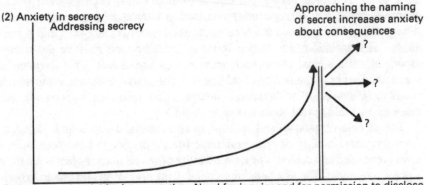

(2) Anxiety in secrecy
Addressing secrecy

Approaching the naming
of secret increases anxiety
about consequences

?

?

?

Patient never 'ready' for interpretation. Need for inquiry and for permission to disclose

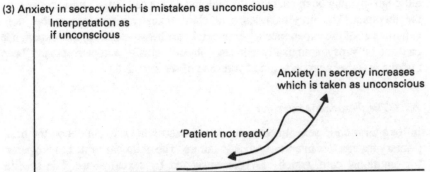

(3) Anxiety in secrecy which is mistaken as unconscious

Interpretation as
if unconscious

Anxiety in secrecy increases
which is taken as unconscious

'Patient not ready'

Therapist picks up secret fear and is himself not ready to address secret of abuse

Figure 7.2 Anxiety in unconscious and secrecy

privacy as treatment of the specific secondary trauma in child sexual abuse becomes an act of tight-rope walking between the traumatic re-enactment of secrecy and the equally traumatic invasion into fragile elements of the developing privacy of the self. The non-intrusion into the developing space of privacy is the prerequisite for the integration and development of the true self, of individuation and autonomy which can lead to true relating and to a rise in a sense of self.

The therapeutic task is to interpret whenever the transference is in the domain of privacy. The very moment the therapeutic interaction enters the domain of secrecy the task is to create and maintain external reality. This balancing act creates technical difficulties. The therapist needs to differentiate continuously between communications in the domain of secrecy and communications in the domain of privacy. When the therapist continues actively to remind a child who is in a transference state of privacy of the sexual abuse in order to create reality as the basis for interpretation, the therapist commits psychological re-abuse by intruding into the space of privacy, violating the child's integrity, attacking the child's development of a true self. Conversely when the therapist does not actively remind the child of the external reality of the abuse, but continues to interpret in the domain of secrecy the result is anti-therapeutic therapy. By interpreting in the domain of secrecy the therapist re-creates the original context of child sexual abuse where reality was undone in the process itself and where the non-abusing parent did not want to know what really happened. This was clearly an example of a young mother who had been abused and who had been in therapy for several years: 'The therapist always told me how I felt, but he never wanted to listen. He never wanted to know what really happened'.

The dilemma between intruding into the domain of the privacy of self or colluding with the secrecy creates an often most excruciating transference–counter-transference interaction. I have been interpreting with increased feelings that whatever I interpreted was really not what the situation was about. I felt that I was interpreting in the context of secrecy. I felt increasingly desperate to meta-communicate about these feelings and to say that whatever the patient brought at that time was not what I felt it was really all about. When I then said that I felt that the patient was really communicating the secrecy of sexual abuse I often felt instantly that I should not have said what I had just voiced. But when I continued to interpret and did not comment about secrecy I felt that therapy was phoney and false.

As a result I was constantly torn between naming the abuse and then feeling like stuffing the facts down the patient's throat and becoming the sexual abuser or not naming the abuse and continuing to interpret whatever the patient brought. I then got equally desperate, torn and enraged because I felt that all my inter-pretations were pseudo-therapy and had actually nothing to do with what was really going on. I became the non-abusing mother who did not want to know and I felt I was joining through anti-therapeutic therapy the patient's system of secrecy.

The despair, rage and confusion in the counter-transference was re-creating the very psychic state of the patient who had experienced the trap of the no-win situation of child sexual abuse as syndrome of secrecy. The specific trans-ference–counter-transference interaction in individual therapy and counselling mirrors the original interaction in child sexual abuse as syndrome of secrecy in which the reality experience of the child says that reality is not reality. The transference–counter-transference interaction which communicates that reality is non-reality reality requires the therapist to be able to oscillate constantly between interpreting when secrecy has shifted into privacy and creating reality when the process shifts back into secrecy again.

The inherent dilemma of therapist and patient in the specific transference–counter-transference interaction of child sexual abuse can make it structurally impossible for the therapist to interpret the transference. The therapist may have to make a meta-communication about the transference–counter-transference interaction to the patient in which the therapist states to the patient his own dilemma in the counter-transference. In meta-communications about my own counter-transference I have shared my own confusion, helplessness and rage with the sexually abused patient. I told the patient that I felt I could be of no help; that I did not know whether I should talk about the sexual abuse or whether I should not, suggesting that this dilemma may reflect what the patient wanted to com-municate. I felt that if I reminded the patient of the sexual abuse I would violate the patient's privacy of self and would myself become the abuser. If I interpreted or kept silent I would gloss over the real issues of sexual abuse by interpreting peripheral events and I would collude with the secrecy. I would then conduct false therapy and become like the mother who had not wanted to know what really happened in external reality between the father and the child. If this is done in the appropriate context, the meta-communication of confusion, helplessness and rage of the therapist in his own counter-transference can have powerful therapeutic effects.

In the psychotherapy of child sexual abuse patients can easily induce pseudo-therapy by seducing the therapist into an unidentified re-enactment of secrecy. Some children will in the transference–counter-transference interaction induce in the therapist the lack of ability to differentiate between secrecy and privacy, resulting in anti-therapeutic therapy of secrecy of which the therapist may not be aware. The structure and the content of individual therapy of child sexual abuse make it quite understandable that sexually abused children and patients can be less motivated to trust to be helped in individual therapy and that individual therapists may find it difficult to deal with these cases (see The interactional nature of motivation, 2.4.1). Some of the problems in individual psychotherapy can be alleviated when concurrent group therapy takes the function of creating the reality aspect of sexual abuse, preventing a therapy of secrecy in individual therapy in the differentiated and complementary use of individual and group therapy in the context of a Primary Therapeutic Intervention. (See Concurrent forms of therapy, 7.1.)

7.3.4 The need for behaviour modification

In long-term child sexual abuse children, and especially young children, can learn to equate any interpersonal relating with sexual relating. Sexualised behaviour can be conscious but it is often quite unconscious. It can lead to vicious circles of secondary victimisation. In ordinary social contexts open sexualised behaviour is regarded as anti-social behaviour. Children who act out sexually are at high risk of being rejected in foster families, in children's homes and in other social settings. Often foster parents, residential staff, teachers and others cannot cope with open sexualised behaviour of children. In addition all sexually abused children who re-enact sexualised behaviour and give sexualised messages put themselves at high risk of re-abuse and sexual victimisation. This holds in particular for mentally handicapped children who are unable to prevent further sexual abuse, especially when they are placed in residential institutions.

The treatment of sexualised behaviour as anti-social symptom, and the re-introduction of modesty, require specific symptom-oriented treatment. In older children behaviour-oriented work can be aimed directly at the child, trying to make children aware of at times very subtle forms of sexualised relating and to help them to modify this behaviour. In young children it is much easier to help parents, foster parents or residential staff to deal with the sexualised behaviour within the child–carer dyad. Whenever the sexualised behaviour occurs the carer should try to substitute this behaviour by non-sexualised forms of interactions of emotional care. Symptom-oriented programmes need to address the specific needs of the individual child.

The following example illustrates secondary damage and victimisation as a result of sexualised behaviour. A 3-year-old girl who had been sexually abused by her father had been placed in foster care. When she started to feel secure and began to form emotional relationships within the family, she re-enacted the sexual abuse. She became completely obsessed with the penis of her 6-year-old foster brother. She offered to touch his penis and to suck him and she followed the boy each time he went to the toilet. The boy and the very caring and capable foster parents became increasingly distressed. The effects on the boy seriously threatened the long-term placement. A regime was implemented that whenever the girl began to sexualise and to go for the boy's penis, the foster mother would take her aside and substitute the sexualised interaction by a parental interaction. The foster mother took the child on her arm, gave her a physical cuddle and distracted her into a non-sexualised interaction. Later a direct scheme of positive reward was introduced for each time the girl came directly to the foster mother for a cuddle instead of diving for the boy's penis. This symptom-oriented mother–child work was embedded in supportive family work for the foster family and the child. Despite good progress in treatment the sexualised behaviour of this girl was so strong and so disturbing to the foster brother that the girl needed to be placed in another family. This example demonstrates the importance of dealing instantly and intensively with sexualised behaviour as anti-social symptom. It also illustrates the great difficulties of re-introducing modesty in severely sexually abused children.

7.4 Working with sexual abusers

7.4.1 The context for group treatment and individual therapy

In the long run any therapeutic approach to child sexual abuse is only as good as the therapy for abusers. If we want effectively to break the cycle of sexual abusing and being abused, a context needs to be created in which abusers are able to disclose and to find therapeutic help. Group therapy with sexual abusers needs to run parallel with family therapy and individual work in the context of a Primary Therapeutic Intervention. Group therapy is most suited to break through the barrier of secrecy and to introduce a sense of reality into the treatment, counteracting the reality avoiding tendencies of sexual abusers. Abusers in groups have to admit openly to the addiction and have to own up to being sexual abusers in front of other group members and the therapist. We also know from other forms of addiction that group pressure from other addicts and the self-help component are important elements of any treatment of addiction. (See Aims and steps in the Primary Therapeutic Intervention, 6.2; Concurrent forms of therapy, 7.1.)

Although sexual abuse as syndrome of addiction shares crucial elements of other addictions, the specific element of child sexual abuse as interlocking syndrome of secrecy and addiction in which a structurally dependent child is the 'drug' puts an infinitely greater pressure on the treatment to succeed and to stop the abuser as addict from further abusing. The role of legal interventions in other forms of addiction may be doubtful. The specific situation of child sexual abuse in which the child is the 'drug' requires tight control and legal backup for the treatment of sexual abusers in order to prevent a relapse into the addiction which cannot be tolerated. The process of treatment of sexual abusers with legal backup poses specific problems for court-ordered therapy. Therapy needs to be designed as a precondition for the reassessment of the possibility of rehabilitation and not as a precondition for rehabilitation itself. (See Syndrome of secrecy, 2.1; Syndrome of addiction, 2.2; The interlocking process between secrecy and addiction, 2.3; see Court-ordered therapy, 12.16.)

It is important that therapy of sexual abusers in the context of a Primary Therapeutic Intervention is designed in a way in which the therapist has at any stage recourse to the legal process in order to re-evaluate the progress of therapy. The therapist needs to be free to declare at any stage that therapy has failed and to hand the case back to the legal process for re-evaluation. Probation orders or the process of plea bargaining in which the conditions for treatment need to be well defined and controlled are helpful legal backup for a Primary Therapeutic Intervention. Continuous evaluation of progress or failure is of crucial importance and needs to include regular feedback sessions with the abuser.

In the treatment of sexual abusers as addicts it is important that the focus of control is firmly with the legal process which forms the structural umbrella under which the abuser can choose to comply with given structures of therapy. For any therapeutic process the possibility of choice is absolutely vital. In child sexual abuse the abuser cannot choose as a free agent between therapy or non-therapy. The choice can only lie between accepting the preconditions for legally supported therapy in the context of a Primary Therapeutic Intervention or choosing for a Primary Punitive Approach, because continued sexual abuse cannot be accepted. (See Three basic types of intervention, 4.1; Aims and steps in the Primary Therapeutic Intervention, 6.2.)

The legal process can support the therapy of the Primary Therapeutic Intervention in a twofold way. In structural terms it provides the holding context for the therapeutic process. The legal process also establishes legal responsibility which later helps abusers in therapy to own up on a psychological level. Legal proof and admissions which can be read in court reports also serve as fall-back positions for renewed secrecy and denial in the process of treatment. Questions like 'What would you read in the court proceedings about what you have said at that time?' can help abusers to stay with the reality of the sexual abuse when they have relapsed into secondary or tertiary denial. (See Proof and belief, admission and owning up, 1.5; Dealing with primary denial 10.6; Relapse into secrecy and secondary denial, 12.13; Tertiary denial by fathers, 12.14.)

The treatment of abusers in child sexual abuse as syndrome of addiction requires it to be stated openly and explicitly that even at the end of successful therapy abusers may not be cured. As in other addictions sexual abusers can remain under certain circumstances of stress and in certain trigger situations in danger of sexually abusing again.

7.4.2 Aims and goals for treatment

The overall goal in the group treatment of sexual abusers relates to child sexual abuse as syndrome of addiction. Five structural steps are required.

1 The abuser needs to establish the facts of the addiction and the sexual addiction as fact.
2 The abuser needs to share openly with other group members the precise sequence and the accompanying fantasies of the abusive circle from the trigger-event to the exit ritual.
3 The abuser needs to take full responsibility for his addiction and needs to own up fully to his sexual abusive actions and fantasies.
4 The abuser needs to see himself as an addict over time who uses sexual abuse as a drug which serves tension relief and reality avoidance.
5 The abuser needs to see that even at the end of treatment he may not be cured and may have to avoid high-risk situations which could lead to relapse into sexual abuse.

Group work needs to address the following seven areas:

1 *Owning up.*   The abuser needs to take full psychological responsibility for his sexual actions in the abuse. This responsibility taking should go parallel to concurrent family work with the child (see Aims and steps in the Primary Therapeutic Intervention, 6.2).

2 *Trigger-events and fantasies.*   The abuser needs to find out precisely which events, fantasies and circumstances trigger the urge to abuse.

3 *Conflict avoiding and tension relieving behaviour and fantasies which maintain the abuse.*   The abuser needs to analyse the different steps of the process of sexual abuse itself. It is especially important to deal with sexually stimulating and arousing fantasies or sensations which precede the abuse. Special attention needs to be drawn to accompanying fantasies of violence and victimisation. A step-by-step behavioural analysis of the process which induces and maintains the sexual interaction is necessary in order to develop alternative behaviour and to learn to avoid possible high-risk situations.

4 *Underlying meaning structures and life experiences.*   The abuser needs to link the abuse to predisposing events in his own life. Many sexual abusers have been sexually abused themselves or have been members of families in which siblings have been sexually abused. (See Siblings in families of child sexual abuse, 14.1; The Hansel-and-Gretel Syndrome and sexual abuse by older brothers, 14.2.)

Many abusers have been physically abused and others have developed personality disturbances under severe emotional abuse and deprivation. A combination of severe rejection and interpersonal eroticisation in early childhood can lead to low frustration tolerance and narcissistic hurt which finds relief in sexual abuse. There are obviously many different predisposing life events which can contribute to becoming a sexual abuser. They need to be identified as long as they form an important maintaining factor for the addiction to sexual abuse.

5 *Partner problems and the attitude towards women.*   On the interpersonal level abusers need to work on marital and partner issues and on their attitude towards women and children. Discrepancies between adults' sexual demands and practices and emotional immaturity and dependence need to be addressed. Issues of responsibility, autonomy, individuation and separation form a centre-piece of therapy. The work on partner issues is impossible without addressing the abuser's general attitude towards women and children. (See The family process, Chapter 3, and particularly, Confusion on different levels of dependency, 3.1.)

6 *Work on parenting.*   The second area of interpersonal work needs to address parental issues. Abusers must examine how they can reverse the process in which children's demand for emotional care is answered by sexual abuse. Paternal

boundaries need to be clarified. The abuser needs to learn to respect the child's privacy, integrity and individuality. He needs to become able to bear feelings of jealousy, autonomy and independence from children who want to live a life without sexual abuse. Central to the work on parenting is the need to work on the abuser's ability to recognise and to empathise with the child's needs for emotional care.

7 *Preventive work on addictive trigger situations and trigger fantasies.* Abusers need to identify external risk situations which can trigger sexual abuse when internal tensions have risen sufficiently. On the behavioural level they need to develop coping mechanisms with which they can achieve tension relief in a more acceptable way. The sexual abuser needs to develop strategies to avoid external risk situations in which he is alone with the abused child or other children.

It is crucial to address the behavioural aspects of the treatment which relates to the addictive quality of child sexual abuse. Physical and body contact can immediately lead to sexualised reactions. The abuser can then be driven to construct a context of secrecy for renewed abuse. Equally important is the avoidance of arousing trigger fantasies which the abuser needs to learn to recognise and to control. Arousing trigger fantasies often lead to the abuser actively seeking to create an external environment in which he can re-abuse.

7.4.3 Therapy group structure

Closed groups or slow open groups for abusers have the same basic advantages and disadvantages as described in the group work with children (see Group structure of therapy groups, 7.2.4). In addition there are some specific aspects in groups for abusers. The use of male therapists only or the inclusion of female therapists needs to be seen in a different perspective. For some aspects of the work it can be very helpful to have a woman therapist present or to conduct the group as a partner group which includes the female partners of the abusers. Groups of men on their own are always in danger of deteriorating into macho pseudo-football-club meetings where the real issues of child sexual abuse can be increasingly avoided in a group syndrome of denial or in dangerous anti-therapeutic sexualisation. The presence of women will force the abusers to face up to their responsibility with all its consequences for the child and the family. The inclusion of a female therapist or of female partners of the abusers avoids the need for repeated and quasi religious and ritualised 'confessions' by the abusers as they need to be made in some other forms of treatment of addicts. The presence of the female partners of the abusers in therapy can actively promote the central aim to face up to reality and to the conflicts and tensions of child sexual abuse as syndrome of addiction with several layers and mechanisms of reality avoidance (see Syndrome of secrecy, and of addiction, 2.1, 2.2, 2.3).

Although the presence of female partners has advantages with respect to reality testing and owning up, certain gender-specific aspects of the work need to be addressed in abuser groups only. Abusers can be much less open in talking in front of their partners about specific sexual aspects of the abuse and about the therapeutically important masturbation fantasies and fantasies during the sexual abuse. It is therefore very helpful to have under the overall umbrella of partner therapy differentiated mixed group sessions and single-sex sessions separately for abusers and for their partners. The single-sex sessions should address specific sexual practices, fantasies and attitudes of the abusers and gender-specific problems of abusers which need to be addressed. The mixed group sessions need to include complementary topics of marital and parental problems. Both types of sessions feed each other. Issues raised in one setting can be taken up and worked on in the other group.

7.4.4 The treatment process

In the treatment process we can distinguish four phases:

1 External acceptance.
2 Bargaining and minimising.
3 Acceptance.
4 Reconstruction.

Phase 1: external acceptance

At the beginning of the group each abuser needs to share what he has done with the group. The joining ritual needs to include the abuser talking about the nature and the duration of the abuse and about the child he has abused. It is also important to ask the abuser right at the beginning to share with the group what exactly he had done, why in his opinion he sexually abused the child and what he got out of it. The first acknowledgment of the sexual abuse can still be experienced by the abuser as alien and can be delivered in a mechanical way. Telling the initial story can be like the admission in court which is more a split-off experience than the expression of psychological acceptance and owning up. Nevertheless the joining ritual sets the scene for therapy. It breaks the secrecy and brings the facts of the abuse into the sessions.

It is important that abusers tell the full external facts right from the beginning and that they are not let off with half-told facts. This is crucial because once abusers get used to the group they often develop and employ different techniques of splitting and denial in the struggle to avoid owning up fully to the abuse. It can be very helpful to employ the group process as much as possible in order to assist the abuser to own up unreservedly. As in other forms of addiction fellow abusers are much more able to be to the point and tough and empathic simultaneously and they can help fellow abusers who begin to deny or to play down the abuse.

Phase 2: bargaining and minimising

After the initial phase of external acceptance sexual abusers often move into the second phase of bargaining and minimising. We need to be prepared for an infinite number of at times powerful reality- and responsibility-avoiding moves.

a. *Minimising:*   Abusers may straightforwardly and instantly begin to minimise again what they have done.

b. *Bargaining:*   They often attempt to bargain in order to trade off some of the responsibility either by listing the good things they have done to the abused child or by making the abuse less severe than other people's abuse.

c. *Blaming:*   They often blame the abused child for the abuse saying that the child has wanted it and has been sexually provocative and seductive.

d. *Seduction:*   They may try to seduce the therapists by being the 'goody-goodies' who are especially helpful in the group and who offer themselves as allies to the therapist against other group members whom they try to bring into the position of 'baddy baddies'.

e. *Pleading:*   Sexual abusers may try to plead special circumstances which should explain why they got into the abuse against their will and with less responsibility for it.

f. *False remorse:*   One of the most difficult moves is false remorse. Like alcoholics who typically feel terribly sorry for themselves and who say they will never drink again, sexual abusers can show remorse which cannot be trusted. They may even mean the regret at that very moment but the regret and remorse may not last long or it may only be put in order to be forgiven and let off quickly, without having to face the real issues.

g. *Hostility:*   Sexual abusers often show outright hostility, attacking the treatment process as rubbish and the therapists as useless. They may try to become gang-leaders of the group, which they want to lead into a state of group aggression or group denial.

h. *Somatisation:*   Abusers can use somatisation of different forms to avoid therapy completely. Somatisation can also be used to distract from difficult issues the abuser does not want to face. Or he may use somatic complaints in the hope of being treated in a less confronting way if the group wants him to own up.

Sexual abusers can be very creative in developing avoidance strategies. These are only some of the unlimited range of avoidance techniques which abusers use in the second phase of bargaining and minimising during the treatment of child sexual abuse. In the bargaining and minimising phase the group process is of paramount importance. Sexual abusers, like other addicts, know each others' weaknesses and their problems of owning up much better than non-abusers. It is also more acceptable for sexual abusers to be confronted by fellow abusers who can easily put their finger exactly on the avoided issue.

Phase 3: acceptance

The phase of acceptance is characterised by a much more realistic view on the relationship between the sexual abuser and the child and the abuser and his partner. Sexual abusers can allow themselves to stop bargaining and minimising. They can bear to face what they have done and they can move to focus on understanding the predisposing life events and the maintaining cycles of behaviours, trigger events and interactions which keep the abuse going and which continue to make the sexual abuser vulnerable to renewed child sexual abuse. They begin to make sense of their own motives and their own part in the abuse. Increased acceptance of the abuse and increased understanding of themseves become mutually reinforcing. Abusers can then begin to understand what they have done to the sexually abused child and to their partners.

Phase 4: reconstruction

Once the abuser has accepted psychological responsibility for his own addiction and for the abuse he has inflicted on the child and once he has owned up to the effects the abuse and the disclosure had on the child and on the family he can begin to develop new ways of behaving and relating. In the reconstruction phase concurrent forms of family therapy and partner therapy can be particularly important. Family therapy or partner therapy can address the issues which led and maintained the abuse in the family. Successful concurrent family and partner work can lead to therapeutic divorce and separation as an expression of success-ful therapy.

The success or failure of a group member in trying to work on new ways of relating and behaving can feed the group process in a very creative way. The group can support the abuser in developing alternative strategies and can help to deal with the anxiety about new situations within the group first before the abuser dares to put himself into a new and anxiety provoking situation in external reality. The group can also help to deal with disappointment and failure when new ways of behaviour do not work or when new ways of relating fail or when the abuser falls back into old habits.

The crucial and at the same time the most difficult phase to negotiate is the second phase of bargaining and minimising. Some sexual abusers are never able to face up fully to the reality of their own addiction and to the reality of the abuse they have inflicted on the child. They can for a long time continue to attempt to trick themselves out of therapy. The backup of the legal process is vital for supporting the second phase of bargaining and minimising. Only the threat of being handed back to the legal system as a result of treatment failure and of becoming candidates for a Primary Punitive Intervention may put great enough pressure on some sexual abusers to face up to the abuse. At this stage the addictive quality of child sexual abuse becomes most evident.

A prolonged second phase of bargaining and of avoidance to own up to the abuse makes it crucial to distinguish between therapy as precondition for certain rehabilitation or as precondition for a reassessment whether rehabilitation is possible. The condition of therapy must never carry the promise of certain rehabilitation or of access to the child. Therapy can only be the precondition for a reassessment whether rehabilitation and access are possible or not (see Court-ordered therapy, 12.16). If treatment itself was already a sufficient precondition for rehabilitation many abusers would stay in the second phase throughout therapy. They could easily seduce courts and other members of the professional network that they have changed without having ever really owned up to the reality of the addiction and the abuse. Treatment as a precondition for rehabilitation would put therapists into a bind and put them under pressure to get abusers over the stumbling block of the second phase. The therapeutic effect of therapy is paralysed when failed therapy reflects as much on the therapist as on the sexual abuser who needs to learn to become fully responsible independently of what others do. An abuser–therapist interdependence which takes any responsibility away from the abuser can never be therapeutic in the treatment of addiction.

7.4.5 Therapeutic techniques

Many different therapeutic techniques can be used in the group therapy of sexual abusers, of which I want to mention the following five methods.

1 Role play.   It can be very helpful to use role play to help abusers to illustrate how they got into the abuse and to demonstrate situations they find difficult to verbalise. We need to be aware that child sexual abuse as syndrome of secrecy and addiction includes many situations of conflict avoidance and the inability to face up to unresolved problems and conflicts. Role play can be used to confront the abuser with reality and to help to understand the abuse, to work on problem solving and on conflict resolution and to develop and to try alternative forms of behaving and relating.

2 Psycho-drama.   In some cases psycho-drama techniques can be very impor-tant and useful to work on family-of-origin issues. Carefully used techniques of psycho-drama can be especially helpful for recalling traumatic events of abusers from their own childhood. The process of psycho-drama can make this event a true group experience. In the treatment of child sexual abuse as syndrome of addiction these shared group experiences can foster the self-help component in

the group. It can trigger powerful therapeutic group processes when it enables other group members to relate similar experiences.

3 Behavioural techniques.   Once the abuser has identified the trigger fantasies and the trigger events for the abuse, behavioural techniques can be helpful for developing small and manageable, practical, step-by-step solutions to previously unmanageable situations of stress and conflict. The behavioural aspect of the work can become especially important when abusers need to develop coping mechanisms in relation to arousing fantasies and to situations when they are alone with the child and in relation to physical touch and body contact between the abuser and children.

Although the origins of the abuse may lie in complex previous experiences of the abuser, sexual abuse as syndrome of addiction is also maintained and triggered by the behavioural component of the abusive cycle in itself. Abusers may initially need to avoid certain high-risk situations with children such as bathing them or being with them on their own in the house.

4 Interpretations of past experience.   Sharing of past experience and the understanding of life events which have made the abuser vulnerable to sexual abuse play an essential part in the group process. It is important to understand basic meaning systems which have developed in the abusers past in order to achieve change in the life script of the abuser which assists his change of behaviour and his way of relating. Interpretations of past traumatic life events and concurrent work on behavioural change are therefore necessary complementary elements in the treatment of sexual abusers.

5 Social skills.   Sexual abusers can lack important interpersonal skills. Low self-esteem and emotional immaturity can make the resolution of partner conflicts and the fulfilment of parental demands very difficult. Sexual abusers need to learn social skills to deal with these areas, which often include the inability to approach and to communicate with adult women in a relaxed and acceptable way. As well as being denigrating and dismissive, sexual abusers are in fact often frightened of women and need to develop social skills to cope appropriately.

Part two

Practical problems

Chapter eight

Preparation for disclosure

8.1 Crisis of disclosure – crisis of professionals and family crisis

We usually overlook that the crisis of disclosure contains two very distinct elements. The first crisis is the crisis of the professionals, the second the crisis of the family. The crisis of the professional network is a different crisis from the family crisis. It is we professionals who may have just learned about the abuse and who feel we have to act immediately. In child sexual abuse as syndrome of secrecy the disclosure of the secret is often equated with the fact of the abuse itself. We forget that in child sexual abuse as syndrome of secrecy the child may have had to live with the abuse not only for days, but probably for months and years. We react out of our own professional crisis triggered by the fact that we have just learned about the abuse and often quite inappropriately take immediate action, intervening blindly into a process of secrecy we do not fully understand. This process is reinforced by professional guidelines which require professionals to act immediately. Such 'panic guidelines' are unfortunately mainly the expression of the solidified professional crisis. The uncoordinated intervention which acts out the professional's own crisis usually leads to a failure of the intervention with secondary traumatisation of the child and the family. (See Three basic types of intervention, 4.1; The interprofessional process, 5.1; The inter-professional process in context, 5.2.)

When a child discloses or when professionals first suspect sexual abuse they need to deal with the professional crisis first. For this purpose I have developed the 'Child Sexual Abuse Crisis Intervention Kit'. (The Kit needs to be placed in a locker next to the First Aid Box, containing a large mug and spoon, a supply of freshly ground coffee, milk and a double amount of sugar.)

1 It is important not to act immediately but to think first.
2 It is equally important not to run away from the child either and to try not to convey our own panic.
3 It might be helpful to use the 'Child Sexual Abuse Crisis Intervention Kit': to get a large mug of coffee, and to sit down and hold on tightly to the mug.
4 As long as we hold on to the mug we fortunately cannot touch the telephone. This gives us time to think about what the child has said and what we have

seen. We can consider whether we really have enough information and enough well-documented facts about the child and the abuse. We can assess whether we have already a well-founded second-line suspicion or whether we need more information before we can intervene (see First-line suspicion and second-line suspicion, 8.3).

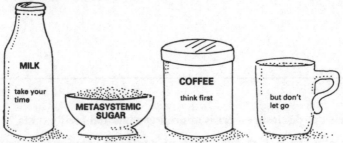

Figure 8.1 Child Sexual Abuse Crisis Intervention Kit

Time and again professionals realise later during the intervention, and usually too late, that they had insufficient facts to intervene. At the first vague suspicion of child sexual abuse they often rush into action without listening carefully enough to the child. With a suspicion in mind it can be very difficult to remain calm and to link up with the child and to illicit factual information first. The entire intervention is in limbo when the failure to differentiate between the professional crisis and the family crisis prevents professionals from collecting sufficient evidence prior to any intervention.

'Child abuse has time'. This phrase was coined in relation to physical abuse by Henry Kempe. In physical abuse children are much more at risk of their life than in sexual abuse. But even in physical abuse young children often die not because professionals intervene too late. They often die long after initial disclosure as a result of the lack of clear and problem-oriented co-operation in the professional network. 'Child sexual abuse has time' does not mean that we may not have to intervene instantly in some cases. It means that many cases which seem to require instant professional response do so because we as professionals have ourselves induced the family crisis in acting prematurely and chaotically out of our own crisis in the professional network. (see The individual process, Chapter 2; The family process, Chapter 3.)

The premature induction of the family crisis of disclosure by professionals does not only happen intentionally. A sudden raising of the eyes, the hasty asking of a question, sudden body language and panicky comments on a child's sexual communication can easily be picked up by the child. The professionals non-verbal and unintentional verbal behaviour can induce the awareness in the child that we suspect the secret of child sexual abuse. This can lead to premature disclosure and to denial and unsubstantiated allegations.

The professional crisis will only induce a premature family crisis of disclosure when our own panic reactions give the message to the child that we suspect the secret of sexual abuse. Professionals are very often unaware of the powerful effects of the indirect messages the child picks up from our response to their secret communications. (See The interactional nature of motivation, 2.4.1; Giving explicit licence to communicate, 2.4.2; The unconscious and secrecy, 2.4.4.)

Some children, and especially older children, make very acute and intentional full disclosures and we need to act immediately. Yet many of these disclosures are unwillingly triggered by professionals who are unaware that they are doing so. Distinguishing the professional crisis from the family crisis allows us to prepare the intervention. Inducing the family crisis of disclosure after we have dealt with the professional crisis first enables the professional network to use the family crisis of disclosure to achieve a Primary Therapeutic Intervention. Paradoxically, later and slower interventions often lead to earlier and quicker help for the child whereas hurried interventions end in failure to help and to protect. (See The interprofessional process in context, 5.2; and see Three basic types of intervention, 4.1.)

A common source of failure in the confusion between the professional crisis and the family crisis lies in the early involvement of family members, especially mothers. Professionals may contact mothers prematurely in the belief that mothers are always the natural allies of the child. If it is the mother who brings the abused child she is usually the ally of the child. In all other situations no family member must be contacted before the professional network has dealt with its own crisis first. Otherwise mothers will let the abuser know of the suspicion. The premature involvement of mothers and other family members usually leads to denial and to an increased pressure on the child to keep the secret.

8.2 Steps in the crisis intervention of disclosure

When children initiate full disclosures the crisis intervention by professionals includes seven steps. It has eight steps when the disclosure is induced by professionals. The eight steps are:

1 Looking for signs and symptoms and believing the child's communication.
2 Firming up on a partial disclosure or transforming a vague first-line suspicion into a well-founded second-line suspicion (see Section 8.3). Task: INFORMATION GATHERING, NO ACTION. Need for Anonymous Diagnostic Interprofessional Consultation – ADIC (see 8.4).
3 Planning the intervention at the stage of a second-line suspicion. Task: PREPARATION FOR ACTION of disclosure. Need for pre-intervention meeting (see 8.7).
4 Co-ordination of the professional network.
5 Disclosure interview with the child.
6 Opening up towards the abuser and the family.
7 Responsibility session with the abuser and the family.
8 Specific treatment.

The second step varies depending on whether sexual abuse has become an issue through the suspicions of professionals or through a full, acute and intentional disclosure by the child. In cases of suspicion by professionals based on a partial disclosure of the child, the Trusted Person (see 8.6) to whom the child has partially disclosed or who suspects child sexual abuse, may have to clarify the grounds for any further intervention using the Anonymous Diagnostic Interprofessional Consultation (see 8.4). When children themselves disclose fully to the Trusted Person, we would need to talk to the child on her or his own in order to decide whether there are sufficient grounds for a well-founded second-line suspicion. It would depend on the extent of the initial disclosure of the child and on the circumstances under which the child discloses whether a separate full disclosure interview would be necessary subsequently. (See The use of the 'trusted person', 8.6; Anonymous Diagnostic Interprofessional Consultation, 8.4.)

It may seem strange to include as the first step in the crisis intervention of child sexual abuse the need to look for signs and symptoms. The interactional nature of motivation strongly influences whether professionals become suspicious or not. Partial disclosures from children often become full disclosures only when the attitude of the professional conveys to the child that she has explicit licence to disclose the abuse and when the child can trust enough to be believed and to be helped. (See The interactional nature of motivation, 2.4.1; Giving explicit licence to communicate, 2.4.2.)

8.3 First-line suspicion, second-line suspicion and partial disclosure

A suspicion of child sexual abuse is not just a sudden feeling or thought. Forming a suspicion is already a complex process, which requires careful factual information and evaluation. In cases of suspicion the process of disclosure begins in the professional network. In partial disclosures children try consciously to test a specific professional as the Trusted Person in order to see whether they can proceed to a full disclosure. In both situations professionals may see or hear certain things which lead to an initial suspicion of possible sexual abuse. Suspicions can be aroused by drawings of children, especially young children, by school essays of older children, by sexualised behaviour of all ages, by indirect verbal references or by other forms of direct or indirect communication. Suspicions in professionals are always based on their own perception of symptoms and behaviour in the child which may indicate sexual abuse. The child may be unaware of the communications or it may be part of an intentional partial disclosure.

Initial vague first-line suspicions from which professionals draw first inferences of possible child sexual abuse need to be carefully documented. Any grounds for a first-line suspicion need to be examined with regard to their factual value before they are shared with other professionals. This is the point when the 'Child Sexual Abuse Crisis Intervention Kit' comes into action (see Crisis of disclosure – crisis of professionals and family crisis, 8.1).

A first-line suspicion *always* requires further information gathering and clarification before any intervention can be considered. An Open or Anonymous Diagnostic Interprofessional Consultation should therefore become the next routine step in the interprofessional process (see ADIC and ODIC, 8.4). A first-line suspicion must never be shared with family members but needs to remain firmly within the professional network. It should never lead to the action-planning pre-intervention meeting (see The pre-intervention meeting, 8.7). An interprofessional diagnostic consultation is usually necessary before a vague first-line suspicion can over time lead to the firm conclusion of a well-founded second-line suspicion. On the level of a well-founded and well- documented second-line suspicion, concrete preparations for the intervention need to be taken within the professional network. A well-founded second-line suspicion needs to lead to the action-oriented pre-intervention meeting.

First-line suspicion		Second-line suspicion
Vague	*Evidence*	Well founded and well documented
Further information gathering to gain sense of reality and seriousness of suspicion	*Aim*	Planning for action of disclosure
Professional network	*Directed at*	Family intervention
Must not be part of action-oriented decision-making process	*Crucial to avoid*	Must not yet openly alert or involve any family member
Open or Anonymous Diagnostic Interprofessional Consultation (ODIC and ADIC)	*Interprofessional process required*	Pre-intervention meeting
Any professional who can assist in clarifying degree of reality and seriousness of suspicion	*Professionals involved*	All professionals who are already involved or who may need to become involved during the crisis intervention of disclosure

Figure 8.2 First-line suspicion and second-line suspicion

Unintentional sexualised behaviour or intentional partial disclosures by children which lead to suspicions in professionals have the great advantage that they have not yet induced the opening crisis of disclosure in the child. The sexual abuse is still a secret and we have not yet entered into the communication with the child giving her the message that we have understood that the child wants to tell us the secret of ongoing sexual abuse. We have not yet conveyed the message 'I know that you have a secret' and further 'I know that you know that I know that you have a secret which you may be too frightened to disclose openly'. We therefore have not yet communicated with the child in a way which triggers the acute crisis of disclosure. Once the full disclosure is triggered when we openly talk to the child about our suspicions, older children are often too frightened to go back home and young children usually begin to talk to family members at home about the conversation they had with us about the abuse. In both cases we as professionals have triggered the full crisis of disclosure prematurely and we would need to act immediately.

Suspicions by professionals and the partial disclosure by children give professionals the time to think and to prepare the intervention on the interprofessional level and towards the child and the family before the intervention gets underway. Within the professional network we can ask for an ODIC or ADIC in cases of first-line suspicions and can organise a pre-intervention meeting in well-founded second-line suspicions.

Our own professional reaction towards an initial suspicion can induce a crisis of disclosure in the child when the child breaks the secrecy in response to our own reaction to the child's initial communication (see The interactional nature of motivation, 2.4.1). Clinical judgement needs to be used to get as much information as possible from the child to harden any vague first-line suspicion without crossing the line to a full disclosure at this stage. When a small child draws a man with an erect penis we can approach the child and ask about the man with the erect penis in the context of many other questions. We can ask in a very casual and more light-hearted way: 'Oh that's a nice picture. Who is that?'. We can ask amongst other things about the penis 'what is that?', putting this question in a context in which it is not central but seemingly peripheral and embedded in comments on other things. Without triggering in the child the suspicion that we suspect sexual abuse we can then ask detailed questions about the facts of possible sexual abuse. We can go on exploring vague first-line suspicions of sexual abuse with the aim of converting them into well-founded second-line suspicions as long as the child talks about what looks like a penis without anxiety or alarm and without any indication that she becomes aware that we are enquiring about possible sexual abuse.

We can and should continue to explore our suspicion as long as we do not induce by our own way of questioning and through our own personal behaviour the full awareness in the child that we suspect sexual abuse. We need to be extremely alert however. At the first sign of the child becoming aware that we are talking about sexual abuse we must be prepared to switch back immediately and instantly to distract from our exploration of the issue. If the child is still drawing we can ask 'What other colour do you want to use next?', defusing any danger of inducing the full awareness in the child that we are exploring the possible secret of sexual abuse.

It is we professionals who induce the crisis of disclosure when we ask in panic about a sexual drawing or when we convey our own feeling of crisis by different verbal or non-verbal means. Our own communication will then alert the child that we suspect sexual abuse and we as professionals will inadvertently trigger a premature and uncontrolled crisis of disclosure. We then need to act immediately and often prematurely before we have prepared other colleagues who need to be involved.

Partial disclosures in older children are conscious and intentional ways of testing. In contrast to communications by small children we need to remain very neutral, neither rejecting the communication nor fostering further elaboration. Further questioning of older children can easily lead to instant denial or to an immediate and premature full disclosure before we have planned and co-ordinated the intervention and the professional network. To take the case of a 13-year-old girl who writes a school essay about her sexual abuse, putting it into a covered form of a nightmare. The casual questioning or commenting which can be helpful in exploring the unintentional sexual drawing in the young child cannot be used for the older child who is much more intellectually and socially aware. We cannot begin to elaborate on explicit sexual topics in the school essay without instantly making the child aware that we suspect that she is communicating about possible sexual abuse.

If a teacher asks the child immediately and directly in front of the whole class about the sexual communication in the essay, he can induce an immediate and probably uncontrolled crisis of disclosure when the child breaks down in front of all the other children in the class. This would be a very undesirable moment for the disclosure. The same reaction of the teacher can lead to the opposite reaction of the child who could close up again in fear and who might never dare again to communicate the abuse to anybody for months or years. The best way to react to this situation is to keep silent initially, to register that the child seems to be communicating about sexual abuse and closely to observe the child and her behaviour. It is important to document the child's communication carefully. The teacher needs to photocopy the essay and he should react with heightened awareness of possible further clues about sexual abuse. He then needs to clarify with the support of the headmaster or the educational social worker in an ODIC or ADIC whether statutory and legal colleagues in the network think that enough evidence has been collected for a well founded second-line suspicion in order to proceed to the planning stage of a pre-intervention meeting and to a subsequent full disclosure.

The teacher, the headmaster, the school nurse or the educational social worker needs to co-ordinate the professional network within the school and ask whether other colleagues have had similar communications which may support the suspicion. When we involve other colleagues we need to bear in mind that these colleagues in turn may react with an immediate professional crisis which can lead to a premature disclosure (see The interprofessional process, 5.1; From secrecy to privacy, 6.4). In the meantime the teacher can seek contact with the child about other areas of interests and activities in the context of the normal school curriculum and he can look out for further signs of sexual abuse. He can try to comunicate in general ways to the child that he has understood that she has chosen him as Trusted Person. This may later help the child openly to disclose the abuse. A full disclosure may then be triggered in good time by the showing of a child sexual abuse prevention film (see The use of prevention films in suspicion and disclosure, 8.12).

The two examples of the young child's sexual drawing and the older child's essay about sexual abuse are only two of an infinite number of different situations in which the suspicion of child sexual abuse can arise and in which children may make partial disclosures. The basic process applies to all cases of suspicion and partial disclosures. They all become full disclosures through an interactional process between the professional and the child. The important practical point to bear in mind is that partial disclosures and vague first-line suspicions give us the time to substantiate the suspicion and to transform a vague first-line suspicion into a well-founded second-line suspicion before any action towards the family is taken. We need to learn that the induction of the full disclosure as an inter-actional process between the child and the professionals can often be controlled by the professionals involved. We can influence the time and the setting of the disclosure according to the needs of a Primary Therapeutic Intervention much more often than we think. (see Three basic types of intervention, 4.1; The interactional nature of motivation, 2.4.1; Aims and steps in the Primary Therapeutic Intervention, 6.2.)

Careful examination has shown that in many cases of sexual abuse in which professionals thought the child had induced the disclosure, the disclosure had in fact started with specific actions and reactions of the professional. We therefore need to use explicitly the state of suspicions and partial disclosures as important periods to prepare and to plan the intervention before we trigger any full disclosure towards the child and the family. To act on unfounded and vague first-line suspicions or to create guidelines for interventions which require actions on vague first-line suspicions often leads to intervention failure, to false allegations, to denial and to secondary damage in the child as consequence of anti-therapeutic therapy, abuse-promoting child protection and crime-promoting crime prevention (see The interprofessional process in context, 5.2).

Finally we should never forget that a vague first-line suspicion may turn out to be quite unfounded. The secondary damage to children and to families where we have intervened falsely can be horrendous and must lead to the ethical obligation to transform any vague first-line suspicion into a well-founded second-line suspicion before we intervene (see From secrecy to privacy, 6.4).

8.4 ADIC and ODIC: Anonymous and Open Diagnostic Interprofessional Consultation

In child sexual abuse as syndrome of secrecy we have a clear need for the right and for the procedure of an Open or Anonymous Diagnostic Interprofessional Consultation in professional networks prior to the intervention in cases of vague first-line suspicions and partial disclosures. In the Anonymous Diagnostic Interprofessional Consultation the case is discussed within the professional network in a problem-oriented way without immediately identifying and naming the child concerned.

The ADIC addresses the need to mediate between the different and seemingly opposing needs for confidentiality and privacy in medical, therapeutic and educational settings, and the need of child protective agencies and of the police to gain legally valid facts in order to be able to protect children from unlawful and harmful child sexual abuse. In child sexual abuse as syndrome of secrecy the right to confidentiality and privacy, and the equally valid but opposing need for openness in order to establish facts and to protect, can be transformed from seemingly mutually exclusive requirements into a complementary process when we introduce the professional right to anonymous consultations.

Anonymity can guarantee confidentiality and can provide open facts at the same time. In the ADIC any professional who has a vague first-line suspicion of child sexual abuse can clarify for herself and for other members of the professional network the degree of reality in her suspicion. In an ADIC ways of substantiating or disproving a first-line suspicion can be discussed and the professional network can agree on specific criteria under which the specific case would become a well-founded second-line suspicion. The ADIC gives the professional who only has a vague first-line suspicion the necessary sounding board to clarify her own mind before any intervention is considered. The questions of 'how real is real?' and 'am I really perceiving external reality of possible abuse?' are pertinent in child sexual abuse as syndrome of secrecy. The confusion about reality and non-reality in professionals mirrors the intrinsic problem of creating external reality in child sexual abuse.

On the other hand the ADIC gives child protective and legal agencies the possibility of determining in each specific case the exact nature and the degree of factual information which is required for the case to increase the chance of successful disclosure. The ADIC allows and requires the development of criteria for successful disclosure prior to the intervention. It can therefore serve as an important tool for developing objectifiable criteria for intervening and it can equally be used to evaluate the intervention.

The second function of the Anonymous Diagnostic Interprofessional Consultation is to help other professionals in the network to avoid the confusion between the family crisis and their own crisis in the opening crisis intervention of disclosure. In child sexual abuse as syndrome of secrecy, only the moment of naming the facts of the sexual abuse is the point at which the abuse is created as fact for the family. The secrecy becomes open reality through the naming event in the domain of languague. This is also true for professionals who prematurely trigger a disclosure at the first moment of suspicion of sexual abuse, when they act out their own professional crisis. The ADIC helps the professional network to deal with their own crisis of disclosure first and to concentrate on a goal-oriented and problem-solving intervention before the intervention itself gets underway. (see The individual process in context, 2.4; The interprofessional process in context, 5.2.)

The following rules of the ADIC should always be observed:

1 During the ADIC the therapeutic argument and the child protective or legal side must be equally represented in order to avoid anti-therapeutic therapy, abuse-promoting child protection or crime-promoting crime prevention (see Beyond circularity, legal abuse and psychological damage, 1.1 and Responsibility, participation, guilt, blame and power, 1.2)
2 The ADIC requires absolute respect for the therapeutic and confidential considerations and the professionals who represent these aspects and for the legal considerations of protection and crime prevention and for the professionals who stand for this linear part of child sexual abuse (see The interprofessional process, 5.1).
3 The right of anonymity which reflects the right to confidentiality and privacy of children and families can only be respected as long as the suspicion remains a vague first-line suspicion.
4 The professional who has asked for the ADIC needs to disclose the name when a suspicion has become a well-founded second-line suspicion and when the professional network has in a pre-intervention meeting agreed on the form, on the aims and on the structure of the intervention and has concluded that protective and legal action is necessary.

Many professionals are rightly frightened that the very moment they openly voice the very first suspicion of child sexual abuse, any control over the further process is immediately taken away with often disastrous results. The ADIC does not only help doctors, therapists, teachers, nursery nurses and other child professionals to clarify their suspicion and to link in with legal and child protective agencies. It can also be extremely helpful to social workers in child protective agencies to avoid intervening prematurely in chaotic and irresponsible ways at the first moment of suspicion of child sexual abuse. The ADIC can give statutory and legal professionals the chance to examine the exact details of any suspicion determining the degree of facts they need before they intervene.

The interlocking professional–family crisis in child sexual abuse as syndrome of secrecy often triggers interventions by child protection workers and by the police on the level of first-line suspicions on which they would never intervene in any other form of child abuse. In physical abuse no social worker or police would take action on the information of a vague first-line suspicion that a child has broken an arm or has received blue marks. The social worker and police would want to know more about how the child might have received the injuries and would want to firm up on the suspicion of non-accidental injury before they would take any action towards the child and the family. The ADIC is crucial to assist legal and child protective workers to develop clear factual and rational criteria for cases of well-founded second-line suspicions in child sexual abuse as syndrome of secrecy.

The ADIC can also help to identify cases of unfounded first-line suspicions which need to be dismissed. Once criteria for dismissal and for second-line suspicions are developed by all agencies it will be possible to act complementarily in a problem-oriented Primary Therapeutic Intervention (see Three basic types of intervention, 4.1).

When we do not know the colleagues from other agencies with whom we need to co-operate and when we do not know their reactions we can use the simple and helpful device to phone these professionals and to discuss the initial suspicion in general terms in the form of an ADIC. We can say to a child protection worker or a police officer 'I actually wanted to talk to you generally about co-operation in sexual abuse. What would you do if I had a case?' and then describing in general terms the scenario of a specific case. This helps the professional colleagues from other agencies to think in a problem-oriented way about a Primary Therapeutic Intervention without having to think about instant action (see Aims and steps in the Primary Therapeutic Intervention, 6.2). Sometimes I would say to a professional from another agency that I have just seen a child but that I am not sure at all yet whether my perception constitutes a real suspicion of sexual abuse and that everything is still extremely unclear. I would follow on by saying that I just wanted to know what to do if I did have a clear suspicion. Having prepared the colleague anonymously for the need for a problem-oriented planning and co-ordination of the intervention in this particular case I would later go back and discuss the case openly.

This use of the ADIC is not a cynical or unprofessional way of dealing with colleagues. Nor is it in any way a device to prevent the disclosure of child sexual abuse. It only serves to recognise that other professionals may panic at times as much as I do. In their own professional crisis they can easily take over and can block any problem-oriented approach if they are not prepared first. Non-therapeutic action responses can be avoided if the problem-oriented thinking about a specific case can be separated from the professional's own crisis and the often immediate urge for action which usually overrides every thought about preparation and rational planning. This use of the ADIC therefore serves as useful and rational breathing space to prepare the entire professional network for a goal-oriented Primary Therapeutic Intervention (see The interprofessional process in context, 5.2).

In professional networks with well-established multi-professional structures of co-operation, all interprofessional diagnostic consultations can become Open Diagnostic Interprofessional Consultations (ODIC) as long as this does not lead to inappropriate and premature interventions at the stage of vague first-line suspicions.

8.5 Explicit therapeutic permission to disclose

Talking to children in order to evaluate a disclosure puts professionals under great pressure to get true and objective information. The distinction between talking to children in order to give explicit therapeutic permission to communicate about the experience of sexual abuse, and the distinct though connected task of interviewing children for legal and child protective purposes, is easily confused. Interviewing for legal purposes and communicating therapeutically for treatment can take very different forms and we need to be very clear about the specific aims of our exercise. We need to distinguish between the task of assessing the child's mental health and the need to gain objective information for legal or statutory purposes which will be admissible in court. The task of talking to the child in the context of a therapeutic endeavour and the need for legal interviewing must not be confused.

In child sexual abuse as syndrome of secrecy we cannot expect that children disclose sexual abuse when they are asked directly and openly about their experience. Often we will get no valid answer when we ask strictly neutral questions right from the beginning in a way which would be required in normal interviewing for legal and child protective procedures as Jones and McQuiston (1985) have described so well. We often need to give the child the explicit permission to communicate first. This means addressing all the anxieties which prevent the child from disclosing. The child needs to know that we know why the child is worried, why she may be frightened and disturbed and still does not talk. Child professionals need to know that there are many reasons why a child may be too frightened and why she may be 'motivated not to be motivated' to disclose and why the child may not trust us to help. In child sexual abuse as syndrome of secrecy the child needs to know that we know the reasons why the child may be unable to disclose. (See The interactional nature of motivation, 2.4.1.)

Giving explicit permission to communicate means on the contextual level addressing child sexual abuse as syndrome of secrecy. In practical terms we need to communicate in varied and repeated ways the message that 'I know that you know that I know'. 'I know that you have many reasons to be too frightened to disclose. And I know that you know that I am aware of this fact' is the structural communication of secrecy which can take different forms. Often the use of the 'Story of the Other Child' can give the message that 'I know that the child is too frightened to disclose in an indirect but open way'. (See Giving explicit licence to communicate, 2.4.2.)

Giving the explicit therapeutic permission to communicate means addressing the following seven aspects of secrecy which prevent the child from disclosing:

1 We need to introduce 'an idea' about a secret.

2 We need to address the anxiety about secrecy.
3 We need to address the anxiety about non-believing.
4 We need to address the anxieties about threats.
5 We need to address the anxieties about the consequences of the disclosure.
6 We need to address the anxiety about using explicit sexual language by introducing sexual language ourselves.
7 We need to address the sexual abuse itself.

If a child in therapy indicates ongoing child sexual abuse we need to switch from the interpretive mode to the investigative mode (see The unconscious and secrecy, 2.4.4). I would say something like 'You know I just can't concentrate today. It is very strange, I am just not sure but somehow something goes through my mind a girl has said to me a while ago. I have just remembered and it is still in my mind'. I would be very vague and just introduce 'an idea' to communicate to the child that I am talking about something totally out of context which comes only from myself and from my own mind and has nothing to do with the child. The crucial element of introducing 'an idea' is the communication that this idea is the professional's idea which has nothing whatsoever to do with the child. This is crucial in order not to put any pressure on to the child to say something the child feels we want to hear; nor to put any of our own ideas into the child's mind; and finally not to increase the child's anxiety by communicating that we are talking about the child's own sexual abuse. In order to stress this aspect I would watch the child's reaction very closely and may repeatedly say 'it is just my own strange idea' or 'I just have to think about it and I am only telling you about it because I can't quite concentrate at this moment'. I therefore repeatedly and explicitly make it clear that the following story is my own story as a professional. The subsequent story telling becomes explicitly my personal problem as the professional.

The subsequent story becomes a metaphor which communicates to the child that I know about sexual abuse as syndrome of secrecy and about the anxieties related to it. The story then serves to give the child the explicit therapeutic permission to communicate about her experience of sexual abuse.

In the story I would always use 'The Other Child' as the third person. I would probably continue saying something like 'you know, this girl wanted to tell me something but she wasn't quite sure and then she said she wanted to talk about things but somehow she was worried because she felt she should not talk and that it was a secret' (addressing the anxiety about secrecy).

'But then she went on and she said that she wasn't sure anyway because she felt if she were to talk she was really worried that I may not believe her' (addressing the anxiety about non-believing).

'And anyway she had tried to tell people earlier and she had been called a liar and she was really scared. And you know what then happened was that she said that she was really frightened to talk to me because something terrible might happen to her' (addressing the anxiety about threats).

'And then she said she was very scared anyway that something horrible would happen, if she were to talk about it, not only to her but also to her mummy and her daddy. And she really didn't want to talk at all. And she didn't. And you know I was very confused and did not know what it was all about' (addressing the anxieties about the consequences of disclosure).

'But then later she said that in fact somebody had touched her and then that he had actually touched her not only at her hands and her face but had also touched her private parts and between her legs.' At that stage I would ask the child about the names she has for the different sex organs and would use the names the child uses for male and female sexual parts. I would continue with the Story of the Other Child who felt that it was naughty to talk about private parts (addressing the anxiety to talk in explicit sexual terms).

In telling 'The Story of the Other Child' I would always observe the child very closely for any sign of rising anxiety. I would reiterate the Other Child's anxiety saying 'Yes, you know the other girl was really *very* scared to talk about things.' I would always adapt the story about The Other Child instantly according to the actual reaction of the child to what I say. I would mirror the child's response to 'The Story of the Other Child' in the story of The Other Child itself. When the child gets too frightened I would react by saying 'you know and then the child got so scared she couldn't tell me any more. And I quite understood that it was very scary. And she could not tell me any more at that time and she couldn't even listen to it. And do you know how long it took her to tell me again? Three months.'

At any stage of telling the story, clinical judgement is of paramount importance for determining how far to go and how to convey in an appropriate way to the child the possible anxieties, to talk about sexual abuse according to the specific situation. 'Telling the story' to an older child of 13 will look very different from communicating the same areas of anxieties to a young child of 3 years. When I have told the story without the child disclosing her own story of abuse I would let the story stay in the room as a message and a metaphor for the child. The Story of the Other Child is like a coloured balloon I let fly. It rises and then floats above us in the room. It is *my* balloon but both the child and I can look at it. My balloon carries the story of another child who has been sexually abused. And I talk about it for my very own reasons. But while I create this balloon the child can look at it and understand 'the story' as explicit permission to communicate her own sexual abuse. 'I know that you know that I know' is the indirect message. But openly I talk about balloons and stories and about my own problems. And when I see that the child has understood the metaphor or when she gets too frightened the balloon may disappear again. It was still my balloon and I would say something like 'stupid me that all these thoughts came into my head'. 'I do not know why that just came to my mind, it is just very strange'. Then I would go on to continue what we had done before.

Sometimes the child shows open signs of increased anxiety. I would then go on saying 'well it is probably all funny in my head but could it be that something like that has happened to you?'. Some children have then burst into tears and have started to disclose. At this very moment we need to switch and need to allow the child to tell her own story in her own words without any leading questions or suggestions from us. When the child starts to disclose it is of paramount importance to switch instantly from a metaphoric mode of telling the story to a factual and reality-oriented mode of legally interviewing children in order to establish the objective facts of the abuse and the abuse as fact. After the child's disclosure I would say to the child that we probably will have to think together with other people about what she had just told me and I would proceed to prepare a full disclosure interview (see Organising the disclosure interview, 9.3).

When children are still too frightened to disclose they sometimes just listen and leave it at that. Often children do not disclose at all at this stage. When we continue to have strong clinical suspicions of sexual abuse we must not take the child's 'no' for an answer, that abuse has not happened. It needs to be our professional skill to know that this denial may still be due to the anxieties and fears which make the child motivated not to disclose. 'No' may therefore not mean that sexual abuse has not happened but that the child is too frightened to disclose. I would communicate this to the child at the end of 'Telling the Story'. I would follow up the child's 'no' by saying 'that is exactly what the other child said, she said "no". And do you know what happened then? Then later on she said yes, "yes", that it had happened. And do you know how long it took her to tell? It took her 6 weeks until she talked to me about it. And then she said that she had said "no" in the beginning because she thought: how could she trust me? And you know I think she was right. How did she know that she could trust me? So she said "no".' If the child does still not disclose I would abandon the subject and would go on to other topics.

I am fully aware that the use of the metaphor in Telling the Story of the Other Child will inevitably be misunderstood by many readers as obstructing the course of justice or as manipulating the child and putting things into the child's mind. Telling the story does neither. In the context of child sexual abuse as a syndrome of secrecy it gives the child the explicit permission to disclose the abuse which she otherwise may never dare to do (see The interlocking process between the explicit therapeutic permission to communicate and legal interviewing, 9.1). The permission to communicate in the domain of mental health does not and must not follow legal standards of neutral interviewing. If done in the way described it is not suggestive, nor leading. It is using a metaphor of the professional to serve as permission to disclose for the child.

'Giving explicit therapeutic permission to disclose' is different from legal interviewing. 'Giving explicit therapeutic permission to communicate' addresses the specific psychological difficulties in child sexual abuse as syndrome of secrecy. The ending of Telling the Story is therefore very important. In contrast to a legal interview we must not take 'no' for an answer, nor are we allowed to push the child by giving the message that we now expect her to disclose because otherwise we cannot help. We also need to have a truly open mind about whether sexual abuse has happened or not. We need to give the child the time and the space to take in the metaphor as permission to communicate and to come out in her own time. We should use the meantime to prepare the network for a possible disclosure.

When we tell the 'Story of the Other Child' we give the sexually abused child who is too frightened to disclose the following messages:

1   If the child has been sexually abused we want her to know that we know that sexual abuse may have happened or may be ongoing.
2   We want to let the child know that we know about the anxieties and threats which prevent the child from disclosing.
3   We want to let the child know that we can talk about sexual matters openly and in sexual language direct which is accepting and non-panicking, non-denigrating, non-denying and non-punitive.
4   We want to let the child know that we know that she may not trust us, and that she may have only too good reasons not to trust us immediately.
5   We want to give the child the message that we know that it may take time for the child to get used to the idea of disclosing the secret of the abuse and that it may take time to deal with all the anxieties of disclosing and with the fears about not being believed, protected and helped in a way in which the child would feel safe.
6   In Telling the Story we communicate to the child that we do not take 'no' for an answer because we know the predicament of wanting to disclose and at the same time of being too frightened of the consequences of disclosure.
7   Finally we want to give the child the permission to come out with possible sexual abuse in her own time, giving her the message that we will not forget that sexual abuse may still be going on.

I had reactions to 'Telling the Story' which varied from immediate disclosure of a 14-year-old girl to still lasting denial in cases where I still think sexual abuse has taken place but where no professional has been able to provide hard enough evidence to intervene.

Sometimes adolescents have disclosed many months later. In one case a 16-year-old girl phoned me after 18 months with an urgent request to speak to me. I had moved to another clinic and she had found my new address, had managed to phone, had crossed London on her own although she had been considered intellectually sub-normal. She then disclosed a history of several years of sexual abuse. She had been asked by others directly and told me that she had been too frightened to disclose. The entire professional network had been worried about possible sexual abuse for a long time. A case conference 18 months prior to the child's disclosure had decided to try to get a well-founded second-line suspicion. Police felt unable to intervene and the child had been referred to the GP and to the local child psychiatrist, to the school nurse and to the educational social worker, who had all tried to link up with the child. She had been sent to the local Child Guidance Clinic and did not dare to disclose either.

She told me she was frightened of men, only to continue to tell me as a man that she had not dared to disclose to the female school nurse and the female education welfare officer who had both asked her repeatedly. It had taken the girl more than a year to pluck up courage and to work through her anxiety to disclose. Then she came back to me as the Trusted Person who had given the original 'explicit therapeutic permission to communicate' 18 months earlier. She came and gave a full and legally and therapeutically valid account about her abuse. (See The use of the 'trusted person', 8.6.)

Even if a sexually abused child never does disclose, the Story of the Other Child can still have great therapeutic effect. It may be the first time in the child's life that somebody has talked about sexual abuse, believing and naming the possibility that sexual abuse may have happened at all. In addition we communicate our knowledge about the child's predicament about disclosing when we address all the areas of anxiety which may prevent the child from disclosing. The story will often for the first time address possible sexual abuse as fact and as a real experience of the child. This can enable the child to deal in a covert way with her anxieties and with the traumas of the abuse. The story can then be an important therapeutic contribution to clarify the emotional and cognitive confusion in the child's mind about the abuse.

Telling the Story led in some cases to the other important conclusion and to the clear clinical judgement over time that the child had not been sexually abused. If no sexual abuse has happened, 'the story' has no consequences as long as the professional strictly owns this story as his own story which comes from his own mind without putting it as the child's reality. 'The story' is therefore not a communication about real sexual abuse. It is a metaphor. It is very important that the story maintains its metaphoric value, otherwise the Story becomes a confused and, probably for the child, damaging affair which also can bring professionals into conflict with legal colleagues and with the parents and the family of the child.

Telling the Story requires the professional:

1 To be able to have a truly open mind about the presence or absence of sexual abuse.
2 To be able to use 'the story' as metaphor without confusing it with reality.
3 To be able to assess instantly in the process of telling the story the child's reactions to the story and to react on the spot by integrating the child's response into the ongoing story.
4 To be able to communicate with the child on a verbal and non-verbal level appropriate for the age and stage of the child's development.
5 To be able to switch from a metaphoric level into a neutral way of factual legal interviewing once the child discloses her own story of sexual abuse.

The individualised 'story of the other child' can in general terms be substituted by the use of prevention films or other prevention materials. This is often very helpful in the context of suspicions in schools and nurseries (see The use of prevention films in suspicion and disclosure, 8.12). To ask the child to draw or to write a story about 'My really very worst nightmare' can similarly give sexually abused children the psychological space which serves as explicit permission to describe under the disguise of fantasy the secret reality of sexual abuse. These are only some examples of how to give the child explicit licence to communicate about possible ongoing sexual abuse.

The story of 'the other child' and other materials as metaphor and indirect communication about suspected sexual abuse

Figure 8.3 Giving permission to disclose

8.6 The use of the 'trusted person'

Settings and situations in which sexually abused children show disturbed and sexualised behaviour or in which they make partial disclosures which lead to the suspicion of child sexual abuse in professionals are not random settings or situations. Nor is the specific professional exchangeable. It is most important to understand that in child sexual abuse as a syndrome of secrecy the professionals to whom the child makes a partial disclosure or in whose presence the child displays disturbed or sexualised behaviour are selected and specifically chosen professionals. The person in whose presence the child displays these symptoms unconsciously or makes a conscious and intentional partial disclosure is the specifically chosen 'Trusted Person'. 'Trusted Persons' are the professionals in whose presence sexually abused children feel safe enough to begin to communicate the secret reality of sexual abuse.

The Trusted Person who has the first suspicion of sexual abuse is therefore the most important professional for the child for the entire process of the disclosure. If we think about even minor secrets of any negative kind in our own lives and the time we need and the courage we have to pluck up to disclose these secrets to another person, we can imagine what devastating effects a referral to a stranger can have on a child who has just partially disclosed to a Trusted Person. The Trusted Person is the *expert* for *this child*. The Trusted Person needs to link up with the *expert for sexual abuse*. In cases of vague first-line suspicions it is the Trusted Person who needs the Anonymous Diagnostic Interprofessional Consultation in order to create a well-founded second-line suspicion as a precondition for intervention (see ADIC, 8.4). It would be quite wrong for a nursery nurse or a teacher to hand the child over to any doctor, social worker or police officer as 'experts' in child sexual abuse. Instead the Trusted Person needs to be helped by 'experts' and by the professional network to find ways in which a first-line suspicion can be made substantial. To use the Trusted Person as key professional in the process of disclosure can mean that we have to consult colleagues in nurseries or in schools or therapists for weeks or months until a vague first-line suspicion becomes well-founded enough to merit an intervention.

Once the intervention gets underway the full disclosure interview must take place in the presence of the Trusted Person. The child *must not* be referred from the nursery nurse, the teacher or therapist to a social worker or the police or any other expert, who then interviews the child without the nursery nurse, the teacher or the therapist being present. The presence of the Trusted Person is vital for the disclosure process. The Trusted Person does not have to conduct the disclosure interview. The presence of the Trusted Person as special and important attachment figure can however avoid the increase of anxiety which otherwise often leads to understandable lying and denial when children are referred for disclosure interviews to people they have never met before and of whom they are frightened.

The Trusted Person as an attachment figure provides emotional backup and gives the child explicit licence to disclose the abuse. The Trusted Person can also remind the child of the drawings, of the behaviour or of the essay and the words or the situation which have led to the suspicion in the Trusted Person. In reminding the child of these situations the Trusted Person as expert for the child provides the emotional and cognitive continuity under which other professionals as experts for abuse may be able to conduct a full disclosure interview.

The Trusted Person is often an important attachment figure of 'the world in between', in between home which is too close and the strange world outside where a child does not dare to trust. It is usually somebody at school, in the nursery, in youth clubs or church groups or in medical and therapeutic settings. The Trusted Person can be a dinner lady at school. If this is the case this dinner lady is the most important person for the child during the entire disclosure process.

The role of the Trusted Person for the disclosure process can not be underestimated. The role of the Trusted Person must be clearly distinguished from the role of all other professionals who undertake specific tasks during the process of disclosure. Again it is a matter of differentiation in which the Trusted Person is the expert for the particular child and the other professionals are experts in sexual abuse and in conducting disclosure interviews. Both functions are complementary. The Trusted Person also needs to be part of the handover meeting if after a full disclosure the further intervention requires the referral of the child and the withdrawal of the Trusted Person from her central role during disclosure (see The handover meeting, 9.14).

8.7 The pre-intervention meeting

The pre-intervention meeting needs to take place when a vague first-line suspicion has been substantiated into a second-line suspicion and when a full disclosure needs to be considered. The pre-intervention meeting of the professional network needs to include all agencies which might have to become involved during the intervention. The task of the pre-intervention meeting is to plan the intervention and to co-ordinate the different tasks of the different professionals. The decision making in the pre-intervention meeting is action-oriented, unlike the ADIC which is oriented towards information gathering. The pre-intervention meeting, as an interprofessional meeting prior to the actual intervention involving the child and the family, helps to avoid a crisis in the professional network later on.

The pre-intervention meeting needs to decide on the basic structure of the intervention and on the necessary steps involved (see The family and the professional network, Chapter 4). Agreement needs to be reached about which professional is responsible for which action, who should confront the alleged abuser, what happens to the child and where the child will stay if she cannot go home. How will the mother be involved and which statutory issues have to be dealt with? A way of giving quick feedback needs to be established and it is important to nominate a key worker or a monitor person to co-ordinate the initial stages of the crisis intervention of disclosure.

The pre-intervention meeting needs to clarify the following seven points within the professional network:

1 Who will talk to the child about the facts of the abuse and about the possible further events?
2 What role will the mother have during disclosure?
3 Where will the child go if the intervention requires removal of the child?
4 What are the practical consequences of denial?
5 Who will talk to the abuser and the parents and where?
6 What different role and functions have the police, legal agencies and child protective services in this particular case and how will they co-operate at any stage of the disclosure?
7 Who will monitor the overall intervention and how can a Primary Therapeutic Intervention be safeguarded from changing into a Primary Punitive

Intervention or a Primary Child Protective Intervention, especially when the child does not return home? (see Three basic types of intervention, 4.1).

The most important task of the pre-intervention meeting is directed towards the interprofessional process itself. Structural institutional conflicts between different agencies, conflicts-by-proxy between individual professionals and institutionalised conflicts-by-proxy need to be openly addressed (see The interprofessional process, 5.1). Conflict-resolutions-by-proxy need to be achieved as a precondition for any subsequent Primary Therapeutic Intervention. If it is impossible during the pre-intervention meeting to achieve conflict-resolutions-by-proxy within the professional network, different professionals and agencies will react with non-therapeutic action responses which will lead to certain intervention failure and to the denial of the abuse. (see Mutual influence and interlocking professional–family process, 4.2; The interprofessional process in context, 5.2; Changing interprofessional and institutional co-operation, 5.3.)

8.8 Allegations of children in children's homes, in reconstructed families and in families of separation and divorce

Clinical experience has shown that children who make allegations of sexual abuse in the family usually do not lie but speak the truth. There are however three groups of children where we need to be careful when we assess allegations of child sexual abuse. Allegations (1) of older children in children's homes, (2) of adolescents in newly reconstructed families and (3) of children in families of separation and divorce need to be treated with caution. On the other hand all three groups are high-risk groups for child sexual abuse and even if they have not been sexually abused in this setting they have often been sexually abused by someone else before. The diagnosis in these cases can therefore pose special problems and difficulties.

1 Emotionally deprived adolescents with a long-standing history of institutional care increasingly get hold of the notion that the accusation of sexual abuse against a member of the residential staff will create a lot of attention. Allegations of these children must therefore be judged with caution. On the other hand we find increasingly that many children in children's homes have previously been sexually abused. These children are often only placed in institutional care as result of the consequences of open or undiagnosed child sexual abuse. We also understand increasingly that children who have been sexually abused once are as a consequence of sexualised behaviour or victim behaviour at increased risk of becoming sexually abused again. And child sexual abuse does also happen in institutional care.

2 Adolescent girls in newly reconstructed families are the second group of children who may use the allegation of sexual abuse for alterior motives. Adolescent girls may not like the mother's new partner and can feel displaced by him. The accusation of sexual abuse can quickly help them to get rid of the

newcomer and these allegations have to be treated with caution. On the other hand we know that children in reconstructed families are between two and five times more likely to be sexually abused by stepfathers than children who live with their natural fathers (Finkelhor, 1979). Again we are facing a dilemma of possibly false allegations in children who are also part of a high-risk group.

3 Children in families of separation and divorce are the third group where the allegation of sexual abuse may face us with a dilemma. We see an increasing number of cases where the allegation of sexual abuse is used by mothers to get care and control over the children or to curtail access by fathers in separated families. On the other hand maternal accusations may also be true. The mother may be truly protective and may only want a separation from the father or a termination of access to prevent further sexual abuse of the child.

These situations need to be carefully assessed and we always need to involve both parents directly. Statutory involvement can be necessary to support procedures which bring the mother and the father, as parental couple, into assessment sessions, together with the aim of dealing with the child's safety and protection as long as allegations of sexual abuse are not dismissed or substantiated. (see Suspicion of sexual abuse following access visits to fathers, 8.11.)

8.9 Suspicion of child sexual abuse during individual counselling and therapy

The suspicion of child sexual abuse often arises during individual therapy and counselling. The suspicion affects the therapy and counselling in two ways:

1 The therapist or counsellor needs to be aware that the child may try to give secret information in order to test whether the counsellor or therapist is able to respond, and to take up the issue of sexual abuse on a reality level. Even if the communication is unconscious, the therapist or counsellor needs to switch from an interpretative mode to an investigative mode, first in his own mind and later in explicit communications towards the child. (see Child sexual abuse as syndrome of secrecy, 2.1; The individual process in context, 2.4; Individual counselling and therapy, 7.3.)

2 A full disclosure during ongoing individual therapy requires a change of frame of reference by the therapist. The emergence of a possibly ongoing crime renders the original therapeutic contract of confidentiality void. Under child protective considerations and considering the nature of child sexual abuse as syndrome of secrecy, the therapeutic framework needs to be widened from individual therapy to a family approach. The therapist needs to co-operate with statutory agencies in order to safeguard not only the ongoing therapy but also the protection of the child from further abuse. (see Three basic types of intervention, 4.1; The family process, 3.2; Family therapy and family approach, 6.1.)

Individual therapists who continue to treat sexually abused children without considering issues of protection easily become part of the secrecy system of child sexual abuse. The therapist's collusion with the system of secrecy in child sexual abuse completely redefines the situation. What started as a therapeutic process aimed at psychological change becomes an interaction in which a child tries to disclose external reality and an externally existing traumatic life situation of ongoing sexual abuse. A non-protective response of the therapist does not only mean that therapy has ceased to take place. Continuing therapy of secrecy becomes anti-therapeutic therapy which can increase the disturbance in the child and can add secondary psychological trauma when the therapist does not help the child to disclose the abuse and when she does not allow and assist the child to name the facts of the abuse and to establish the abuse as external fact and reality. (see Rejecting the experience, rejecting the child, 1.3.1; The unconscious and secrecy, 2.4.4; The interprofessional process in context, 5.2.)

The switch from an interpretative mode to an investigative mode does not mean that the therapist instantly initiates a process of disclosure. This would be quite inappropriate and would be as damaging as any other premature disclosure which is based on a weak first-line suspicion. Switching from an interpretative mode to an investigative mode requires that the therapist is aware of possible further secret communications of the child about sexual abuse. The therapist needs to gather factual information which could substantiate or defuse the vague first-line suspicion. Verbal communications, drawings or explicit sexual play need to be carefully recorded. This material needs to be presented in an Anonymous Diagnostic Interprofessional Consultation which should help the therapist to assess whether what he is perceiving is in fact material which indicates child sexual abuse as external reality.

External consultation for individual counsellors and therapists is vital. I myself found it sometimes very difficult as therapist and as participant in the transference–counter-transference interaction in individual therapy to assess whether what I was perceiving were in fact indicators for external reality of ongoing sexual abuse or just indicators for internal psychological events. (See Child sexual abuse as syndrome of secrecy from the child, 2.1; Anonymous Diagnostic Interprofessional Consultation, 8.4.)

The need to ask questions and not to interpret does not mean that the therapist herself immediately introduces the topic of sexual abuse. Nor must the therapist become insensitive and stop taking the lead from the child. Sexually abused children who start to trust therapists will inevitably bring their sexual abuse into the session although it may come into therapy in very hidden and secret ways. We therefore do not need to be worried that the child will not bring material which we could take as a lead. Individual counsellors and therapists however need to be skilled to recognise and to respond to the hidden and often very subtle signs of ongoing child sexual abuse.

The Anonymous Diagnostic Interprofessional Consultation (ADIC) links the interprofessional process and therapy. The ADIC should help the therapist to structure his thinking and to determine what he and professionals from other agencies need to know in order to come to a well-founded second-line suspicion with the following pre-intervention meeting and a full disclosure. In individual therapy it has sometimes been very helpful to suggest that the child draws or writes down the worst ever nightmare (s)he has had. Very often sexually abused children will use the 'fantasy-space' given to them to communicate about their real experience of child sexual abuse.

When children reveal information which indicates child sexual abuse therapists must not instantly begin to talk openly about child sexual abuse. Therapists need to be aware that asking open questions about sexual abuse in a hasty and panicky way can induce the crisis of disclosure in the child which is triggered by the professional's own crisis of having to deal with child sexual abuse (see Crisis of disclosure – crisis of professionals and family crisis, 8.1). The process from the first suspicion to the full disclosure can therefore take many weeks and even months and the disclosure must be prepared carefully as in any other context (see Steps in the crisis intervention of disclosure, 8.2).

8.10 Suspicion of sexual abuse during family sessions

If events in family therapy lead to the suspicion of sexual abuse, family therapists need to switch mode from working on interpersonal aspects of changing family relationships to working in a linear mode of establishing the facts of external reality. Children who are structurally dependent on their parents will not disclose sexual abuse in family sessions and the disclosure of child sexual abuse must not be attempted within conjoint family sessions. (See From mad to bad, Chapter 1; The individual process, Chapter 2; Aims and steps in the Primary Therapeutic Intervention, 6.2; First-line suspicion, second-line suspicion and partial disclosure, 8.3.)

Family therapists need to widen the approach from a family therapy approach which addresses only interactional aspects of family relationships to a family approach which contains circular and relationship aspects of the family process as well as linear aspects in the legal and statutory domain as an expression of the structural dependence of children resulting from a linear biological lack of maturation. (See Responsibility, participation, guilt, blame and power, 1.2; Family therapy and family approach, 6.1.)

When family therapists become suspicious that child sexual abuse may lie behind a family problem they need to involve other professionals. They should try to find out from other sources, such as schools or nurseries, whether other people have similar suspicions and whether the child already has a relationship to one specific professional who would be the Trusted Person (see The use of the 'trusted person', 8.6).

Family therapists, like other professionals, may not be sure whether what they see is really an indicator of possible child sexual abuse. They may need consultation for themselves in order to find out what they need to look for. An Anonymous Diagnostic Interprofessional Consultation may be the first step in coming to a firm second-line suspicion as a precondition for any further intervention. (See Anonymous Diagnostic Interprofessional Consultation, 8.4; Steps in the crisis intervention of disclosure, 8.2; First-line suspicion, second-line suspicion and partial disclosure, 8.3.)

The family therapist needs to find a situation in which she herself can talk to the child on her own or where she can use another professional who has natural regular one to one contact with the child as Trusted Person, who may become involved in helping the child to disclose. Trying to confront and disclose sexual abuse for the first time in the context of a conjoint family session will most likely lead to instant denial, to increased secrecy and to termination of therapy. If therapy continues, it results in increased pressure on the child to keep the sexual abuse secret. Family therapy then becomes anti-therapeutic therapy (see The interprofessional process in context, 5.2).

8.10.1 The unmentioned creation of reality

In very exceptional situations in families with older adolescents or young adults where statutory and child protective issues are no longer central and with older adolescents and young adults who are able to stand up for themselves when they have ceased to be structurally dependent on their parents, experienced therapists can try to disclose sexual abuse in the context of conjoint family sessions.

This must remain the exception to the rule. On rare occasions I have used two opposite methods. One is to lead a very general discussion about sexual abuse to a point at which I would discuss what would happen if sexual abuse had happened in this family. I would use newspaper stories, television news or other events to induce the seemingly unrelated topic of child sexual abuse which I would transform from a subtle and unoutspoken hypothetical 'what if' mode to the reality mode. When I as clinician feel confident that sexual abuse has taken place, and when I think that the abused late adolescent or young adult will be able to stand up for herself I will switch without announcing or acknowledging the switch, starting to talk openly about sexual abuse.

Without any explanation or any other meta-communication about whether the abuse has taken place or not, I would just talk about it as if it were fact. The main criterion of whether the family accepts this disclosure is the degree of normality and matter of factness I am able to introduce. I would try to give the family an indirect message like 'I am getting bored stiff, you are the tenth family this week who shows exactly the same pattern, which is always related to child sexual abuse.'

The matter of factness also demands that we make no big fuss but play down the switch from the hypothetical to the factual mode. I would at first use comments such as 'you remind me of the other family', relating some facts of abuse I think are relevant to this family. On the basis of my own attitude of normality the main technique would be to avoid questions about whether the abuse has taken place or not but to ask questions about specific facts of the abuse. I would ask the mother, 'who suffers most in the family' and I would ask the child whether she felt it had been more difficult for her or for her father to keep the secret.

The basic principle of this kind of intervention is to treat sexual abuse of late adolescents and young adults as if it were an everyday fact, giving constantly reassuring and normalising messages to the different family members when anxieties and defences increase in the process. This way of working is based on undermining the defences of the family members and on decreasing their anxieties. It induces the disclosure through the totally unexpected move of normalising the most exceptional situation. In this approach the family gets disarmed through the surprise of dealing with the greatest secret as an everyday event where the therapist does not question sexual abuse as fact, but where he immediately starts to ask differentiating questions about different experiences and effects on different family members which take the basic fact of the abuse for granted. Carl Whitaker would probably be the only family therapist who could make this move without any problems.

8.10.2 'The maximal drama of normality'

The other extreme of using the same principle of normalising would be to create a 'maximal drama of normality'. I would change the normal course of the family session and say 'I don't know what is happening here today. I just saw a family like you', then going on to talk the family through the abuse saying things like 'you are exactly like the other family I have just seen'. It is important to intersperse differentiating questions such as 'for whom was it worst to keep it bottled up?' and 'when was it most difficult to bear the secret and what will you do now?', using a constant flood of normalising statements. We can also use a specific symptom in the late adolescent or young adult to say that we are surprised to see this symptom again and that we have seen this in many cases of child sexual abuse. We then ask the family not whether sexual abuse has taken place but how it came that this happened to them as well.

The meta-communication in the subtle introduction 'unmentioned creation of reality' and in the opposite of producing a 'maximal crisis of normality' is the same. The meta-communication gives the family the open and explicit licence to communicate about sexual abuse. It gives them the message that I know that sexual abuse may have happened and that I want them to know that I as therapist can deal with child sexual abuse in a non-punitive and non-persecutory way. Using the meta-communication as explicit licence for the family of late adolescents and young adults to communicate about sexual abuse requires one to be extremely flexible and non-dogmatic in reactions to the family's response to us breaking the secret. If families begin to deny the abuse I would switch to the hypothetical 'as if' mode and to a therapy of denial (see Dealing with primary denial, 10.6).

Having mentioned two ways in which it can be possible to disclose sexual abuse in conjoint family sessions I would like to exclude any misunderstanding by saying that this approach is in my opinion only ethical and will only lead to disclosure in families with late adolescents and young adults who are beyond the stage of structural dependency and beyond the age where child protective considerations are relevant. Even then this strategy needs to be used most carefully in order to avoid denial or justified rejection by the family in unfounded suspicions of sexual abuse when therapists have read the signs incorrectly. Therapists therefore need to be very sure clinically that sexual abuse has really happened before they proceed as described.

The general rule remains that the suspicion of ongoing child sexual abuse in structurally dependent children in family therapy needs to lead to a switch from the therapeutic mode into an investigative mode with the child being seen on her or his own as in any other situation of arising vague first-line suspicions. If conjoint family sessions are used inappropriately for attempted disclosures of child sexual abuse the result will be anti-therapeutic therapy and failure to protect (see Interprofessional process in context, 5.2).

8.11 Suspicion of sexual abuse following access visits to fathers

Although allegations of child sexual abuse by mothers may be made falsely as part of marital conflicts in families of separation and divorce, child sexual abuse does also happen to children during access visits to fathers in divorce. If the suspicion of child sexual abuse during access visits is raised by mothers or by professionals, it is important not to act prematurely. Mothers often stop access without any firm evidence and professionals take instant non-therapeutic action responses in unsubstantiated allegations. (see Steps in the crisis intervention of disclosure, 8.2; Suspicion and partial disclosure, 8.3; The interprofessional process in context, 5.2.)

The diagnosis of sexual abuse during access visits is in some respects easier than in ongoing intrafamilial abuse. The time of the suspected abuse can be very accurately determined and mothers are usually very co-operative. The abuse will take place on the day of the child's visit to the father. Before the matter is in any way raised with the child or the father a medical examination of the child should be organised immediately after return from one of the access visits. This will often be on a Monday morning when the examination could take place in the context of a routine school medical examination. Nursery staff can send the child with some unspecific complaints to a doctor who is qualified to collect forensic evidence and who has been informed prior to the intervention and has agreed to co-operate. This procedure will usually be unproblematic when mothers assist in the process. To the child some general reasons such as the school medical or a general medical check-up can be used (see Forensic proof and medical examination, 9.5).

If this procedure is followed with patience and without panic it may in the long run be much more effective than instantly curtailing access following premature verbal confrontations and accusations against the father. Any premature action against divorced fathers who have access to the child also needs to take into account that courts often restore access if the suspicion is not well-founded enough. The danger of sexual abuse can then be enhanced and the intervention can lead to crime-promoting crime prevention and abuse-promoting child protection if sexual abuse continues in secrecy. On the other hand if the suspicion is unfounded and if the allegations are only part of an ongoing separation battle between the parents, the child must not be prevented from retaining a possibly very important relationship with the father.

8.12 The use of prevention films as diagnostic tools in suspicion and disclosure

Prevention films and other prevention materials may have some preventive effect in extrafamilial abuse and in interfamilial abuse of older children. Prevention films have certainly helped to alert adults and to raise awareness, especially in parents and teachers. In cases of long-term child sexual abuse in the family and for young children, prevention films and other prevention materials certainly serve the function of facilitating early disclosure of ongoing sexual abuse of children. The use of prevention films and other prevention materials gives sexually abused children the open and explicit permission to communicate about ongoing abuse (see Explicit therapeutic permission to disclose, 8.5).

8.12.1 Early detection

The function of early detection is central when we use prevention films. Sexually abused children who see prevention films may react to the showing of the film with high anxiety or with other behaviour which can lead to a vague first-line suspicion or a well-founded second-line suspicion of ongoing sexual abuse. Prevention films or any other prevention materials should only be used by professionals who are fully aware that the presentation of the material may lead to the suspicion and disclosure of ongoing sexual abuse in children who watch the film. Prevention films and other materials should therefore only be used in small groups where each child is closely observed for signs of distress and for behaviour which may indicate sexual abuse.

Any vague first-line suspicion which arises during the film can be followed up by discussing with the group of children who have seen the film whether anything similar to what had happened in the film could happen to them, and what they would do if it had happened. The general discussion of possible ways to disclose sexual abuse may initially need to exclude the child who is suspected of having been abused from direct participation. Asking the possibly abused child directly right from the beginning can lead to instant denial. The general discussion with a close friend of the suspected child about what she or a friend would do if she had been sexually abused, playing through all the possibilities of how a child could find help and how children can disclose can help the abused child to feel increasingly confident to disclose to this friend or directly to professionals.

The use of prevention films and prevention materials for early detection has often led to disclosures within the session in which the film was shown and the material presented. The primary use of prevention films and other prevention material for early detection and disclosure requires a careful preparation and co-ordination of the entire professional network for the eventuality of disclosure. It is irresponsible to show prevention films or to work with prevention materials without being prepared to watch out for indicators of ongoing sexual abuse in the children who are involved and without taking the possibility of disclosures into account and preparing the professional network accordingly.

8.12.2 Giving explicit licence and permission to disclose

The function of prevention films and other prevention material which tells stories about other children who are sexually abused has on a generalised level exactly the same function as telling a child 'The Story of the Other Child'. Showing prevention films or telling 'The Story of the Other Child' equally serve as explicit therapeutic permission to communicate about sexual abuse. While 'The Story of the Other Child' can be individualised and can be used during the therapuetic process the prevention film has usually a more generalised function for early detection and disclosure in schools and in children's groups, in youth organisations and churches. (See Giving explicit licence to communicate, 2.4.2; Explicit therapeutic permission to disclose, 8.5.)

Prevention films and other prevention material can also be used in specific cases of vague first-line suspicions. Prevention material for the whole group can be used to deal with a suspicion of sexual abuse concerning a specific child in the group, especially in group situations in 'the world in between' of playgroups, nurseries, schools and youth clubs where children attend regular events. (See First-line suspicion, second-line suspicion and partial disclosure, 8.3.)

Teachers who have a vague suspicion of sexual abuse of one of the children in the class can use the showing of a prevention film to observe the particular child in question. In order to be able to respond more effectively it can be helpful for the head of the school or for the educational social worker to be present. They may have the task of linking up with others in the professional network and to co-ordinate the intervention even if they are not the 'Trusted Person'. Showing the prevention film or working with other prevention materials can lead to a full disclosure but as in the individualised 'Story of the Other Child' the child may not react immediately. It can take weeks or months until the suspicion has become well-founded enough for professionals to initiate a disclosure or until the child discloses herself. (See The use of the 'trusted person', 8.6.)

8.13 Preparing fellow professionals for impending disclosure

We may often have to prepare professionals of other agencies with whom we have not worked before for an impending disclosure. At these moments we need to keep the distinction between the crisis of the professionals and the family crisis firmly in mind. In order to control and contain the professional crisis it can be very helpful to approach the unknown policeman, the unknown social worker, the headmistress who is not used to dealing with sexual abuse or the nursery worker, by addressing the potential professional crisis first before thinking about what to do with the family. We can approach our fellow professionals with the problem of suspected child sexual abuse without immediately giving the name of the child. This allows the professional network to remain problem oriented. The Anonymous Diagnostic Interprofessional Consultation (ADIC) helps to avoid taking premature actions which are driven by the professional's own crisis. (See Crisis of disclosure – crisis of professionals and family crisis, 8.1; Anonymous Diagnostic Interprofessional Consultation, 8.4.)

We may say that the situation is not yet very acute even if it is in fact relatively urgent. This line of action is not taken in order to deceive fellow professionals, nor to delay a necessary and urgent intervention. This way of working helps in a multi-professional framework to deal with the crucial distinction between the professional crisis and the family crisis. Introducing the problem of child sexual abuse at first without name, or time scale, gives our fellow professionals time to think in a problem-oriented and differentiated way about their own task in relation to the tasks of other professionals and to the family.

I find it useful to prepare a fellow professional in four areas.

1 I would tell the story of a possible suspicion giving all the evidence I have, but in general terms and without naming names.
2 I would outline what I think my own professional responsibility and role would be in a possible crisis intervention.
3 I would ask the fellow professional from the other agency what he thinks his task would be and how he thinks his task would relate to my task and to the task of any other professional.
4 Finally I would ask the professional how he would want to achieve the task he has identified as his specific professional task.

In child sexual abuse as syndrome of secrecy and addiction we often have only one chance of disclosure and in the majority of cases we rely on admissions of abusers even if we have medical evidence. The anonymous preparation of a fellow professional for an impending intervention reflects in a very ethical and problem-solving way the specific nature of child sexual abuse as syndrome of secrecy. The differentiation between the professional crisis and the family crisis, and the differentiation between interprofessional work directed towards information gathering and work preparing for the intervention in the family, and the need to differentiate between the information-oriented Anonymous Diagnostic Interprofessional Consultation and the action-oriented pre-intervention meeting often require the anonymous preparation of a fellow professional. The anonymous preparation of a colleague in another agency can avoid premature disclosure and an uncoordinated approach which often leads to non-thrapeutic action responses out of the initial crisis in the professional network. (See The interprofessional process, 5.1, 5.2; Steps in the crisis intervention of disclosure, 8.2; Suspicion and partial disclosure, 8.3.)

Chapter nine

Disclosure

9.1 The interlocking process between the explicit therapeutic permission to communicate and legal interviewing

The confusion between talking to children in a way in which we give explicit therapeutic permission to disclose child sexual abuse as syndrome of secrecy and legal interviewing of children according to the legal requirements of the rules of evidence which holds up in court leads to a high failure rate in identifying child sexual abuse. Giving explicit therapeutic permission to disclose sexual abuse and legal interviewing of children for legal purposes are complementary processes. Showing prevention films and telling 'The Story of the Other Child' as explicit permission to communicate often need to happen first before children will trust and disclose their own sexual abuse. The very moment a child starts to disclose her own abuse, professionals need to switch from the metaphorical mode into the reality mode of neutral questioning which allows the child to relate her own experience in a way which is factual and non-suggestive (see Explicit therapeutic permission to disclose, 8.5).

Telling 'The Story of the Other Child' is no different from showing children prevention films on child sexual abuse. Prevention films do not only have exactly the same effect as the individualised 'Story of the Other Child'. Prevention films do in fact follow exactly the same principle. A story of another child is shown who has been sexually abused. Seeing this story is often understood by sexually abused children as explicit permission to disclose their own abuse (see The use of prevention films, 8.12).

Prevention films which give children explicit licence to communicate are not seen as putting ideas in children's minds when they lead to disclosure. 'Telling the Story' as explicit therapeutic permission to disclose needs to be seen in the same way as prevention films and prevention books. As permission to communicate about sexual abuse as syndrome of secrecy, they foster a process which is complementary to the legal interviewing of children (see Child sexual abuse as syndrome of secrecy, 2.1).

To take the necessary time to collect sufficient facts for a well-founded second-line suspicion prior to a full disclosure often leads to quicker and more effective help than rushing into action at the stage of a vague first-line suspicion out of the crisis in the professional network. Talking to children in order to give the explicit therapeutic licence to disclose is often a much earlier process than the legal interviewing of children at the time of disclosure. Talking to children in order to give the explicit permission to communicate happens at the stage of a vague first-line suspicion when premature attempts at legal interviewing would most likely lead to early denial and to crime-promoting crime prevention or abuse-promoting child protection (see The interprofessional process in context, 5.2).

The often thought-blocking urgency to establish legal facts pushes professionals into premature legal interviewing of children. It is overlooked that an anxious child may disclose more readily, openly and fully when we have previously talked to her in a way which has given the child explicit permission to reveal child sexual abuse as syndrome of secrecy. Children have often already talked about sexual abuse in secret ways before they come out openly during the legal interview. The better the child is prepared by having received the explicit permission to communicate, the less will be the anxiety of disclosing and the more successfully will a later legal interview reveal the necessary facts.

Legal, child protective and treatment agencies will need to understand the difference between legal interviewing of children and the need for talking to children as metaphorical permission to disclose child sexual abuse as syndrome of secrecy before the complementary nature of the two forms of communicating with children can be clearly acknowledged as two distinct and equally necessary processes. The reference to the analogous nature of prevention films as metaphor to give children explicit permission to disclose will help to differentiate between the two processes. To give children explicit permission to disclose by telling 'The Story of the Other Child' obstructs the course of justice as little as showing prevention films. Nor does 'The Story of the Other Child' put anything suggestive in the child's mind as long as it is unmistakably clear to the child that it is purely the professional's own thought. 'The Story of the Other Child' and prevention films equally use the metaphor of a third person to communicate indirectly above sexual abuse and to give the permission to disclose without manipulating the child.

Legal and therapeutic agencies will be able to use the differentiated process to further the legal and child protective process as well as therapy, if we understand that giving children the explicit licence to disclose and the legal interviewing of children are complementary processes which are both needed. Ideally both processes could be used by one professional with appropiate skills. It can even be used within a legal disclosure interview as long as the different functions and processes of the two forms of communictions are clearly distinguished by the interviewing professional.

9.2 Legal interviewing of children

Legal interviewing of children in order to obtain objective information in a way which is accepted by child protective agencies and in courts is different from giving children explicit therapeutic permission to disclose in the domain of child mental health. Legal interviewing of children takes place in the context of the legal domain and it is part of the process of a full disclosure interview. A prolonged stage of suspicion and partial disclosure may precede and the disclosure may even be the result of an earlier telling of 'The Story of the Other Child' as explicit therapeutic permission for the child to disclose.

Interviewing children for legal facts may be very different according to the age and stage of development. In a 15-year-old girl the interview will usually involve direct and neutral questioning, taking very much the form of an adult interview. In small children non-verbal communications such as drawings and playing are essential to the diagnostic process. Jones and McQuiston (1985) have stressed the importance of patience and the fact that the interview may have to extend over several sessions.

In order to establish rapport with the child in the beginning, periods of free play are important to establish a personal relationship with the interviewer. Cues need to be taken from the child and not to be put into the child's mind. On the other hand, clues given by the child about sexual abuse have to be followed up closely and instantly with neutral clarifying questions. This is very important because children sometimes give us only one chance. A child for example may show us a special sequence of play. If we do not take up this sequence instantly and follow it up closely it may become impossible to establish any facts of the abuse by further abstract neutral questioning and encouragement of the child. It is crucially important to communicate on the actual cognitive, intellectual, psycho-social and psycho-sexual developmental level of the child. We need to take into account that young children may respond to questions about objective facts very much in the context of the relationship aspects with the interviewer. A child may therefore easily tell us what she thinks we want to hear. This can happen irrespective of whether we ask neutral questions or not. It is related to the child's general stage and level of development.

During the interview we can use four main types of questions:

1 Open questions.
2 Closed questions.
3 Choice questions.
4 Hypothetical questions.

Open questions enable children to relate their own point of view. The question 'What happened when you went to see your daddy last Sunday?' does not suggest any particular answer. The closed question 'Did your daddy put his finger into your fanny?' clearly suggests the possibility of sexual abuse and can only be answered by 'yes' or 'no'. The choice question 'Did he put his finger on the fanny or down between your legs?' suggests in a similar way one of two given possibilities. Hypothetical questions like 'If he had put his finger into the doll's fanny would the girl doll have told her mummy?' raises a topic which is introduced by the interviewer.

For the strict legal process only responses to open questions are admissible. Children however will often not reveal factual information when asked strictly neutral questions. Other types of questions are necessary and can be used to facilitate the process but they need to be followed directly by an open question. For example 'Did he touch you with his hand?' then needs to be followed by the open question 'What did he do?'. A constant switch between the different modes of questioning is therefore necessary (see Jones and McQuiston, 1985).

Especially in young children, drawings, play and behaviour during the use of anatomically correct dolls and other diagnostic materials are crucial (see The use of anatomically correct dolls, 9.4). Older children may be helped by describing their worst nightmare and by working with ambiguous picture cards through which sexually abused children describe their abuse. All children who are legally interviewed need the explicit licence and permission to communicate their secret before they can fully disclose.

9.3 Organising the disclosure interview

The disclosure interview should be conducted conjointly by the social worker with statutory responsibility, in the presence of the Trusted Person to whom the child has initially disclosed or in whose presence the child has displayed the symptoms which led to the initial suspicion, and if required in the presence of the police if legal evidence is needed (see The use of the 'trusted person', 8.6).

The use of a one-way mirror can be very helpful with young pre-school children. It means that only the child, the interviewer and the Trusted Person need be in the interview room. Everybody else can be behind the screen. The advantages of the use of a one-way mirror with young children should determine the venue of the disclosure interview rather than territorial considerations of the different agencies involved. This does not hold for older children, who are much more aware of the people behind the screen. With older children we need to assess whether it is more helpful to have everyone involved in the interview room. When the police officer is not the person who conducts the interview, arrangements can be made to ensure that the information is gained in a legally acceptable way. Communication between the people behind the screen and the interviewer can be by telephone, by earbug, by written messages or by means of introducing breaks through knocking at the door of the interview room.

It can be helpful to video a formal disclosure interview. Video material becomes increasingly acceptable in several countries, at least as supporting evidence in wardship cases and in care proceedings. The confrontation of alleged abusers with the video-taped evidence can be a powerful tool to help abusers to admit. The surprise effect and the effect of seeing the child on the video does in some cases help abusers who had previously denied to change their mind and to admit to the abuse.

The mother of the child needs always to be involved although she may have different roles according to the specific situation. If the mother herself has brought the child and has initiated the disclosure she herself is the Trusted Person. She should be in the room during the disclosure interview if a brief assessment prior to the disclosure interview has shown that she will be able to support the child during the session. We need to be aware that even supportive mothers are often so upset during the interview that they give children the direct or indirect message not to disclose. Or children get so anxious that they close up in order to protect their mothers. (See Disclosure by children, 9.6; Disclosure by mothers, 9.7; Disclosure by professionals, 9.8.)

When the mother is not the Trusted Person the mother should ideally be behind a one-way mirror in order to witness the disclosure. The family secret is broken when the mother hears the story directly from the child herself. In child sexual abuse as syndrome of secrecy it is most important for mothers actually to see and to witness directly what the child is doing and saying. Only hearing the facts of the abuse from the child herself may enable mothers to believe that sexual abuse has really happened. If the mother is behind the screen, it is important to have talked to her on her own beforehand in preparation for the interview. The professional network needs to have agreed, prior to joining up with the mother behind the screen, about the possible action to be taken for the child and about the possible involvement of the mother in the subsequent intervention. It is important to have one professional especially allocated to the mother behind the screen, in order to help and to support her during an often extremely upsetting event. (See Child sexual abuse as syndrome of secrecy, 2.1; The individual process in context, 2.4; Family pattern, 3.2).

If the mother is behind the one-way mirror during the interview mother and child need to be brought together instantly after the interview and the facts the child has just disclosed need to be retold to the mother openly and fully in front of the child. This handover meeting helps mothers to come to terms with the facts of the abuse and with the abuse as fact. The handover meeting gives children the permission to talk about the abuse to their mothers and it helps mothers to become protective towards the child during the difficult time of disclosure. (See Proof and belief, 1.5; The handover meeting, 9.14).

A handover meeting at the end of the disclosure interview is also necessary when the child is placed outside the family with other carers. The new carers need to be told in front of the child about the events during the interview in order to be able to help the child with the aftermath of the disclosure.

Prior to the disclosure interview the professionals need to agree on how to approach the alleged abuser. If the abuse has been committed by a father, a stepfather or another member of the family at home, one member of the professional network needs to confront the abuser immediately after the disclosure interiew. This needs to happen before the mother or the child can talk to him. There is a great danger of subsequent denial by the abuser when the mother or the child are able to contact the father before he has been confronted by a professional. (See The interprofessional process in context, 5.2; Steps in the crisis intervention of disclosure, 8.2.)

We must not forget siblings. Only too often siblings of sexually abused children are left out and are forgotten in the process. Siblings of sexually abused children need to be involved in the disclosure process for several reasons.

1 In the turmoil of investigations and separations in families of child sexual abuse, all siblings are affected by the disclosure of sexual abuse and the subsequent family crisis.
2 Children who have not been abused may nevertheless have known about the abuse and are part of the secrecy system of child sexual abuse. They therefore need to be involved in the disclosure.
3 Finally we must not forget that brothers and sisters of sexually abused children may themselves have been sexually abused.

We need to assess in each case how to include siblings in the disclosure. They certainly need to be part of the initial family meeting. Sometimes they may also need to be involved in the initial disclosure interview, either behind the screen with a special person assessing the child's reaction to the disclosure of the sibling or even in the interview room. In several cases in which I have involved siblings in the disclosure interviews behind the screen or in the room, they themselves have disclosed abuse as well.

Usually it is more appropriate to have separate disclosure interviews. In the case of a 3-year-old girl who demonstrated oral intercourse during the disclosure interview, I had decided to include her elder brothers of 8 and 11 years because it was already known that a cousin of the girl had also been sexually abused by the girl's father. Previously there had been no suspicion that any of the boys had been sexually abused as well. During the interview with the dolls the oldest brother started to behave in a way which led to a clear suspicion that he may also have been abused. Subsequently this suspicion became increasingly well-founded and finally led to the disclosure of long-term sexual abuse by the boy's father. (See Clinical example, Section 9.4; Siblings in families of child sexual abuse, 14.1.)

The rate of admission of abusers increases the better the intervention is prepared by the professional network, the more facts are available and the more the person who confronts the suspected abuser feels supported by the professional network and by the facts of the evidence before him. This interactional element has a very important effect on the rate of admissions in child sexual abuse. We need to keep in mind that health and mental health professionals, and especially therapists, are often not the best qualified professionals to confront abusers. Well-trained social workers or police officers may be much better at undertaking this task. Good preparation of the intervention and a careful documentation of facts with which we can confront the abuser together with a certain surprise effect of the meeting often help abusers to admit to the abuse.

We need to keep in mind that the professional who confronts the father and the parents does this as an expert in her own name and not in the name of the child. The professional needs to meet the alleged abuser as an expert who conveys that the child has shown certain symptoms and has said certain things which the professional herself can only explain through sexual abuse. It is imperative to use the facts from the assessment of the child without giving the child the responsibility for the allegation by the professional. The accusation needs to be made by the professional in her own name as illustrated in Figure 9.1.

It is important that the professional makes the allegation in her own name and as result of her own professional judgement, in order to avoid the child becoming the centre of conflict between professionals and parents about the allegation of child sexual abuse. Otherwise the child is forced into an impossible no-win situation between her loyalty to the parents and the wish to disclose. This unfortunately common situation often leads to the scapegoating of the child or to the child's withdrawal of the disclosure. When the professionals confront the abuser in their own name using the material from the child to back their own conclusion of abuse, the child cannot be triangulated and the abuser has to deal with the professional as the person who makes the allegation. It is then much more difficult to scapegoat the child.

Abusers often make counter-accusations that the child has always been a pathological liar and that she always had a dirty fantasy. In this situation the professional needs to confront the abuser as a professional with his own professional conclusions that child sexual abuse has most likely taken place. This judgement is the professional's judgement and has nothing to do with the child. To keep the confrontation on the level between the alleged abuser and the professional maintains the appropriate level between two adults about responsible or irresponsible parenting. The child remains in the position of a structurally dependent child who needs representation and protection by an adult in a parenting capacity.

9.4 The use of anatomically correct dolls, drawings and other diagnostic materials

Anatomically correct dolls do not solve any problem in the evaluation of child sexual abuse if they are not used with competence, skill and sensitively in the overall context of communicating with children and and in the context of child sexual abuse as syndrome of secrecy. They can become very helpful when they are used by a professional who is skilled and competent in communicating with children about issues of secrecy with or without the dolls. To put it into a metaphor: the cake is the knowledge about communicating with children on the level of their current psycho-social development and about communicating with children about child sexual abuse as syndrome of secrecy. The anatomical dolls

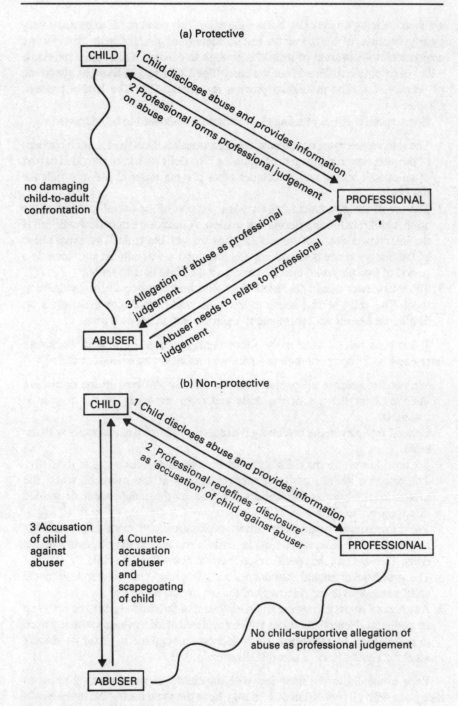

Figure 9.1 Confronting the alleged abuser

are then the icing on the cake, but not the cake. This point needs to be made very clearly because of the common rescue fantasy of professionals that putting anatomical dolls in front of a child is enough to conduct a disclosure interview with young children. This is not the case. (See Child sexual abuse as syndrome of secrecy, 2.1; The individual process in context, 2.4; The family process, Chapter 3.)

Some specific issues of using the anatomical dolls need to be addressed.

1 The interviewer must not present the anatomical dolls as the essential element of the interview right from the beginning. The dolls should be provided as part of an overall setting which includes other playing material and materials for drawing.
2 The use of the anatomical dolls needs to be part of the overall context of the adult–child relationship during the session. A disclosure interview will fail if the interviewer does not emotionally link up with the child. The initial phase of the interview needs to address this issue and we usually need to include a period of free play with the child and give the child time to settle.
3 The interviewer should not handle the dolls himself, especially not undressing them. The child herself needs to have the chance to discover the dolls, to familiarise herself with them and to undress them in her own time.

It has been helpful to keep the following seven steps in mind in disclosure interviews with young children in which we use anatomically correct dolls:

1 We need to prepare all people who are directly involved in the disclosure interviews for the use of the dolls and other explicitly sexual diagnostic materials.
2 General free play in the beginning is necessary to link up emotionally with the child.
3 We need to wait for the child's spontaneous or guided discovery of the dolls.
4 The specific sexual abuse diagnosis begins at the moment when the professional observes the child's reaction to the independent or guided discovery of the dolls.
5 The professional begins her active exploration and evaluation with her response to her observations of the child's reaction to the discovery of the dolls. The lead and the specific clues need to come from the child.
6 The professional should introduce sexual language only in response to the child's reactions to the discovery of the sex organs of the dolls.
7 Any sign of anxiety, freezing and withdrawal of the child needs to be taken up immediately. Neutral questions which are aimed at information gathering need to be followed by questions which address and explore in anxiety-reducing ways the child's fears of possible disasters.

Prior to the disclosure interview with the child a separate meeting needs to take place with all professionals who may be in the room during the interview. It is important to prepare the Trusted Person and any other professional who will be in the room for the use of the anatomically correct dolls and for the use of explicit sexual language. Professionals, as much as others, may be embarrassed or upset by the use of the dolls or by hearing the child's story of sexual abuse.

The preparation of all professionals is necessary in order to avoid their apprehensive or upset reaction making the child frightened and withdrawn during the interview. If professionals, and especially if mothers, get upset during the interview, the child will instantly pick up this communication, which usually leads to a failure to disclose. The preparation of the professionals in the room is therefore an integral and crucial part of the procedure of using the dolls. If mothers are involved I would always talk to them separately from the child prior to the interview and would show them the dolls and let them undress the dolls to see what they look like. I would also use explicit sexual language to prepare mothers or fellow professionals for the interview.

I start the interview by talking about non-related issues with the aim of linking up with the child and making contact through general play and conversation. The dolls are usually not openly visible. They are in a closed box to which the child has free access. This is helpful because the child is not instantly confronted with the dolls and I have time to make emotional contact with the child. The specific diagnostic sequence begins with the child's discovery of the dolls.

If the child does not approach the box to find out what is in it, I initiate a 'guided discovery' of the doll's genitals which represent the suspected abuser. I would in a throw-away sentence say to the child 'I think there are some more toys in the box'. I may say this just as a digression from talking to the adults about something unrelated to the abuse. I would then watch the child's discovery of the dolls. Sometimes children immediately start to undress the dolls. In other cases the child may need some encouragement and again this encouragement should not happen in concentrating on the dolls. I may even try to avoid directly playing with the child at that stage, but may address the Trusted Person and let the child play by herself. If the child does not start to undress the dolls I would again say in a throw-away remark 'look, they have got some lovely buttons and I wonder whether you can undo buttons'.

It is very important not to concentrate on the dolls at this stage, but to allow the child to discover the dolls and to undress them in her own time and only to punctuate the process if necessary. This is so crucial because one of the most diagnostically valuable moments is the child's first reaction to her own discovery of the sex organs of the dolls when she starts to unclothe them. The very first reaction of the child to seeing the genitals of the dolls often gives crucial information about sexual abuse. The child may become instantly tearful and frightened. Some children become frozen with fear. Some talk spontaneously in a way which openly indicates sexual abuse. Some children get suddenly very excited and start to play in a very explicit sexualised way. Others show in their very initial reaction that, most likely, they have not been sexually abused. There are many verbal or non-verbal indicators of sexual abuse triggered by the very first discovery of the sex organs of the anatomical dolls.

The strongest reaction is usually displayed in the very first response to the discovery of the penis of the adult male doll. A 3-year-old girl who was suspected of having been sexually abused by her father undressed the dolls whilst I was talking to the nursery nurse. I only watched the girl from the side, letting her get on with the discovery and the undressing of the dolls herself, without giving her any open attention, only prompting her about the buttons. The girl undressed first the mother doll and then the father doll. She showed an immediate reaction of extreme excitement to the naked father doll. She looked up at me with a searching glance. In a quick move she put the penis of the father doll fully into her mouth, moving it in and out repeatedly. In doing so she closely watched my reactions and seemed to be relieved and calm when I reacted to her reactions to the discovery of the dolls in a very casual way, asking her what she had got there in her mouth. She looked at me intently and whispered 'a willy'.

Responding to the child's own reaction to the discovery of the dolls I established the facts of the sexual abuse by neutrally asking the child about what was happening, always following her lead. Her whispered answer 'a willy' already indicated that she was either frightened or knew that she was talking about a secret. In the process of the interview it became clear that she knew that she was communicating a secret. I then asked 'what happens to the willy'. She put it in and out of her mouth again looking apprehensive and excited. When I asked her who was doing this to her, she replied 'the daddy doll', then following on saying spontaneously 'this is not the real daddy'. In this disclosure interview the very quick interaction at the moment when the child had put the penis of the daddy doll into her mouth led to a clear and undisputed disclosure of sexual abuse by the father.

It can take more than one session to get a disclosure and the use of anatomically correct dolls is no short cut in this process. The child needs to be well settled and needs to be comfortable and understood before the specific disclosure process can begin. Prompting the child at some stage during the interview to discover the dolls and prompting to undress them by talking about buttons can sometimes be helpful. If the child's reaction to the discovery of the dolls is paralysing anxiety and avoidance the interviewer must not push the child back into using the dolls but needs to deal with the anxiety about approaching the dolls first. To give the child explicit therapeutic permission to communicate and to address the child's anxieties as outlined in Section 8.5 can in some cases be a complementary and necessary element at this point in the interview if we want to achieve an objective and valid diagnostic evaluation.

Other tools of non-verbal communication about sexual abuse may need to be employed when a child reacts with open fear to the discovery of the sex organs of the dolls. We can ask the child to draw her family. Sometimes children draw explicit sexual scenes which lead to a subsequent full and open disclosure of sexual abuse. We can ask the child to draw her worst nightmare or to draw the most scary thing they could see through a keyhole. We can use ambiguous pictures which the child may relate to sexual abuse and we can use other play material which addresses the problems of communicating child sexual abuse as syndrome of secrecy.

Put into context the use of anatomical dolls in the evaluation of child sexual abuse can be extremely helpful. But it also shows that the dolls are only one tool amongst others and that they can only be used in an overall context of communicating appropriately with the child. Other ways and alleys of communication may have to be explored as well.

9.5 Forensic proof and medical examination

Unequivocal medical and forensic evidence is not only helpful to the child protective and legal process, it is also of great therapeutic value. To be able to confront the abuser with unequivocal proof of sexual abuse and with factual evidence spares the child from having to give evidence and to make legally conclusive statements. It also makes it impossible that the abuser, the child or any other family member withdraw the accusation again under psychological pressure following the initial disclosure.

For forensic reasons an immediate medical inspection and examination of the vaginal and anal area may be necessary. Swabs for sperm and for other material from the abuser need to be taken from the thighs, the vaginal and anal areas and if necessary from the hands and from other parts of the body. A forensic examination should only be conducted by a well trained doctor and after careful preparation of the child. During the examination only a minimum of people should be present including the doctor, the Trusted Person, whose presence is extremely important, and a minimum of the necessary medical personnel. It is often less frightening for the child if the examination is conducted by a woman doctor. However, the medical examination through a skilled and sensitive doctor takes clear precedence over the gender of the examiner. If there is no indication of sexual abuse over the last 3 days, the advantages and disadvantages of an immediate medical examination need to be carefully considered in each case.

Whether the medical examination is conducted by a paediatrician or a police surgeon needs to be decided according to the setting and the skills of the doctors involved. The advantage of involving a police surgeon is the fact that a police surgeon may be able to collect additional forensic evidence such as hairs or fibres from the clothes of the abuser which can lead to unequivocal proof. The advantage of the investigation by a paediatrician on a paediatric ward can lie in the less threatening setting in which the examination takes place and in the special expertise of paediatricians in physically examining frightened children who need to be soothed and reassured. A well functioning professional network will attempt to combine both advantages. In some areas local authorities are setting up special units for the investigations of child sexual abuse similar to the special units for rape victims. Close co-operation between police surgeons and other medical practitioners is absolutely vital in order to avoid a repetition of the examination which, if repeated after several days or weeks, may be of very limited value anyway.

The medical examination can have two very different starting points. The examination can follow a suspicion or allegation of sexual abuse or a routine examination may itself lead to a first suspicion. When the primary suspicion originates from the medical examination we may have unequivocal medical evidence but we may have no idea who may have abused the child. In cases in which a child is sent for a medical examination following a suspicion or a partial disclosure, the medical examination is already part of the disclosure process itself. If a first suspicion arises from a medical examination the results of the medical examination need to be recorded carefully. Even if the examination gives clear evidence of child sexual abuse, doctors must not initiate a disclosure towards the family at this point. The results of the medical examination must be taken in the context of the overall planning of the intervention. (See Preparation for disclosure, Chapter 8.)

The value of medical evidence needs to be put into context. First we have only a minority of less than 20 per cent of cases with unequivocal medical evidence. Even if we have medical evidence of sexual abuse, we still have no forensic proof as to the identity of the abuser. Medical evidence of sexual abuse is very different from forensic proof which identifies the abuser. In all cases of doubtful or proven medical evidence in which we have no forensic evidence about the abuser the medical evidence can only be taken as one factor amongst others in the assessment and evaluation. Medical evidence without forensic proof as to the identity of the abuser needs to be taken as one part of the evidence which needs to be judged in the context of child sexual abuse as a syndrome of secrecy. It needs to be assessed whether the medical evidence has to count as a weak first-line suspicion or as a well-founded second-line suspicion and the intervention needs to proceed accordingly. (See The individual process, Chapter 2; First-line suspicion and second-line suspicion, 8.3.)

The first-line or second-line suspicion from the medical examination is no different from any other suspicion and requires the same steps in the preparation of the intervention. Professionals need some idea as to the identity of the abuser. Without having any idea who the abuser could be, the opening crisis intervention can be very difficult. The structure of the intervention in medically proven cases of sexual abuse would be very different if the child had been abused outside the family or by a family member. (See Family pattern, 3.2; Extrafamilial child sexual abuse, Chapter 13.)

9.6 Disclosure by children

A full disclosure is usually triggered by the mother, by the child or by professionals. The three different forms of disclosure need to be handled differently. Children often disclose directly to a professional or to another adult outside the family who becomes the Trusted Person. Or the child discloses indirectly via a friend or a peer at school in whom the child has confided. Intentional disclosures are more frequent in older children and adolescents who disclose in settings and to professionals of the 'world in between'; that is between home where they are too frightened to disclose and the world outside where they do not know people and do not trust to be helped. This brings school teachers, nursery teachers and other professionals in the educational system into the centre of disclosure work (see Disclosure at school, 9.9).

When a child makes an intentional full disclosure we need to sit down with the child and talk to her on her own and listen patiently to what the child has to disclose. At the moment of crisis the child will be very open and will be prepared to tell more than at any other time. The first professional who sits down with the child must not panic and must not think how he can instantly involve other professionals at that stage. He should take all the time necessary to listen fully to the child. It is important to realise that the person to whom the child discloses has become the Trusted Person. (See Child sexual abuse as syndrome of secrecy, 2.1; The individual process in context, 2.4; The use of the 'trusted person', 8.6.)

If the Trusted Person remains with the child throughout the disclosure process none of the facts the child has disclosed will get lost. Many professionals are instantly worried about whether they may interfere with child protective or legal requirements, and make the common mistake of not sitting down calmly with the child and listening to what the child has to say. Children then get hastily referred. Without having established what children have to disclose to the Trusted Person they are sent off to total strangers they do not know. Children who are hastily referred to social workers, police or other 'experts' who are strangers often close up again.

When the child has told her story, and when the Trusted Person has the feeling that the child has told the whole story, the Trusted Person needs to talk to the child about the next steps which need to be taken. If the child is pre-adolescent or a young adolescent, other professionals need to be involved within hours and the disclosure may have to be made to the family on the very same day. With older adolescents it may sometimes be possible to make a contract to delay the disclosure towards the family until the next day. It may be possible to say that we will have to think about what the child has told us and that we will have to talk to some other colleagues about what needs to happen next. The professional needs to give the child the exact time at which she will see her the next day and she needs to promise the child not to disclose towards the family until after the specified time of the next meeting. This contract gives the professional the time to prepare the crisis intervention in the family and to co-ordinate the professional network. However, this procedure will only be possible in a small number of cases where the child is mature enough and not too upset and where the professional network needs time for preparation. (See The family and the professional network, Chapter 4; The pre-intervention meeting, 8.7; Preparing fellow professionals for impending disclosure, 8.13.)

In the majority of cases the disclosure towards the family needs to take place the same day. When the child has confided in the Trusted Person, the Trusted Person should explain to the child carefully the most likely following steps, including the intervention by other professionals. The Trusted Person then needs to activate the professional network. The first step is to organise a formal disclosure interview with all professionals involved in which the child repeats once what she has disclosed to the Trusted Person. If there are any indications that sexual abuse has taken place over the last 3 days, a medical examination should take place as soon as possible (see Forensic proof and medical examination, 9.5).

We need to be aware that initial disclosures by children are very often only partial disclosures. Children come out with lesser abuse first before they trust to tell the full story, often much later. Some children say initially that they have only been abused once and they might implicate a stranger. Only later when they trust do they disclose long term abuse by friends, family members and fathers (see Clinical example, the P family, 4.2.3).

The disclosure to the family needs to follow as soon as the professional network has planned and co-ordinated the intervention. At first professionals need to assess what role the mother should have in the disclosure interview. The mother needs to be contacted and asked to come to the place where the child has disclosed without being already told over the phone the reason for the emergency. On the mother's arrival one professional needs to talk to the mother on her own, separately from the child, in order to inform her about the child's disclosure and to assess from the mother's reaction how much she will be an ally of the child during the following formal disclosure interview or how much she may link up with the abuser against the child. If the mother does not believe, or expresses hostility towards, the child she certainly should not be in the room during the disclosure interview because she will give open or indirect messages to the child not to disclose. Even mothers who are assessed as being allies of the child may be so upset themselves that they will frighten the child, who might be prevented from disclosing. After the child's disclosure the abuser should then be confronted with the disclosure of the abuse as soon as possible and without prior contact with either the mother or the child. (See Organising the disclosure interview, 9.3.)

9.7 Disclosure by mothers

If the mother is the person who informs the professionals she needs to be regarded as the Trusted Person. It is with her whom the professionals should talk first.

1 It is best to talk initially to the mother on her own in detail and without panic

about the specific allegations of the child or the specific things the mother has seen about the abuse.

2   The family situation and the most likely reaction of the abuser towards the confrontation with the allegation of child sexual abuse need to be clarified with the mother.

3   The professionals need to discuss with the mother the likely steps of the crisis intervention.

If the mother is too upset herself the professionals may need to help her to help the child to disclose. Otherwise the mother herself as Trusted Person can prepare the child in the presence of the professionals for the disclosure interview which should follow. If the mother is not too upset she as Trusted Person should be present in the interview room during the disclosure interview. (See The use of the 'trusted person', 8.6.)

We need to keep in mind that protective mothers can also be very upset and may need a lot of help and attention in their own right during the disclosure interview. Also, protective mothers can feel extremely torn between their loyalties towards the abused child and the abuser. The need to assess whether the child can go home or not and how child protective issues will be affected by an admission or by denial of the alleged abuser need to be discussed with the mother right at the beginning. The difficult question of whether the mother will choose for the child or whether she would link up with the abuser against the child if he denies needs to be explicitly addressed with the mother. Any further action can only follow an assessment which also needs to take into account that the mother's allegations can in certain circumstances be false. (See Allegations in separation and divorce, 8.8; Munchausen Syndrome-by-proxy in sexually abused mothers, 14.6.)

9.8 Disclosure by professionals

The first task of a full disclosure induced by professionals is to establish the facts of the sexual abuse in a structured disclosure interview. The advantage of a disclosure by professionals lies in the fact that professionals can often determine the point in time when they are ready to trigger the disclosure. Weak first-line suspicions can be firmed up sufficiently over time into well-founded second-line suspicions and the professional network can be prepared and co-ordinated fully before the family crisis of disclosure is induced. The disadvantages of a disclosure induced by professionals lie in the need to establish the facts of the abuse from the child on her own, often without any support from the mother or other family members. (See Child sexual abuse as syndrome of secrecy, 2.1; The family process, Chapter 3; The family and the professional network, Chapter 4; The professional network, Chapter 5.)

Repeated interviewing of children should be avoided. Since the time and the place of the disclosure interview are very much determined by professionals, repeated interviewing should not be necessary. Repeated interviewing may not only lead to psychological damage. Children often change the story because they get confused and interpret repeated questioning as threatening. Young children may tell different stories because the repeated questioning is seen by the child as not having given a good enough answer at the first interview. Children often fall back into lying and denial in order to avoid the anxiety and the confusion of repeated interviews.

We need to distinguish between the repetition of the formal disclosure interview and a possible repetition of an initial disclosure of the child who has confided in the Trusted Person. It can be crucial that the Trusted Person talk to the child on her own, inducing the disclosure prior to the formal disclosure interview which, as a multi-professional interview, can be very threatening and frightening to the child. After the Trusted Person has induced the disclosures in the child she can help the child to repeat the disclosure and talk about the abuse, which the child might often not do unless the Trusted Person has talked to her before. The Trusted Person can help the child to relate the facts of the abuse in the often frightening and intimidating setting of an official disclosure interview in which the child needs to talk to people she has never met before. (See The use of the 'trusted person', 8.6.)

In disclosures initiated by professionals the mother needs to be approached in the same way as in disclosures initiated by children (see Disclosure by children, 9.6.). The professionals often have the opportunity to assess prior to the disclosure whether the mother might be protective or not. We need to bear in mind that in a disclosure initiated by the professionals the mother is not necessarily the Trusted Person and unfortunately can not be taken automatically as a natural ally of the child. The best procedure during the disclosure interview can be to place the mother behind the one-way mirror or to conduct the interview without the mother, retelling the story to the mother in a handover meeting immediately after the disclosure interview (see The handover meeting, 9.14).

9.9 Disclosure at school

School for older children and nursery for young children are the most important places of the 'world in between', in between home and the strange world outside where children increasingly disclose child sexual abuse. It is very important that teachers and other staff in schools and nurseries are trained to detect signs and symptoms of sexual abuse and that they know how to handle suspicions and children's disclosures. (See Preparation for disclosure, Chapter 8; Organising the disclosure interview, 9.3; Disclosure by children, 9.6.)

Educational social workers and headteachers need to co-ordinate the professional network within the school. They also need to become the professionals who link in with the statutory and legal system outside the school. If sexual abuse is disclosed at school, the triad of social worker, police and health worker needs to become a quartet which includes the headmaster or the educational social worker.

The educational social worker is in an ideal position to co-ordinate the professional network within the school. Teachers, school nurses and other staff in the school need to be able to turn to them to share their initial suspicions. School heads and educational social workers need to prepare the disclosure interview in co-operation with social services and the police. The teacher to whom the child has disclosed or in whose class the child induced the first suspicion needs to be involved as a Trusted Person. (See Steps in the crisis intervention of disclosure 8.2; First-line suspicion and second-line suspicion, 8.3; The use of the 'trusted person', 8.6.)

The need for training of professionals in the educational system needs to be stressed because teachers have so far had only a marginal role in professional networks which are involved in dealing with physical abuse and neglect. Educational professionals are becoming a crucial group in the complex multi-professional network of child sexual abuse.

9.10 Suspicion and disclosure in in-patient settings and children's homes

Dealing with suspicion and disclosure in in-patient settings and children's homes has certain advantages.

1 During the time in the in-patient or residential setting the child can be relatively easily protected from immediate further abuse.
2 In an in-patient or residential setting a slowly emerging vague first-line suspicion of sexual abuse can easily be followed up and monitored without any need for further action until the first-line suspicion becomes a well-founded second-line suspicion.
3 Concurrent forms of therapy in a Primary Therapeutic Intervention can be more easily organised (see The Primary Therapeutic Intervention, Chapter 6; Concurrent forms of therapy, 7.1).

There are five major disadvantages when we deal with suspicions of child sexual abuse in in-patient or residential settings.

1 It can be difficult to safeguard the increased need for privacy and confidentiality for the child (see From secrecy to privacy, 6.4).
2 The process of disclosure is complicated by the need for an internal institutional disclosure which needs to include (a) a staff meeting, (b) a meeting with the abused child and the staff and (c) a meeting of all staff and all children of the unit in addition to the official disclosure interview and the responsibility meeting with the family (see Preparation for disclosure, Chapter 8).
3 The heightened intensity of identification of different staff members with different aspects of the child's problems and of the family process creates the

danger of greatly intensified conflicts-by-proxy in the residential staff group. It can be extremely difficult to keep appropriate boundaries for nursing staff and key workers who are directly involved with the sexually abused child over many hours of the day (see The interprofessional process, 5.1).

4 Splitting can easily occur between workers in direct daily contact with the child and professionals who are in contact with the family during family work (see The interprofessional process in context, 5.2).

5 Staff members who have been sexually abused as children themselves are to a much greater degree confronted with possible personal problems of identification than staff in out-patient clinics or in non-residential settings (see Sexually abused professionals, 11.2).

Children and adolescents in in-patient and residential settings will test whether they can trust to disclose, and certain behaviours and symptoms can lead to initial first-line suspicions of child sexual abuse in members of staff. In this situation the child needs the explicit therapeutic licence and permission to communicate before she is able to disclose fully and openly (see Child sexual abuse as syndrome of secrecy, 2.1; The individual process in context, 2.4). The advantage of the immediate safety of the child in an in-patient or residential setting and the close contact with the child allow a more natural progression from an initial first-line suspicion and partial disclosure to a second-line suspicion and full disclosure. This advantage can be offset by an extreme degree of behavioural disturbance which can severely influence the other children and the staff in the unit, especially when the sexually abused child creates a general sexualisation of the entire atmosphere in the unit.

In in-patient settings sexually abused staff members very quickly pick up the abused child's communication and identify, often quite unconsciously but immediately and strongly, with the abused child. Sexualisation in an in-patient or residential unit affects the staff–child relationship and the relationships within the staff group itself. Sexually abused children are often able to split and polarise staff in a way which can lead to severe conflicts-by-proxy. This is based on the subtle forms in which sexualising children can emotionally seduce some staff members while creating hostility in others. This leads to collusions between different staff members and to at times strong but hidden, and therefore even more destructive, female–male splitting.

The first suspicion of child sexual abuse in residential and in-patient settings often creates a split between staff members who want to disclose immediately and staff who identify instantly with the child's anxiety to disclose. Strong conflict-by-proxy can occur about the question of whether and how the initial first-line suspicion should be taken up. Staff members in the unit who begin to suspect child sexual abuse must never share their suspicion with the child without prior explicit agreement and preparation of the professional staff group. Conflicts-by-proxy within the staff group of the unit need to be dealt with before any disclosure can be induced towards the child and the family. (See The interactional nature of motivation, 2.4.1; The interprofessional process, 5.1; Crisis of disclosure – crisis of professionals and family crisis, 8.1; Steps in the crisis intervention of disclosure, 8.2; Anonymous Diagnostic Interprofessional Consultation, 8.4.)

If the child herself has not clearly chosen a Trusted Person amongst the staff the first task of the staff group is to allocate one 'special person' to become the Trusted Person who talks to the child in privacy on her own regularly in order slowly to follow up the first-line suspicion. The 'special person' needs to link up with the child and give the child explicit licence to disclose the abuse. The Trusted Person does not need to be the key worker or the individual therapist. It can be any staff member who is well integrated in the staff group and who does not induce splitting within the staff. (See Explicit therapeutic permission to disclose, 8.5; The use of the 'trusted person' 8.6.)

Splitting will happen if the Trusted Person joins the child's system of secrecy. Any information therefore needs to be shared in the entire staff group. The staff group in turn needs to keep this information confidential towards all other children and initially also towards the abused child herself. Possible conflicts about the right time and about the appropriate form of disclosure need to be identified as conflicts-by-proxy in order to achieve a therapeutic conflict-resolution-by-proxy. The conflict-resolution-by-proxy should help the staff group to anticipate the child's problems and the family conflicts which will follow after disclosure.

The often close and enmeshed staff–staff and staff–child relationships in residential settings and in in-patient units can make the conflicts-by-proxy very heavy. Conflict-resolutions-by-proxy may only be achieved with difficulty. Outside assistance may be necessary in order to avoid institutionalised conflicts-by-proxy. Outside consultation may allow different staff members openly to declare their primary identifications so that the mirroring conflicts in the professional staff group can be used in the consultation process as mirroring the child's problems and the family process. The acknowledgement of the mirroring process can then be most helpful in achieving a conflict-resolution-by-proxy as a precondition for the Primary Therapeutic Intervention. (See The inter-professional process, 5.1; The Primary Therapeutic Intervention, Chapter 6.)

All members of staff need to be involved in the second stage of the disclosure process. When a child has disclosed sexual abuse to a staff member it is important that a staff meeting take place with possibly all staff members of the unit in which the worker to whom the child has disclosed supports the child in retelling the disclosure in order to break the secret towards the entire staff group. It is essential that the child has the actual experience of the sexual abuse being talked about once openly in front of all staff members so that the child knows that the secret is broken and that the child hears from the staff that the staff know that sexual abuse has taken place. The meeting as 'naming event' needs to find explicit sexual language which establishes the abuse as fact within the unit. It has the same reality-creating function as the first family meeting, as described below in 9.11.

(See Naming, creating and maintaining sexual abuse as reality, 2.4.3; Aims and steps in the Primary Therapeutic Intervention, 6.2.)

In residential settings it is especially difficult to distinguish between the need to avoid secrecy and the child's right to privacy. Staff members who identify with the child may wish for secrecy. They may use the argument of the abused child's right to privacy to collude with secrecy and non-disclosure. On the other hand staff members who want to disclose immediately and prematurely may violate boundaries of privacy of other staff members and of the abused child herself. Once the child has disclosed, staff need to consider how the sexual abuse can openly become part of the therapeutic process for the child within the unit. As long as the secret of sexual abuse separates the abused child from other children and defines her as different therapy will be hindered by the isolation and separateness in which the abused child will remain (see From secrecy to privacy, 6.4).

Some children deal with the internal disclosure in the unit in a much more open way than others. They themselves may begin to disclose to other youngsters and the disclosure meeting in the unit with all staff and children becomes much less difficult. Some sexualising and promiscuous children may even have to be protected from secondary victimisation as a result of their uninhibited public announcements of their abuse. Other children are much more frightened to talk and it can be very helpful if one of the staff members takes the responsibility to help the abused child to disclose in a unit meeting with all the other children present. Staff may need to find and to use the words for the child first before the child can talk herself. A staff member may say things like 'Susan wanted to tell you something very important today about herself which she finds very difficult. Do you want to tell, Susan?'. When the child is too frightened or upset to respond the professional should never push the child to talk. But he must also not abandon the disclosure process in the unit because this would not help the child. The aspect of secrecy will always make it difficult to disclose and there never seems to be a 'right time' for disclosure. It is important to follow on and to say things like 'I am sure it is very difficult for you Susan. I would be scared if I were you to talk because you may think that others will think badly about you or that they won't like you any more. What Susan wanted to tell you today is that something very difficult has happened to her. In fact somebody has sexually interfered with her in a way which was very upsetting to her. In fact it was actually her father, wasn't it Susan?'

The initial disclosure can lead to great upset in the abused child, and also in other children. It is important to have in mind that other children may also have been sexually abused. I would always go round and ask each single child one by one by name, saying for example, 'Anna, do you understand what Susan has said? Did anything of that kind ever happen to you as well?' Other children often disclose their own sexual abuse in a crisis of disclosure of a peer in the group and the professional network needs to be prepared for this eventuality. The initial upset after the disclosure in the group is usually followed by great relief for the child in having shed the burden of secrecy. Often other children become very protective and supportive towards the abused child. It can be helpful to spell out to the abused child and the other residents that the abuse has only been disclosed because it is so much linked to the symptoms and the problems of the abused child in the unit. The effects of the sexual abuse can then openly become part of the therapeutic process for the child.

The rule needs to be observed that any internal disclosure to the residential children's group can only be initiated after careful preparation of the abused child. This does not necessarily mean that staff should wait with the internal disclosure until the abused child gives clear and explicit permission. It needs to be our professional skill to know that due to the anxieties in child sexual abuse as syndrome of secrecy the abused child may be unable to give this permission and that a staff member *in loco parentis* has to take responsibility for the internal disclosure. (See The individual process, Chapter 2.)

When the suspicion of child sexual abuse arises within an in-patient setting, outside statutory and legal agencies need to become involved in the usual way. A full disclosure with the child within the unit should if possible go in parallel with or should precede the external disclosure in order to prepare the child for the possible further steps in the Primary Therapeutic Intervention. An external disclosure needs to take place first if there is any danger that the internal disclosure in the unit is communicated in an uncontrolled way to the family or if child protective or legal considerations require an early involvement of outside statutory and legal agencies. The step from the disclosure of the child to the disclosure with the family needs to be equally prepared and co-ordinated within the professional staff group first. Whether the internal disclosure meeting within the unit or the first family meeting as responsibility meeting comes first depends on the child's contact and the relationship to her family and on the specific needs for child protection. In adolescents the disclosure within the unit may precede the family meeting, while in young children the family disclosure usually needs to take place first before the abuse is disclosed in the unit (see Steps in the crisis intervention of disclosure, 8.2).

After the full disclosure the child may need concurrent forms of therapy to deal with the abuse. If possible the child should attend a special sexual abuse group outside the institution to allow her to deal with the specific problems of child sexual abuse as syndrome of secrecy in privacy. Attending a specific group for sexually abused children outside the unit can greatly help the therapeutic move from secrecy to privacy. It can be more difficult to achieve this crucial step in exclusive treatment within the residential or in-patient setting.

The work outside the unit can be seen structurally as the place where the child is allowed to develop privacy and autonomy while close co-operation between all professionals involved avoids the re-introduction of secrecy. As long as close co-operation between the staff of the unit and the outside therapists is maintained, splitting can be avoided through explicit differentiation of the tasks and functions of the two settings. When the tasks are seen as complementary the child will have the permission to develop an unviolated sense of self in privacy and autonomy. Any secrecy between outside therapists and unit staff will inevitably lead to conflicts-by-proxy in the professional network and to non-therapeutic therapy. The advantage of concurrent treatment in the unit and outside to foster the child's sense of privacy and self does not mean that this task cannot also be achieved by treatment, which is entirely conducted within the unit. (See The interprofessional process in context, 5.2; Concurrent forms of therapy, 7.1; Group work with children, 7.2; Individual counselling and therapy, 7.3.)

9.11 The first family meeting as reality-creating responsibility meeting

Even if continuing family therapy is not provided, the highest priority in any Primary Therapeutic Intervention is to bring together all family members involved in one or two conjoint family meetings in which the secret of the abuse is named. The family meeting as naming event needs to achieve clarification in the following five areas (see The Primary Therapeutic Intervention, Chapter 6):

1 The first task of the family meeting is to establish the facts of the abuse and to clarify what has really happened. This is forgotten or is even actively avoided in most approaches at present. Each family member may have made separate statements to professionals, police, social workers, doctors or others. These statements may be of considerable length and it may have taken hours or days to collect them. In addition, different professionals or the different agencies involved often have talked amongst themselves about the facts of the abuse at length and may have exchanged lengthy written reports; it may have been in the newspapers. Despite all these activities in terms of family relationships the sexual abuse is still a family secret. It has never been talked about openly between the persons most concerned: between father, mother and the children directly or indirectly involved. Furthermore, the child may have indicated in the past that abuse was happening. She may even have told the mother or other family members, and up to now no family member may ever have believed the child. (See The family process, Chapter 3.)

In the first family meeting as naming event everything written down beforehand needs to be named aloud. No fact should be taken as known or shared, least of all the fact of the sexual abuse itself, even if the father has been to court and has admitted to it. Admitting the abuse in court establishes the legal reality of the sexual abuse as fact. Naming and establishing the external reality of the abuse is the precondition for further therapeutic work and the legal process is in that sense therapeutic. Creating legal reality does not automatically create psychological reality for the abuser, the child and the family. This only happens in a commonly shared family meeting which creates the shared psychological reality for all family members involved. (See Proof and belief, admission and owning up, 1.5; The individual process, Chapter 2; Working with sexual abusers, 7.4).

The family meeting as naming event needs to introduce sexual language. It needs to establish first the fact of the sexual abuse and the circumstances under which it happened and where it took place and where everybody else was at the time. Words like 'sexual relationship' between abuser and child should be explicitly used to help the family to find an open way of approaching the subject for which families do not have words and a language to communicate. It may not be necessary to go into more anatomical details of the sexual act itself than to mention the word 'intercourse' or 'putting the penis into the child's bottom'. The content has to be explicit but emotionally as neutral as possible. The aim is to establish facts in a non-persecuting and accepting way (see Giving explicit licence to communicate, 2.4.2).

2 The second task for the meeting is to help the abuser to take sole responsibility for the sexual act itself in a way which is outspoken and which, in the presence of other family members and especially the mother, takes away from the child any responsibility for the abuse. The issue of the responsibility of the abuser needs to be very outspoken because often mothers take the blame on themselves or children get blamed either for the abuse itself or for the secondary damage following family breakup. If children do not get blamed by others, they often hold themselves responsible for the sexual relationship as well as for the consequences of the disclosure.

3 The third task is to help both parents – mother and father – to come to an agreement about the degree of their involvement as equal parents who are both responsible for the care of their children. On the father's side one of the most caring actions during the crisis intervention may be to agree to give the child some space and not to be involved in the daily care. In that case a father who agrees to move out for a while may be taking the most caring paternal action possible. On the other hand a mother who does not immediately go for divorce, even if from a marital point of view she may want it, but who gives the child time to deal with the trauma of the abuse first and to adapt to the new situation with the father still involved, may take the most caring maternal step in a given situation.

4 The fourth task of the family meeting is to talk openly in front of everybody about any separations in the family. Any separation should be put into the specific context of child sexual abuse as interlocking syndrome of secrecy and addiction in order to make sure that the therapeutic implications for the separations are understood by everybody in the family and that any actual separation is not seen by the child as punishment for the abuse. Even if no legal or statutory separation of family members has taken place, at least temporary separation will be necessary in the developing intense family process after disclosure.

Separations can involve marital separation as well as the separation of the child when the child does not want to return home. If the father leaves home it is important to convey unambiguously to the child, and especially to any sibling, that the father's leaving is not to be blamed on the abused child. If the abused child leaves the family the family meeting needs to convey to the child that she is not leaving because no one in the family wants her, nor that she is pushed out of the family as punishment for the abuse or for secondary problems arising from disclosure, but that she is leaving because the father has been irresponsible and cannot be trusted for the time being. (See Three basic types of intervention, 4.1)

5 Finally, the fifth task is to make a therapeutic contract which contains agreements about the degree of contact between family members and about visiting arrangements in cases of separation. It also needs to be clarified for all family members which professionals will be involved in what capacity, to what degree and intensity, and what the possible long-term plans are for the family.

Achieving the five practical tasks of the conjoint family meeting has fundamental therapeutic effect in the short and long term. The first family meeting as reality-creating naming event and as responsibility meeting can be conducted by any professional who dares to confront child sexual abuse with an open mind rather than with preconceived notions or revenge feelings, which quite understandably interfere only too easily with attempts to find a positive and problem-oriented solution to child sexual abuse. The greatest danger is to identify too closely with either the child or the mother. Signs of professionals beginning to mirror family conflicts and starting to take up conflicts-by-proxy should alarm all professionals involved and should lead to immediate clarification of aims and means. (See The professional network, Chapter 5; Family therapy and family approach, 6.1; Aims and steps in the Primary Therapeutic Intervention, 6.2.)

When abusers admit to sexual abuse a family meeting should take place as soon as possible and if possible within hours in order to establish the abuse as family reality. The reality-creating responsibility meeting can take place in a social services office, in a hospital, in a school or in a nursery as appropriately as in a police station. It is highly effective legally and therapeutically and it does not interfere with the legal process in any way to get the whole family to the police station as soon as the father has made a statement and to hold a family meeting as naming event, asking the abuser no more than to repeat the statement he has just made to the police. By establishing the facts of the abuse in front of the child and the family the abuse will become a shared family fact for all family members and will become family reality. The family secret of child sexual abuse will be broken. Time and again we see how abusers, mothers and children withdraw the statement they have made in isolation. Once the fact of the abuse is shared in front of all other family members and in the presence of one outsider it will not be withdrawn. An early family meeting as naming event is therefore as much fostering the legal process as it is advancing therapy (see Management and therapy, 5.2.1).

It is much easier and quicker to achieve the first three therapeutic steps of the Primary Therapeutic Intervention in the acute crisis of disclosure:

1 to establish the facts of the abuse and the abuse as openly shared fact for all family members;
2 to find the language which gives the child and other family members explicit permission to communicate about the abuse;
3 for the abuser to take sole and explicit responsibility for the sexual act itself.

We need to give children the explicit licence and permission to communicate about their experience of sexual abuse before they can talk about the abuse in other contexts such as group treatment or individual therapy. The reality-creating responsibility meeting which is held instantly after the abuser has admitted to the abuse is especially therapeutic when the abuser is subsequently unavailable following imprisonment or family breakup or when he is uncooperative in subsequent treatment. The family meeting as naming event should therefore, if at all possible, be part of the very initial crisis intervention of disclosure irrespective of any subsequent form of long-term therapy. Close multi-professional co-operation is crucial in order to create a complementary approach which can support a Primary Therapeutic Intervention (see The professional network, Chapter 5).

Delayed first family meetings as responsibility sessions in legally acknowledged cases can start off like cases of denial. Abusers are often too frightened and find it too difficult to come out with the facts of the abuse and to admit to their responsibility when they are asked directly. This holds especially for sexual abusers in conflict-avoiding families. It can be helpful to turn to the mother or to other siblings first and to ask the question 'What would we read in the police reports?' or to ask family members to guess what the abuser would really have to say if he said what was in the back of his mind. Once the family has started to talk in hypothetical terms the therapist can increasingly intersperse phrases like 'sure we do not know what is in your father's mind, it is our guess and I will ask your father in a moment'. Abusers then find it more easy to come in themselves and to take responsibility and to help establish the facts of the abuse (see Family and responsibility-session-by-proxy, 9.13; Dealing with primary denial, 10.6; Relapse into secrecy and secondary denial, 12.13).

9.12 Organising the first family meeting

Social workers with statutory responsibility and other professionals who are involved in the daily care of the children, and if possible therapists, should be present at the first family meeting as naming event and responsibility meeting. If the first family session takes place immediately after disclosure in the police station the police officer who has taken the statement from the abuser and who may help the abuser to read out the statement becomes the most important legal and therapeutic person in the specific context of the meeting in the police station as therapeutic non-therapy. (See The interprofessional process in context, 5.2; Three basic types of intervention, 4.1; The Primary Therapeutic Intervention, Chapter 6.)

If the first family session as responsibility meeting takes place at a later stage when the father or the child has left the family, brief meetings with the different family sub-units need to take place immediately before the conjoint session. These brief meetings of 5 or 10 minutes have two tasks. (1) The aim of the conjoint family session needs to be explained, saying that in order to be able to think about the future it is important to talk about what has happened in the family. (2) It is important to state explicitly that the meeting may become very difficult, that it may become a bit frightening at times and that if the therapist were in the position of the family members he would be as scared as they may be. This message is very important as meta-communication to the family that the therapist knows about the anxieties of different family members, that she knows that different family members may be frightened of disasters during the session and may be even more frightened of the outcome and the consequences of the meeting. The anticipation of the anxieties and the feared disasters as part of crisis work enables family members to subject themselves to situations of intense family crisis which would otherwise be too threatening. This holds especially for sexually abused children and often also for the abuser.

In practical terms it is helpful to ask the different family sub-groups to arrive at slightly different times and to provide different waiting areas so that the family sub-groups do not have to wait together or do not meet before the actual family session. At the beginning of the conjoint sessions it is usually helpful to ask all family members and professionals, except the abuser, into the office or the consulting room first and to ask them to leave the chair next to the door free for the abuser. After everybody else is seated and settled and after any possible additional clarification I would leave the room and ask the abuser, as the last person, to join the family. This carefully chosen procedure avoids an increase of anxiety which otherwise may trigger the refusal of different family members to take part in the session. This procedure also avoids uncontrolled and premature social contact between the abuser and the child. Uncontrolled social contact before the responsibility meeting can easily lead to renewed family collusion. Or the abuser may give direct or indirect threats and messages to the child to rejoin the family system of secrecy.

In the acute crisis of disclosure, defence mechanisms of family members are usually weak. Psychological orientation and orientation in terms of interpersonal relationships are lost. The moment of individual and family crisis is therefore the moment where psychological and interpersonal change can take place much more easily than at any other point in time. In the acute crisis of disclosure abusers will admit much more readily than later. Underlying individual and family problems surface infinitely more easily in the context of crisis. It is usually not very difficult to get vital information about facts of the abuse and about the underlying individual problems and dysfunctional family relationships when the crisis is not seen as negative by professionals and not dampened down aimlessly but is used in a problem-solving way to facilitate a Primary Therapeutic Intervention.

Many individual and interpersonal problems become unobtainable again once individual defences have been re-established and once underlying interpersonal problems have disappeared under re-established old dysfunctional family patterns. Unfortunately many professionals do not use the acute family crisis to gain facts and to be therapeutic in a goal-oriented way. We try to dampen down the family crisis first with the aim of getting facts and therapeutic change later, helping family members inadvertently to re-establish individual defences and homeostatic rearrangements of family relationships.

The considerable acceleration and intensification of the overall treatment process by using the family crisis of disclosure to its full potential require the clear distinction between the crisis of the professionals and the family crisis. If professionals have dealt with their own professional crisis first and when they know what they want to achieve in the family crisis of disclosure and how they want to achieve it they will not need to dampen down the family crisis out of their own anxiety and confusion. They will be able to use the crisis of the family members to achieve the first important steps of the Primary Therapeutic Intervention. (See The Primary Therapeutic Intervention, Chapter 6; Crisis of disclosure – crisis of professionals and family crisis, 8.1.)

9.13 Family and responsibility-session-by-proxy

In child sexual abuse as syndrome of secrecy it is still necessary for the child and for other family members to establish the facts of the abuse in order to establish the abuse as family reality and to deal with the issue of responsibility even when the abuser is not available for a responsibility session due to imprisonment or because he has left and is unwilling to co-operate or in cases of denial and extrafamilial abuse. The responsibility-session-by-proxy is conducted in the absence of the abuser. It breaks the family secret and gives the child and other family members the explicit permission to communicate about the abuse and to make use of subsequent therapy. (See Chapter 1, Sections 1.2, 1.3, 1.5; Child sexual abuse as syndrome of secrecy, 2.1; The individual process in context, 2.4; Aims and steps in the Primary Therapeutic Intervention, 6.2).

In the responsibility-session-by-proxy the professional who conducts the family meeting establishes the facts of the abuse and the abuse as fact by asking family members and especially the mother as the non-abusing parent or both parents when the abuser is not the father, or asks siblings or even the abused child, what the abuser would say about the facts of the abuse and about the issue of responsibility if he were present. In the responsibility-session-by-proxy the therapist always works on the hypothetical level of 'if the abuser were present what would he say?'. (See The use of different family therapy techniques, 12.10.)

In responsibility-sessions-by-proxy of intrafamilial abuse I would ask 'What would your father say about what has happened and whose responsibility would he say it was if he were here?' In legally established cases it is often helpful to ask 'What do you think we would read in the police statement?' or ' What do you think your father has said to the judge has happened and whose responsibility do you think he said it was?' The professional can on the hypothetical 'as if' level establish the facts of the abuse and the abuse as family reality. He can also deal with the issues of responsibility, participation, guilt, blame and power. Without a responsibility-session-by-proxy abused children may still feel in loyalty conflicts whether they are allowed to deal openly with the abuse in treatment or whether the abuse should remain a family secret. The responsibility-session-by-proxy often establishes for the first time the abuse as an acknowledged external reality for the child and the family.

The introduction of guessing on a hypothetical level is another important technique in addition to the hypothetical questioning on the 'as if' level. In conflict-avoiding families the child or other family members will often respond to the hypothetical questioning by saying that the father would deny that sexual abuse has taken place at all even when the absent abuser has openly admitted to the abuse. Or children say that they do not know what the abuser would say. I would respond to the continuing denial by saying something like 'Sure, you cannot know for certain what your father would say and you cannot read his mind or speak for him. But you know him much better than I do and what is your guess he would have said?' Even stronger denial needs to be taken up on an even more anxiety-reducing hypothetical and more removed level. I would go one step further back and say something like 'What is your guess your father would say if he were here and if he did not have to be worried about what would happen in the family and if he was really honest as he was with the police and if he said what was really in the back of his mind?' (See Proof and belief, admission and owning up, 1.5; Dealing with primary denial, 10.6.)

The degree of the need to work on the hypothetical level and on the level of guessing corresponds to the degree of denial due to the level of anxiety and conflict avoidance in families of child sexual abuse. In conflict-avoiding families with a great discrepancy between the self-image of family relationships and with a high degree of anxiety and denial, a responsibility-session-by-proxy needs to use increasingly hypothetical questioning which is seemingly further removed from confronting the reality of the abuse. In cases of high anxiety the family-session-by-proxy in proven cases of sexual abuse may look very much like a session of primary denial. (See The family process, Chapter 3.)

The responsibility-session-by-proxy can be conducted with any family sub-group and even with the abused child alone. This is especially important when an initial Primary Child Protective Intervention in which the child has been taken into care needs to be turned into a Primary Therapeutic Intervention. (See The family and the professional network, Chapter 4; Turning a Primary Child Protective Intervention into a Primary Therapeutic Intervention, 11.11.)

9.14 The handover meeting

Referrals from one agency to another disrupt the continuity of the intervention and often lead to renewed secrecy and denial and to the breakdown of the intervention. Especially the Trusted Person and the person who has conducted the disclosure interview, and other professionals who have been involved in the initial stages of the crisis of disclosure, become very special and important persons to the sexually abused child and the family. The shared experience of disclosing the secret of child sexual abuse and of creating the abuse as family reality leads to a strong attachment of the child to the Trusted Person. The dilemma between the need for continuity during the intervention in order to avoid a relapse into secrecy, and the unavoidable fact that children and families need to be referred on, can be bridged by the handover meeting (see The use of the 'trusted person', 8.6).

In the handover meeting the professional previously involved meets the new professional who will be involved in the future in the presence of the child and the family. The outgoing professional who was initially involved can help the family and the child to tell the history of their involvement during the intervention in front of the incoming professional. The outgoing professional will especially talk about the way the sexual abuse came to light and how it was talked about. The most difficult aspects of the sexual abuse as syndrome of secrecy and addiction which are most likely to relapse into secrecy and the most personal aspects of the relationship between the outgoing professional which have developed during the intervention need to be explicitly mentioned and talked about.

Handover meetings are usually greatly appreciated by the child and the family. When I am the person to hand over to a fellow professional I often involve the child or the family by asking them to remind me of the particular situation in which we met for the first time. Or I ask the child and the family to remind me of conversations we had on the day of the disclosure or at certain crucial points in our contact. I also will lay first links between the child and the family and the incoming professional. I often ask the child or the family to tell the incoming professional about certain important situations or conversations we had which may be relevant for her to know. If the child or the family finds it difficult to relate those events, I will help them to do so. Or I will do it for them fully acknowledging the anxieties, shame and the difficult feelings which are related to talking about what we have gone through in dealing with the abuse. When the outgoing professional shares his involvement with the family with the incoming professional in front of the family he does not break the therapeutic confidentiality. On the contrary the handover meeting avoids the relapse into secrecy and provides continuity in the professional intervention.

The handover meeting has four important effects:

1 *Avoiding secrecy.*   To retell in the presence of the incoming professional the stories and facts which the child or the family has told the outgoing professional in the crisis intervention avoids the children or families withdrawing back into secrecy when a new professional takes over from the initially involved professional.

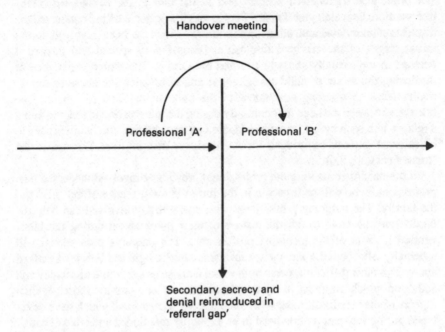

Figure 9.2 The handover meeting

2 Explicit permission to communicate.   The very fact that the outgoing professional talks to the incoming professional in front of the family and the child about the sexual abuse, and about the history of the disclosure and his involvement with the family and the child, encourages the child and the family to link up with the incoming professional. It is important for the child and the family to see the reactions of the new professional to the telling of the story of the sexual abuse by them and by the outgoing professional. An accepting, understanding and non-punitive reaction by the incoming professional to the reports gives the child and the family the explicit permission to communicate about the abuse to this new professional.

3 Experience 'travels'.   Handing on the facts and the emotional experience with the family and the child from the outgoing to the incoming professional in front of the child and family has the effect that their experience 'travels' into the new professional. The continuity of knowledge and experience is maintained and the incoming new professional immediately becomes the new and true Trusted Person. It is a very interesting and sometimes moving, and certainly extremely helpful, process.

4 Avoidance of splitting.   The handover meeting has the important effect of avoiding splitting between the outgoing 'good professional' and the incoming 'bad professional' who takes over. It is important that the family knows that the incoming professional knows all the important experiences that the outgoing professional has had with the family and that the outgoing professional approves of the new attachment between the child, the family and the incoming professional. This knowledge avoids the splitting of the 'good professional' and the 'bad professional' which would enable the child or the family to exclude the incoming professional, which often leads to the breakdown of the intervention.

The handover meeting is a process similar to that which gives an absent parent, who is told on return by the present parent in front of the child about a specific significant event between the child and the present parent, the same authority to deal with the factual and emotional aspects of the aftermath of this event as the parent who had been involved. It is an important experience for the family to see the outgoing and the incoming professional united as a professional couple. This helps to avoid secrecy and secondary denial, gives explicit permission to communicate, makes the experience travel and avoids splitting when children and their families have to be referred on.

A handover meeting needs to take place in all cases where the mother or other immediate carers are not present in the room during the disclosure interview. The presence behind the screen does not make the link of continuity for the child and requires a full handover meeting immediately after the disclosure interview. Handover meetings need to take place at any stage of the intervention with the child and the family in order to make the experience 'travel' down the referral line without losing the emotional or factual importance in the contact between the professional, the child and the family. (See The Primary Therapeutic Intervention, Chapter 6; Organising the disclosure interview, 9.3.)

Chapter ten

Following disclosure

10.1 Abusers leaving home

The first move in any separation after disclosure should be for the abuser to leave home without automatically going to prison. A court-ordered injunction against the abuser to leave home until it is safe to return without the abuser automatically going to prison should become standard practice in child sexual abuse. In child sexual abuse as syndrome of secrecy and addiction an initial separation between the abuser and the abused child may be necessary before rehabilitation can be attempted. The abuser should leave the family because he as an adult has to take full responsibility for the sexual abuse and for the consequences of his actions. It is often of paramount importance for the child to stay at home in order to keep important attachments within the family and within the social network and school which the child would lose if she were to be placed elsewhere. If the child stays at home, inadvertent secondary traumatisation can be avoided, which often occurs in a Primary Child Protective Intervention. Legal procedure should therefore be used to remove the abuser and not the child. Children are often removed because the availability of children's homes makes it easier to arrange alternative placements for the child than for the abuser. This points to the urgent need to create accommodation for sexual abusers with an integrated treatment component for abusers. (See Child sexual abuse as syndrome of secrecy, and of addiction, 2.1, 2.2, 2.3; Three basic types of intervention, 4.1.)

For the abuser to leave home following disclosure can be the most caring paternal act possible under the circumstances. In a problem-oriented Primary Therapeutic Intervention an abuser who leaves home but remains available can be allowed controlled contact with his family within the overall context of the family-oriented treatment approach. The abuser who leaves the family without going to prison can also avoid secondary hardship for the family as a result of loss of income and of secondary social stigmatisation of the family when abusers are imprisoned. (See Family process, Chapter 3; The Primary Therapeutic Intervention, Chapter 6.)

Under certain circumstances it can be more helpful for the child to leave home. Hostility between mother and daughter and maternal non-believing can in some cases be so intense that it is more therapeutic for the child to leave home during the crisis intervention than to stay. A mother of a 16-year-old girl who had been sexually abused by her father and who had lived in a children's home for a year insisted: 'the problem was between my daughter and myself, not between her and her father. If she had stayed at home with me and my husband had left instead, I would have killed her.' The mother's assessment of the severe mother–daughter conflict and a much less hostile relationship between the father and the daughter in this case were shared by all family members including the daughter (see Proof and belief, admission and owning up, 1.5).

The second constellation in which it can be more protective for the child to leave the family is cases in which the child is blamed by all family members including the mother and siblings for the consequences of the disclosure and for subsequent family breakdown. In one family the hostility of the brothers who missed their father and of the mother who missed her husband as partner became so intense that it was less traumatic for the sexually abused child to leave the family than to stay. Scapegoating and blaming can in extreme cases be more harmful for the child than a therapeutic removal from home during the crisis intervention. The attempt by parents to change the overall direction of a Primary Therapeutic Intervention into a Primary Child Protective Intervention is the third constellation in which it can be better for the child to leave home. The rejection by both parents and the common subsequent secondary denial of the abuse can place the child in a position where alternative parenting must be considered. Finally, adolescents who disclose sexual abuse often do not want to return home but choose to stay in alternative placements. This can be beneficial in some cases of older adolescents as long as it is clearly ensured that the alternative placement does not change a Primary Therapeutic Intervention into a Primary Child Protective Intervention. (See The family and the professional network, Chapter 4.)

The four main reasons for the removal of the child are listed here to illustrate the exception to the rule. The rule should be the removal of the abuser rather than of the child. This again illustrates the urgent demand for the creation of 'men's houses' which cater for the therapeutic needs of sexual abusers in the initial phase of the crisis of disclosure.

10.2 Placement in children's homes

To separate sexually abused children from their families is as a rule only the second best solution to the abuser leaving home. If the child is separated from the family a full explanation for the reasons of separation needs to be given to the child. Otherwise the child will feel blamed, punished and abandoned. If the child is placed in a children's home or in a foster family with other children it is often necessary for all professionals involved in the child's primary care to agree upon a cover story for the child towards school and other settings with the rule that this cover story will be held up by all professionals involved, whereas the child is free to say as much as she wants to disclose. The situation of children who have been placed in care as a consequence of a disclosure needs to be handled differently from sexual abuse which is disclosed in residential care or in-patient settings (see Suspicion and disclosure in in-patient settings and children's homes, 9.10).

In children's homes or in other residential settings one of the primary care-takers needs to be allocated as the 'special person' to the child. The 'special person' needs to know all about the abuse in order to give the abused child the chance to speak out when she feels ready or in need. Professionals working in residential settings and hospitals need to be aware that sexually abused children may under the notion of special protection be suspiciously watched and may in subtle ways be treated in a discriminatory way by other children and by resi-dential staff. The special treatment can reflect the staff's own difficulties in dealing with a sexually experienced, but emotionally immature, child or adoles-cent. In addition any sexually abused child will confront carers of both sexes with their own sexuality (see The P family, 4.2.3).

When sexually abused children feel safe they may begin to display strong sexualised behaviour which threatens residential workers who have to work in close proximity to the child for many hours every day. Professionals can be in danger of being seduced. They often react in a hostile way towards a child who shows sexualised behaviour. It is important to be aware that children tend to try to re-create the sexually abusive pattern in the residential setting and they may make false allegations of sexual abuse against members of staff they like but by whom they feel disappointed. Allegations of child sexual abuse can bring staff members into great problems because sexual abuse in residential settings does occur and sexually abused children are especially vulnerable to further abuse (see Allegations of children in children's homes, 8.8).

When sexually abused children and especially adolescents are admitted to residential care it is important that the staff be aware of the danger that children may unconsciously attempt to re-create the sexually abusive pattern in the staff group. Mirroring processes of the sexually abusive family pattern in the staff which induce splitting, conflicts-by-proxy and a sexualised atmosphere in the unit need to be identified early on. (See The interprofessional process, 5.1; Mutual influence and interlocking professional–family process, 4.2.)

If sexually abused children are placed away from home the protective function of the relationships to siblings, friends and peers at school is easily forgotten. It is very important to enable – and if necessary to organise – contact with siblings and friends as freely as possible. Close contact to the mother is vital and should initially take the form of therapeutic meetings in which the sexual abuse and its consequences are dealt with. Initial social visits by parents prior to the first family meeting can be counter-therapeutic. Family members often use these contacts to threaten the child or to re-create the previous pattern of denial and secrecy. If an immediate family meeting after disclosure is impossible a responsibility-meeting-by-proxy needs to be organised (see Family and responsibility-session-by-proxy, 9.13).

Under no circumstances should there be any reason to cut the contact between the child and her mother, siblings and friends, except where mothers do not believe the child and blame and reject her for the problems following disclosure. In these cases mother–child therapy is urgently required. Meetings with the abuser should under all circumstances have the nature and the aim of well-structured therapeutic family sessions as part of the Primary Therapeutic Intervention. (See Aims and steps in the Primary Therapeutic Intervention, 6.2; Mothers who do not believe, 12.12.)

Change of school can be helpful or can be an additional punishment. It is often helpful when the abuse is widely known and when the child is stigmatised and scapegoated by peers and other children in the community. Change of school can be an additional trauma where it amounts to a further loss of important friends and attachment figures. The school situation therefore needs most careful consideration and constant re-evaluation.

10.3 Placement with foster parents

The sexual nature of sexual abuse, the confusion between emotional and sexual behaviour in the child's way of relating, and the strong tendency of many sexually abused children to re-create the sexually abusive pattern in other settings demand that the greatest care and attention be given to the selection, the preparation and the support of foster families. Even experienced foster parents may need continual assistance.

Sexually abused children may only be able to relate in sexual ways. In particular, adolescent girls can act out sexually to a degree which can also threaten stable partner relationships of foster parents. Foster fathers can be in danger of being seduced. If they resist they may nevertheless, and especially by older girls, be accused of re-abuse. Foster mothers can unwillingly assist in re-creating the original family pattern by reacting with open or subtle hostility and rejection towards the sexually abused child. (See The individual process in context, 2.4; The family process, Chapter 3; The need for behaviour modification, 7.3.4.)

Acting-out in sexual abuse can creep into family life rather unnoticed and secretly. The onset can be extremely subtle and it can be very difficult to name and to identify the sexualised behaviour. Foster parents may not feel able or may not feel it is appropriate to talk openly about sexualisation and sexual problems in relation to the foster child. This makes it more difficult to deal with the effects on the marriage and the family. Foster parents may not have a language themselves to communicate about sexual abuse and they often feel inadequate and threatened by the child's behaviour. Sexualisation as re-creation of the original family pattern creeps into the foster family in a much more dangerous way, re-creating also the dynamic of secrecy. When foster parents feel able to talk about sexual abuse they often do not know how much they should talk about it directly to the child and to outsiders.

We must not forget the sometimes profound effect on other children in the foster family. One sexually abused 3-year-old girl was placed with foster parents who themselves had a 6-year-old boy. When the girl began to feel safe she started to be completely absorbed and obsessed with the boy's penis. She followed him everywhere in the house trying to unzip his trousers. She wanted to be with him when he went to the loo and continuously tried to touch or to suck his penis. Although the foster parents were very resourceful they needed much support and counselling to be able to deal with the situation.

It is dangerous and irresponsible to place sexually abused children with foster families without careful preparation and help to enable the foster parents to recognise sexual acting-out and to deal with the effect on the child, on the family and on the marital relationship. It can even be unethical when the placement leads to severe partner problems in the foster family or to family breakdown following an unrecognised re-creation of the sexualised family process which the sexually abused child can induce in the foster family. Foster families may need continuous support, counselling and even family therapy to be able to deal with severely sexually abused children. The specific skills which are needed to deal with sexualised behaviour certainly raise the issue of the need for professional training for foster parents who care for sexually abused children and adolescents. (See Working with foster parents, 12.17.)

10.4 Placement with relatives

We need to think about the implications of placing sexually abused children with uncles, aunts, grandparents or other relatives. Placements with relatives are often considered with the good intention of bringing sexually abused children in the crisis of disclosure into a familiar environment where they already know the carers. The expectation is that the child is better cared for by relatives than by professionals or foster parents.

Placing a sexually abused child with relatives can precipitate intense conflicts within the wider family, which reflects the conflicts in the nuclear family of child sexual abuse. Relatives of sexually abused children often find it impossible to resist being drawn into the blaming game and into siding with one parent against the other. When the child is placed with relatives from the mother's side the child may have to deny any positive aspects of her relationship with and any attachment to her father. The family may reject any contact with the abuser and it can be extremely difficult to hold a responsibility session with the father when the maternal relatives strongly object. When the child is placed with relatives from the father's side the child can come under pressure to minimise the abuse and its consequences. The child may even feel obliged to deny again that sexual abuse has happened at all. (See The family process, Chapter 3).

Placements with relatives can create additional pressures and confusions for the child. She may be rejected when she talks about the abuser and she may be pushed into traumatic loyalty conflicts and into secondary taboos which prevents her from dealing openly with her experience of sexual abuse. Members of the extended family are therefore often not the best people to place sexually abused children in the acute crisis of disclosure. Although each single case needs to be assessed on its own merits, an accepting and neutral setting which gives the child emotional containment and psychological space is often better suited for the time of the initial crisis intervention after disclosure.

Some children who are placed with foster parents can come into severe loyalty conflicts and they might be unable to accept an alternative family setting. They need the even more neutral setting of a children's home. In this situation a well-run children's home can be the very first choice of placement in the context of an overall Primary Therapeutic Intervention as long as the danger signs of a change into a Primary Child Protective Intervention are clearly recognised and dealt with (see Three basic types of intervention, 4.1).

10.5 Mothers who want instant divorce

Mothers who demand instant divorce at disclosure do so mainly for two reasons. The first group consists of mothers who are truly protective and who want to stay with the child having clearly chosen for the child and against the abuser. In these cases the mothers will most likely stick to their decision and a successful Primary Therapeutic Intervention may lead to a therapeutic divorce in which the child does not become triangulated in the conflict between the divorcing partners. These mothers are also often mothers who themselves disclose the abuse and bring as Trusted Person their child to the professionals with the request for help. Usually the abuse will not have been very long-standing. (See The family process, Chapter 3; The use of the 'trusted person', 8.6; Helping protective mothers, 12.11.)

The second group of mothers who demand instant divorce do so as an expression of acting-out in reaction to the shock of the disclosure. In the immediate crisis of the disclosure these mothers feel pushed to choose for the child and against their husband although they might be much more attached to their husbands than to the child. I have seen many mothers who have asked for instant divorce at the point of disclosure, only to go back secretly after several weeks or months and to link up with the abuser again. Despite the initial demand for instant divorce they later choose for the husband and against the child, actively inducing a Primary Child Protective Intervention. It can be crucial to address right from the beginning, head on, the danger of a possible subsequent collusion between the parents in order to avoid a collusion of secrecy between the mother and the abuser later in the intervention, when it becomes very difficult to reintegrate the collusive family sub-system into a problem-oriented Primary Therapeutic Intervention. (See The family and the professional network, Chapter 4.)

When I come to the conclusion that the mother is, despite her demand for instant divorce, still attached to her husband I would prevent the collusion of secrecy by immediately naming the attachment. I would ask something like 'when do you miss your husband most – during the week or at weekends?' 'Do you miss him more when you are with the children or when you are on your own?' 'Do you miss him more as partner or as a co-parent?' All these and other choice questions assume that the mother misses her husband anyway. The questions address the differentiation between different situations in which the mother may miss the father. I would not ask the mother whether or not she misses her husband. Equally I would not ask the children whether or not they miss their father but when they miss him most. Initially I often get the response from mothers that they do not miss their husbands at all and that they will never miss them. Children usually give similar answers out of loyalty to their mother. I then ask the question once removed: 'If you ever were to miss your husband, when would you miss him? Obviously you do not miss him now and you cannot imagine ever missing him, but if you were ever to miss him when would that be most likely to happen?' The denial of missing the father as father or husband requires switching to hypothetical questions to find the areas of attachment between the mother and the abuser which may soon bring them back together again (see The use of different family therapy techniques, 12.10).

Putting the question to the mother: 'When do you miss your husband most?' gives the mother the indirect message that I know that she may at some stage miss her husband as partner and co-parent. It gives her the message that I understand this and that I find it quite normal and that I do not morally reject her for her possibly missing the abuser. Beginning from my side to address this issue gives the mother the permission to miss the abuser and to talk openly about positive feelings and attachments towards him which she may not dare to express otherwise. The questions convey to the mother that she does not need to be secretive about a continuing attachment to the abuser. It gives the message that it is more understandable and normal still to be attached than otherwise and that this attachment does not make her a bad mother.

After an initial denial mothers often begin to talk about how much they miss the abuser as partner and co-parent and the marital and parental relationship then becomes accessible in a Primary Therapeutic Intervention. Working openly on marital and parental issues with the mother on her own safeguards a continued Primary Therapeutic Intervention as long as professionals can bear to allow the mother still to have positive feelings and a continued attachment to the father despite the abuse. Confronting the denial of attachment which lies behind many initial instant requests for divorce also allows the children to admit openly that they may still miss their father.

Dealing instantly with the continuing attachment of family members to the abuser in spite of the maternal request for immediate divorce does not mean that the mother will finally stay with the husband. Early openness about continuing attachments between family members and the abuser in the crisis of disclosure keeps marital and parental problems available for therapeutic renegotiation. The partner relationship can then either end in an open and therapeutic separation and divorce or in the rehabilitation of the family. (See Aims and steps in the Primary Therapeutic Intervention, 6.2; Basic mechanisms in the therapeutic process, 6.3.)

One of the main reasons why mothers ask for instant divorce might have little to do with their degree of protectiveness but might have all to do with what they perceive as expectations from professionals. Expectations or at times even demands by professionals for mothers to separate from abusers can be the strongest motive for mothers to ask for instant divorce. Mothers feel that this course of action is expected from them and that it increases their chances not be threatened with the removal of the child. Suggestions and demands by professionals which influence the mother towards instant divorce are moralistic acting-out and constitute unprofessional behaviour of the professionals involved. It often drives the attachment of mothers to the abuser underground and leads to intervention failure. Encouragement to divorce constitutes unprofessional behaviour in the same way as pressurising mothers to stay with their partners. The task of child protection can be more jeopardised than helped by the moralistic behaviour of professionals. The more professionals feel that mothers think that the professionals expect them to ask for instant divorce, the more that the professionals need to give the mother the permission to miss her partner as described in this chapter.

10.6 Dealing with primary denial

Denial by abusers, by children and families is common in child sexual abuse. It often ends up in deadlock between the family, the abuser and the professionals. Denial carries a high risk of secondary damage to the child when children are wrongly removed or are left in families with ongoing abuse. Denial is often the result of premature interventions by professionals who act prematurely out of their own crisis. (See Crisis of disclosure – crisis of professionals and family crisis, 8.1; Steps in the crisis intervention of disclosure, 8.2; The professional network, Chapter 5.)

Out of helplessness, professionals either collude with the denial and drop the case or get into symmetrical battles of continued accusations against the abuser and the family which the abuser and the family constantly deny. As long as professionals and families remain locked into fruitless mutual accusations children are further traumatised by ongoing sexual abuse at home or by second-ary vicimisation after removal in a Primary Child Protective Intervention. These deadlocked conflicts become damaging and exhausting not only to the child but also to the family and to professionals. (See Child sexual abuse as syndrome of secrecy, and of addiction 2.1, 2.2, 2.3; Three basic types of intervention, 4.1.)

In a problem-oriented approach symmetrical escalation and professional burn-out can be avoided. Denial work needs to integrate linear aspects of legal responsibility for the abuse and circular aspects of family relationships. It is important neither to drop the case nor to push it into fruitless accusations against the abuser and the family. In denial work we need to address the anxieties which lead to the denial as necessary behaviour. It is important to understand the function of the denial for the child, for the abuser and for the mother.

(1) The family process

A

Strong indicators for sexual abuse which is denied

B

Child removed from family

C

6—12 weeks/months later child back in family

No change in family. Child more at risk of abuse with less chance of protection

Figure 10.1(a) Abuse-promoting child protection and crime-promoting crime prevention in cases of denial

(2) The professional process: First case conference/first court decision/first etc.: 'child in danger, needs to be removed'.

Second case conference/ second court decision/second etc.: 'child in no danger, needs to go home'.

All change in professional network everybody exhausted and ready to join denial

Figure 10.1(b) Abuse-promoting child protection and crime-promoting crime prevention in cases of denial

The abuse might be denied by the abuser, by the mother, by the child and by other family members. Each party might deny different aspects of the abuse. It might be total denial that any abuse has taken place at all or it can be partial denial

1 of the abusive circumstances,
2 of the damaging effects,
3 of the addictive and repetitive nature of sexual abuse, and
4 of the abuser's responsibility.

Mothers, abusers, children and other family members often say that some touching had taken place but it was not abuse. They argue that the child has not been harmed and that it will not happen again and they may say that the father was not responsible for what has happened – 'It was when he was drunk' or 'It was when he was asleep' are common excuses made not only by abusers but also by mothers, children and other family members. Partial denial can be similar to minimising and to other defence mechanisms abusers use in the treatment of legally established cases of abuse (see Working with sexual abusers, 7.4).

The key to the understanding of and to working with denial lies in the understanding of the function of denial for every family member. Abusers, children, mothers and other family members deny because they are frightened of disastrous consequences if they admit to the abuse. It is important to understand that the denial has different functions for different family members.

The degree of disastrous consequences increases, the closer the relationship between the abuser and the non-abusing parent as caregiver and between the abuser and the child. If the abuser is the husband or partner or the non-abusing parent and caregiver, the mother will lose more than in cases where no relationship exists between the mother and the abuser. Non-abusing parents and other family members will always disclose abuse by strangers. If mothers disclose sexual abuse by their husband they risk losing their partner and the family breadwinner. They risk loss of social status and of social support and they may lose self-esteem for having been a partner of an abuser. It can mean the loss of a son, of self-respect and of family honour for grandparents and other relatives. For a child who might not have anything to lose by disclosing stranger abuse, the disclosure of intrafamilial abuse often does not only mean the end of sexual abuse, it also leads to the loss of the father and often of the mother and siblings as well. (See Child sexual abuse as syndrome of secrecy, 2.1; Helping protective mothers, 12.11.)

The function of denial can relate to anxieties about:

1 The legal consequences,
2 Consequences for the family and relatives,
3 Psychological consequences,
4 Social consequences, and
5 Financial consequences and consequences on work and professional career.

	Abuser	Mother	Child
(1) Legal	– imprisonment	– care order on child and other siblings	– care order
(2) Family	– loss of partner – loss of children – loss of support by other relatives	– loss of partner – loss of child(ren) – loss of co-parent – loss of support by other relatives	– loss of father – loss of mother – loss of siblings – fear of not being believed – fear of retribution – fear of violence and punishment – fear of violence within the family – fear of abuser's and others' well-being (e.g. abuser's threat of suicide)
(3) Psychological	– suicide – letdown of partner – self-respect – own history of sexual abuse – fear of loneliness and isolation – inability to cope – inability to face addiction and tension relief through abuse	– self-respect – letdown of child – self-blame – having married an abuser – own history of sexual abuse – fear of loneliness and isolation – need to care without partner	– fear of being blamed – fear of being scapegoated – self-blame – fear of loneliness and isolation – loyalty
(4) Social	– reprisal – reputation – stigma – isolation	– reputation – stigma – isolation – problems of being a single parent	– reaction of peers – treatment at school – loss of friends
(5) Financial and professional	– loss of job – loss of earnings – loss of professional licence – loss of reputation	– financial hardship – effects on own work and professional career	

Figure 10.2 Denial: feared consequences of disclosure

Figure 10.2 shows the large range of anxieties which prevent abusers, non-abusing mothers and abused children from disclosing. Some of the feared disasters might be so great that no family member will ever disclose. Working with each family member on the feared disasters as reason for denial has led to disclosures by abusers, mothers and children. Treatment of denial therefore means treatment of the feared disasters in the family. Treatment of denial can take time and often needs to be measured in months and years rather than days and weeks.

Even when family members admit to abuse legally it might not be taken as psychological owning up. The work on psychological denial is one of the corner-stones of therapy, which will only cease at the end of successful treatment. Denial as conscious lying in the context of legal and child protective measures must not be confused with denial as psychological defence mechanism (See Proof and belief, admission and owning up, 1.5; The unconscious and secrecy, 2.4.4.)

Abusers often use the following six areas of denial to disclaim responsibility for the abuse.

1 Primary denial of any abuse. The abuser denies that any abuse has taken place.
2 Denial of severity of facts. Abusers describe less severe acts than have really happened.
3 Denial of knowledge of the abuse. Abusers say that the abuse happened when they were drunk or when they were asleep and they deny that they can be held responsible for what might have happened.
4 Denial of the abusive nature of the abuse. Abusers argue that what they did was not abuse but normal.
5 Denial of the harmful effects of the abuse. Abusers maintain that what they did was not abuse because it did not harm the child.
6 Denial of responsibility. Abusers make children responsible for the abuse by saying that they have triggered the abuse by their behaviour.

The following 14 steps illustrate one way in which we can maintain a goal-oriented stance in the work with denial in family meetings. In denial work important therapeutic effects can be achieved if we can accept that dealing with denial may take time and may require patience and stamina (see The individual process in context, 2.4).

1 Addressing the underlying anxiety of feared disasters

The first step in working with denial addresses the anxiety about the legal threat to the abuser and the fear of possible family disasters which would happen if the abuser, the child or other family member admitted that child sexual abuse has taken place. I would ask 'What would be the biggest disaster that could happen in your family if sexual abuse had taken place?' At that stage the father may already interrupt and repeat that sexual abuse had in fact not happened. It is of vital importance not to react in   symmetrical way. I would therefore say 'sure, I hear what you are saying and I do not know whether abuse has taken place or not. I only know that those things do happen these days and that the issue has been raised. So what would be the greatest disaster in your family if sexual abuse had happened?' Usually I would turn with this question to the mother or to non-abused siblings or to the child, but not to the suspected abuser. Family members will quickly come out with fears about imprisonment, divorce, suicide, murder, violence, social stigma and other secondary effects of family breakdown.

In very defensive families with high anxiety levels I often put alternatives to family members which indicate maximal disaster. I ask for instance 'Would your father kill himself or would he kill you?' What seems a cruel and unprofessional suggestion has on an indirect level the effect of giving the child and other family members permission to think about the worst disaster they really fear and which they may be too frightened to mention. Even if the child or other family members have lesser fears the example of the ultimate disaster gives the child and the family the contextual message

a   that I know that family members might have strong fears,
b   that these fears are common,
c   that I know about them,
d   that I don't get frightened or punitive about them.

Very often this initial process already decreases the anxiety of children and families considerably.

2 Understanding the function of the denial as necessary for the abuser and the family

When family members have disclosed fears of imprisonment and other disasters we can understand and discuss the function of the denial as necessary to avoid a major disaster, and we can make it clear that we do not expect any family member to disclose. We can say to the father 'I now understand that it is important that you say "no" even if sexual abuse had happened. I am not saying that it has happened, but if it had happened you would have to go to prison. You obviously would not want to go to prison and your family may not want you imprisoned either. It is therefore necessary that you go on to deny sexual abuse even if it had happened. In fact it could be foolish to disclose because the person who discloses would be blamed for having caused the disaster.'

It is possible to make sense of the denial as a function of feared disasters which family members voice and we can understand and share with the family the need and the function of maintaining the denial. We also need to give the child and the family the message that we know that they deny not because they are malicious or stupid but because they feel the denial is necessary to avoid the feared disaster. (See From mad to bad, Chapter 1.)

3 Working on the hypothetical 'as if' level

The next step is to make clear that we are not police officers, and that we are at this stage not interested in finding out whether sexual abuse has happened or not. Even if it had happened we would not expect the child and the family to disclose. I sometimes go so far as to say that the father is not allowed to admit even if sexual abuse had taken place because of the possible disaster a disclosure would bring about. I would continue to work on the hypothetical level and explore in full what would happen to the child and the family if abuse had happened and if it were disclosed. We often need to deal with a great number of different fears of different family members about different disasters which might happen if sexual abuse were disclosed.

4 Not taking 'no' for an answer

The work on the hypothetical 'as if' level allows us not to take 'No' for an answer. We can make the crucial distinction between the two possible different meanings of the 'No'. It can mean that no sexual abuse has happened but it can also mean that sexual abuse has happened but that the child, the abuser and the family are too frightened to disclose. We can establish that sexual abuse might well have happened and might well be a reality in the family despite the 'No'. The statement 'Sexual abuse might have happened despite the "no" or it might not have happened. But even if it has happened I would not expect anything else than a denial' does not only free the family to think about their own anxieties. It also frees the professionals to have an open mind as to whether sexual abuse has taken place or not.

5 Not pushing for facts and confessions

Once allegations have been made openly and once these allegations have been denied in a direct confrontation with the abuser and the family in direct questioning we need to abandon our wish to get facts and need to turn around completely and do seemingly exactly the opposite from what we need to do.

Paradoxically we can only get the facts in cases of denial if we do not want to get the facts immediately. Once the direct approach with direct questioning has failed and once the suspected abuser has denied sexual abuse, further pushing in order to obtain confessions will only lead to a hardening of the denial and to increased secrecy and hostility. We need to address the anxieties about the disaster in the context of the denial. We need truly to abandon for the time being getting at the facts of possible abuse. When we understand the anxieties behind the denial and the function of it we do not need to push for facts or confessions at this stage but can concentrate on the context of the anxieties which prevent family members from disclosing.

6 Introducing the concept of responsibility

Working on the hypothetical 'as if' level, the question of responsibility can be raised as in an ordinary first session as reality-creating responsibility session. In denial work we can deal on a hypothetical level with the issues of responsibility, participation, guilt, blame and power with the same therapeutic effect for the child even if the denial remains intact. We can follow all the steps of the Primary Therapeutic Intervention as if the family had disclosed the abuse. The question to the child 'If the abuse had happened, do you think it would be your or your father's responsibility?' already addresses in potentially highly therapeutic ways important therapeutic goals in the treatment of child sexual abuse. On the hypothetical 'as if' level many important issues of family relationships and individual psychological problems can be addressed openly, as in the treatment of established abuse. (See Aims and steps in the Primary Therapeutic Intervention, 6.2; The first family meeting as reality-creating responsibility meeting, 9.11.)

7 Normalising secrecy

In the next step I try to normalise the context of secrecy. I always ask about birthday presents and about how ordinary secrets are dealt with in the family. I ask, 'Who is good at keeping secrets in your family and who is bad at it?' One question which often creates a much more relaxed atmosphere, and even laughter, is, 'If you were paid to keep secrets who would be rich in your family and who would be poor?'

At this step we can explore how ordinary secrets are dealt with in the family and we can begin to differentiate between family members who are good at keeping secrets and others who are bad at it. This differentiation is preparing the ground for the possibility that some family members might disclose the secret of sexual abuse more easily than others. The broadening of the topic of secrecy into ordinary family secrets and the use of normalising phrases like 'who is an expert and who is useless at keeping secrets?' usually leads to an instant decrease in tension and to visible relief and relaxation in all family members.

8 Reframing as 'bottling up'

I like to reframe the question of 'who is good at keeping a family secret?' into the question, 'who is good at bottling up secrets?'. This reframing has the function of turning secrecy into something which people may find difficult to handle because it may be difficult to bottle up. I like to use the concept of 'bottling up' because it is a very concrete metaphor. 'Bottling up' can be illustrated in a very physical and bodily way which all family members, including small children, can understand. I usually support the talking about bottling-up by non-verbal gestures of pushing something down inside me which wants to come up. I then ask the family, 'Who is really good at bottling up, keeping all the pressure in and who is hopeless at it?'

9 Suffering from secrecy

Even young children can understand that bottling-up a secret can lead to great pressure and can create tummy pain which makes people suffer. I often ask small children of 3 to 5, 'Who do you think gets most tummy pain from bottling up and keeping things deep down very much?' The notion of bottling up many secrets or one big secret creates a notion that family members might suffer from keeping important secrets, and that they may understandably want to get rid of these pains, upsets and pressures.

10 Disclosure of normal secrets and 'slip-ups'

Following the discussion of how good or bad people are in bottling up we can ask about occasions where family members have 'slipped up'. 'Slip-ups' happen when secrets are bottled up too much. This is another very concrete metaphor which children of all ages can easily understand. The metaphor of 'slip-ups' helps even very resistant families to relate incidents where family members have 'slipped up' and accidentally told a normal secret they were not supposed to disclose.

The discussion about bottling up of normal family secrets around birthdays and other events quite often leads to real fun in the session when family members relate typical stories of somebody 'slipping up' about a surprise they should have kept to themselves. The usual effect is that the anxiety level of all family members decreases visibly. Talking about 'slipping up' gives the message to the abused child and the family that 'slip-ups' do happen and are normal in other contexts.

11 Structural differences between adults and children

We then need to differentiate between 'slipping up' of adults and 'slipping up' of children. It is helpful to overemphasise the difference between dependent and biologically immature children and adults by stressing that children and even adolescents are quite often irrational and illogical. This is not because they are bad or malicious but for the simple and normal reasons that they are immature, which in turn is the reason why they are still children and adolescents. Children often do not know what they are doing and saying and they can be out of control. They still need parents and they are different from adults who are logical and in control of themselves as grown-up people. I would highlight the structural difference between children and parents, even so far as deliberately putting down the child or the adolescent. The seeming denigration of the child has the function of normalising the fact that children and adolescents are illogical, that their minds work differently from those of adults.

Talking about differences in maturity carries the message that children may be unable to withstand the pressure of bottling up and may slip up without knowing. The 'slipping-up' as disclosure of secrets then becomes the normal function of the child's immaturity for which the child is not responsible. Stressing the issue that the child's or the adolescent's mind works differently from that of adults helps to avoid a subsequent disclosure which leads to blaming the child, because children cannot help it. Adults are different, they can keep secrets.

12 Whom would the child trust?

The question of whom the child might trust to tell a very big secret often frees children to entertain for the first time the idea that they could find somebody to whom they could disclose. Several children who disclosed after denial work later talked about the importance of this question. It had freed them for the first time to begin to think about a person they knew to whom they could disclose.

13 When would the child trust to disclose?

We can reflect in the same hypothetical way on how long it might take the child to disclose difficult secrets, whether it would take weeks or months or years. In addressing the questions of trust and dealing with all the anxieties which could prevent the child from disclosing, we can initiate a process in the session and in the child's mind in which the child can begin to find possible solutions for a future disclosure. (See The interactional nature of motivation, 2.4.1; Giving explicit licence to communicate, 2.4.2; Explicit therapeutic permission to disclose, 8.5.)

14 When and whom would the abuser trust?

I sometimes ask abusers the same question about when and in whom they would trust to confide if sexual abuse had happened. Sometimes I put it indirectly and ask the mother 'Who would your husband trust to confide in if sexual abuse had happened? How long would it take him to disclose and under what circumstances would he dare to do so?' In raising the issue we can already begin to deal with possible solutions to the dilemma of the denial for the abuser.

In consultation sessions with professionals from child protective agencies we finally need to turn to the abuser with the additional question, 'What do you think the agency would need to know for it to be safe for you to live with the child or to have access?' Sometimes I have asked suspected abusers to put themselves into the place of Directors of Social Services, saying 'If you were the Director of Social Services what would you need to know in that position of responsibility from somebody who has been accused of having sexually abused a child to be sure that the child is safe?'(See Dealing with statutory hierarchies in professional–family meetings, 11.10.)

If legal agencies and courts are involved we can put the suspected abuser into the judge's chair. Hypothetical questioning of the suspected abuser in the assumed role of the judge can create serious and acceptable child protective and potentially therapeutic solutions for children in families of denial. Suspected abusers who live at home may agree that it would only be safe if they moved out. They may agree to supervised access and they often develop a differentiated list of conditions for a step-by-step rehabilitation and treatment for themselves and for the family. (See Therapy and consultation, 5.4; Practical problems in consultations, 11.5; Dealing with statutory hierarchies in professional–family meetings, 11.6.)

Denial work is like digging the river bed all the way along but keeping the lock of denial still closed. The only step which remains is to open the lock in the actual disclosure. Denial work aims at decreasing the level of anxiety and the degree of defensiveness in the family. Decreased levels of anxiety increase the likelihood of disclosure and help professionals and the family to remain problem-oriented.

In some cases full disclosure by children has taken place within weeks. Denial work can be highly therapeutic even if it does not lead to an immediate disclosure. The hypothetical 'as if' – work is therapeutic when it conveys to the child that somebody in the world has not taken 'no' for an answer and believes that sexual abuse may have happened even if everybody including the child denies it. Denial work does not only address ongoing sexual abuse behind the denial and the anxieties which prevent its disclosure. It also addresses on a hypothetical level all but the first aims and steps in the Primary Therapeutic Intervention.

A further important therapeutic effect results from the message to the child that the interviewer also understands the child's predicament. The child's wish to disclose and to be protected from further abuse is counter balanced by the fear of a disaster for herself, the suspected abuser and the family.

Denial work is certainly only the second best way of working with cases of sexual abuse, but it is less hopeless than we often think. It can give professionals the necessary time and space to remain problem-oriented and effective. Denial work with children, abusers and other family members can become highly problem-oriented and therapeutic when professionals can avoid the escalation of symmetrical battles about whether abuse has taken place or not. Denial work has the following six important effects:

1 It names child sexual abuse as a possible family reality even if it has been denied.
2 Denial work helps the child and other family members to make sense of the denial. It makes sense of the anxieties which prevent family members from disclosing and names the predicament of wanting to disclose without creating major family disasters.

3 Denial work addresses the issues of responsibility, participation, guilt and blame which are crucial treatment issues in child sexual abuse.
4 Above all, denial work frees the child, the family and the professionals to begin to think in problem-oriented terms. The ability to think in a problem-oriented way is one of the first faculties to vanish in the battle of denial.
5 Denial work prepares possible ways for the child and sometimes for the abuser to disclose. Children can, under the cover of denial, work secretly on their anxieties until they feel confident enough to disclose.
6 Denial work enables children, often for the first time, to think specifically about a possible person and possible circumstances under which they might be able to disclose.

We need to learn to understand that in denial work we often need to wait a long time for a full disclosure. In the mean time we can address most aims and goals of the Primary Therapeutic Intervention and can help the child and sometimes the abuser eventually to disclose. Professionals need to accept the following three main difficulties:

1 The process of disclosure after denial can take many weeks and months, and even years.
2 Any symmetrical and oppositional battle with the abuser and the family on the question of whether abuse has happened or not needs to be avoided.
3 Professionals need to have patience and must not try in desperation to push or or drop the case altogether.

Denial work in child sexual abuse also requires a truly open mind as to whether sexual abuse has in fact taken place or not. Addressing the context of denial rather than the content of possible sexual abuse demands that professionals are able to work with children, abusers and families over weeks and months without disclosure. This process gives all professionals involved the chance permanently to assess their own reasons for suspicion.

It can happen that professionals come to the conclusion that their suspicions were unfounded. I worked with one family for 9 months until I was convinced that no child sexual abuse had taken place. The accusation was part of a Munchausen-syndrome-by-proxy (see Section 14.6) of the mother who had herself been sexually abused as a child. In another case it took a girl more than 18 months after the first denial session to disclose fully in a way which could not be dismissed. I had seen her in individual denial-work and had gone over the same 14 areas with which I deal in family sessions. Denial work with families usually needs to be followed by individual denial-work which covers the same areas. Denial work can also be done from the beginning separately with only the child or the suspected abuser and other family members. (See Giving explicit licence to communicate, 2.4.2; Explicit therapeutic permission to disclose, 8.5; The use of prevention films in suspicion and disclosure, 8.12.)

Denial work allows professionals to learn from mistakes through which they themselves have often induced the denial. The added difficulties of denial work should help professionals to refrain from premature interventions on the level of a vague first-line suspicion. We need to be aware that many cases of denial are triggered by insufficient preparations in the professional network and by other mistakes during the intervention. (See The interactional nature of motivation, 2.4.1; The professional network, Chapter 5; Preparation for disclosure, Chapter 8.)

Frequent secondary denial after initial admission and disclosure is an import-ant argument for an early family meeting as reality-creating responsibility meet-ing. We see time and again that fathers, children and mothers reveal child sexual abuse in the acute crisis only to withdraw the disclosure again later. An early family meeting will prevent the disclosed abuse from relapsing into secondary denial. (See The first family meeting as reality-creating responsibility meeting, 9.11; Relapse into secondary denial, 12.13.)

Denial will be a central feature in child sexual abuse as long as we have no better-developed treatment facilities for sexual abusers. Abusers will only admit when they are dealt with in a problem-oriented Primary Therapeutic Intervention. For the sake of sexually abused children we need to make the case for problem-oriented approaches to the treatment of abusers. Treatment for abusers is an important task for probation officers and adult psychiatrists who need to become part of the standard multi-professional network in child sexual abuse.

Chapter eleven

Interprofessional problems

11.1 Finding the appropriate sexual language to communicate about the abuse

Not only families but also professionals need to find an appropriate explicit sexual language in which they can communicate about sexual abuse. It is most interesting to see how very experienced and skilled professionals find it difficult to address directly and openly the sexual aspects of sexual abuse. I often see very experienced professionals getting themselves increasingly muddled up talking about 'it' happened and who did 'it' and how often 'it' took place. They are unable to use explicit sexual language in an appropriate way. Other professionals instantly use sexual language in an insensitive way which instantly increases the anxiety in the family and which can easily lead to denial.

The difficulty of finding the appropriate sexual language has a parallel situation in the medical examination of sexually abused children. Inexperienced doctors either do not dare to look at the anus or the vagina of a girl at all, or they are in danger of metaphorically diving between the child's legs in a way which can be most anxiety provoking and frightening for the child. Mental health and legal professionals need to find their own explicit sexual language in the same way as paediatricians and police surgeons need to find appropriate ways of conducting a medical examination. This means neither avoiding the sexual nature of sexual abuse nor diving insensitively between the child's legs literally or metaphorically.

It can be difficult for female professionals to have to sit with a sexual abuser in a room and to have to talk about the abuser 'putting his penis into the child's anus'. Male therapists can find it difficult to have to talk to a well-developed adolescent girl about the experience of how it was when 'your father had sexual intercourse with you and when you took his penis into your mouth'.

The sexual nature of child sexual abuse can make appropriate and explicit communication very difficult for professionals. Our own shame and embarrassment and feelings of voyeurism can interfere with a neutral professional stance. We therefore need to give ourselves and our professional colleagues the 'licence to communicate openly about sexual abuse'. It is for this reason that I often start workshops on child sexual abuse by relating some of the very personal experiences I have had in dealing with sexually abused children and their families. Telling colleagues about my own experiences and difficulties of working with child sexual abuse serves as direct and explicit licence and permission for fellow professionals to communicate in open sexual language about sexual abuse. We need to unlearn feeling embarrassed, voyeuristic or ashamed and need to learn to find a neutral and factual professional language. (See Preface.)

Dealing with child sexual abuse in the family does not start with the child or with the family but begins with ourselves and our own ability to deal with our own attitude towards sex and child sexual abuse and with our own ability as professionals to find the appropriate language. Because sex is by its very nature such an emotive and private topic we may need each other's help. Quite often it has been helpful to practise repeatedly in role plays how we can talk openly with a child about sexual abuse, how a woman can talk to a sexual abuser explicitly about sexual abuse and how a man can talk to a nearly grown-up adolescent girl about her sexual experiences in a way which is explicit, appropriate and helpful. We also need to give each other the space to admit that we may find this task difficult and that it may take time to become relaxed in dealing with the explicit sexual nature of sexual abuse. Professionals will only be able to be therapeutic and children and families will only open up when professionals have first found an appropriate open sexual language and an attitude first which makes them feel comfortable in dealing with the subject. Only then will abused children, abusers and families be able to find their own language to talk about sexual abuse in their families. (See The interactional nature of motivation, 2.4.1; Does the gender of the therapist matter?, 12.15.)

11.2 Sexually abused professionals

The problem of professionals who have been sexually abused as children themselves and who are confronted with sexually abused children in their work is still not fully recognised. It is an issue which needs urgent attention. It is perfectly acceptable for professionals to disclose other life events which may have an influence on their work such as personal bereavement and marital separations. But it is as yet nearly impossible for professionals to disclose their own experience of child sexual abuse.

The effects of child sexual abuse as syndrome of secrecy also apply for professionals who have been abused themselves and it can be extremely difficult for sexually abused professionals to deal with their own experience of sexual abuse as a precondition for their professional work with sexually abused children. It can be equally difficult for professionals who know that they are not ready yet to deal as professionals with child sexual abuse to refuse doing the work which for personal reasons they are unable to do. Often they cannot even disclose why they cannot deal with sexual abuse because a personal disclosure would be counted against them professionally. (See The individual process, Chapter 2.)

If the behaviour of a co-professional leads to the suspicion that this colleague might have been sexually abused herself or himself it would be quite inappropriate to treat this colleague in any way differently from any other colleague. If professional colleagues have been able to deal with their own sexual abuse, this experience may also help them to understand professionally sexually abused children. Nevertheless processes of identification with sexually abused children can create problems for some sexually abused colleagues who have been unable to deal with their own abuse. For these colleagues primary identifications with the victim or the feeling of re-enactment of their own sexual abuse can be extremely stressful. The personal reactions of one professional colleague can influence the entire professional network considerably. The result can be extreme conflicts-by-proxy in the professional network and great personal distress (see The professional network, Chapter 5).

We need to achieve a professional attitude where it is professionally acknowledged and accepted that colleagues might be sexually abused themselves. We then need to refrain from pathologising. We need to come to a point where it becomes acceptable to decline sexual abuse work in cases where professionals have suffered long-term sexual abuse to a degree which interferes with their professional stance. Many professional colleagues suffer from the consequences of child sexual abuse. Others have been less affected. The personal experience of child sexual abuse can certainly lead to stronger primary identifications with defendants, clients and patients and to greater dangers of conflicts-by-proxy.

If the personal experience of sexual abuse of a colleague interferes with the professional task we can approach the problem through a senior of the colleague concerned or through a close colleague who would with the appropriate care and discretion attempt to introduce the subject of identification and the possible need for help. The problem of a sexually abused colleague who finds it difficult to function professionally can be dealt with appropriately and with integrity and confidentiality when the abused colleague works in an institutional context which allows a personal and confidential approach by senior colleagues.

Matters can become difficult for professionals who work outside hierarchical structures such as GPs or judges or when abused professionals themselves are in senior positions. The problem of the sexually abused senior professional in the legal field, in courts, in child protective agencies, in the educational system and in the child health and child mental health institutions is still fully taboo. Nevertheless the acting out of the abused professional's own trauma can jeopardise the overall therapeutic approach and can influence the work of other professionals who are unable and not in a position to address the possible sexual abuse of the colleague concerned.

It is difficult enough to address the problem of sexually abused professionals in the areas of health, mental health, education and social work. It is nearly impossible but most urgent to address the issue in the legal system where lawyers, juries, magistrates and judges deal with criminal cases and child protective procedures in child sexual abuse in professional isolation and independence without being allowed to refuse a case which may lead to a re-enactment of their own experience of child sexual abuse.

Sometimes it is possible to address this difficult and potentially very destructive situation in a distressed colleague in an indirect way which addresses the suspected sexual abuse without mentioning it openly. In the context of case conferences, meetings or workshops with professionals I try to address the suspected sexual abuse of a colleague indirectly by talking in general terms about possible long-term consequences of child sexual abuse which seemingly relate to the topic in general, or to some clinical case I may take as an example but in which I do in fact address the co-professional's own sexual abuse. As in cases of suspicion in children where we use 'The Story of the Other Child' we can talk to the colleague using a general case or a case of a specific child as a means of communicating about how adults who have been sexually abused can find some help. In talking about 'the general case of sexual abuse' we can address all the problems we see in the co-professional which arise out of her or his own identification with the sexually abused child. When we communicate about secrecy in the indirect form we may not only assist sexually abused colleagues to find help in their own right but we may also influence and hopefully stop the acting-out as a result of primary identification with the sexually abused child. Working in this way has led to confidential disclosures and in some cases to the arrangement of specific help for the colleagues in their own right. (See The interactional nature of motivation, 2.4.1; Giving explicit licence to communicate, 2.4.2.)

11.3 Interprofessional support

Not only sexually abused colleagues need support. All professionals who work in this field need some support which should address the following six main areas:

1 In child sexual abuse as syndrome of secrecy it can be very difficult to maintain a clear sense of reality. Mirroring processes from the child and the family quite often make it difficult to decide whether what we perceive is really external reality or whether it is our own fantasy. It is extremely important to have a fellow professional to whom we can talk in order to clarify our own thinking when we have a suspicion of sexual abuse and when we enter into the process of disclosure and treatment. The confusion of professionals between reality and fantasy is mirroring the processes arising from the basic nature of child sexual abuse as syndrome of secrecy. I sometimes need to say to somebody aloud 'I think I have seen a child playing sexualised in this or that way. Do you think this could indicate sexual abuse or do you think all of this is only in my head?' This kind of clarification with a colleague is essentially necessary to avoid either joining the child's and the family's system of secrecy or conversely to avoid rushing into a premature intervention when the

suspicion has not yet reached the level of a firm second-line suspicion. (See The individual process, Chapter 2; Preparation for disclosure, Chapter 8.)

Clarification of external reality can also be necessary during therapy. I had several families and children who in the process of therapy fell back into denial and relapsed into secrecy. It is then necessary to have a colleague outside the therapeutic system with whom I can check whether my perception of reality or fantasy, which mirrors the therapeutic process of confusion between external reality and non-reality, is part of a collusion with the child's denial or whether it is the expression of external reality (see Individual counselling and therapy, 7.3).

2 The work with child sexual abuse can be emotionally draining. Personal identifications in sexual abuse can induce unrealistic fears, rescue fantasies and subsequent burn-out even when we are aware of our own identifications and of the mirroring processes in the professional network and even when we have reached conflict-resolutions-by-proxy. All professionals need a place to deal with the effects which the work with sexually abused children has on themselves (see The professional network, Chapter 5).

3 Mirroring processes in child sexual abuse as syndrome of secrecy always threatens to split the professional network and can lead to scapegoating amongst professionals. We constantly need to support each other in order to be able to admit that we all make mistakes. Even if we are skilled, competent and responsible in our own profession, the skills and responsibilities needed for dealing with child sexual abuse are greater than any task, skill and responsibility of any individual professional and agency can cover. In child sexual abuse as truly multi-professional and metasystemic problem we need to be able to share our doubts about whether we are acting appropriately with professional colleagues from other professions and agencies who can assist us in putting our own thoughts and actions into the context of the overall intervention (see Preface and Introduction; From mad to bad, Chapter 1).

4 We need to be extremely responsible with ourselves in terms of indicating our own boundaries and limits under which we can work when we want to avoid personal and professional burn-out. This must not provide any excuse for opting out from professional responsibilities. But we do need interprofessional support constantly to reassess our own personal and professional limits, which we must not overstep. To be kind to ourselves is quite often one of the most difficult tasks for professionals who are involved in intensely demanding work with sexually abused children and their families. Burnt-out professionals are lost professionals. To be kind and responsible with oneself can therefore indicate a highly professional attitude. (See The interprofessional process, 5.1.)

5 Gender issues between men and women and sexualisation of children require clarification of personal attitudes towards sexuality and about specific personal and gender responses towards the sexual nature of child sexual abuse.

Child sexual abuse as syndrome of secrecy is still reflected in the taboo between professionals in talking freely about the sexual aspects of sexual abuse in the interprofessional work. This in turn is reflected in the fact that sexually abused professionals cannot yet freely disclose their own sexual abuse without being stigmatised. Gender issues and the problem of handling sexualised behaviour of sexually abused children do need interprofessional discussion, clarification, support and consultation. (See Does the gender of the therapist matter?, 12.15.)

6 The specific multi-professional problems of management and treatment in a metasystemic approach often require interprofessional support to clarify positions towards other professionals and towards the family. The confusing and complex process where certain steps in therapy, and where actions towards child protection and crime prevention, can in different contexts lead to exactly the opposite outcome of the intended intervention requires support to clarify each professional's position in the multi-dimensional orbit of the overall intervention. (See Family process, Chapter 3; The family and the professional network, Chapter 4; The orofessional network, Chapter 5.)

In child sexual abuse we must not work on our own. Even having only one colleague with whom we can discuss aspects of interprofessional support can be most helpful and can prevent professional acting-out and personal burn-out. Working in a coherent team gives the best opportunity for personal and professional support, especially if we can work together regularly over a period of time with colleagues from other professions who need to be involved.

Interprofessional support in working with child sexual abuse is no luxury. If we do not learn to be responsible with ourselves we will not be able to conduct this most complex professional task responsibly. The result can be severe conflicts-by-proxy and acting-out in non-therapeutic action responses according to the formal competence and formal responsibilities of agencies and professions. This often results in anti-therapeutic therapy in crime-promoting crime prevention and abuse-promoting child protection and in secondary damage to the child and the family. Interprofessional support is therefore a basic requirement and needs to be an integral part of the overall intervention because the task in child sexual abuse is greater than the skill and the responsibility of any single agency and professional can cover. If people do have to work on their own it is therefore very important that they organise some structured support and supervision from outside or from senior colleagues.

11.4 The problem of the 'expert'

Experts create as many problems as they solve – only different ones. Experts in dealing with child sexual abuse are a mixed blessing. To accept the notion of experts in child sexual abuse easily creates the false expectation that somebody who knows could tell others who do not know. The notion of the 'experts' makes us easily forget that the debate is not between the ones who can see and the ones who cannot. The dialogue in child sexual abuse as complex metasystemic problem is one between the half-blind and the blind when we think about our ability to avoid secondary damage to children and families and to achieve the aims and goals of the Primary Therapeutic Intervention. (See Preface, Introduction; From mad to bad, Chapter 1).

The notion of the 'expert' creates a false belief in the possibility that in child sexual abuse we can find mono-professional solutions. Even if we have expert knowledge in particular areas of sexual abuse we can only be experts in our own particular domain and only on a particular problem of the overall metasystemic needs of the intervention. I only have skills and responsibilities for a very small part of the Primary Therapeutic Intervention. The tasks, the skills and the responsibilities in the overall intervention are larger than any single professional or agency can cover. The notion of the 'expert' also creates even greater pressure on other professionals who are not regarded as 'experts' quickly to become experts, which in turn may lead to even more severe mistakes. (See The interprofessional process in context, 5.2.)

Becoming an 'expert' in child sexual abuse as multi-professional problem means to respect the expertise, the skill and the responsibilities of fellow professionals from other agencies and professions. When 'experts' in child sexual abuse become experts in knowing that they can only be experts in a very limited part of the overall problem, they also allow fellow professionals to trust their own expertise and the experience they have gained in other areas of their work which they can use in sexual abuse work. This holds especially for experience in working with physical abuse. Many of these skills can be used in sexual abuse work although they have to be put into the very specific and different context of child sexual abuse as syndrome of secrecy and addiction. Nevertheless the emergence of 'experts' in child sexual abuse threatens to deskill colleagues who have much more expertise and skills than others and they themselves credit themselves with (see Changing interprofessional and institutional co-operation, 5.3).

The referral of suspected cases of sexual abuse away from the Trusted Person to the 'experts for the evaluation and assessment of child sexual abuse' can be encouraged by guidelines which have been created to avoid inappropriate handling of disclosures and therapy. Many of these guidelines are worrying examples of how highly professional work can in the metasystemic intervention of child sexual abuse turn into exactly the opposite. In child sexual abuse as syndrome of secrecy the referral away from the Trusted Person as 'expert for the child' to 'experts for sexual abuse' can lead directly to a *decrease* of disclosures if we do not distinguish between the role of the 'expert for the child' and the task of the 'expert for sexual abuse'. (See Preparation for disclosure, Chapter 8; The use of the 'trusted person', 8.6.)

11.5 Practical problems in consultations

When a referral for 'therapy' turns out to be in fact an indirect request for consultation I would initially never see the child or the family. I would always meet the professionals first for consultation. Conflicts-by-proxy usually come up fairly quickly and we can try to achieve a conflict-resolution-by-proxy (see The professional network, Chapter 5).

When child protective agencies ask for assistance in decision making about a particular family I would invite the statutory social worker and the family to attend the consultation together. The consultation would have to address in hierarchical order:

1 The interprofessional process.
2 The professional–family process.
3 The family process.

In a brief meeting with the professionals on their own prior to the professional–family meeting we need to clarify first whether there are any structural institutional conflicts or conflicts-by-proxy in the professional network and in the social worker's own hierarchy. Following the assessment of the interprofessional process I would turn to the professional–family process. In the professional–family meeting I ask the social worker in the presence of the family about her formal responsibility and about the actual issues involved in the decision-making process with regards to the child and the family. I ask questions like 'What decisions need to be made and how can I assist in your decision-making process?' With this question I do not only clarify the task. I also give explicitly and implicitly the message to the family that I am at the service of the professional colleague and answerable to her. This often counteracts right from the beginning possible attempts by families to split the professional network into 'the good therapist' versus 'the bad child protection worker'. In a third step I would turn to the family and I would address the family process and the individual problems in the presence of the referring professional. In consultation we can only assess and treat children and families in the context of the stated aims and goals of the consultation. In consultation the professional colleague and not the family is the client even when the family is present. Therapeutic work in the context of statutory involvement can never be therapy. The family has come as a result of the statutory involvement and not as a free agent. All therapeutic work can therefore only be seen in the context of the consultation to the professional colleague. (See The interprofessional process, 5.1; Changing interprofessional and institutional co-operation, 5.3).

The family of a 13-year-old girl and a 14-year-old boy who had been sexually abused by their father was brought by the social worker who had asked for assistance to assess whether it was safe for the children to return home. Although the father had moved out from home the suspicion had arisen as to whether the uncle who lived in the house had also abused the children. The social worker brought the family for consultation to the professional–family meeting. At first I turned to the social worker to ask about the specific problems in the decision-making process she and her agency had in the case. She talked about the need to assess the degree of protectiveness of the adults and the dangers of renewed secrecy and re-abuse. Having established the task of the consultation with the social worker I turned to the family and conducted a family interview. Because the uncle denied all allegations of abuse I conducted a denial interview addressing all the anxieties which may prevent the uncle and the children from disclosing (see Dealing with primary denial, 10.6).

After an exploration of the family process as in a family session proper, at the end of the meeting I turned back to the social worker as my client and asked what she and the hierarchy in her agency needed to know to be able to decide whether under the given circumstances of denial it was safe for the children to return home. I then assisted the social worker to establish the specific preconditions and the criteria for change for the family under which she and her agency felt that it would be safe for the children to return home.

This consultation to the professional–family system was as much therapeutic as any family therapy session proper could have been. The important difference from therapy was the metasystemic context of statutory decision making in which the meeting took place. The family session needed to be put at the beginning and at the end into the context of the professional–family process and the interprofessional process of consultation.

11.6 Dealing with professional hierarchies in consultations

When we consult the professional network or when we ourselves receive consultation we always need to include the hierarchies of all agencies involved. It is of little use to consult a junior social worker, a junior police officer, a junior doctor or a junior teacher without considering the hierarchy. Otherwise we may agree on a common approach in the professional network and we may achieve potentially highly therapeutic conflict-resolutions-by-proxy amongst the junior professionals who are directly involved in the case, only to throw the entire intervention into disarray at the moment when we become effective because the respective hierarchies who had not been involved in the process from the beginning are unable to understand and to agree with the proposed problem solution (see The professional network, Chapter 5).

We always need to deal with hierarchies on two levels: first on the level of the professional network as separate sub-system and second on the level of the professional–family process. I often get requests for consultations to assist child protection workers in the decision-making process of sexual abuse cases. Whenever we discuss problem solutions for specific cases where statutory responsibilities are involved we need to consult on possible problems within the professional hierarchy first. It is mandatory to ask questions like 'If your senior and your deputy director who is responsible for fieldwork were here and would listen in, what would they say to this suggestion?' Addressing interprofessional issues first often reveals that seemingly unresolvable conflicts between the professionals and the family originate in fact in conflicts within professional hierarchy with different opinions on different levels of responsibility.

When a conflict-by-proxy within a social services hierarchy or within any other professional hierarchy emerges, the interprofessional conflict-by-proxy which is in hierarchical terms a higher-order conflict needs to be resolved first before any further problem-oriented decision can be reached on the hierarchically lower professional–family level. As long as the interprofessional conflicts are not resolved first, the non-integrated and disagreeing professional hierarchies will interfere to the detriment of the family and the junior professionals. This process can threaten to change the basic nature of the intervention at the point when the junior professionals embark on a problem-oriented approach towards the family. (See The family and the professional network, Chapter 4; The interprofessional process, 5.1.)

Conflicts-by-proxy within professional hierarchies can best be tackled by direct consultation to the junior colleague and his or her senior. For practical reasons this does not often happen. We then need to follow an indirect route which can in addition help the junior professional to become more autonomous. First we need to discuss the possible problem resolution of the conflict-by-proxy with the junior on his own. If the consultation reveals that a conflict-resolution-by-proxy according to the steps of the Primary Therapeutic Intervention might be resisted by the hierarchy we can help the fieldworker to develop 'predictions of bad outcome' and the complementary 'predictions of good outcome'. This can assist the professional network to become problem-oriented again. (See The Primary Therapeutic Intervention, Chapter 6; Changing interprofessional and institutional co-operation, 5.3; Therapy and consultation, 5.4.)

11.7 Preparing court reports

Court reports in child sexual abuse cases are often very difficult to write. Although the responsibility of courts is only to consider the legal aspects of the case, courts make crucial decisions which deeply influence the ways in which other professionals are able to fulfil their own separate professional tasks. As the highest agency in the hierarchy of linear professional sub-systems, courts deeply determine the basic structure of the overall intervention. They often influence through legal decisions long-term aspects of the child's mental health and of family relationships. (See Three basic types of intervention, 4.1; Aims and steps in the Primary Therapeutic Intervention, 6.2).

Court reports must not only contain recommendations which assist the legal decision-making process. The report also needs to point out the effects of the court decision on all other sub-systems in the network. To assist legal colleagues and courts to place themselves within the wider context of an overall Primary Therapeutic Intervention, the recommendations of the report need to state the possible long-term consequences of the different possible legal decisions on the legal process itself, on the work and the task of other professional sub-groups and on the child and the family. In court reports non-legal professionals need to put the different possible legal options of the court into a wider context in order to point out which court decisions could lead to crime-promoting crime prevention and would force child protection workers into abuse-promoting child protection and therapists into anti-therapeutic therapy (see The professional process in context, 5.2).

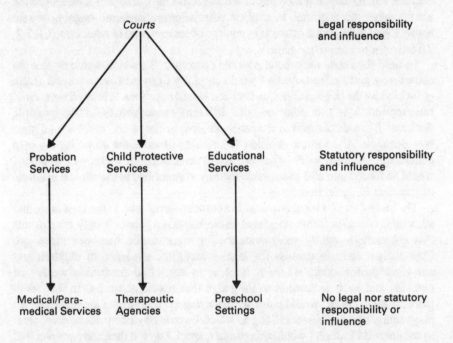

Figure 11.1 Hierarchy of linear professional responsibility and influence

Recommendations in court reports in child sexual abuse cases need to contain four elements:

1 A court report needs to list all possible legal outcomes equally.
2 Each of the possible outcomes needs to be examined in terms of their consequence for the basic structure of the wider professional intervention.
3 Possible legal outcomes which may lead to crime-promoting crime prevention, to abuse-promoting child protection and to anti-therapeutic therapy need to be linked to the 'predictions of bad outcome'.
4 Possible decisions which can assist in creating the framework for a Primary Therapeutic Intervention need to be supported by 'predictions of good outcome' (see Changing interprofessional and institutional co-operation, 5.3).

I would usually list the different possible outcomes and would discuss each of them separately. In a specific case I may predict that the possible decision 'A' of a father being allowed to return home without treatment could lead to possible further sexual abuse and to the severe psychological disturbance of the child. I would need to state that the court decision 'A' itself could directly increase the likelihood of further crime and may lead to crime-promoting crime prevention. I would need to state that the court would have to take full responsibility not only for the legal decision 'A' itself but also for the long-term consequences of the decision and for the increased risk of crime-promoting crime prevention when the abuser takes the acquittal as explicit permission to continue ongoing sexual abuse. (See Child sexual abuse as syndrome of secrecy, and of addiction, 2.1, 2.2, 2.3.)

I would then state the second possible outcome, 'B', which would be that the abuser may go to prison. Again I would carefully examine from a mental health point of view the implications this decision would have for a Primary Therapeutic Intervention. I would point out the different consequences of the possible decision 'B' in distinction to the other possible decision 'A' and I would state how decision 'A' and how decision 'B' would influence the scope for my own genuine professional work, whether I could do therapeutic therapy or whether I would be forced into anti-therapeutic therapy as described in the clinical example of Jonathan O. in Section 5.3.2.

The mere fact of a legal acquittal in court can never lead to the invariable and automatic conclusion that no sexual abuse has taken place. It only ever means that not enough legally valid evidence for a conviction has been presented. Courts often have to dismiss for legal reasons the evidence of children and non-legal professionals where it is clear to any child protection worker or clinician and even sometimes to the judge that sexual abuse has in fact taken place. In those cases I would point out that certain procedures in the legal domain may require certain legal decisions on which I would obviously not be competent to comment and which I would accept and respect. I would then add however that the court would also have to take full and sole responsibility for the likely consequences of the specific legal decision which either may further the overall therapeutic process or may lead to blocking and undermining any child protection or therapy. This is not to blame courts and colleagues in the legal professions, nor to be antagonistic, but to help courts to see their own responsibility as part of a truly multi-professional process which as a whole is bigger and goes beyond the skills, tasks and responsibilities of each single professional sub-group involved in dealing with child sexual abuse. (See From mad to bad, Chapter 1; Changing institutional co-operation 5.3.)

Listing in a court report all the possible legal outcomes with the most likely effects on the child protective and therapeutic process can assist courts to see their own action in the context which they may otherwise find difficult to see. It therefore helps lawyers, judges and magistrates, who are particularly isolated from the ongoing overall process of the intervention, to link in to a problem-oriented Primary Therapeutic Intervention. By describing the influence of possible court decisions on the overall intervention the court report assists in integrating the separated and isolated legal process into a part of the multi-professional intervention. It also leaves the responsibility for the likely outcome of a non-therapeutic or non-protective decision by the courts truly with the courts where it belongs as the highest linear sub-system in the professional network.

When courts make decisions against my professional judgement as mental-health professional which change therapy into anti-therapeutic therapy I usually write back to the court with a request for advice as to how a therapist could deal with a legal outcome which in my opinion would force therapists to conduct anti-therapeutic therapy as stated in my report. I would invite the court to give child protective or therapeutic advice when child protection workers or therapists are prevented by the decision of the court from conducting true child protection and true therapy (see Trusting one's own expertise, 5.3.3).

In the vast majority of cases of intrafamilial child sexual abuse a problem oriented non-custodial sentence is preferable by far. Some legal safeguards are usually necessary to prevent further crime and to get abusers and families into the treatment of a Primary Therapeutic Intervention. Although a probation order or plea bargaining may seem a soft option these solutions can often provide a better safeguard against re-abuse than suspended or custodial sentences. A probation order or plea bargaining can include certain conditions for protection and treatment and it is possible to order and to supervise therapy. It is also possible to go back to court and to declare failure of treatment when the abuser withdraws from therapy or when therapy fails. Plea bargaining and probation orders allow the implementation of continuous reassessment of progress or failure of treatment and rehabilitation which is not possible in suspended sentences, and in most cases they fit best into an integrated problem-oriented approach of therapy and child protection in child sexual abuse as syndrome of secrecy and addiction (see Working with sexual abusers, 7.4; Court-ordered therapy, 12.16).

11.8 Specific issues in case conferences

Case conferences and pre-intervention meetings of professionals in child sexual abuse cases are often attended by a great number of professionals. The largest case conference I was part of included 23 professionals. In particular, networks involved in disorganised and conflict-regulating families have the tendency to mirror the family process and nobody is allowed to take responsibility nor to leave the field and everybody has to stay involved. Paralysing conflicts-by-proxy amongst professionals are often expressed in the inability to agree on the seriousness of the problem, to take appropriate responsibility and to agree on clear problem-oriented action (See The Family process, Chapter 3; The interprofessional process, 5.1; The pre-intervention meeting, 8.7.)

In case conferences processes occur in the professional network which often mirror the family process. Different professionals always identify with different family members and different aspects of family life. This can lead to open conflicts-by-proxy or to subtle mutual undermining by members of the case conference. The most frequent conflict-by-proxy prior to disclosure is the tension between the pressure to disclose immediately and the wish to leave the family as it is. A second common conflict-by-proxy is the conflict between professionals who want to protect the child by instant removal and others who want the child to stay at home and have therapy. A third common conflict-by-proxy is between the wish to convince oneself and others that no sexual abuse has taken place at all and the wish to acknowledge sexual abuse as external reality (see Child sexual abuse as syndrome of secrecy, 2.1).

Case conferences of child sexual abuse often have double agendas and mirror the syndrome of secrecy. A 9-year-old boy in a single-parent family had partially disclosed sexual abuse by his father at school. The family was well known to social services and the father had regular support from the social worker. During the time in which the social worker worked with the father and son in supportive family therapy, many panic signs and distress calls from school and teachers were given that the child was impossible to handle at school and that school wanted the boy to be taken into care. In the case conference the school argued that the boy was physically neglected and not appropriately cared for. In full identification with the protective aspect of child abuse, the school tried to undermine the social worker who in identification with the parental function rejected the accusation that the boy was neglected and insisted that therapy was needed to improve the father–child relationship.

The conflict-by-proxy between school and social worker during the case conference dealt on both sides only with the question of possible physical neglect of the child. It later became clear that both equally had double agendas in which the neglect was clearly secondary to the secret agenda of sexual abuse which neither brought into the open. It was in fact the sexualised behaviour of the boy at school with which the teachers felt unable to cope. But they did not openly raise the issue. The social worker as child protection worker wanted to achieve protection by continuing therapy which became anti-therapeutic therapy when the separate issue of protection in possibly ongoing child sexual abuse remained taboo.

Each part of the professional network reflected the denial of the possibility of sexual abuse out of their different primary identifications. At the same time all professionals were talking about 'it' without naming 'it' and getting increasingly deeper into mirroring conflicts-by-proxy. The fact that the conflict-by-proxy was acted out instead of being recognised as such made it impossible to find a conflict-resolution-by-proxy. The unrecognised conflict-by-proxy made it appear that there was only the choice between joining the family system of secrecy and denial or proceeding with a Primary Child Protective Intervention and removing the child from the father. (See The interprofessional process in context, 5.2; Three basic types of intervention, 4.1.)

After the case conference the relationship between school and social services deteriorated. The unidentified conflict-by-proxy affected the multi-professional co-operation negatively and threatened to lead to an institutionalised conflict-by-proxy until a consultation to the overall network of school and social services revealed the double agenda. The interagency consultation helped the professional network to acknowledge the real problem of potential sexual abuse. The identification of the conflicts between the school and social services as conflicts-by-proxy led to a conflict-resolution-by-proxy. It resulted in a problem-oriented co-operation with the plan to assess the symptoms of the suspected sexual abuse in a way which would not collude with the family's denial and which would not lead to a premature disclosure either. It was decided that child protective action would have to be taken if the vague first-line suspicion of sexual abuse of the boy by his father became a well founded second-line suspicion and it was discussed how the child protective action could relate to therapy and vice versa. (See Preparation for disclosure, Chapter 8.)

It has been helpful to take the following three-step approach when conflicts have arisen in case conferences or in pre-intervention meetings (see The inter-professional process, 5.1).

1 Acknowledging the existence of the conflict. We need to ask: 'There is a conflict in this meeting. What is the present conflict telling us about the family problems?' This question needs to be asked openly as a meta-communication about the inter-professional process.

2 Identifying the nature of the conflict. It then becomes possible to distinguish whether the particular conflict is a conflict-by-proxy, an institutional-conflict-by-proxy or a structural institutional conflict.

3 Conflict resolution. If the conflict has been identified as a conflict-by-proxy which is mirroring the family process the members of the case conference need to enter into a conflict-resolution-by-proxy. Professionals need to give each other space and permission to express their personal identifications with different aspects of the individual problem and family life.

Somebody needs to say openly, 'You find ten reasons why the father's return to the family in this case, at this point in time and in this specific family would be anti-therapeutic and non-protective', asking the opponent in the conflict-by-proxy to do the same with the opposite argument for the return of the father. In the conflict-resolution-by-proxy conflictual issues cease to be oppositional. This does not only assist in our professional task, it also helps to prevent institutionalised conflicts-by-proxy and professional burn-out (see The inter-professional process, 5.1).

In case conferences of child sexual abuse many different conflicts-by-proxy are often going on at the same time. It is therefore important to try to separate the different areas and to deal with them one by one. In trying to identify the different problems I have found it very helpful to orientate myself to the different aims and steps of the Primary Therapeutic Intervention (see Aims and steps in the Primary Therapeutic Intervention, 6.2).

In case conferences the expression of professional identifications and open conflicts-by-proxy need to be fostered as an important problem-oriented multi-professional tool. Chairpersons of case conferences need to give attending professionals the explicit permission to use their different identifications and to express conflicts-by-proxy openly. This can happen in a four-step approach:

1 It has been extremely helpful to predict openly, right at the beginning of a case conference, that mirroring processes of the family process will occur in the attending professionals which are based on different identifications of different professionals with different aspects of the case.
2 Chairpersons in case conferences in child sexual abuse should always state in advance that contrary to present professional custom the expression of primary identifications of different professionals with different family members and different aspects of family life is considered highly professional, and is welcome and should be voiced.
3 It should be explicitly stated that the mirroring process of identification will necessarily lead to conflicts between the professionals. It needs to be conveyed that the open expression of conflict in the case conference is very welcome and considered to be highly professional.
4 In a fourth step it needs to be said that these conflicts are not primary conflicts between professionals but conflicts-by-proxy. The open expression of the conflicts-by-proxy can lead to positive and creative conflict-resolutions-by-proxy as a precondition for a Primary Therapeutic Intervention.

The open encouragement to mirror the family process in conflicts-by-proxy opens the way for conflict-resolutions-by-proxy. This process nearly always leads to a creative problem-oriented and conflict-solving outcome of the case conference. It avoids counterproductive and unrecognised conflicts-by-proxy in which professionals undermine each other to the detriment of the child and the family.

Absent members are one of the most difficult problems in case conferences. Even if professionals who attend the case conference achieve a conflict-resolution-by-proxy, absent professionals can collude with the wish of the family for secrecy. They can easily induce renewed splitting in the professional network as illustrated in the clinical example in Section 5.1 (see The interprofessional process, 5.1). It is crucial for case conferences of child sexual abuse that all professionals and agencies are represented who are involved with any intensity in a legal, statutory or therapeutic role. If important professionals are absent it is crucial for the members present at the case conference to take into account the possible identifications of the absent professionals and the resulting possible conflict-by-proxy. Otherwise, absent professionals can undermine any Primary Therapeutic Intervention on which the case conference may have agreed.

11.9 'The goodies' and 'the baddies': splits in the professional network

The nature of child sexual abuse as a truly multi-professional problem and as syndrome of secrecy and addiction easily lends itself to splitting within the professional network in professionals who are seen by the family as 'goodies' and other professionals who are seen as 'baddies'. Abusers, children and families often blame the first professional who names the sexual abuse as fact that he has in fact created the abuse and is to blame for the family crisis. The blaming and scapegoating of the family often lead in a mirroring process to blaming and scapegoating between different professionals within the professional network. The splitting within different professionals between 'goodies' and 'baddies' and the interprofessional scapegoating can be the result of conflicts-by-proxy, of institutional-conflicts-by-proxy and of structural institutional conflicts. Interprofessional scapegoating is also often the result of the confusion between therapy and consultation. (See Child sexual abuse as syndrome of secrecy, and of addiction, 2.1, 2.2, 2.3; The interprofessional process, 5.1; Therapy and consultation, 5.4.)

1 Interprofessional scapegoating as an expression of structural institutional conflicts is usually the result of the confusion between different domains and levels of institutional and professional responsibility. Courts often dismiss in the legal domain reports and applications by social workers, which are appropriately written from a child protective point of view and not from a legal point of view. Social workers are frequently left in the impossible bind of being undermined by courts in their professional opinion, having their application dismissed and nevertheless at the same time being expected to take full responsibility for the protection of the child. As result of interprofessional undermining this judge becomes, in the eyes of the abusers and parents, the 'goodie' and the social worker is turned into the scapegoat. In another situation a therapist may want to keep confidentiality and may not want to disclose information to child protective services. For the family this therapist will easily remain the 'goodie' who helps the family, in contrast to child protective services who want to rip the family apart.

   Scapegoating as an expression of structural institutional conflicts is the result of the confusion between different professional domains in which professionals of one domain do not respect the skills and the responsibilities of fellow professionals of another domain. In the first example the confusion lies between the legal domain and child protection where courts undermine child protective efforts. The second example illustrates structural conflicts between child protection and therapy where the therapist uses the excuse of confidentiality to build herself up as 'better child protector' who is helpful to the family against the child protection worker who is the 'worst child protector', who destroys families. In the first case the undermining legal action will lead to crime-promoting crime prevention; in the second example therapy will result in anti-therapeutic therapy. In both situations it will be impossible for the child protection worker to conduct effective child protection.

To come to a solution structural institutional conflicts need to be taken up at an interprofessional level. The splitting needs to be identified by all professionals involved as a structural institutional conflict which needs to be solved through working parties, changes in laws and procedures etc. (See The interprofessional process in context, 5.2.)

2 Scapegoating amongst professionals and splitting in the professional network as an expression of conflicts-by-proxy or institutional-conflicts-by-proxy are the result of identifications of different professionals with different aspects of the family process. One professional becomes the 'good helper' and the other the 'bad punisher'. A paediatrician may for a seemingly medical or therapeutic reason, but in fact out of his primary identification with protective needs for the child, demand instant protection. If a statutory social worker does not intervene instantly she will be accused of being a 'bad child protector', leaving the child at risk in the family. On the other hand the same doctor may, out of the different primary identification with aspects of parental needs, not want child protection workers to intervene at all. When the same social worker does intervene in this case she will again be accused of being a 'bad child protector', destroying families, whom the 'good doctor' wants to help.

3 Scapegoating within professional networks which is induced by the family process can also be expressed in the confusion between therapy and consultation. Abusers and families will try to turn therapists who have been asked by child protective services to help assess the case into the 'good professional', playing him against child protective agencies and legal courts as the 'bad professionals'. If therapists behave in this situation as if they were free agents to the family and not consultants to the child protective services, they feed into the destructive splitting by the family in which they are seduced as 'goodies' against child protective services, who become the 'baddies'. Any confusion in the professional network between therapy and consultation needs to be recognised as soon as possible and must be dealt with accordingly. (See Therapy and consultation, 5.4; Practical problems in consultation, 11.5.)

11.10 Dealing with statutory hierarchies in professional–family meetings

Even if the confusion between therapy and consultation is avoided, families in consultation sessions with professionals will still try to split the professionals along statutory and therapeutic functions into the 'bad' social worker and the 'good' therapist. This often happens at the point when the statutory worker has to talk about her statutory responsibility to protect the child with the need to decide about care and access for the child. (See Therapy and consultation, 5.4.)

A simple but very effective move of the consulting professional to help the statutory social worker to get out of the scapegoat position is to decentralise the child protection worker and to depersonalise the linear function of statutory responsibility by introducing 'Mr and Mrs Authority' or 'the law'. I often say to a social worker something like 'Sure your agency has to take a decision which is in fact not your decision but the decision of your hierarchy. What will your director or your senior officer responsible for child abuse want to know from you about this case in order to be able to make a decision whether this child can return home?' Or I would introduce 'the law'. I would ask 'What do you think the law would say?' or 'What do you think the judge would need to hear to be convinced that it is safe for the child to return home?', or 'What do you think the judge would have to know to be able to follow the law?'

Sometimes I have used an empty chair and have said to the most hostile and antagonistic family member 'Well, if "the law" were sitting here what would she want to know from you and the child protection worker to be satisfied that things are safe for your child?' Consulting with 'the law' in this hypothetical but very concrete way decentralises the social worker and puts him as much as the family and the consulting professional under the same metasystemic rule of 'the law'. This created a problem-oriented focus for the professionals and the family under which legal and therapeutic aspects can be discussed with the family without putting the statutory social worker into a scapegoat position.

One of the most successful ways to maintain a metasystemic perspective of a Primary Therapeutic Intervention is to put the abuser or the alleged abuser himself into the chair of the judge. This often livens up the session considerably. It can even lead to much and unexpected fun. I would ask the abuser or the suspected abuser to change chairs and to take on the role of judge who has to decide in a case like the one before us. I would say to the father 'Assume you are now the judge.' I would then outline the case to him with all pros and cons and would finish by saying 'What do you think you as judge would have to know and what do you think would have to happen for you as judge for you to be sure that it is safe for this child to return home?'

Abusers or suspected abusers often do not want to assume this role initially but with some help of playfulness and humour it can be very successful. It is interesting that abusers or suspected abusers in the role of the judge or 'the law' often offer very appropriate problem-oriented suggestions which at times are even rather tough proposals and conditions for the abuser. When appropriate conditions are introduced it is important to check immediately with the statutory worker how she thinks her hierarchy would react to these suggestions (see Dealing with professional hierarchies in consultation, 11.6).

When these techniques do not work it is still important for the consulting profession to help the social worker to avoid destructive personalised conflict by reminding the family and the professionals who are present that it is not the social worker's or the consulting professional's task to decide but that of 'the higher authority outside the room' (see The 'goodies' and the 'baddies', 11.9).

When we move the linear and statutory function away from the child protection worker in the room on to the abstract level of 'Mr and Mrs Authority' or
'The Law' we do three things:
1 We help the statutory social worker to remove himself from an often very
   destructive and personalised conflict with the family.
2 The consulting professional can firmly join the statutory colleague by stress-

(1) *Theraputic statutory work*

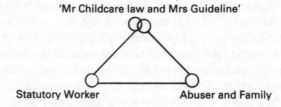

'Mr Childcare law and Mrs Guideline'

Statutory Worker   Abuser and Family

(2) *Court-ordered assessment and therapy*

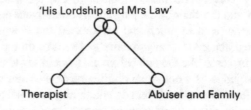

'His Lordship and Mrs Law'

Therapist   Abuser and Family

(3) *Consultation*

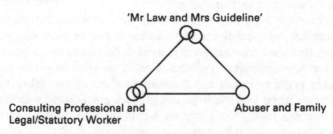

'Mr Law and Mrs Guideline'

Consulting Professional and   Abuser and Family
Legal/Statutory Worker

Figure 11.2 Professional–family hierarchy in therapeutic statutory work,
courtwork and consultation

ing the functional aspects which helps to prevent the family from splitting the professionals into the 'good' versus the 'bad' professional. I may underline this joining by saying 'obviously we all have the best interests of the child in mind'. I may even include the parents and the abuser by adding 'You as responsible parents would obviously only want the best for your child whatever has happened'.

3 Introducing the depersonalised and functional 'The Law' helps both social worker and family to gain a meta-perspective in which relationship aspects and legal aspects become complementary and can be used to help the child and the family in a problem-oriented Primary Therapeutic Intervention.

11.11 Turning a Primary Punitive Intervention (PPI) and a Primary Child Protective Intervention (PCI) into a Primary Therapeutic Intervention (PTI)

The explicitly stated aims and goals of the Primary Therapeutic Intervention enable us to turn a Primary Punitive Intervention (PPI) or a Primary Child Protective Intervention (PCI) at any stage into a Primary Therapeutic Intervention (PTI). We only need to reframe the PPI or the PCI and relate the intervention to the aims and steps in the Primary Therapeutic Intervention. (See Three basic types of intervention, 4.1; Family therapy and family approach, 6.1; Aims and steps in the Primary Therapeutic Intervention, 6.2.)

As a result of a Primary Punitive Intervention abusers are often sent to prison. We can reframe the situation and can declare that the fact that the abuser is detained in prison means that the first treatment step in the Primary Therapeutic Intervention of stopping the abuse has been achieved. It also means that the remaining six aims and steps of the Primary Therapeutic Intervention are still to be accomplished. I would turn a Primary Punitive Intervention with an imprisoned father into a Primary Therapeutic Intervention by openly acknowledging that the first step has been achieved and would suggest turning to the preparations of the responsibility meeting with the father as a second step in therapy.

The mental translation and reinterpretation of the abuser's imprisonment as a result of a Primary Punitive Intervention into the first step of a Primary Therapeutic Intervention led to the move to ask for family meetings in prisons and for the temporary release of prisoners for family sessions. We asked prison authorities to allow one or two family sessions as reality-creating responsibility meetings with the father in prison, and the fathers and the families were prepared for the meetings, in close co-operation between child protective agencies and prison probation services.

The redefinition of a Primary Punitive Intervention as a Primary Therapeutic Intervention can lead to some practical problems. It can be very difficult to find space and rooms in prisons where a family meeting can take place in an atmosphere of privacy. Some travelling for the family and other professionals is

often involved and child protective services and prison probation services need
to develop new forms of co-operation. Usually it is easier to proceed when the
prison gives permission for the abuser to attend the family sessions locally. The
mental reframing of a Primary Punitive Intervention into a Primary Therapeutic
Intervention enables and frees professionals to use any given possible situation
and even the most confused constellation as a new starting point for a problem-
oriented Primary Therapeutic Intervention.

It is usually easier to turn a Primary Child Protective Intervention into a
Primary Therapeutic Intervention. Again it is the mental reinterpretation of the
situation by professionals rather than the external setting which defines the nature
of the intervention. Even after the switch from a Primary Child Protective
Intervention to a Primary Therapeutic Intervention the child may still remain in
a children's home or in foster care. Whether a child remains formally in care is
as an independent fact irrelevant and there is usually nothing good or bad about
a placement as such. Placements and care orders become therapeutic or damaging
only in the context in which they are taken. A responsibility session or a
responsibility-session-by-proxy needs to be the first step in the switch from a
Primary Child Protective Intervention into a Primary Therapeutic Intervention
with the aim of helping the child to understand that she has not been removed
from her family as punishment for the abuse. The responsibility needs to be
allocated firmly to the abuser (see The first family meeting as responsibility
meeting, 9.11; Responsibility session-by-proxy, 9.13).

The child's removal can then be reinterpreted as giving the abuser the chance
to become a better father before the child can return home. When we turn a
Primary Child Protective Intervention into a Primary Therapeutic Intervention
we also need to make important practical arrangements to enable the abused child
to maintain close contact with the mother, with siblings, peers and with the wider
social environment (see Placement in children's homes, 10.2).

The most difficult task in the switch from a Primary Punitive Intervention and
a Primary Child Protective Intervention to a Primary Therapeutic Intervention
usually lies in the interprofessional co-operation in the newly redefined Primary
Therapeutic Intervention. Fellow professionals in continuing conflicts-by-proxy,
in institutionalised conflicts-by-proxy or in structural institutional conflicts often
resist change to a Primary Therapeutic Intervention (See The professional network, Chapter 5).

The resistance to the transformation often reflects the different identifications
of different professionals with different family members who themselves may
not want to change to a Primary Therapeutic Intervention. Adolescents may
refuse to see their fathers and mothers and other relatives equally often resist the
changing of a Primary Punitive Intervention into a Primary Therapeutic Intervention. The same can happen when parents have formed a coalition against the
child in a Primary Child Protective Intervention which they may not want to
change in order to avoid further marital and family conflict. It is therefore

important to have both the interprofessional process and the family process in mind when we try to change a Primary Punitive Intervention or a Primary Child Protective Intervention into a Primary Therapeutic Intervention (see Mutual influence and interlocking professional–family process, 4.2).

Chapter twelve

Treatment issues

12.1 Creating a therapeutic sub-system

A family approach in distinction to a family therapy approach does not necessarily mean that all or even most therapy takes the form of conjoint family sessions. Legal, therapeutic and practical considerations often make it necessary to see different family members or sub-groups separately. Although the therapeutic process always needs to be considered as an overall family process, family-oriented treatment usually includes work with family sub-groups, group work and individual sessions to deal with the differentiated needs of different family members and with the increasing intensity of conflicts and anxieties in the family. Different forms of therapy and different treatment constellations enable therapists to take into account the different needs of different family members at different stages in therapy. In the treatment of child sexual abuse as syndrome of secrecy different concurrent forms of therapy can be seen as therapeutic boundaries in the treatment process from secrecy to privacy. (See Family therapy and family approach, 6.1; Aims and steps in the Primary Therapeutic Intervention, 6.2; From secrecy to privacy, 6.4; Concurrent forms of therapy, 7.1.)

Conjoint family sessions are especially important in the opening phase after disclosure. Although different family sub-groups may be seen separately it needs to be clarified with all family members that important issues which emerge in the work with family sub-groups might need to be shared in conjoint sessions with other family members in order to prevent a relapse into secondary denial and secrecy. (See The first family meeting as reality-creating responsibility meeting, 9.11; Responsibility-session-by-proxy, 9.13.)

The therapeutic approach as part of a metasystemic framework of child sexual abuse as syndrome of secrecy and addiction needs to be supported by and co-ordinated with legal authorities including police and child protective agencies. The co-operation of therapists with statutory agencies who can secure access to the child and with legal agencies who can support the treatment of abusers seems essential for successful therapy. (See Three basic types of intervention, 4.1; The interprofessional process in context, 5.2.)

The Primary Therapeutic Intervention usually involves different professionals from different therapeutic, statutory and legal agencies. A social worker may be responsible for child protection, a probation officer may work with the father, a counsellor or a GP may see the mother and a therapist may conduct conjoint family sessions. All different forms of individual work need to be integrated into a family perspective. The family perspective needs to be created and maintained throughout close co-operation between all professionals involved. It often helps individual family members to talk about difficult issues in concurrent conjoint family meetings when the professional who is dealing with the individual family member is also present in the family session. The presence of individual or group therapists in family meetings assists in avoiding secondary secrecy and splitting. The family process is constantly kept in mind while the individual need for confidentiality, privacy, autonomy and individuation towards other family members is fostered and maintained.

Even the decision not to disclose a specific issue of an individual family member in a family meeting can become a family-oriented act when it serves to reinforce appropriate boundaries, giving family members the right to individuation and privacy within the family. To keep facts from other family members can be seen as 'therapeutic collusion' with one family member. As long as these secrets are shared fully between the professionals of the treatment team the secret becomes, as the individual privacy of a family member, part of the therapeutic process. The therapeutic team needs to have regular meetings to co-ordinate the overall approach in order to safeguard therapy and to avoid conflicts-by-proxy. (See Mutual influence and interlocking professional–family process, 4.2; The interprofessional process, 5.1; Concurrent forms of therapy, 7.1.)

12.2 Picking up bits and pieces in therapy

The basic aims and steps in the Primary Therapeutic Intervention look very stringent but clinical cases often do not work out that way. In therapy we often have to pick up bits and pieces when professionals and family members have initially triggered a Primary Child Protective Intervention or a Primary Punitive Intervention. (See Three basic types of intervention, 4.1; Aims and steps in the Primary Therapeutic Intervention, 6.2; Turning a Primary Punitive and a Primary Child Protective Intervention into a Primary Therapeutic Intervention, 11.11.)

In many cases we cannot proceed because the abuse is denied altogether. Courts and child protection workers often do not approve of an early conjoint family meeting as responsibility meeting for the abuser in order to establish the abuse as family reality. In other cases the abuser has left the family or the mother refuses to meet with the abuser and there are many obstacles of this kind. Picking up the bits and pieces of the intervention and reframing them according to the different aims and steps of the Primary Therapeutic Intervention allow us to become therapeutic at any point of the intervention. (See The first family meeting as responsibility meeting, 9.11; Dealing with primary denial, 10.6.)

We are often able to work with the mother and the child right from the beginning. The work on the mother–child dyad or with any other carer and the child needs to begin with a 'responsibility-session-by-proxy'. It is helpful to employ indirect family therapy techniques in order to create a hypothetical presence of the abuser before moving into direct work between carer and child. The responsibility-session-by-proxy in the absence of the abuser needs to establish the facts of the abuse and should address issues of responsibility, guilt and blame for the abuse. When the abuser has admitted to the abuse but is uncooperative in further work or when he is absent and in prison we need to ask the mother to tell the child what she thinks the abuser would say if he were present in the session. With family sub-groups we often need to work with indirect strategic and systemic family therapy techniques with the aim of naming the facts of the abuse, in order to create sexual abuse as family reality. (See Responsibility-session-by-proxy, 9.13; The use of different family therapy techniques, 12.10.)

The aims and goals of the Primary Therapeutic Intervention can help us to start the therapeutic process wherever the situation allows. The sequence of the therapeutic steps is then often very different from the one described in Section 6.2. But we can achieve the same result as long as we eventually cover all aims and goals. Flexibility in the handling of the sequence of the therapeutic aims and steps of the Primary Therapeutic Intervention frees professions to be therapeutically effective in situations which initially seem hopeless, messy, anti-therapeutic and in bits and pieces (see Turning a Primary Punitive Intervention and a Primary Child Protective Intervention into a Primary Therapeutic Intervention, 11.11).

Wherever and whenever treatment begins and even if it is many months or years after the disclosure, we need to conduct one or two family meetings in which the child hears from the abuser himself the open acknowledgement that sexual abuse has taken place. In cases of denial abusers need to take hypothetical responsibility in a treatment session of denial (see Dealing with primary denial, 10.6). The direct experience of open parental acknowledgement of sexual abuse seems vitally important for sexually abused children. Time and again sexually abused children and even adults say, 'If only I could ask my father once in my life what happened and what he did to me and if I could tell him once how I felt. And if only once I could tell my mother how I tried to tell her.' In sexually abused children the need to hear the abuser himself naming the abuse and admitting to the facts of the secret are extremely strong.

12.3 From crisis intervention to long-term therapy

Sexual abuse is often disclosed in the 'world in between', between the family where the child is often not believed and strangers whom the child cannot trust to help. This means that teachers, youth leaders, nursery nurses, GPs etc. will get increasingly involved in disclosures of child sexual abuse. The teacher or the nursery nurse to whom the child discloses and who has become the Trusted Person is often not the professional who would be involved in the long-term treatment of sexually abused children. (See Steps in the crisis intervention of disclosure, 8.2; The use of the 'trusted person', 8.6; Disclosure at school, 9.9.)

In the preparation of the intervention we need to establish explicitly the time-limited task and role of the initial professional as Trusted Person who remains involved until the disclosure work is concluded in the 'handover meeting'. The clarification of roles during the crisis intervention and in long-term treatment is part of the task of the action-directed 'pre-intervention meeting'. The clear limitation of the task of the Trusted Person during the crisis intervention and the handover meeting is important because it allows professionals from the 'world in between' whose task, timetable and training make it impossible or undesirable to be involved long term, nevertheless to remain the Trusted Person for the child until the disclosure work is completed. The knowledge that their involvement is limited makes professionals from the 'world in between' more motivated to co-operate in a Primary Therapeutic Intervention. (See The interactional nature of motivation, 2.4.1; The pre-intervention meeting, 8.7; The handover meeting, 9.14).

The often emotionally draining task of the Trusted Person can be made bearable when it is clear that the task is concluded at the end of the disclosure stage in the handover meeting. The clear limitation of the task as Trusted Person can keep professionals involved who would otherwise withdraw the moment the case is referred to 'the expert'. It can help other professionals who, as Trusted Persons, would be in danger of getting over-involved from getting lost and from blocking the therapeutic intervention. In one case a GP got so involved with the counselling of a sexually abused patient that he saw her for many sessions, even late at night and during days when he was supposed to have time off. This led to the danger of re-enacting the secrecy and sexualisation of the original dynamic of the sexual abuse. The GP described how he became increasingly drawn into the case to a degree which even had repercussions in his private life and in his professional standing amongst his colleagues. Consultation on the case enabled him to terminate his over-involvement and to hand over to a therapist for long-term treatment.

Sometimes the Trusted Person remains involved in a 'grandfather' position with an indirect supporting and monitoring function. This can be extremely helpful when the Trusted Person, without conducting the therapy himself, protects the treatment by fostering and encouraging children and families to attend therapy. Children and families often turn to the original Trusted Person to complain about the therapist and the therapeutic team. The Trusted Person can then encourage the child and the family to stick to the treatment. He can also have an important liaison role when problems arise during therapy. This holds especially for GPs, headmasters and other professionals in trusted authority positions with regular access to the child and the family.

The Trusted Person can become central and extremely important again in renewed crisis and breakdown of therapy. The Trusted Person in the disclosure might again be able to link up with the child and the family and revitalise the threatened therapeutic approach. When treatment contacts have broken down he can make a referral to another therapeutic team. This would require the very important step of a second 'handover meeting' to a new therapist or a new therapeutic network. Even a minimal but sustained involvement over time by the Trusted Person in 'grandfather' position can have quite disproportional therapeutic effects as long as the Trusted Person co-operates closely with the professional network. (See The interprofessional process, 5.1; Mutual influence and interlocking professional–family process, 4.2.)

In some cases the person who conducts the disclosure interview becomes the second Trusted Person. This is due to the intensity of disclosure interviews when new facts are disclosed and extremely frightening secrets of sexual abuse are shared for the first time. In these cases the role in subsequent handover meetings can often be better performed by the second Trusted Person.

12.4 The need for child psychiatric assessments

At present child psychiatrists often get involved for reasons which have little to do with the genuine child psychiatric task of assessing children's mental state and conducting therapy. Police, lawyers, magistrates and judges often do not yet know how to communicate in the legal domain with children and child psychiatrists, and child mental health professionals get involved because they are considered to be competent in communicating with children. Conducting disclosure interviews and legal interviewing has little to do with traditional child psychiatric work and it is important to be aware of this fact. The fact-finding task of child psychiatrists should therefore be transitional until legal professionals are sufficiently trained and competent to conduct disclosure interviews and to ascertain facts from young children (see From mad to bad, Chapter 1).

Genuine child psychiatric involvement is necessary (1) in the assessment of primary psychiatric disturbance as a result of the abuse itself; (2) in the assessment of secondary trauma through the intervention; and (3) for forensic purposes.

1 Child psychiatric assessment of primary psychiatric disturbance is necessary in all severe cases of child sexual abuse. Not all sexually abused children are psychiatrically disturbed through the abuse. The very narrow normative definition of child sexual abuse can lead to a definite legal label of sexual abuse in a child who is not psychiatrically disturbed (see Legal abuse and psychological damage, 1.1).

When professionals are concerned about the child's mental health, child psychiatrists need to assess whether the child suffers from psychiatric disturbance which requires therapy. The very specific nature of child sexual abuse as syndrome of secrecy has the effect that all children are confused by the experience to some degree and need some form of protection work. Usually the more structured, educational and time-limited protection work should be considered first. Psychiatrically disturbed children can then be assessed for subsequent, more long-term and less structured, psycho-therapeutic work. (See Child sexual abuse as syndrome of secrecy, 2.1; Therapy and protection work, 7.2.2.)

2 The assessment of secondary psychiatric disturbance is as important as the assessment of primary trauma. Social stigmatisation in schools and in the wider social network, interprofessional conflicts and the choice of the basic type of intervention can lead to fundamental changes in the child's life circumstances which often includes extrafamilial placements, changes of carers and of school. In addition the reaction of family members and relatives to the disclosure can lead to scapegoating, rejection and blaming of the child. Secondary disturbance can also be the result of the child's learned victim behaviour and of sexualised behaviour which is regarded as an anti-social symptom. Secondary disturbance can be triggered by the professional network, by the family or by the child. It can be the starting point for entirely new cycles of secondary traumatisation. (See Primary and secondary damage, 1.4; The need for behaviour modification, 7.3.4.)

3 Child psychiatrists have a genuine mental health task as part of forensic child psychiatric work. This includes the assessment of developmental stages and of the mental state of the child in relation to the reliability and validity of children's communications for legal purposes.

A second child psychiatric task in forensic work relates to the assessment of possible effects of the participation in the legal process on the child's mental health. A third forensic task includes possible recommendations for therapy and a fourth and not least important task relates to decisions about the child's external life circumstance such as placements, changes in carers and changes of schools.

The child psychiatric assessment must include the assessment of the individual child and of the entire family. The inclusion of all family members is necessary to assess the relationship and the attachment between the abuser and the child, to assess the protectiveness and the attachment in the mother–child relationship and evaluate the ameliorating or damaging effects of siblings who may protect or blame the abused child (see Siblings in families of child sexual abuse, 14.1).

The assessment also needs to enclose an evaluation of the influence of the professional network on the child and the family. Professional carers and the functioning of the professional network need to be included in order to assess the protective potential or the danger of secondary damage as result of the inter-professional process and the professional–family process. (See The interprofessional process, 5.1; The family and the professional network, Chapter 4.)

12.5 Minimal work with parents in a statutory context

Protection work or therapy with sexually abused children always needs to be accompanied by some minimal work with the carers. The work should include both parents when the father is still available or the mother on her own when the father has left or is in prison. Clinical experience has shown that protection work or therapy with children will otherwise be disrupted and fail. Changes in children as a result of individual therapy or group treatment cannot be integrated into the relationship between the child and parent without the parents' help. Mothers and fathers can feel very threatened by changes in children who attend therapy and children need the parents' permission and licence to be and behave differently.

Parents who cannot allow their children to be different will either stop the child from attending therapy or will bring them into unresolvable loyalty conflicts. The choice for the child between changing in therapy and thereby losing the parent or choosing for the parent at the cost of therapeutic change often results in the child stopping attending therapy. Minimal family work to help parents and carers to work on specific issues related to the abuse and on their relationship with the child is therefore essential. (See The Primary Therapeutic Intervention, Chapter 6; Concurrent forms of therapy, 7.1.)

Mothers whose husbands are in prison find themselves suddenly not only without husband but often also without breadwinner. They need help to deal with both aspects as individuals in their own right and in their roles as mothers. Otherwise the child is easily blamed and is held responsible for the family breakdown as a consequence of the disclosure. I have seen mothers turning against their abused children by allying with the abuser in prison and ousting the child from the family. This leaves the child in the desperate situation of having lost both parents, being blamed for the abuse, being separated from siblings and being the odd one out amongst peers. Mothers may also have to come to terms with having lost their husbands as partners and being attacked by the child for having failed to prevent the abuse. (See The family process Chapter 3; Helping protective mothers, 12.11; Mothers who do not believe, 12.12; Mutual influence and interlocking professional–family process, 4.2.)

It becomes increasingly urgent to create treatment structures for abusers in the community and in prisons in order to be able to turn Primary Punitive Interventions into Primary Therapeutic Interventions. Abusers in prison are often still open to work on their problems but all is lost once they come out of prison and return to the community and to their partners without having received treatment in prison. Sexually abused children in these families are at high risk. In the eyes of society and the law the abuser has paid for the crime and there is often no way to help the child without parental agreement, which they may want to withhold. At this stage the family may close up again and the same or another child, or a child in another relationship that the abuser may initiate with another woman, can find herself in an identical situation of sexual abuse. (See Working with sexual abusers, 7.4; Turning a PPI or a PCI into a PTI, 11.11.)

If during imprisonment direct help for the abuser and the family is not available, a family meeting should be arranged by the local professionals 2–6 weeks prior to the abuser's release. This meeting needs to take the form of a responsibility meeting. The professionals most suitable to conduct this meeting are often the local social worker in co-operation with the probation officer. It has been shown to be possible and prison governors in different countries have started to become increasingly co-operative and helpful in this matter. However if it is not possible to arrange a meeting prior to the abuser's release, a family meeting as responsibility meeting needs to be arranged on the very day of the release.

The day of the abuser's discharge from prison assumes, in terms of family relationships, the quality of a crisis. It is a time of great uncertainty and an optimal moment to engage parents and families in treatment. This chance will be lost once the abuser has settled back into the community. The aims of the family meeting would be exactly the same as a family meeting immediately after disclosure. (See Aims and steps in the Primary Therapeutic Intervention, 6.2; The first family meeting as reality-creating responsibility meeting, 9.11.)

12.6 Setting up groups

12.6.1 Children's groups

It is often difficult to start the first children's group because there are not enough children of about the same age and stage of psycho-social development. Children are referred at different times and it can be difficult to find a common starting date for a sufficient number of children. It also happens that a professional who would want to start a group cannot find a co-worker immediately, and finally there may be problems in organising the actual attendance of the children (see Group work with children, 7.2).

When we started the first group we initially had only one child who wanted to come to a group which did not yet exist. I saw this child in family meetings, announcing that we would set up a group as soon as possible. In a holding operation I then saw the child individually once a fortnight in counselling sessions. When the second child was referred I did the same until we had a third referral. I then asked each child whether she would like to meet other children with similar experiences and I brought the three abused children together in a first group session.

Three children are the minimum number for a proper group. Two children do not yet really form a group and sessions with two children can become very difficult pseudo group sessions. From three children upwards we can conduct proper group treatment, increasing the number to not more than 6–8 children. We felt that the ideal number of children attending was 5 or 6. Eight children was the maximum and was at times already too many to give each child the appropriate attention within the time limit of the session, but this may differ for different approaches and different therapists.

In the beginning it can be helpful to organise the groups as slow open groups. This means starting with the first three children and then adding the other children one by one as they are referred. Slow open groups are especially appropriate with small numbers of referral and when professionals want to run only one ongoing group. The advantage of a slow open group is that older group members can, at a later stage, introduce newcomers and can help them to become integrated in the group much better than the therapists can. The best way of integrating a new child has been to ask an older group member to repeat her or his own story which gives the new member the permission to talk about her own abuse and helps the child to open up and to tell about her or his own experience.

The initial opening up and talking about the facts of the abuse is of great importance. Until the child has openly spoken out in the group and until the group has explicitly acknowledged the facts of the abuse the abuse remains a secret. The more group therapists delay talking about the facts of the abuse, the more difficult it becomes to avoid joining the children's system of secrecy continuing to talk about 'it'. As a rule children should be encouraged in the very first, or at least second, session to share the facts of the abuse with the group. This may seem to be pushing the issue but experience has shown that whether children do relate their story easily or not is much more dependent on the attitude and on the anxieties of the therapist than on the anxieties of the child. If therapists create a group ethos where talking about sexual abuse is the normal way of joining the group and of becoming a group member, the opening-up and sharing might still be difficult but will usually be a relief and a therapeutic experience for the child. There may be exceptions where we need to proceed differently but it is important to keep in mind that children become only full members of the group and the therapeutic process about the abuse will only be established once the child has openly talked about the secret of the abuse, establishing the sexual abuse as fact in the group context. (See Child Sexual abuse as syndrome of secrecy, 2.1; The individual process in context, 2.4.)

If several children in the same age group are referred at about the same time we may want to start a closed group where all group members start at the same time without new members joining later. The advantage of closed groups lies in the fact that all children are at the same treatment stage. For instance, in the beginning only one opening ritual is needed to open up the abuse for all group members and to find an appropriate sexual language to talk about the abuse.

Although it is usually easier to work as a co-therapist couple it may happen that initially only one professional is available. I myself, for instance, started a group on my own to be joined later by a female co-therapist. If groups are taken by single therapists they need to be aware of the advantages and disadvantages of being either male or female. If the respective advantages and disadvantages of being a single male or female therapist, with the aspects of modelling and the transference–counter-transference interaction, are kept in mind there is no reason why a single therapist of either sex could not be highly effective and therapeutic (see Does the gender of the therapist matter?, 12.15).

Co-therapists have the advantage that they can model in reality and can represent symbolically both paternal and maternal aspects. But there is also the danger that sexually abused children split the therapist couple. Groups of sexually abused children can, even more than other groups, challenge the sexuality of the therapists. This can lead to severe hidden sexual conflicts between the therapist couple which get acted out in a very subtle process which can seriously threaten therapy. It can at times induce the worst of macho-ness in male therapists and male-hating behaviour in female therapists. It is important for the therapists to have a supervisor or a third team member in a team to whom they can talk when splitting and conflicts-by-proxy occur. (See The interprofessional process, 5.1.)

The last but often not the least practical problem is physically to get the children to the group. Children who after disclosure have gone into care may have to be brought to the group by social workers or other professionals involved. During the initial stages of therapy we often have to deal with single-parent families where the abuser has left. Families with children who remain at home may need practical help to get the children to the group.

The specific aims and goals of each group can be adapted to the specific needs of the children involved when the assessment has shown that some children need only protection work whereas others need more intensive therapy. The group can be structured either as a therapy group which includes protection work but expands into more free sessions over a longer period of time; or the group is set up primarily as a structured and more short-term protection group and the more disturbed children are subsequently seen individually or join a follow-on therapy group. The nature of the initial group depends on the availability of resources and on the needs of the referred children. Protection groups need to become part of the routine work of child protective teams who can also offer therapy groups if the skills and resources are available. (See Group work with children, 7.2.)

Different agencies need to co-operate in order to provide the necessary concurrent individual, group and family work for children, abusers, parents and carers. Child protection teams, child psychiatric teams and colleagues from probation services and from adult psychiatry need to pool their different skills and resources in order to establish a comprehensive therapeutic service. The rules of close co-operation between all agencies involved need to be most carefully observed in order to avoid otherwise certain splitting and conflicts-by-proxy. (See Mutual influence and interlocking professional–family process, 4.2; The interprofessional process, 5.1; Family therapy and family approach, 6.1; Aims and steps in the Primary Therapeutic Intervention, 6.2.)

12.6.2 Carer groups

Groups for abusers, non-abusing parents and for carers need to run parallel to children's groups. For children in care, in children's homes or in foster care, separate groups for the carers need to be arranged in parallel to the children's group. It is usually the most practical solution to have the carers' group and the children's group running at the same time. The arrangement of concurrent groups also enhances the chance of attendance.

The aim of carers' groups is to help carers in the following six areas:

1 Carers need to be able to talk about behavioural problems of the child which relate directly or indirectly to the abuse. Sexualised behaviour in particular can create severe problems for carers and other people in the child's social environment.
2 Carers need to be able to talk openly about the way in which the child's sexualised behaviour influences family and marital life in foster families and group life and staff relationships in children's homes.
3 Carers need to be able to use open sexual language and need to learn to recognise and to deal with sexualised behaviour in a way which does not endanger family life or the work and life in children's homes.
4 Carers often need to clarify their own personal response to the sexual nature of sexual abuse. If children have been placed in foster care as a result of the abuse, foster parents need to become part of the carers' group. When sexual abuse has happened in foster care, foster parents need to join the groups for parents and for abusers and not the carers' group.
5 Carers need to know how much they should tell other members of the life-group and how they can deal with neighbours, schools, nurseries and friends of the abused child.
6 Finally, carers need to talk about how much they should talk about the abuse with the child and how they can substitute sexualised behaviour through non-sexualised emotional care and attention.

The decision whether a carer should join a carers' group or a parents' group depends on the point in time when the carer has become involved. In general all carers who have been involved in a parenting function during ongoing abuse should join the groups for parents and abusers respectively. All carers who have become involved subsequently are better placed in a group for carers. The distinction between carers' group and parents' group is based on the fundamentally different way in which issues of responsibility, participation, guilt and blame are experienced and dealt with.

Relatives who take over *in loco parentis* only after disclosure may nevertheless need to join the parents' group. They are often so much party to the family crisis of disclosure that they react more like parents who have been involved prior to disclosure than like carers who are in a more neutral position towards the family and the abuser. (See Responsibility, participation, guilt, blame and power, 1.2; Implications for practice, 1.3; Primary and secondary damage, 1.4; Placement in children's homes, 10.2; Placement with foster parents, 10.3; Placement with relatives, 10.4.)

12.6.3 Parents and abuser groups

Mothers, non-abusing fathers and abusers need groups where they, like the children, can, in privacy and separate from other family members and from the family meetings, work on partner problems, on sexual issues and personal experiences which are of no concern for the children. Different combinations of groups are possible. Single-sex parents' groups give the opportunity for either sex to talk in more depth and with more mutual understanding about gender-related problems in sexual abuse. The danger of single-sex group work is that the very structure of the group increases the split between the partners. The advantage of couple groups lies in the increased therapeutic intensity of working on the partner conflicts of the parents. Mixed-sex groups also make it more difficult for abusers to avoid facing their responsibility for the abuse, which they may try to do in single-sex men-only groups. On the other hand single-sex group sessions are needed to deal with the gender-specific problems and with the problem of being abusing or non-abusing parents. (See Proof and belief, admission and owning up, 1.5; Child sexual abuse as syndrome of addiction, 2.2; The family process, Chapter 3; Working with sexual abusers, 7.4.)

In practical terms it is helpful to use a combination of mixed- and single-sex sessions in which the mixed-sex couple sessions initially address the facts of the abuse and, later, partner issues. Separate single-sex meetings of mothers and fathers deal with gender-specific problems and with issues of being an abusing or non-abusing parent. The aims and goals of the group work for parents and abusers need to be related to the aims and goals of the Primary Therapeutic Intervention (see Aims and steps in the Primary Therapeutic Intervention, 6.2).

12.7 Linking group treatment and individual sessions with family meetings

Whether simultaneous individual work or group treatment and family sessions become non-therapeutic does not depend on the fact of the parallel treatment of two different treatment modes, nor does it depend on the family. It is primarily a function of processes between the different therapists. As long as the rule is observed that confidentiality between group and family sessions is maintained while at the same time the therapists of the different settings are entirely open with each other, the different treatment modes will serve to differentiate between different needs of family members and different aspects of family life rather than leading to splitting and undermining of one form of therapy by the other. Undermining happens when therapists of different orientation fail to differentiate between the different functions of different modes of therapy or when they fail to co-operate fully, introducing the splitting in the therapeutic system on the level of the interprofessional process. (See Family therapy and family approach, 6.1; Concurrent forms of therapy, 7.1.)

Therapists who are running groups and who are at the same time involved in family sessions need to be aware that they are in different positions towards the child or the adult in the two different settings. In children's groups therapists are much more *in loco parentis* modelling reality and developing a symbolic parental transference–counter-transference relationship. In family sessions therapists are much more neutral and removed. They are more grandparental figures working with mutual projections in the family. In order to enable a clear transition for family members and therapists between the two different modes of therapy very simple 'rituals of differentiation' have been shown to be effective and helpful. (See Concurrent forms of therapy, 7.1)

If individual work or group treatment and family sessions are conducted by different therapists it is vital that all therapists involved in a given family meet regularly in order to avoid splitting and conflicts-by-proxy and to promote the therapeutic process in conflict-resolutions-by-proxy. (See The interprofessional process, 5.1.)

12.8 Special problems in individual counselling and therapy

It happens increasingly often that sexual abuse is suspected and disclosed in individual counselling and therapy. Older children can indicate consciously that sexual abuse is happening. Both older and younger children may unintentionally indicate sexual abuse verbally or non-verbally through sexualised behaviour, play or drawings.

When a vague first-line suspicion of child sexual abuse in individual counselling or therapy arises we need to examine first whether we are dealing with a secret communication or an unconscious communication. When the child is trying to communicate secrecy it is important not to interpret the secret communication about external reality as internal fantasies and feelings. We need to switch from an interpretative mode to an investigative mode taking the secret communication of the child as a communication of facts to which we need to respond in an indirect and oblique way. This means neither ignoring nor interpreting the suspicion or the partial disclosure, nor asking head-on immediately. If we ask children immediately and directly about sexual abuse they will often close up and express denial. (See The unconscious and secrecy, 2.4.4; Individual counselling and therapy, 7.3; First-line suspicion, second-line suspicion and partial disclosure, 8.3.)

In individual therapy we need to respond to a first-line suspicion of child sexual abuse at first on the level of a meta-communication which gives the child the indirect licence and permission to disclose the abuse. We need to find a way to let the child know that we know that the child knows that she is trying to communicate the external reality of child sexual abuse which is anxiety provoking in its real consequences if the abuse is disclosed. We therefore need to communicate to the child that we understand the anxieties which prevent the child from disclosing. (See The interactional nature of motivation, 2.4.1; Giving explicit licence to communicate, 2.4.2.)

We can deal with a first secret communication of the child in different ways. One way would be to address directly the anxiety about the secrecy. The therapist can communicate that he knows that the child may have something in mind, which she may be too frightened to reveal for fear of what would happen after disclosure. We would need to put to the child the question 'What would happen to you and what would happen to other family members if you told your greatest secret?' We need to deal first with the fears of the greatest possible disaster as a result of disclosure before we can address the content of what the child might have to disclose.

An even more indirect and therefore even less anxiety-producing way of dealing with a first-line suspicion is by 'telling the story of the other child'. I would stop interpreting and would move into 'story telling' in which I would address all possible anxieties and dilemmas of the child in front of me projected on to another child. I would use 'the story of the other child' indirectly to let the child in therapy know that I know of some of her anxieties and dilemmas of disclosing or keeping the secret. This meta-communication helps children to test whether they can trust that we will understand them and it helps children to prepare themselves for a later full disclosure. (See Explicit therapeutic permission to disclose, 8.5.)

We need to ask clarifying questions about facts of children's communications in a casual and matter-of-fact way when young children re-enact the abuse in sexualised behaviour, play or drawings and in sexualised transference–countertransference interactions. If a young child produces sexual drawings or plays sexually we can ask: 'who is doing this?' as long as we ourselves do not introduce the issue of sexual abuse but follow the child's lead and communication. In these situations psychotherapeutic skills of following rather than leading the child's communication are vital. Using psychotherapeutic skills we need however to switch the basic interactional mode from an interpretative mode to an indirect investigative mode. Whether we trigger the crisis of disclosure in the child immediately, involuntarily and prematurely depends primarily on the way in which we ask special questions about the child's play. It is crucially important to control the tone of voice and to be aware of the subtle non-verbal communication which accompanies the verbal exchange (see Crisis of disclosure – crisis of professionals and family crisis. 8.1).

When a child has triggered a first-line suspicion, the therapist needs to think about how best to establish the full facts. This is necessary both for therapeutic and for child protective purposes. When we deal with secrecy we need to establish the presence of a secret as external fact, in order to be able to address subsequently the psychological dimension of fantasy about the external reality of the secret. We need to establish the fact of the abuse as a basis for the child's anxieties and fantasies in order to be able to interpret the fears, anxieties and fantasies which children have about the abuse and about what happens if they disclose. Establishing the facts of the secret communication is exactly the opposite constellation of the ordinary therapeutic process of interpreting. It is necessary to establish the external facts of the abuse for therapeutic purposes because therapists will otherwise enter into a pseudo-therapy of secrecy, where the therapist joins the child's system of secrecy which itself is often the very basis for the child's disturbance. (See Child sexual abuse as syndrome of secrecy, 2.1; From secrecy to privacy, 6.4; Individual counselling and therapy, 7.3.)

I have been involved in cases where children's communication about the external reality of child sexual abuse has been taken as fantasy with the result that the child got increasingly confused and disturbed. The aim of therapy to facilitate congruent reorientation between distorted internal psychological reality and external facts was entirely lost. Not establishing the external facts of sexual abuse first before interpreting is like talking about the death of a child's mother as fantasy in which the child's communication about the dead mother is constantly interpreted as an internal psychological event and as the child's wish to kill the mother, when the child needs to talk about how she feels regarding the fact that the mother has died. We create a dynamic which structurally increases the psychological confusion and disturbance in the child when we do not establish the external reality of the presence of an important secret first before we interpret emotional responses and fantasies around this secret. It becomes impossible to help children to adapt emotionally to the external reality of child sexual abuse as syndrome of secrecy if we confuse secrecy with the unconscious. (See The unconscious and secrecy, 2.4.4.)

One of the problems for therapists lies in the nature of the transference–counter-transference interaction in child sexual abuse. The transference–counter-transference interaction itself may re-create the confusion about fantasy and reality of sexual abuse which is part of the original traumatic experience in child sexual abuse as syndrome of secrecy for the child. Processes of accommodation and structural confusion in the child's mind, whether the abuse is real or not, can confuse the therapist as much as the child. This confusion can seduce the therapist to treat the transference–counter-transference interaction of secrecy as the child's communication of fantasy. (See The individual process in context, 2.4; Individual counselling and therapy, 7.3.)

Establishing reality is also necessary from a child protective point of view. Therapists need to be aware that the therapeutic contract with the child and the family ceases in its original form when a possibly ongoing crime of child sexual abuse is suspected. It is quite understandable that counsellors and therapists who have worked in traditional and accepted ways resent having to adapt to the suggestion that the suspicion of ongoing sexual abuse invalidates basic notions of confidentiality and interpretative modes of working in therapy with children. Nevertheless for therapeutic and child protective reasons the counsellor and therapist will need to step out of the traditional role and will have to involve other agencies in the professional network.

The earlier other professionals are notified about the possible disclosure, the better the network can be prepared. However the danger of over- reacting and of premature interventions by statutory and legal professionals needs to be borne in mind as much as the danger of therapists using this over-reaction as a justification not to involve child protective services and to continue traditional therapy and counselling as if nothing had happened. This may not only be unethical. It will also lead to anti-therapeutic therapy and to secondary psychological damage in the case of ongoing child sexual abuse. (See The interprofessional process, 5.1; The interprofessional process in context, 5.2.)

The Anonymous Diagnostic Interprofessional Consultation (ADIC) is the most appropriate way to proceed. The ADIC allows the safeguarding of the necessary confidentiality until a firm second-line suspicion has been formed. The ADIC enables the involvement of other professionals in attempts to establish the facts of sexual abuse and to plan the intervention prior to a subsequent disclosure. It also prevents other agencies from seizing inappropriate control and from intervening prematurely. (See Anonymous Diagnostic Interprofessional Consultation, 8.4; Steps in the crisis intervention of disclosure, 8.2.)

In older adolescents and young adults child protective considerations are less important. From a therapeutic point of view it is nonetheless as important to establish the facts of the abuse in order to establish the abuse as fact although a disclosure within the therapeutic process may precede any external disclosure. I have been involved in cases where older adolescents have first disclosed within therapy and counselling. The confidentiality of counselling and therapy had then been used to consider all the consequences and possible ways of disclosing externally before the abuse had been opened up to the family and if necessary to other professionals. This 'therapeutic collusion' is justified from a child protective and therapeutic point of view in adolescents who are mature enough to keep the reality of the abuse within therapy without immediately panicking and precipitating an unprepared and uncontrolled disclosure to the family. The disadvantage of this procedure lies in the danger that therapists get too easily drawn into a collusion of secrecy with the child with the result that no external disclosure takes place at all. Therapists often get increasingly drawn into the dysfunctional and damaging secrecy system of sexually abused adolescents which makes the therapeutic move from secrecy to privacy increasingly difficult. (See From Secrecy to Privacy, 6.4)

It should be the rule that therapists or counsellors who work with late adolescents or young adults take at least one other professional, as an external representation of reality and as a guardian against a therapy of secrecy, into their confidence. The non-involved colleague has the task of preventing the therapist from embarking on anti-therapeutic therapy of secrecy instead of moving into the therapeutic realm of privacy. The danger for therapists in individual therapy of getting drawn into systems of secrecy by clients and patients who have experienced long-term sexual abuse cannot be underestimated. In anti-therapeutic therapy secrecy is finally reframed as confidentiality.

If sexual abuse is a past event, child protective aspects are obviously less important. The problem however, is that initially children often admit to sexual abuse only as a past event. They can also maintain that it has only happened once, when in fact sexual abuse is ongoing and has happened for many years. To the child's detriment therapists are often only too willing to join the child in their denial that sexual abuse is still ongoing. It is therefore important that therapists keep an open mind about a child's contention of past sexual abuse. Therapists need to be aware that this contention may in fact be the understandable denial of ongoing sexual abuse when the child feels she or he cannot trust us or trust us yet to reveal the full facts.

When the therapist has formed a firm second-line suspicion following an Anonymous Diagnostic Interprofessional Consultation she needs to prepare the professional network in a pre-intervention meeting for possible necessary action. After the pre-intervention meeting the therapist can take up the sexual abuse directly and openly in order to trigger a full disclosure. This changes the contract of confidentiality in therapy to the duty of child protection as part of an overall Primary Therapeutic Intervention. (See Three basic types of intervention, 4.1; The primary therapeutic intervention, Chapter 6; The pre-intervention meeting, 8.7.)

The timing and the circumstances of inducing a full disclosure can often be controlled. Professionals can often make sure that the full disclosure is only triggered after careful preparation and co-ordination of the professional network involved. Other professionals need to take into account the fact that individual therapists and counsellors are usually very protective of their patients. Under normal circumstances this is part of the positive aspects of the therapeutic alliance. In child sexual abuse as syndrome of secrecy it can destruct a Primary Therapeutic Intervention which needs to include child protection and therapy in a complementary way. The mechanism of conflict-resolution-by-proxy using mirroring processes of primary identifications of different professionals with different aspects of the patient and of the family life needs to be employed in order to avoid otherwise destructive and anti-therapeutic conflicts-by-proxy amongst professionals. (See The interactional nature of motivation, 2.4.1; The interprofessional process, 5.1; The interprofessional process in context, 5.2.)

12.9 The problem of re-introducing modesty

In severe sexual abuse, symptom-oriented work needs to deal with the behavioural aspects of sexualisation in children. This work is absolutely vital because sexualised behaviour and victim behaviour make the child much more vulnerable to further abuse and to sexual assault by strangers. It often precipitates social stigmatisation and rejection in schools, by teachers and peers and can make the child an outcast in her wider social environment. In addition sexualised behaviour can trigger off re-abuse in foster care and children's homes. It often results in foster breakdown and leads to rejection and isolation of children in residential care. The re-introduction of modesty in sexualised behaviour and the treatment of victim behaviour is therefore not only an important therapeutic task. It has even greater preventive value.

In young children the re-introduction of modesty can probably best be dealt with in the context of the carer–child dyad substituting emotional care for the child's sexualised behaviour. In older children direct behavioural approaches with positive reinforcement and gratification for non-sexualised behaviour and social skills training may be more appropriate (see The need for behaviour modification, 7.3.4).

The direct work on the sexualised behaviour needs to go together with other concurrent forms of therapy. The danger of secondary victimisation demands that the behavioural symptoms of sexualisation be treated as a high priority. It is often impossible to separate the symptoms of sexualisation from the overall therapeutic process in which children need to unlearn sexual responses when they ask for emotional care. Carers in turn need to learn to respond immediately to sexualised interactions and demands with emotional care. In the introduction I have spoken of the 'internal switch' which translates the input 'sex' into the output 'cuddle'. This process needs to become part of the symptom-oriented treatment of sexualised behaviour. (See Introduction; Confusion on different levels of dependency, 3.1.)

The treatment of sexualised behaviour is so difficult because the sexual nature of sexual abuse has strong habit-forming effects. The habit forming and addictive psychological stimulus in sexual abuse often makes the re-introduction of modesty extremely difficult. The habit-forming tendency of sexualised behaviour in the child corresponds to the difficulty of professionals and carers in dealing with the child's anti-social sexualised symptoms in an open and non-punitive way.

The treatment of sexualised behaviour is often a race against time. The strong anti-social character of sexualised symptoms can lead to early secondary victimisation of severely sexually abused children before we are able to deal with sexualised behaviour in therapy. A mono-therapeutic approach is usually insufficient and symptom-oriented work and the treatment of relationship aspects need to be addressed simultaneously in concurrent forms of therapy (see Concurrent forms of therapy, 7.1).

12.10 The use of different family therapy techniques

The clear distinction between a family approach and a family therapy approach has helped the avoidance of ideological battles about the use of different family therapy approaches and methods of change to the exclusion of others. The metasystemic perspective has allowed us to acknowledge that all therapists are better in some ways of working than in others and that we need to examine our own specific preferences and skills in order to relate these to the overall therapeutic task.

The metasystemic perspective has also enabled us to examine the usefulness of specific different family therapy techniques for specific different situations in the treatment of families of child sexual abuse. It has allowed us to remain problem-oriented and to acquire skills which are needed to deal with specific tasks rather than bending and distorting the tasks according to certain fixed ways of working. The different family therapy techniques and methods of change are not used on the level of theoretical conceptualisation of different schools. The different methods are used for goal-oriented change in professional networks, in families and in family members according to the practical requirements to change aspects of the professional process, the professional–family process, the family process and the individual process. (See From mad to bad, Chapter 1; The professional network, Chapter 5; Family therapy and family approach, 6.1.)

1 Direct intensification: the first family session in acknowledged abuse

Direct structural techniques which intensify underlying conflicts and which deal openly and directly with structural issues of responsibility and intergenerational boundaries within the session are extremely helpful in first family sessions as reality-creating responsibility sessions. The task of the first family session as reality-creating responsibility session is to break the secrecy and to establish the full facts of the abuse, and by doing so to establish the abuse as an open family reality. The first session also needs to deal with the issue of the abuser's sole responsibility for the abuse. In openly admitted cases of child sexual abuse, the use of indirect strategic or systemic techniques would be quite inappropriate and would ignore central features of child sexual abuse as syndrome of secrecy and addiction. The use of strategic and Milan-systemic techniques in the reality-creating responsibility session of openly acknowledged cases of child sexual abuse would structurally repeat the context of child sexual abuse where external reality and conflict are never openly and directly named and confronted as such. The use of direct structural techniques in the responsibility session creates in the very process sexual abuse as a family reality. (See The individual process, Chapter 2; Aims and steps in the Primary Therapeutic Intervention, 6.2; The first family meeting as reality-creating responsibility meeting, 9.11.)

The use of indirect strategic or Milan-systemic methods in the initial steps of the Primary Therapeutic Intervention would exactly feed into the dysfunctional mode of indirect communication of sexual abuse as syndrome of secrecy and addiction which avoids naming reality as such. Reality avoidance in sexual abuse and the linear element of responsibility require the use of direct and intensifying reality-confronting techniques in the initial responsibility sessions. The secrecy of child sexual abuse needs to be lifted, the facts of the abuse need to be told, the abuse as family reality needs to be established and children need to hear directly and openly in front of all other family members, from the abuser himself, that sexual abuse has in fact happened and that he takes responsibility for it. To achieve these goals the use of structural techniques is eminently helpful.

2 Anticipatory problem-solving questions: anxiety reduction in primary and secondary denial

The treatment of denial requires working in exactly the opposite way to the direct structural mode of the openly acknowledged responsibility session. We need to address the anxieties which have led to the denial rather than aiming directly at the facts of the abuse itself. We will only get the facts if we postpone our wish to get the facts and address the context of the abuse instead. Strategic and Milan-systemic techniques greatly facilitate possible indirect ways out of the trap of denial and create hypothetical solutions to the problem. In denial work the linear aspects of reality creation and responsibility taking become part of the circular element of the family process. The feared family disaster resulting from a possible disclosure needs to be addressed first before we can at a later stage return to linear issues of responsibility and factual information about the abuse (see Dealing with primary denial, 10.6).

In denial work it seems impossible to use structural modes of working. We need to address the underlying disaster of a possible disclosure first. We need to ask hypothetical questions, such as 'What would be the biggest disaster if sexual abuse had happened?', 'How long would it take and in which situation would it be safe to come out?' and 'Would your father think that he had done wrong if it had happened?' In dealing with denial we need to identify the trap for the child, for the abuser and for the family, which prevent family members from disclosing. We need to deal with the fear of real or imagined family disasters when we want to help the family to find possible hypothetical solutions which can help the child, the abuser or other family members to disclose in future and under safer and more controlled circumstances (see The interactional nature of motivation, 2.4.1).

The stronger the denial the more important is the application of increasingly indirect strategic and Milan-systemic methods. In cases of strong denial I would put the possibility of disclosure into the indefinite future and would say, 'Most likely you would never be able to disclose if sexual abuse had happened. But if you were ever able to do so what would be the worst thing which could happen?'

Often I myself choose the worst possible disaster and put it to the family. With increasing degrees of denial I also use increasingly peripheral family members as allies. In a family with a low degree of denial I would probably address the father himself saying, 'What would be the worst disaster for yourself if sexual abuse had happened?' In very hostile families I would never ask the suspected abuser himself initially and certainly not the child, who would feel much too trapped by loyalty conflicts. I would use the least involved family member or even a professional if I see the family in the context of a consultation, asking, 'What do you think the biggest disaster would be for the father if sexual abuse had happened and he admitted to it? And what do you think would be the greatest threat to the child if she disclosed?'

Questioning on the hypothetical 'as if' level avoids symmetrical escalation and intensification. The anxiety-reducing effects of strategic and Milan-systemic techniques are precisely what is needed in denial work. In contrast to desirable intensifications in structural moves of open disclosure and responsibility sessions, hypothetical questioning decreases potential conflict and decreases anxiety levels. It enables family members to begin to think again about the future and helps children to find safer ways to disclose.

In the treatment of denial therapists need continuously to avoid symmetrical escalations about the question of whether sexual abuse has happened or not by saying, 'Sure I hear you say it has not happened, but there are these allegations and we have to think about it. What do you think would be the biggest disaster if sexual abuse had happened?' The therapist may need to accompany the emotional de-escalation by all sorts of verbal and non-verbal reassurances without ever losing the thread of the enquiry. Only the use of strategic and Milan-systemic techniques will allow professionals to begin to understand the function of the denial and the involvement of the different family members in the denial. On the hypothetical 'as if' level it is also possible to conduct hypothetical responsibility sessions and to become therapeutic in terms of the aims and goals of the Primary Therapeutic Intervention (see Dealing with primary denial, 10.6).

Similar methods can be used when families and family members relapse into secondary or tertiary denial after previous disclosure. We can ask, 'What would be the biggest disaster if you were to repeat what you had said in the beginning?' Again with increasing degrees of denial we need to go for the worst disaster, the longest time span until disclosure and the most peripheral family member. (See Relapse into secrecy and secondary denial, 12.13; Tertiary denial by fathers, 12.14.)

3 Involving absent family members: family-sessions-by-proxy

In family sessions without the abuser, or in family-sessions-by-proxy with only the child, we can introduce the absent family members by the use of strategic and Milan-systemic techniques. We can include absent abusers by asking, 'What if your father were here? What would he say? Would he say that he is responsible for the abuse or that you are responsible? What would he say had happened between him and you?' This way of questioning can be followed up by circular questioning in the hypothetical mode such as, 'If your husband were here who would he say has been most upset by what has happened?' (See Individual therapy and family-therapy-by-proxy with children on their own, 7.3.1; Family and responsibility-session-by-proxy, 9.13.)

4 Positive connotation and paradoxical injunction: tertiary denial

Cases of tertiary denial by fathers or other relatives are situations in which techniques of positive connotation need to be applied to extreme degrees and where they have an invaluable therapeutic function. The treatment of tertiary denial soon becomes symmetrical and breaks down without the use of very strong positive connotations of the tertiary denial. As in some cases of primary denial, we may in tertiary denial use some openly paradoxical methods as well. I have said to fathers that they are not allowed to come off the denial because otherwise there may be violence, death and disaster in a family. I have told children that their denial is very helpful because it keeps the family together even at the cost of their self-sacrifice. Under such positive connotations I have explored the real anxieties and the possible disasters which the disclosure would bring about. In tertiary denial it is obvious that the denial is not a function of the linear issues of legal threats of punishment, but that denial in sexual abuse is also part of the interpersonal and psychological pattern of child sexual abuse as syndrome of secrecy and addiction. (See The individual process, Chapter 2; Tertiary denial by fathers, 12.14.)

5 Hypothetical linking between family and professional network: consultations to professionals with statutory and legal responsibility

Questioning in the subjunctive mode can be very helpful in consultation sessions in which the professional with statutory responsibility and the family are present. Questions like 'What would Mrs Smith as social worker with statutory responsibility have to know from you, Mr Jones, for it to be safe for your children to be with you on your own?' avoids the dangers of collusion of the consulting professional against the professional with statutory responsibility and prevents the split between the 'good professional' and the 'bad professional'. At the same time it involves family members actively in a problem-oriented way instead of making them receivers of orders from the higher authority of social workers or courts. Elements of the consultation which address the professional–family process can be conducted in hypothetical circular questioning of the family about what professionals with statutory and legal responsibility would need to know or would need to do in order to protect children and to prevent further abuse. (See Legal abuse and psychological damage, 1.1; Therapy and consultation, 5.4; Practical problems in consultations, 11.5.)

6 Anticipatory guessing: dealing with statutory hierarchies

In consultations to professionals the possible reactions of statutory and legal hierarchies need to be explored first. Before we explore the professional–family process we need to know how a senior social worker would react, or how the director of an independent child protective agency would respond to the field workers' proposed way of dealing with the case. In these situations it has been extremely helpful to use hypothetical questioning, asking the social worker, 'What would your senior say if she were to hear what we are discussing now?' In the hypothetical mode we can find out whether we are dealing with conflicts-by-proxy, institutionalised-conflicts-by-proxy or possible institutional conflicts in the professional hierarchy (see The Interprofessional Process, 5.1; Dealing with Professional Hierarchies in Consultations, 11.6).

It is possible to help statutory or legal workers to find possible solutions to problems within the professional hierarchy and possible danger points to proposed ways of handling of the case by using hypothetical anticipatory problem-solving questioning such as, 'Obviously your senior would have to take direct legal action due to the existing procedures. How do you think this would influence your own work and how do you think you could convince your senior that a problem-solving approach would require a different handling of the situation?' And 'What would you do if your senior were to proceed as she thinks fit, which might be exactly opposite to how you said you would like to approach the problem?' I then have a second session in the hypothetical anticipatory problem-solving mode with the same worker in order to see whether the inter-professional problems have been resolved and whether the hierarchy has become part of an overall agreed Primary Therapeutic Intervention. The indirect hypo-thetical questioning about interprofessional hierarchies often leads to the request by the agency for a case-oriented consultation to members of the professional hierarchy.

7 Decentralising and the 'one-down' position: maintaining a metasystemic perspective as statutory and legal worker

Legal and statutory workers can themselves avoid oppositional and symmetrical conflicts with abusers and families by putting themselves under the higher authority of 'the law' or 'the guidelines'.

This process again requires hypothetical anticipatory problem-solving questioning and circular questioning in the hypothetical mode in which the statutory worker says 'I am only here because the law requires me to be here and I have to deal with the situation because of the guidelines'. The worker can continue by explaining the law and the guidelines and (s)he can say, 'When do you think the law and the guidelines would allow me to let your child return home?' and, 'How much do you think your mum and dad would have to be able to talk about their own problems, and how much do you think your mum would have to learn to listen to you until you think the courts would say that things have really changed in your family?'

Introducing the higher authority as a linear, statutory and legal element requires the use of hypothetical and strategic techniques, which then allow the statutory worker to decentralise herself and to maintain a truly metasystemic stance. She can become truly therapeutic and can remain a truly statutory worker at the same time. Hypothetical questioning and the mastery of strategic and Milan-systemic techniques in these circumstances are invaluable assets and form the basic requirement for the ability to maintain a truly metasystemic stance in child sexual abuse as a legal, statutory and therapeutic problem. The delegation of the linear and legal aspects of responsibilities of statutory workers into the hierarchy of 'The Law' enables social workers and probation officers to conduct therapy without confusing their double role as controlling and helping agents. (See From mad to bad, Chapter 1; Dealing with professional hierarchies in consultations, 11.6; The 'goodies' and the 'baddies': splits in the professional network, 11.9.)

8 Interprofessional communication and information gathering: preparing fellow professionals for disclosure

One of the most helpful ways of using anticipatory problem-solving questioning is the Anonymous Diagnostic Interprofessional Consultation. It can be very helpful to prepare a statutory social worker or a policeman or a child psychiatrist for a possible intervention by asking, 'I have got a child whom I will see again today where I am not sure at all of what is going on. But what would you do if my gut feeling of possible sexual abuse became a vague first-line suspicion or a well-founded second-line suspicion?', 'What would I have to know and what would I have to be able to tell you before you were to intervene?', 'If I had enough information how would you want me to proceed to organise a pre-intervention meeting?'

It is possible to pre-warn fellow professionals under the heading of a hypothetical case and to deal with the crisis of the professional network and with the interprofessional aspects of the preparation for the intervention first before the case is actually disclosed and named. Putting a hypothetical case first clearly separates the professional crisis from the family crisis and the subsequent crisis intervention. (See Anonymous Diagnostic Interprofessional Consultation, 8.4; Preparing fellow professionals for impending disclosure, 8.13.)

9 Interprofessional problem solving: conflict-resolution-by-proxy in the professional network

If we deal with mirroring conflicts-by-proxy in the professional network which have been induced by the family process, hypothetical questioning can be of great help. In a conflict-by-proxy between a probation officer and a social worker I could ask the probation officer who is responsible for the abuser, 'What do you think would be the anxieties of the social worker who is responsible for child protection if you all agreed on the father's rehabilitation at this point?' The interprofessional process and the professional–family process, as well as the family process itself which is mirrored in the conflict-by-proxy, can be explored by hypothetical questioning of the professionals involved in the case (see The interprofessional process, 5.1).

12.11 Helping protective mothers

Child sexual abuse also happens in families where the mother has a close and protective relationship to the child. These protective mothers are often the mothers who themselves discover and disclose the abuse. They are the Trusted Person to the child and should be involved in the assessment and treatment process right from the beginning of the disclosure. In the disclosure interview we may want them to be in the interview room or behind the one-way mirror if they are too upset to be in the room. (See Proof and belief, admission and owning up,

1.5; The use of the 'trusted person' 8.6; Organising the disclosure interview, 9.3; Disclosure by mothers, 9.7.)

Parents in families of child sexual abuse relate to each other in many different ways which can all be affected by the disclosure of sexual abuse. Six main areas need to be considered.

1 The non-abusing mother and the abusing father are parents to all children in the family, including the non-abused siblings.
2 The parental couple in a family are partners in a legal and social unit towards the outside world. Single mothers are still regarded very differently in legal and in social terms and they are often discriminated against.
3 Parents are partners who support each other within the family in their important roles as confidantes and as company for each other.
4 Husbands and wives are a kinship unit which relates to both sets of relatives. In-laws might provide important support socially, financially and in practical terms.
5 Parents are sexual partners and on-going sexual abuse in the family does not make this aspect of their relationship less important.
6 Parents relate to each other in their function as breadwinners in the context of the family as economic unit.

Protective mothers in families of sexual abuse invariably come into conflict between the different aspects of their relationship to the abuser. They are often forced to choose in a way which they find hard or nearly impossible. The pressure to act and to separate from the abuser instantly can come from themselves, from relatives and from friends in the wider social network and not least from professionals in social and legal agencies which might put considerable pressure on the mother to choose between the abuser and the child.

As parents, protective mothers might want to separate from the abuser in order to protect the abused child. However, when they choose separation they may also lose the father as co-parent for the abused child and for all non-abused children. They may lose the father as companion and confidant and as sexual partner. They lose the social status of a person who is a partner in a marital couple. They may also lose the breadwinner and the separation usually means financial and economic set-back or hardship for the remaining members of the single-parent family.

The mother often loses the social, financial or practical support of the wider family of the abuser or of her own relatives. Finally, the mother may just not be used to being alone as an adult, and protective mothers often feel lonely on their own at a time of crises when many pressing problems need to be resolved. Often there are no quick and easy answers for protective mothers on how to deal with the very complex situation at disclosure, and demands by professionals for quick and clear-cut actions might, at best, reflect the professional's understandable wish to dispose of a complicated case as quickly as possible. Considering the emotive nature of child sexual abuse, the influence of the professional network and of the social environment on the mother to come to inappropriate and over-simplistic solutions cannot be under-estimated. (See From mad to bad, Chapter 1; The family and the professional network, Chapter 4; The inter-professional process, 5.1; Following disclosure, Chapter 10; Siblings and families of child sexual abuse, 14.1; Sexually abused mothers of sexually abused children, 14.7.)

Protective mothers often feel that they have to decide instantly and that they have to choose immediately between the partner and the child and that they should ask for instant divorce. But even in cases of truly protective mothers, demands for divorce in the crisis of the disclosure should not be taken up instantly. Also protective mothers can be attached to sexually abusing husbands. They need time and space to think about the partnership issues involved, about family aspects and about the social and financial side of separation and divorce. Once the crisis has subsided it may be important for the mother, the child and the abuser to renegotiate family relationships with the result of the parents staying together or separating in a therapeutic divorce. (See The family process, Chapter 3; Mothers who want instant divorce, 10.5; Aims and steps in the Primary Therapeutic Intervention, 6.2.)

Whether protective mothers divorce or not, a period of separation between child and abuser is usually necessary. In cases of protective mothers all efforts need to be made not to separate the child from the mother and to come to an agreement that the father and not the child moves out. Mothers need support to cope on their own as parents and to deal with personal, financial and social problems resulting from the disclosure. Mothers often have to deal with stigma-tisation from the wider family and from social networks. They also need help to deal with the sexually abused child and siblings who despite the abuse and despite some anger with the abuser often also miss their father.

12.12 Mothers who can not acknowledge abuse

What happens after disclosure depends very much on whether mothers acknowledge or do not acknowledge that sexual abuse has taken place. Belief as a process in the psychological domain is different from proof in the legal domain. It is also different from lying. In some cases where we have unequivical proof and where fathers have been imprisoned for proven sexual abuse, mothers have still not acknowledged that sexual abuse has taken place. Conversely in many cases where sexual abuse has not been fully proven mothers have nevertheless believed the child's disclosure. The question of whether mothers of sexually abused children can acknowledge that their child has been sexually abused is important because further child protective and therapeutic steps in the intervention depend very much on whether mothers as non-abusing parents can acknowledge that sexual abuse has taken place (see Proof and belief, admission and owning up, 1.5).

Mothers who cannot acknowledge abuse may have been abused themselves or they cannot allow themselves to acknowledge it for fear of family-breakdown or other forms of disaster. Mothers often feel guilty for not having protected their children and they fear being blamed and scapegoated by professionals, neighbours and friends, by the wider family and by the abused child herself.

The confusion amongst professionals about the different importance of acknowledgment and belief for protection and for therapy has led to situations where treatment has been terminated with mothers who do not acknowledge abuse. Therapeutic work with the mother–child dyad can be conducted in all cases of child sexual abuse irrespective of whether the mother acknowledges abuse or not. The difference lies in protection work. Mothers who do not acknowledge that abuse has happened cannot be entrusted to protect their child. They cannot see that the child is at risk and it is impossible to contain their protective capacity. Therefore children who are in further danger of abuse may not be able to live with mothers who cannot acknowledge the fact of abuse. There is however no reason to remove a child where the abuser has definitely left or where the legal process carries enough protective influence that no further abuse can take place and where no collusion between the abuser and the mother can put the child at further risk. When the child is protected from further abuse it would be quite inappropriate to remove her from a mother who cannot acknowledge abuse. To remove a child in this situation would be a non-therapeutic action response unless the child is severely blamed, scapegoated or rejected by the mother. (See The family process, Chapter 3.)

When mothers cannot acknowledge abuse we need to conduct denial work. Denial work often leads to psychological and interactional changes which enable the mother to acknowledge and to believe the child and to become protective. Denial work may also show that no change is possible and that the child cannot stay with the mother when the abuser re-enters the family scene. In denial work we need to address all the anxieties and possible disasters which make it impossible for the mother to face the reality of child sexual abuse. (See Dealing with primary denial, 10.6; The use of different family therapy techniques, 12.10.)

Only in extreme cases of hostility towards abused children and in cases of severe blaming and scapegoating can removing a child from a mother be indicated even if there is no danger of re-abuse. We need to keep in mind that many mothers react in this way because they have been sexually abused themselves. Initial hostility and scapegoating towards sexually abused children must therefore never be taken as a *prima facie* cause for removing the child (see Sexually abused mothers of sexually abused children, 14.7).

We need to make a further distinction between not-believing and lying. Some mothers may say that they cannot believe that sexual abuse has taken place but they are in fact lying. Mothers lie when they have openly known about the abuse or when they themselves have been actively abusing. They are non-protective and work on the mother–child dyad will also be non-therapeutic. Usually we will find hostility and scapegoating towards the abused child which will increase rather than decrease during denial work. Intensive denial work will be necessary to assess whether any therapeutic work on the mother–child dyad can be done.

12.13 Relapse into secrecy and secondary denial

Relapse into secrecy and denial after initial open admissions by abusers, children and other family members is a very common problem. The tendency to retreat into secondary secrecy and denial is linked to the nature of child sexual abuse as syndrome of secrecy and addiction. The relapse into secrecy is often a function of the way professionals intervene. (See The individual process, Chapter 2; Three basic types of intervention, 4.1; The professional network, Chapter 5; Preparation for disclosure, Chapter 8; Disclosure, Chapter 9.)

We find the following five common patterns amongst many and varied situations in which sexual abusers and families relapse into secondary secrecy and denial.

1 Relapse into secrecy and denial after isolated disclosure

Mothers, children and sexual abusers often admit to sexual abuse in the initial crisis of the disclosure. These disclosures are usually made in isolation. The father admits to the police and is often retained in custody. The mother talks separately to the police and to child protection workers and so does the child. After a day or two the father, the mother and the child often withdraw their statement and relapse into secondary secrecy and denial. Abusers say that they have made the statement under duress. Children realise the consequences of the disclosure for the family and for themselves. They have often already come under pressure from the family to withdraw the statement and have been blamed and scapegoated for the consequences of the disclosure. Mothers realise that their disclosure takes away their partner, the breadwinner, the co-parent. In addition, family members become socially stigmatised and traumatised through the reaction in the wider family and in the social and professional network.

The relapse into secondary denial can be avoided by an instant family meeting in which the facts of the abuse are established and shared by all family members and where the abuse is established as an open family reality. After an initial family meeting where the facts of the abuse and the abuse as fact are established for all family members concerned the disclosure will hardly ever be withdrawn again. (See The individual process in context, 2.4; Aims and steps in the Primary Therapeutic Intervention, 6.2; The first family meeting as reality-creating responsibility meeting, 9.11.)

2 Relapse into secrecy and denial induced by legal and child protective agencies

Non-believing of courts or child protective agencies can be devastating to children who have tried to disclose. The dismissal of the criminal case on legal grounds gives the indirect message to the abuser, the child and the family that the legal dismissal can also be taken as proof that no abuse has happened at all.

Professionals, family members and abusers interpret the legal ruling as if the courts had officially certified this fact. Legal professionals and courts are often not sufficiently aware that their verdict as highest linear and legal agency has direct influence on the work of all other agencies. A legal dismissal often means that children are not believed at all and that the abuse is considered to be a lie or fantasy. (See From mad to bad, Chapter 1; The interprofessional process in context, 5.2; Preparing court reports, 11.7.)

Legal and child protective dismissals of children's disclosures do not only lead to 'crime-promoting crime prevention' and 'abuse-promoting child protection'. They also drive the entire ongoing process of child sexual abuse back into secondary secrecy and denial. Sexually abused children are trapped and find themselves in hopeless situations where nobody can stop the abuse. This can result in many months and years of further and aggravated abuse. In order to avoid non-believing on legal and child protective levels in clinically ongoing cases of child sexual abuse, all professionals involved need to prepare interventions in child sexual abuse carefully and thoroughly before they proceed. (See Syndrome of secrecy, and of addiction, 2.1, 2.2, 2.3; Preparation for disclosure, Chapter 8; Disclosure, Chapter 9.)

3 Relapse into secondary denial in a Primary Child Protective Intervention

Initially openly acknowledged abuse can lead to secondary denial when no reality-creating responsibility meeting has taken place. Children are removed from the family to prevent further abuse and the situation is often dealt with in a bureaucratic way where all agencies try to cover themselves. (See Three Basic Types of Intervention, 4.1; The first family meeting as responsibility meeting, 9.11.)

If the child protective intervention is not part of a Primary Therapeutic Intervention we often find that children withdraw into renewed secrecy and denial. A process sets in where the sense of reality of sexual abuse as fact slowly and increasingly evaporates. Over time the abuse becomes more and more shadowy. Parents say that the abuse was not really severe at all and it is finally denied again. Children feel lonely and abandoned and comply with the change of story. Earlier statements in which the abuse was admitted are then labelled as professional distortions of what the child has said. The pressure on family members to keep the family together often supports and accelerates this process. The wish to return home leads to secondary denial of children in which mothers and other family members join in only too readily. (See The family process, Chapter 3; The Primary Therapeutic Intervention, Chapter 6.)

It can be very difficult to stop and reverse slowly reappearing secrecy and secondary denial which creeps in over longer periods of time through increased changes of stories and statements and through the slow but powerful induction of conflicts-by-proxy in the professional network. After many weeks or months professionals suddenly find themselves in severe conflicts-by-proxy with each other. Some professionals are seduced to collude with the family's denial of abuse against other professionals who uphold that nothing has changed in the family and that the child is still in danger.

In these cases professionals meet after several months in renewed case conferences where they have to make decisions between a bad and an even worse solution. On one side, they can decide to allow the child access to the abuser and to start a slow rehabilitation of the family in a situation where none of the professionals has been able to influence the basic family process of sexual abuse as syndrome of secrecy and addiction. Rehabilitation means closing eyes to the fact that sexual abuse may continue under self-sacrifice of the child with an increased risk to the child's health and safety. The equally bad or even worse decision is to go for long-term placement of children. Children are separated from their family and usually feel punished for the abuse.

Placements out of these situations often lead to foster breakdown and to damaging careers of multiple placements for the child. Secondary denial of children and families is not hopeless as long as case conferences are able to regain a sense of reality of the abuse and as long as professionals can agree to turn the Primary Child Protective Intervention into a Primary Therapeutic Intervention as described in Section 11.11. On the interprofessional level case conferences can use conflicts-by-proxy and the relapse into secondary secrecy and denial as a basis for conflict-resolutions-by-proxy. The first step on the family level would be to hold a responsibility meeting where the facts of the abuse and the abuse as family fact are re-established in the presence of all family members involved. (See The interprofessional process, 5.1; Special issues in case conferences, 11.8.)

4 Relapse into secrecy and denial as a result of a Primary Punitive Intervention

Sexual abuse is often dealt with in a punitive way. The abuser is punished and sent to prison without being allowed to have any contact with the abused child and the family. The professional network only begins to think about the consequences for the child at the moment of the abuser's return to the family (see Crisis of disclosure – crisis of professionals and family crisis, 8.1).

Professionals often try unsuccessfully to restart treatment at the point of the abuser's return. I myself had to pay for this mistake when in one case a mother slammed the door in my face saying that her husband had paid for the abuse, that she was now pregnant again and that everything was OK between them. This was one of the most worrying situations because it left the previously abused 8-year-old daughter entirely unprotected. Leaving therapy until the abuser is discharged from prison diminishes the chance that therapy is accepted by the family. Primary Punitive Interventions which professionals attempt too late to change into a Primary Therapeutic Intervention often turn into Primary Child Protective Interventions. The only action professionals feel able to take is to remove the child from the family the moment the abuser returns home. This punishes and traumatises the child on top of the victimisation she has suffered from the abuse.

In a Primary Punitive Intervention the relapse into secrecy and secondary denial can be avoided when the Primary Punitive Intervention is turned into a Primary Therapeutic Intervention before the punitive measures have ceased. This means that the first family meeting as reality-creating responsibility meeting needs to take place during the period of imprisonment or probation of the abuser. The very fact of the prison sentence can then be used as a reminder for the abuser and the family that child sexual abuse has in fact taken place. It is possible to ask abusers, children and other family members who have relapsed into secondary denial why the father is in prison. In very defensive families we may have to go further back and deal with the case like an established case of primary denial, asking the abuser 'What would we read has happened if we read the police statement and the judgement of the court which brought you into prison?' (See Turning a Primary Punitive Intervention into a Primary Therapeutic Intervention, 11.11; The use of different family therapy techniques, 12.10.)

5 Relapse into secrecy and denial during therapy

The nature of child sexual abuse as syndrome of secrecy and addiction can also lead to secondary denial in a Primary Therapeutic Intervention . The difficulty for the abuser to face up to the sexual abuse and for the abuser and other family members to deal with the underlying individual and family problems can push the abuse back into secrecy and secondary denial.

Proof and admission on the legal level does not yet constitute believing and owning up in the psychological domain. It is for this reason that an initial family meeting is important in order to establish the facts of the abuse and the abuse as family reality. This initial family meeting in the presence of one outsider enables the therapist to maintain a sense of reality in a therapeutic process where renewed denial creeps in. The therapist who meets psychological denial can then refer back to the first responsibility session and remind the child, the abuser and the family of what was said in the reality-creating responsibility meeting. The therapist may need to go over all the facts of the abuse again in order to maintain sexual abuse as external reality for the abuser and the family. The process of renewed secrecy and the relapse into secondary psychological denial is part of a therapeutic process in child sexual abuse as syndrome of secrecy and addiction which has as its therapeutic core the transition from denial and secrecy to reality, privacy and responsibility. (See Proof and belief, admission and owning up, 1.5; The individual process, Chapter 2; Working with sexual abusers, 7.4.)

12.14 Tertiary denial by fathers

Tertiary denial is the most stressful situation and much more difficult to handle than primary or secondary denial. In tertiary denial abusers have admitted to sexual abuse. They have gone through the legal process and may even have been to prison. Afterwards they say that they have only taken responsibility for the abuse because they wanted to spare the child from going through the ordeal of court proceedings. They maintain that the child has lied and that sexual abuse has never happened. In tertiary denial abusers take responsibility on the legal level but use this admission to reinforce even stronger psychological denial. Abusers admit but never own up. (See Proof and belief, admission and owning up, 1.5; Dealing with primary denial, 10.6; Relapse into secondary denial, 12.13.)

Tertiary denial creates an inescapable trap for the child. It is a real 'who's afraid of Virginia Woolf?' move in which cruel and hurtful attacks on the child's integrity on one level are always undermined and denied again on another level of pseudo kindness and perverted concern. Previously acknowledged facts of sexual abuse become redefined in hindsight as fantasies which are based on mental derailments and on the morally evil nature of the child. Abusers demand from the world to be acknowledged as exceptionally caring and protective people who have sacrificed their life for the lies and the mental disturbance of the child.

Tertiary denial creates a new dimension of pressure for the child. The child is forced to be grateful to the abuser in a way which increases the child's confusion between fantasy and reality to a degree which can lead to most severe secondary psychological disturbance. Tertiary denial is the ultimate structural confusion between reality and fantasy and between victim and abuser. In tertiary denial the abuser can portray himself as the real victim and turns the child into the abuser. This is a further reality-avoiding move (see Syndrome of secrecy, and of addiction, 2.1, 2.2, 2.3).

Tertiary denial poses difficult therapeutic problems. The first problem is the counter-transference of professionals. Joining the abuser's denial means adding to the secondary traumatisation of the child. Maintaining a sense of reality and joining the side of the abused child make it very difficult to maintain a therapeutic stance towards the abuser. It can be very difficult to remain therapeutic in a situation of a strong counter-transference of hate and desperation. In addition abusers in tertiary denial need the strongest possible form of positive connotation and of positive paradoxical injuctions of the denial if we want to remain therapeutic and want to help the child.

We may have to be able to say things like 'Obviously it seems that the abuse has somehow taken place but it is very helpful to say that this is not so because as super father you may want to help the child and the family to forget all about the abuse as quickly as possible.' We can begin to explore the underlying anxiety and the disaster for the abuser if he began owning up psychologically to himself and to the family that sexual abuse has in fact happened as he had admitted legally before. It may be a constant dance between going along with the father's denial and at the same time putting the notion that it may be too frightening and too disastrous to acknowledge that sexual abuse has in fact happened (see The use of different family therapy techniques, 12.10).

In tertiary denial it is very difficult to avoid symmetrical and oppositional positions which can immediately turn very nasty. Conflicts between the abuser and the therapist can become very aggressive and often lead to acute therapy failure and to extreme scapegoating processes of the child. In tertiary denial it can at times be too great a risk to explore the extreme anxieties and disasters that it is possible to do in primary and secondary denial. In tertiary denial we always need to address the extreme low self-esteem and the narcissistic personality of the abuser. Sometimes I would use extreme language which would normally be quite inappropriate in therapy or even in ordinary social conversation. I might say that the father 'may feel a shit' if he would think about what had really happened. This is a meta-communication to let the abuser know that I know that he may in fact suffer from extremely low self-esteem. Often we get the clue from the abuser himself who in denying the abuse paints most denigrating and hateful pictures of sexual abusers, a group of human beings to whom he could never belong.

One of the techniques I have used to gain information in order to understand the personality factors and the life events in the abuser in cases of tertiary denial is to make the abuser into an expert on sexual abuse. We can ask abusers about the personality factors and characteristics sexual abusers have in their opinion. This move allows abusers to externalise their own problems and to attach them to other abusers. It is the analogous process of prescribing the symptom in family therapy. When professionals succeed in taking themselves back and 'one down' and putting the father 'one up' as the expert they may be able to understand the reasons for the need for tertiary denial.

Working with the abuser in tertiary denial can be very slow. It is extremely exhausting and often fails. For the child it is very important to have something much more intensive than one or two responsibility-sessions-by-proxy. We may need to try to get the child into regular individual counselling or therapy. We may only be able to see the child individually when we put to the parents reasons which are unrelated to the sexual abuse such as learning difficulties or behavioural problems at school. We may also be unable to get full parental co-operation. In cases of tertiary denial I sometimes have asked schools and nurseries to act as 'parents by proxy' and to bring the child to therapy. Therapy might be much shielded from the parents who would otherwise disrupt the work with the child. In individual sessions with children we may need to conduct something like 'responsibility-therapy-by-proxy'. Therapists may need to represent both the abuser and the child. They may need to find 10 reasons why the father may have to maintain his denial. We then need to think with the child about another 10 reasons why children may want to agree with this denial even at the cost of their own self-sacrifice. This process attempts to make sense of the denial for the child. We address the denial as functional for the family and as an expression of the personal predicament of the abuser and the child. (See Concurrent forms of therapy, 7.1; Individual therapy and family-therapy-by-proxy with children on their own, 7.3.1; Responsibility-session-by-proxy, 9.13.)

With the child we need to address especially the pressure to agree with the paternal reframing of the child's allegations of sexual abuse as a result of her own mental derailment or badness for which the father has sacrificed himself. We may also need to address constantly the child's own wish to deny the reality of the abuse in order to survive the unbearable discrepancy between the projected image of the father as caring parent and the reality of sexual abuse. This can be very difficult because the father has made the idealised self-image of the family relationships into the myth of the accepted family reality. Tertiary denial attacks in a most extreme way the sense of identity, reality and integrity of the child. It is another situation in which long-term sexual abuse in the family links up with consequences of the concentration-camp syndrome. (See Child sexual abuse as syndrome of secrecy, 2.1; The family process, Chapter 3.)

12.15 Does the gender of the therapist matter?

There have been demands that sexually abused children must only be seen by female therapists and social workers. In my experience no principal contra-indications exists for a sexually abused girl to be seen by a male professional and for a boy to be seen by a female professional as long as female and male workers are aware of the fact that their respective gender has certain specific dis-advantages and advantages (see Group work with children, 7.2; Finding the appropriate language, 11.1; Sexually abused professionals, 11.2).

Male therapists need to be aware of the following three main potential disadvantages:

1 Sexually abused children can be initially very frightened of a male therapist.
2 A male therapist may be in danger of being seduced to respond in a sexualised way to the powerful sexual communications of the abused child whether boy or girl.
3 Male professionals may also be seduced on a parental level to collude as a paternal figure against maternal figures, re-creating in the process the collu-sion and secrecy between the abuser and the child during the abuse which excluded the mother from the process.

The advantages of a male therapist are:

1 It is possible to give sexually abused children the direct experience that the male therapist as a man does not respond in a sexualised or sexual way to the child's emotional needs and that relationships with men can be emotional and caring without being sexually abusive.
2 The child can experience directly that male adults are able to draw appropriate generational boundaries.
3 It is usually easier for male professionals to allow sexually abused children to work on the positive aspects between the abuser and the child as well as allowing aspects of rivalry between the child and the mother for the father as an emotional or sexual partner to surface. However the danger in this situation is that a male therapist may again re-create the collusion against the mother,

especially when the question comes up 'why did my mother not prevent the abuse?'.

The complementary advantages of a female therapist are:

1 A female therapist can give the child the direct experience of a caring and trusting maternal figure who listens and believes the child and to whom the child can bring the trauma of the abuse afflicted by father figures.
2 A female therapist can give the child the experience that she does not gang up with the child against paternal figures, re-creating the parental split in the abuse.
3 A female therapist may be able to listen to the positive experiences the child had with the abuser without becoming horrified and rejecting or rivalrous as the mother may have been.
4 A female therapist may be able to bear the child's hostility and disappointment towards her which is an expression of the child's experience of non-protection and maternal let-down.

The main disadvantages and dangers for a female therapist are:

1 The female therapist may identify more strongly with the victim aspect in sexual abuse. This can give sexually abused boys and girls the message that they are not allowed to communicate about positive aspects in the abusive relationship with the father figure.
2 Children can be more frightened openly to relate the negative aspects of maternal let-down and female rivalry to a female therapist.
3 Female therapists can find it more difficult to tolerate the sometimes extreme hostility which children can develop as a result of feeling unprotected and not understood by their mothers.
4 A female therapist needs to be careful not to collude with the sexually abused child against men as being basically bad when the child goes through phases of anger and hate towards the abuser and men. (See The family process, Chapter 3; Child sexual abuse as syndrome of secrecy, 2.1; Aims and steps in the Primary Therapeutic Intervention, 6.2.)

The reality element of the gender of the therapist certainly is more important in the treatment of child sexual abuse than in other syndromes. In cases where a child is frightened of men, a female therapist is obviously more appropriate. Conversely, I have seen several children who had been sexually abused by fathers and father figures but who nevertheless wanted to be seen by a male professional. This had two different causes. One group had felt unsupported and rejected by the mother and wanted to see a male worker because they were frightened of maternal rejection. The second group showed very sexualised and seductive behaviour and the children were still very much in a repetitive mode of the victim role.

Any automatic same-sex link between the gender of the abused child and the gender of the therapist must be rejected. The treatment of a sexually abused girl by a female worker who is in a state of primary identification with the sexually abused girl or of a boy by a male worker who is in a state of primary identification with the sexually abused boy may be as anti-therapeutic or as damaging to the child as the forced therapy of a girl or a boy by therapists of the opposite sex. Again the issue is one of differentiation between two different sets which both have advantages and disadvantages (see Primary and secondary damage, 1.4).

The confusion between children's needs and professional's own projections and personal reactions to child sexual abuse often leads to inappropriate ideological discussions of the importance of the gender of the therapist. The professional's own personal attitude and her or his own life experience invariably strongly influence and limit the individual professional ability to deal with the sex-related aspects of child sexual abuse. If a professional feels that for her or his own personal reasons she or he can only cope with girls or boys respectively, this preference is perfectly acceptable. This limitation needs to be respected as long as the professional knows that this choice is not based on the child's need but on the professional's own personal capacity to work with only girls or boys. (See Introduction; The interprofessional process, 5.1.)

The distinction between the professional's own needs and the needs of the child gives space for both sex-linked approaches of feminist origin and non-sex linked approaches to child sexual abuse which are rooted in child health and child mental health practice and in work with abusers. We need to differentiate and see the strengths of our work as well as the limitations and weaknesses rather than argue ideological points.

12.16 Court-ordered therapy

Traditionally therapists have refused to undertake therapy with people who have been court-ordered, maintaining that it does not work. In child sexual abuse as syndrome of secrecy and addiction entirely voluntary treatment for abusers and families is usually doomed to failure. Therapists cannot allow themselves to be put into a situation by courts and statutory agencies where they take responsibility for the prevention of further abuse or guarantee psychological change in the abuser.

It is possible to transform the seemingly contradictory relationship between therapy and legal order into a complementary and mutually supportive framework.The impossible bind can be solved if court-ordered therapy is not seen as therapy in traditional terms but as consultation to courts and statutory agencies. Court-ordered therapy can never be therapy in classical terms because the therapist and the abuser and the family are not free agents in relation to each other. They are invariably held together by the conditions of the legal and statutory process, not by traditional therapeutic parameters of motivation. The conceptual distinction between consultation and therapy allows therapists to conduct therapy without taking inappropriate responsibility for the legal and statutory decision-making process at the end of treatment when final decisions about punitive and child protective aspects need to be made. (See Legal abuse and psychological damage, 1.1; Therapy and consultation, 5.4; Practical problems in consulta- tions, 11.5.)

Court-ordered therapy cannot be the precondition for family rehabilitation. It can only be the precondition for an assessment where rehabilitation is possible. The court order to the abuser cannot be 'instead of punishment you have to go into therapy and at the end of therapy you will be allowed to have free access to your child or to live with your child again'. Such orders would bring therapists into impossible binds in which they have to prove themselves, while abusers can sit back and sit out their time without being involved in therapy at all. Therapists would have the impossible responsibility of making sure that the abuser does not abuse again. They would have the equally impossible task of deciding when and whether it would be safe for the abuser to return to live with the child without having recourse to courts and statutory agencies to whom they could return the case for legal reconsideration if therapy were to fail.

The court order needs to be, 'You have to go into therapy and at the end of therapy we the court or others in our name will reassess whether the situation has sufficiently changed or not. We will then decide whether to attempt to rehabili- tate or not.' Therapy as consultation to courts becomes the very precondition for a separate future reassessment in legal and statutory terms by the courts who made the original order. Therapy as consultation needs to start out with clearly defined psychological and interpersonal aims and goals and needs to conclude with a final psychiatric evaluation by the therapist and a recommendation to courts and statutory agencies.

The decision about the possibility of rehabilitation on the legal level needs to be taken by courts and statutory agencies who are responsible for legal and statutory aspects of safety and child protection. The role of the therapist therefore remains that of a consultant. Therapists assist the courts and child protective agencies through therapy and psychological assessments in their decision- making task on legal and child protective matters.

Court-ordered therapy in which therapists have immediate recourse to proba- tion officers and courts when therapy fails creates an effective complementary framework for treatment of convicted abusers. The legal process is necessary in child sexual abuse as interlocking syndrome of secrecy and addiction to support therapeutic work. The ensuing therapy can become truly therapeutic in terms of psychological and interpersonal change when decisions about legal and statutory issues are separate from therapy itself.

Having made the fundamental distinction between therapeutic and legal res- ponsibilities we can now say that the two tasks may nevertheless be fulfilled by one person. A social worker with statutory responsibility can remain truly thera- peutic by introducing the metasystemic triad between himself, the family and 'the authority'. Equally, therapists who conduct court-ordered therapy can create the triad between themselves, the abuser and 'the law' or 'the authority' (Figure 12.1).

In the process of continuous re-evaluation and at the end of therapy the therapist can say, 'If you were to go back to court in your present state do you think the judge would agree that it is now safe for you to return home?' Courts need to spell out clearly the aims and goals for therapy if court-ordered therapy is to be conducted by social workers and probation officers with legal and statutory responsibilities. The court may give therapists the executive power to evaluate whether these steps have been achieved or not and to hand the case back when treatment has failed (see Dealing with professional hierarchies in consultations, 11.6).

This rather authoritative procedure of step-by-step evaluation of treatment progress is very much like the step-by-step evaluation in traditionally known forms of treatment of addiction. In child sexual abuse as interlocking syndrome of secrecy and addiction the access to legal and statutory agencies needs to be open for the therapist at any time. If in other forms of addiction the addict opts out of therapy he only harms himself. In child sexual abuse where the 'drug' is a child, legal and statutory evaluation need to remain involved until the very end of therapy because breakdown of therapy and therapy failure can easily lead to renewed child sexual abuse. (See Responsibility, participation, guilt, blame and power, 1.2; Child sexual abuse as syndrome of secrecy, and of addiction, 2.1, 2.2, 2.3; Working with sexual abusers, 7.4.)

12.17 Working with foster parents

The placement of sexually abused children in foster care without the intensive support of foster parents often leads to foster breakdown. In extreme situations it can lead to re-abuse in foster care. Placing sexually abused children in foster families without adequate family support is in my opinion unethical. Sexual re-enactment of sexually abused children can be detrimental to the foster parents. Sexualised behaviour in the child can induce family and marital conflicts which might result in separation, divorce, re-abuse and family breakdown (see Placement with foster parents, 10.3).

Foster families need to be well prepared and carefully selected before sexually abused children are placed. Foster fathers in particular can become very insecure and frightened or dangerously self-assured as over-compensation when they are not well prepared for dealing with sexually abused children.

Sexually abused children often re-enact sexual behaviour towards other children and children in the foster family need to be considered. In one case an 11-year-old girl instructed a 10-year-old boy in the foster family to have sex with her. In another case a 3-year-old girl started to persecute a 5-year-old boy in the foster family and tried to rub and suck his penis. The placement broke down when the boy became thoroughly frightened and disturbed. Finally the question needs

(a) *Legal process undermining therapy:*
Therapy as a precondition
for rehabilitation

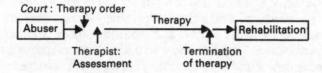

(b) *Legal process facilitating therapy:*
Therapy as a precondition
for assessment of possible
rehabilitation

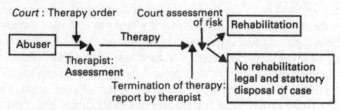

Figure 12.1 Court-ordered therapy and rehabilitation

to be raised whether the marriage can stand the behaviour of the sexually abused child. Marital aspects of the relationship between the foster parents need to be addressed as far as necessary for the placement of the child.

When sexually abused children are placed in foster families a handover meeting needs to take place between the previous Trusted Person, the social worker and the foster family. During the handover meeting the professionals need to help the child and the foster family to find explicit sexual language to communicate appropriately about the abuse. Families often do not communicate about sexual abuse openly and foster families need help to find an appropriate sexual language in order to deal with the child when issues of the abuse need to be raised between the parents and with the child. The handover meeting is vital in order to avoid a relapse into secondary secrecy which makes it a family taboo and impossible to address inappropriate sexualised behaviour of sexually abused children who can induce subtle sexualisation into the foster family, which family members feel too frightened or embarrassed to name openly. Finding the language and creating sexual abuse of the child as family reality by naming the facts of the abuse can be as difficult for foster families as for natural families. (See Aims and steps in the Primary Therapeutic Intervention, 6.2; The use of the 'trusted person', 8.6; The handover meeting, 9.14.)

Once sexually abused children are placed in foster care the following five questions need to be addressed in support sessions for foster parents.

1 How can we talk to the child about the abuse and how can we deal with disturbed and sexualised behaviour?

Sexually abused children are often still loyal to the abuser and feel rejected by their parents for being placed in care. Sexually abused children, like physically abused children, often blame themselves for the placement. Foster parents therefore need to acknowledge the child's loyalties and need to reassure the child on issues of responsibility, blame and guilt. (See Responsibility, participation, guilt, blame and power, 1.2; Implications for practice, 1.3.)

Sexually abused children can be frightened of foster fathers and can be very demanding on foster mothers. The most intolerable behaviour is usually open sexualised behaviour of the child. Sexualised behaviour can be directed at other children in the family and at the foster father and occasionally at the foster mother. Sexually abused children have often learnt that relating to men means sexual relating. When they want care and attention from the foster father they will begin to re-enact their experience by re-enacting sexualised behaviour. Sexualised behaviour of sexually abused children towards foster fathers can subsequently lead to hostility and rejection by foster mothers, creating structural repetitions of the original traumatic family pattern for the child. (See The individual process, Chapter 2; The family process, Chapter 3.)

It is important to support foster parents to set firm boundaries on inappropriate sexualised behaviour of sexually abused children without being frightened of becoming punitive. Foster parents need to be able to talk explicitly about the sexual abuse whenever disturbed behaviour of the child indicates that the abusive experience is influencing the child's behaviour and relationships. It is difficult to find the fine balance between not avoiding raising the subject and becoming persecutory and pushing the issue too far. The inability to raise the issue can lead to the re-introduction of secondary secrecy and to the re-enactment of underhand sexualised behaviour in the child whereas constant reminding of the abuse will prevent children from putting the traumatic experience behind them.

2 How does sexual abuse affect the personal and individual feelings of each foster parent?

Some foster parents find it more difficult than others to talk openly about sexual matters and to use sexual language openly. It is important to explore the personal attitude of both foster parents towards the sexual abuse of the child. Foster fathers need to understand that the child may become seductive towards them or conversely that the child may be very frightened of them. They need to accept the very difficult fact that sexually abused children may be able to arouse sexual feelings in them. Foster fathers need the permission of professionals to be allowed to register sexualised feelings induced by the child. The very moment foster fathers feel sexually aroused in any way by the child they need to talk to their partner who needs to help the child to desexualise the interaction. Foster fathers also need to learn that children who are frightened of men need time and space slowly to get used to the idea that not all father figures respond to emotional demands with sexual abuse.

Foster mothers need help to deal with possible sexualised behaviour of foster children towards their husbands. Sexually abused children can show strong hostility towards foster mothers when they re-enact their relationship to their natural mothers who did not protect them from the abuse. On the other hand sexually abused children can make great emotional demands on foster mothers. They are often emotionally immature despite premature pseudo-adult sexual experiences. Support work might need to address gender-specific problems and feelings between the foster parents which are induced by the re-enactment of the sexually abused child.

3 How does the sexually abused child influence the partner relationship?

Sexually abused children can create problems even in previously stable partner relationships. Abused children may not be aware that they begin to sexualise towards the foster father. The onset can be so subtle that the foster parents are equally unaware of it. Secret sexualisation can creep into the family relationships when the child succeeds in splitting the foster parents. The induction of secrecy can trigger a very dangerous family process. The origins of ensuing marital tensions may not be recognised by either foster parent as conflict-by-proxy and open marital conflict can follow. The extreme effect can be re- abuse and marital breakdown (see The interprofessional process, 5.1).

Foster parents need to be prepared to communicate about possible sexualised behaviour of the child as soon as the foster father becomes aware of any sexual feelings towards the sexually abused child or as soon as the foster mother becomes aware of any sexual acting-out of the child. It is extremely important that both parents get the explicit permission of the placing social worker and the therapist to allow themselves to have these counter-transference feelings which are induced by the child. (See Introduction; Finding the appropriate sexual language to communicate about the abuse, 11.1.)

4 How to deal with the abused child in the presence of other children in the household?

Sexualised behaviour towards other children in the household often leads to foster breakdown. It is quite understandable that foster parents find it unacceptable if a young child openly behaves sexually towards other young children in the family. It is also understandable that foster parents find it intolerable when latency children or young adolescents try to introduce pre-adolescent or adolescent peers into genital-sexual play and behaviour.

Sexualised behaviour towards other children needs to be instantly interrupted by foster parents. It is important that foster parents learn to see the demand for emotional care and non-sexual relating behind the child's sexualised behaviour. Whenever a child shows sexualised behaviour the foster parents need to try to substitute the sexual interaction through emotional care. Sexualised behaviour can be substituted by non-sexualised physical contact and general parental attention. In addition specific symptom-oriented measures might be necessary (see The need for behaviour modification, 7.3.4).

Sexually abused children often have great problems in their peer relationships. They may have felt isolated for many years. They often feel dirty and different from other children and their experience of sexual abuse has separated them from their peers around them. Foster parents therefore need to be aware that sexually abused children need help in building up normal peer relationships (see Group work with children, 7.2).

5 How to talk and to deal with social contexts of school, nursery, youth clubs and neighbours?

Sexually abused children have a right to privacy. This basic fact is often forgotten when sexually abused children get harassed by undue attention from people in the child's social environment. On the other hand it can be necessary to inform key professionals in nurseries, schools and youth clubs about the fact that the child has been sexually abused.

Children often display disturbed and sexualised behaviour in nurseries and schools and it can be very helpful if the nursery teacher, the headmaster and the class teacher know the background. Otherwise sexually abused children can be rejected and punished for anti-social sexualised behaviour which they feel unable to control. A cycle of secondary victimisation is easily induced if key care takers are not informed. They need to be able to make sense of the child's behaviour and to set firm limits on unacceptable behaviour without becoming punitive. We need to stress the child's right for privacy and confidentiality but good communication and shared knowledge of the abuse between foster parents, schools and nurseries can be very helpful and therapeutic.

It needs to be considered most carefully whether the fact of child sexual abuse of children in foster care should be shared with neighbours or family friends. Children become easily scapegoated and excluded for the very fact of having been sexually abused. On the other hand sexualised behaviour towards children of friends and neighbours can lead to rejection and isolation of the child. It can be necessary to take selected parents and family friends into confidence. The danger of unstoppable gossip needs to be carefully weighed against the danger of rejection of the child by other families as a result of specific behaviour problems in the sexually abused child.

When sexual abuse has taken place in the foster family itself, foster fathers and foster families need to be treated like other abusers and families of abuse. In long-term foster placements foster parents are important attachment figures for children. In long-term fostering the legally weak status of foster parents often does not correspond to their psychologically important position as the only meaningful attachment figures for the child.

To deduce from the legal status of foster parents that sexually abused children should under all circumstances be instantly removed and should never have any contact with sexually abusing foster fathers or the family again denies everything we know about attachment, loyalty and the importance of family relationships in long-term fostering. The need to include long-term foster parents fully in a Primary Therapeutic Intervention in the same way as natural parents does not on the other hand mean that sexually abused children should necessarily always return back to the foster family (see Aims and steps in the Primary Therapeutic Intervention, 6.2).

Chapter thirteen

Extrafamilial child sexual abuse

13.1 How to distinguish between intrafamilial and extrafamilial abuse in cases of denial

Sometimes we do not know whether child sexual abuse has happened within the family or outside even if the abuse has been proven by medical and forensic evidence. It can be difficult to come to any firm conclusion and the assessment can be complicated. Once the allegation of child sexual abuse has been denied by an alleged abuser within the family it is important to involve all family members in the assessment of intra or extrafamilial abuse. Siblings of abused children sometimes give important corroborative information which can help clarify the situation and sometimes it emerges that siblings have been sexually abused as well. (See Dealing with primary denial 10.6; Siblings in families of child sexual abuse, 14.1).

The direct inclusion of suspected but denying abusers in the assessment of intrafamilial or extrafamilial sexual abuse is vital. Initial reactions of suspected abusers and of mothers has often proved to be indicative. There are very different and typical reactions of parents and abusers which can help to distinguish intrafamilial child sexual abuse from extrafamilial abuse.

In both situations parents and abusers can show great upset after disclosure. In cases of extrafamilial sexual abuse both parents usually show deep concern for the child. They ask questions as to the person of the abuser and about his possible motives. They always express great concern about possible physical harm and psychological effects. Parents in extrafamilial child sexual abuse are increasingly concerned about AIDS. They also want to know about the short-term and long-term consequences of the abuse on the child's development. Parents usually raise the question of whether other siblings in the family could have been sexually abused as well and how siblings could be protected from similar experiences. Parents in extrafamilial abuse often turn to other siblings and actively question them about whether similar things had happened to them. Fathers in extrafamilial abuse usually turn to professionals for information and for help for the child. They ask many and sometimes desperate and angry questions to understand how abuse could have happened and what it could mean for the child. Parents in extrafamilial abuse often ask for further physical and medical examinations. They nearly always want to know whether the child needs counselling or therapy and what this would do to the child.

The reaction of suspected abusers and parents in long-term intrafamilial abuse is quite different. Parents are not so much upset on behalf of the child but they are concerned about the allegations and about their own way of formulating their denial. I have rarely heard any *questions* asked about the possible perpetrator. I have, however, always heard fierce *accusations* against other people such as adolescent or adult male neighbours and acquaintances or friends of the child.

It seems to be very indicative for intrafamilial child sexual abuse that suspected abusers and parents tend to avoid questions about possible physical harm and about possible long-term psychological effects for the child. If anything the parents already have a specific behaviour of the child in mind which they do not like and which they blame on the abuse. We rarely find the typical reactions we see in parents of extrafamilial child sexual abuse who wonder whether other children might have been sexually abused as well. On the contrary, siblings are often excluded from being questioned and parents try to silence siblings by speaking for them.

In unclear cases of denial parents and suspected abusers in intrafamilial abuse seldom turn to professionals for information and for help for the child. They show a much more apprehensive and often aggressive attitude towards professionals. No questions are usually asked to understand the abuse, nor do parents want further medical examinations. They tend to avoid asking whether the child needs counselling and therapy and they themselves do not ask for guidance on how to deal with the children. They usually wish to be left alone by professionals and want to deal with everything themselves.

The main global differences between parents in cases of denial of intrafamilial and extrafamilial abuse are that parents asked a lot of questions, were very concerned about the consequences for the child and wanted a lot of information and help in cases where extrafamilial abuse was finally diagnosed. The upset of the disclosure was accompanied by a strong sense of helplessness and desperation and often by self-doubt and self-accusations. In contrast, in cases where intrafamilial abuse was finally diagnosed, few questions to obtain information and help were asked. The mood of the parents was much more controlling and aggressive. Neighbours and people in the social environment of the family were accused of sexual abuse and professionals were attacked for their lack of skill and understanding in diagnosing and dealing with supposedly extrafamilial abuse. The different patterns of reactions are shown in Figure 13.1. (See From mad to bad, Chapter 1; The individual process, Chapter 2; The family process, Chapter 3.)

13.2 Traumatic debriefing in extrafamilial child sexual abuse

In mild forms of short-term extrafamilial sexual abuse such as a single incidence of fondling which is taken up by parents immediately, the technique of 'traumatic

Extrafamilial abuse	Intrafamilial abuse
Parental reaction towards child	
(1) Acute concern for the child	(1) Concern about their own denial
(2) Concern about physical harm	(2) Avoidance of questions of physical harm
(3) Concern about psychological damage	(3) Avoidance of questions of psychological damage
(4) Questions on short-term and long-term consequences	(4) Avoidance to learn of short-term or long-term consequences
(5) Concern for siblings who may be abused as well	(5) Exclusion or silencing of siblings
Parental reaction towards abuser	
(1) Questions to the person and personality of the abuser	(1) No specific questions about abuser but often unspecific lament
(2) Often extreme anger of fathers towards abuser, even violent revenge	(2) Legal process to find the abuser avoided
(3) Parents employ legal process to the full	
Parental reaction towards professionals	
(1) Turning to professionals for information and help	(1) Apprehensive and aggressive towards professionals
(2) Questions to understand the abuse	(2) No questions to understand the abuse
(3) Often request for further medical examination and evaluation	(3) No wish for further examination and evaluation
(4) Often request for counselling and therapy	(4) Rejection of professionals
	(5) Attempt to isolate themselves and to manage on their own
Parents' personal reactions	
(1) *Cognitive*: barrage of questions	(1) No questions, denial
(2) *Mood*: helplessness, desperateness	(2) Controlling, aggressive, distancing
(3) *Reflex*: self-doubt, self-accusation, self-blame, sometimes violent fury against abuser	(3) Accusation against the child, professionals and others

Figure 13.1 Parental concern and diagnostic differentiation between intrafamilial and extrafamilial child sexual abuse

debriefing' can be very helpful. Usually the child will have to make a statement to the police and it is important that one or both parents are present. The child needs to be able to go through the events step-by-step, not only for legal but also for therapeutic reasons. By recalling step-by-step the factual details of the abuse the child can begin to form a congruent experience out of the confusing facts and feelings about what has happened. The neutral and detailed questioning about specific facts and little details immediately after disclosure can help to avoid children being overcome by the experience. Subsequent to the disclosure, parents need help in family sessions to deal with any disturbed behaviour of the child. Parents should get assistance to find out when it is appropriate to talk about the abuse and when it is important to allow the child to be able to forget.

The first reaction of parents and professionals to the immediate disclosure of mild forms of short-term extrafamilial child sexual abuse is often to protect the child by talking as little as possible about the abuse. It is important to go over the details of the sexual abuse at least once in the presence of the parents in order to establish the facts of the abuse and to help the parents and the child to be able to talk openly about the abuse whenever it becomes necessary.

Although it is very important that parents in cases of instantly discovered mild forms of extrafamilial abuse feel able and free to raise the abuse openly with children in order to help them to deal with the experience, sexually abused children must also be allowed to forget the abuse and get on with life. After the traumatic debriefing and an initial period of talking, the abuse should only be mentioned openly if the child develops disturbed behaviour which might be related to the abuse. In that case the child might need more intensive professional help. (See From mad to bad, Chapter 1; The individual process in context, 2.4; Aims and steps in the Primary Therapeutic Intervention, 6.2.)

13.3 Dealing with the family process in long-term extrafamilial child sexual abuse

Long-term extrafamilial child sexual abuse can continue for many months and years. In long-term extrafamilial child sexual abuse intensive family work is necessary to deal with predisposing factors which made the child vulnerable to extrafamilial sexual abuse and to address the effects of the abuse on the child and the family. Total helplessness and the feeling of complete loss of parental control in combination with intensive self-blame and guilt feelings are common parental reactions.

In long-term extrafamilial child sexual abuse possible predisposing factors need to be identified. Emotional distance or rejection by parents and neglect can make children vulnerable to seduction by potential sexual abusers who are not seldom part of the social environment of the child. Often parents do not know where their children spend their free time or they have not met the people the child associates with. Parents might be unable to read early enough the signs of change in the child–parent relationship resulting from a long-term sexual abuse outside the family. Absent parents can increase the vulnerability in children to extra-familial sexual abuse. The absence of a father-figure can make boys more vulnerable to falling victim to homosexual abuse by father figures of 'nice uncles' who live in the neighbourhood (see Dealing with children of sex-rings, 13.4).

The family process in the treatment of long-term extrafamilial sexual abuse is in many aspects very similar to the family process in the Primary Therapeutic Intervention of intrafamilial child sexual abuse. The abuse needs to be established as family reality in a first family meeting in order to break through the secrecy of the extrafamilial abuse. As in intrafamilial abuse parents and families need help to find a language to communicate adequately about the sexual nature of the sexual abuse. Although there is no abuser within the family, both parents need to take equal responsibility for the further protection and parenting of the abused child. The sexual abuse can trigger severe marital problems and the relationship between the parents and the abused child needs to be re-evaluated (see Aims and steps in the Primary Therapeutic Intervention, 6.2).

The work on the different dyads in long-term extrafamilial child sexual abuse shows the following specific characteristics.

1 Work on the parental dyad

Parents of children in long-term extrafamilial sexual abuse usually feel that they have lost parental control completely. They feel paralysed in their parenting capacity and do not know how to deal with the abused child. The abuse can shatter their self-confidence and their belief in their ability to be effective and protective parents. Parents do not know how to deal with the fact that sexual abuse has happened over long periods of time under their eyes and often by somebody they have known.

The feeling of loss of control, guilt feelings and self-blame can lead to very different reactions in fathers and in mothers. Fathers are usually much less able to deal with feelings of helplessness and loss of control. They find it much more difficult to face the sexual nature of sexual abuse towards their child. Fathers tend to turn their helplessness and guilt feelings into often murderous anger against the abuser. This anger can be so overwhelming and the rage so overpowering that fathers are in danger of losing control, physically trying to find and attack the abuser. This has happened in several cases in which I have been involved. Fathers also tend to turn their helplessness and loss of control into over-compensating actions towards the abused child. They often become extremely strict, controlling and punitive towards the child in order to 'put things right'.

Mothers usually react very differently. They tend to become much more self-blaming and depressed. They often feel paralysed as mothers and ask others to take over and to help them to understand how it could have happened to them. They certainly do not want to have anything to do with the abuser. Often they do not agree with the father's over-reactions towards the child but feel unable to find an appropriate firm but non-punitive approach to the child themselves.

2 Work on the marital dyad

Self-blaming of parents often leads to mutual blaming of each other. Fathers accuse mothers of being too soft and too little controlling towards the child. Mothers accuse fathers of being absent and not caring about them or about the child. The mutual blaming on the parental level can produce marital conflict. The sexual nature of the abuse confronts the parents with their own sexual relationship and with gender issues which need to be addressed.

3 Work between the parents and the child

Children in long-term extrafamilial child sexual abuse often feel guilty to have let their parents down. At the same time they can develop strong attachments and loyalties to the abuser. In several cases the abusers were old and lonely men in the neighbourhood. The children had felt pity for the abusers and had submitted to their sexual demands not only because they were bribed but also because they felt sorry and wanted to be nice. Several cases of child sexual abuse by young physically or mentally handicapped abusers were based on similar feelings of pity in the abused children. Other children got attached to 'nice uncles' who gave them a lot of attention and treated them with sweets and other bribes.

Parents usually find signs and expressions of children's loyalties towards extrafamilial abusers unbearable and can become very angry, hostile and rejecting towards the child. Children in turn can develop devious and self-punishing behaviour during the abuse and after disclosure which parents find difficult to understand. The fact that the inappropriateness of the sexual relationship between the extrafamilial abuser and the child can nevertheless lead to strong attachments of the child needs to be taken into account and needs to be explained to the parents and dealt with in the child.

In long-term extrafamilial sexual abuse which can last for years, treatment needs to help parents to substitute the inappropriate but often strong emotional attachments of the child to the extrafamilial abuser as adult authority figure and to form closer and more adequate attachments with the child. Initially over-controlling reactions of fathers and openly displayed helplessness by mothers are understandable but therapeutically unhelpful reactions. Treatment between the parents and the child needs to focus on better parental understanding of their child and of the child's needs for parental care and attention. This includes focusing on the external aspects the child's daily life. Parents need to learn to take more interest in their children's social activities. It is of crucial importance for the parents to get themselves actively involved in the child's social life and to spend leisure time together in shared activities. Parents also need to supervise their children and they need to know where they are and who they are mixing with. Family work and work on dyads have the aim of creating a closer emotional relationship between the parents and the child and of fostering a positive and close interest of the parents in the child's activities. This enables children to deal therapeutically with their confused attachment to the abuser.

Family-oriented treatment also has great preventive value. Children need to know that they will be understood and not punished when they want to approach their parents in future for help in situations of threatening re-abuse. The children also need to know that if they are re-abused, a future disclosure will meet with an understanding and protective response.

Finally, it is important to do some work on the peer relationships of the child. Children who have been victims of long-term extrafamilial child sexual abuse have had secret premature sexual experiences which make them feel very different from other children. This aspect needs to be addressed in similar ways to intrafamilial abuse and sexualised behaviour needs to be treated urgently. (See The individual process, Chapter 2; Aims and steps in the Primary Therapeutic Intervention, 6.2; Group work with children, 7.2; The need for behaviour modification, 7.3.4; The problem of re-introducing modesty, 12.9.)

13.4 Children of sex-rings

Sex-rings with boys only are usually formed by paedophile abusers. We may find single abusers or whole groups of abusing adults. Mixed sex-rings which include girls and boys can be run by groups of adults which can also include women. The children are recruited through social networks of schools, youth clubs or friends. Children are bribed, threatened and put under considerable group pressure to maintain secrecy. Sex-rings of large numbers of children can continue for many months and even years without disclosure. It is remarkable how even sex-rings of younger children can be kept secret over long periods of time.

Family-oriented work with children of sex-rings and their parents poses the same problems as for other forms of long-term extrafamilial child sexual abuse as described in Section 13.3. There are, nevertheless, some important differences which need to be addressed.

1 The multi-family meeting

A multi-family meeting needs to be organised as soon as possible after disclosure. The multi-family meeting needs to be attended by all children who have been involved in the sex-ring and by their parents. In addition the key statutory, legal and mental health workers who may be involved should be present. It is most important to co-operate closely with the police. It can be very helpful to have a police officer present who has been part of the investigation. This police officer can be extremely therapeutic in helping to establish the sexual abuse as multi-family reality by naming the offences with which the abuser or the abusers are charged.

The involvement of multiple families and multiple legal and statutory workers and agencies can make the process of disclosure and investigation very confusing for individual parents. The aim of the multi-family meeting is to establish the facts of the abuse and to help parents to find a language to communicate openly with each other and with their children about what happened in the sex-ring. The group experience of the multi-family meeting is an excellent starting point for subsequent treatment. It is often only the experience of the multi-family meeting which 'hits home' to the parents the full reality of the sex-ring. The self-help component of multi-family meetings can be very therapeutic when they help to overcome parents' sense of isolation, confusion and helplessness. Parents are often very confused about what has been told to them and they need explanations about what is happening in the investigation. They also need to see that police, child protective services and therapists are working together in a commonly agreed professional approach. The size of multi-family meetings is obviously dictated by the size of the sex-ring. In large sex-rings more than one parallel meeting might be necessary. The multi-family meeting needs to be carefully prepared in a prior meeting of all professionals involved. (See From mad to bad, Chapter 1; The individual process, Chapter 2; The professional network, Chapter 5; The first family meeting as reality-creative responsibility Meeting, 9.ll; Family and responsibility-session-by-proxy, 9.13.)

A senior social worker with statutory responsibility who has been involved in the disclosure is often the best person to invite the families. He should also open the meeting by stating the aims of the session and by introducing the professionals to the families. A police officer who has been directly involved in taking the statements from the children and the abuser should then list all the offences which have allegedly been committed. A calm and neutral account can be extremely helpful in setting the scene for the ensuing dialogue with the parents, which should be led by a therapist with some experience in child abuse and group work.

The following questions should guide the therapists' dialogue with the parent group:

1 Can parents believe that the sex-ring has happened?
2 Can they believe that their own child has been part of the ring and has been sexually abused?
3 What do they feel about the fact that the abuse has happened under their noses?
4 What do they feel about their own child having been abused?
5 What do they feel about their child not having told them?
6 Who blames their child for the abuse?
7 What does the abuse do to their sense of control and their ability to parent?
8 In which way do the parents feel they are in the same position or in a different position from other parents?
9 Do the mothers feel the same as the fathers feel about the children and the abuser or differently?

These are some of the questions for the initial multi-family meeting as the starting point for subsequent parallel treatment of family meetings and separate groups for parents and children. We need to be aware that emotions can get very high, especially among fathers, and we have to be prepared for mothers and fathers disclosing abuse in their own childhood. The multi-family meeting obviously needs more time than an ordinary family meeting but it should not take longer than 2 hours. It can be very helpful to spend the last part of the meeting in separate groups for parents and children and use the groups to reflect on the large meeting. This first group meeting is a very good starting point for subsequent continuous group therapy for parents and children.

2 Group work for children and parents

In long-term sex-rings the treatment of choice is parallel group work for children and parents. In concurrent forms of therapy multi-family meetings need to be held at intervals of 4–8 weeks. The parent group will centre very much around the same issues as in long-term extrafamilial child sexual abuse, although I have seen stronger male–female splits and mutual blaming for non-protectiveness than in other forms of extrafamilial abuse. In parent groups of sex-rings different parents can help each other to deal with their anger, their sense of helplessness and loss of control and with their guilt feelings and self-blame. The self-help aspect in the parents' group of sex-rings can avoid parental and marital conflicts becoming anti-therapeutic and destructive. In the children's group special attention needs to be drawn to strong mutual attachments and group loyalties of the abused children amongst each other and towards the abuser.

In group therapy for sex-rings the setting of the group can structurally re-enact the abusive group context in the original sex-ring. Peer group pressure to keep the secrecy can therefore be considerable in children's groups of sex-rings. In sex-rings children can be as frightened of punishment and retaliation by other ring members as they are of punishment by parents and the abuser. One child may not dare to disclose more than other children. Children may also be frightened to talk more negatively or more positively about the abuse and the abuser than other children in order to avoid implicating themselves in the context of the peer group. Workers in groups of children from sex-rings therefore need to be prepared to work with considerable degrees of resistance and collusion amongst the children against therapy. Group work with children in the treatment of sex-rings has the same structural disadvantages as individual work in other forms of sexual abuse. Group work in sex-rings re-creates the structural setting of the abuse in the same way as individual therapy does in the individual abuse of children. A concurrent individual session or family therapy is therefore absolutely essential in the treatment of sex-rings. (See Concurrent forms of therapy, 7.1; Individual counselling and therapy, 7.3.)

In the beginning stages of group treatment children of sex-rings often do not dare to disclose their attachment to the abuser. This does not mean that no attachment exists. In one group the boys were asked to write down a list of feelings they had towards the abuser. Very negative and derogative terms at the beginning such as 'fucker' were later followed by much more positive and even moving associations such as 'good to talk to' and 'good to be with'. At the end of the session there was a very sad atmosphere in the group and great concern was expressed towards the abuser.

In sex-rings group loyalty to the abuser can be very strong and it is important to work on the children's guilt feelings about the possible punishment and imprisonment of the abuser. Children in sex-rings often feel that the punishment of the abuser is their fault. In one group all the boys got very worried and the entire group process changed at the time when the abuser came to court and was sentenced to imprisonment. Several boys were upset and sad and this issue needed to be dealt with in the group. Despite all the hate and anger in the parents' group, and despite the demonstration of negative feelings of the children, the abuser had also been a very positive 'nice uncle figure' to whom the children were strongly attached.

3 Work with peer group abuse

In sexual abuse of sex-rings we often have a whole network of abuse which can include mutual sexual abuse of children. Older boys in particular who have been sexually abused themselves in sex-rings can in turn become sexual abusers of younger children. It is of paramount importance to keep in mind that even after disclosure secondary abuse by older children within the sex-ring can continue under ongoing peer group pressure of secrecy (see The individual process, Chapter 2).

Sexually abused members of the sex-ring get induced by the abuser to become abusers themselves. Mutual abuse of children can create a whole secondary network of interlocking abuse. It can be very difficult to disentangle this net, and additional individual therapy and behaviour modification may be necessary to deal with the aspects of abusing and being abused. Secondary sexual abuse among the children can also have severe effects on the parents' groups and therapists need to consider in advance how to react to a possible secondary split into 'victim-parents' and 'abuser-parents'. Very close co-operation with police is necessary to avoid secondary victimisation of boys who have become sexual abusers as a result of induction to abuse in the sex-ring. (See Court-ordered therapy, 12.16; Adolescent sex offenders who are sexually abused themselves, 14.3.)

Chapter fourteen

Special situations

14.1 Siblings in families of child sexual abuse

We must not forget siblings of sexually abused children. In the initial crisis of disclosure all attention is often entirely focused on the abused child whose siblings are easily excluded from the process. For the following six reasons siblings need to be involved in the disclosure process right from the beginning.

1 Brothers and sisters of sexually abused children may have been sexually abused themselves. Often only one child discloses initially and siblings need to be included in the evaluation in order to assess possible multiple abuse of other children in the family (see The family process, Chapter 3).
2 In cases of long-term sexual abuse siblings often know what has happened. If asked they will often not admit to it because they are frightened and know that they are not supposed to know. Witnessing sexual abuse of a sibling or even only knowing about it can in itself be extremely traumatic and children may for their own emotional protection want to forget what they know.

I have seen several siblings, girls and boys who had known about or witnessed sexual abuse of a brother or a sister and who had become very disturbed. In one case a boy developed 'blackouts' and was at one stage suspected of having epilepsy, which was not confirmed. He had been massively traumatised by the knowledge of the abuse of his sister which had lasted for nearly 10 years.

Another boy whose sister had been sexually abused by her father for many years wanted to protect her from boys in the neighbourhood by threatening them with large kitchen knives. This boy desperately identified with his abusing father and needed to pretend for his own protection that his father had not abused his sister. When confronted with the facts he became very frightened and discharged his tension by rocking back and forth, repeating continuously 'He hasn't done it, he hasn't done it, he hasn't done it.' The psychological denial and the identification with his abusing father was so strong that he wanted to be with his father in prison but still found it impossible to face that he was an abuser. Soon after disclosure this boy sexually assaulted a 4-year-old girl in the neighbourhood. (See Proof and belief, admission and owning up, 1.5.)

Children's 'no' to the question whether they have known about the abuse does not mean that they have not been involved, that they do not know or that they have not been affected by it. It often means that they are too frightened to talk. Siblings need to be involved in the initial evaluation in order to establish the degree of their involvement and knowledge of the abuse and to assess the effect the abuse of a sibling had on their mental health and on their emotional, cognitive and psycho-social development.

3 Even in long-term sexual abuse in the family some children do not know that abuse has happened. These children are nonetheless from the very beginning of the disclosure fully affected by child protective and legal investigations and by other events in the family. Non-abused children often suffer the consequences of family breakdown, placements in care and separations as much as sexually abused children. Siblings often experience that their father has suddenly disappeared and they see that sisters or brothers are taken into care with great haste and panic.

Siblings of sexually abused children need to know why often drastic actions are taken and they need to be able to adapt to new situations. Brothers and sisters are often left in the dark about what has really happened. They are confused and forced to make sense out of very anxiety-provoking situations without sufficient explanations and support. Siblings assume that the disappearance of a father or a sister or brother is partly due to their own behaviour and they are frightened that they themselves may suddenly be taken away and removed from the family.

4 One of the important functions of the Primary Therapeutic Intervention is to avoid scapegoating of the abused child by other family members. Siblings of sexually abused children need to be present at the first family meeting as responsibility meeting, where the issue of responsibility for the abuse and the consequences of disclosure are dealt with. Only too often we see that sexually abused children are accused by brothers and sisters for having taken their father away and that they are blamed for the family breakdown. (See Aims and steps in the Primary Therapeutic Intervention, 6.2; Basic mechanisms in the therapeutic process, 6.3; The first family meeting as reality-creating responsibility meeting, 9.11.)

5 In some cases I have seen the opposite reaction to blaming when non-abused children have become excessively protective and over-involved with abused brothers and sisters. Older brothers and sisters can feel entirely responsible for the abuse of younger siblings.

Older siblings often feel guilty for not having protected the younger child from sexual abuse. An 11-year-old girl developed panic attacks and severe obsessional checking behaviour. Sexual abuse of her younger sister was revealed and it emerged that the girl had witnessed the abuse. She was over-protective of her younger sister and tried desperately to keep male adults under control. Over-protective older siblings need to be included in treatment in order to deal with the guilt feeling and with their inappropriate attempts to parent and to protect the abused child. Some sexually abused older siblings did even bear their own abuse without disclosure until the onset of sexual abuse of a younger sibling drove them to overcome their fear of disclosing.

6 Finally we need to keep in mind that all attention is usually focused on the abused child. The physical and emotional care of siblings can be severely neglected during this period. The phenomenon of relative emotional deprivation of siblings is well known from siblings of children with severe and life-threatening illnesses.

I increasingly try to involve siblings in the initial disclosure interview. I often ask all siblings to attend and make a quick initial assessment as to whether it is appropriate to conduct a conjoint disclosure session. In many cases conjoint disclosure interviews are inappropriate. It is then important to organise seperate meetings with the siblings immediately after the disclosure interview with the abused child. This has led to further disclosure of sexual abuse in other siblings. (See Preparation for disclosure, Chapter 8; Disclosure, Chapter 9.)

After the disclosure siblings of sexually abused children need to be involved in further family meetings which deal with the effects of the abuse itself and of the disclosure on each family member and on the family as a whole. The work on parenting should always include non-abused siblings. Siblings have often suffered from the lack of intergenerational boundaries in other ways and have taken on inappropriate parental roles. (See The family process, Chapter 3; Aims and steps in the Primary Therapeutic Intervenion, 6.2.)

14.2 The Hansel-and-Gretel syndrome and sexual abuse by older brothers

Abusing brothers and under-age sex offenders mainly come from four backgrounds:

1 Many under-age sexual abusers have been sexually abused themselves. Certainly boys under the age of 15 who become sexual abusers in any form must always potentially be considered as being sexually abused themselves (see Adolescent sex offenders who are sexually abused themselves, 14.3).

2 Boys in families where siblings have been sexually abused seem at high risk of becoming sexual abusers. Even if these boys have not been abused themselves they often know about the abuse and sometimes have witnessed the sexual interaction. These boys are at high risk of becoming abusers out of identification with the abusing father (see Siblings in families of child sexual abuse, 14.1).

3 Adolescent sex offenders are often boys who grew up in a parent–child relationship which was on the one hand emotionally depriving and at the same time sexualised. These boys then grow up with a very low self-esteem and at the same time with a very low frustration tolerance. In order to gain emotional satisfaction and to release tension these boys resort to sexual abuse of siblings or other children.

4 Many under-age sexual abusers have been severely physically abused and have suffered severe emotional deprivation.

Sexual abuse of younger children by older brothers has two very distinct dynamics. Brothers in late adolescence or early adulthood who are much older than the abused child are often in a quasi-parental authority position and the abuse of younger siblings can be understood very much like abuse by fathers and father figures. We find the same difference in terms of structural dependence and immaturity and the same dynamics of child sexual abuse as syndrome of secrecy for the child and as syndrome of secrecy and addiction for the abuser. In these cases it has been helpful to follow, with the appropriate variations, the same aims and steps in the Primary Therapeutic Intervention that we need to achieve in sexual abuse by fathers and father-figures. (See Responsibility, participation, guilt, blame and power, 1.2; Child sexual abuse as syndrome of secrecy, and of addiction, 2.1, 2.2, 2.3; Aims and steps in the Primary Theapeutic Intervention, 6.2; The first family meeting as responsibility meeting, 9.11; Working with sexual abusers, 7.4.)

Sibling abuse by brothers who are not much older than the abused child can have a very different dynamic and must not be confused with abuse by brothers who are *in loco parentis*. Sexual abuse by nearly-same aged siblings is often an expression of the 'Hansel-and-Gretel syndrome'. Hansel and Gretel were two children who were sent away by their parents and who got lost in the woods and had only each other's company, comfort and care to survive. The abuse by nearly- same aged brothers does not show the characteristics of great difference in maturation between abuser and child and there is no structural dependence in an authority relationship between the abused child and the equally immature abuser.

In the Hansel-and-Gretel syndrome it can be unhelpful to use the terms 'abuser' and 'victim'. Sexual abuse by nearly-same aged brothers is usually part of a general syndrome of emotional deprivation in which both children may also have been severely physically or sexually abused by parent figures. The abuse between nearly-same-aged children is often much more of an equal sexual relationship in which both children try to give and to receive some distorted form of mutual satisfaction, comfort and care. The sexual abuse is a perverted and confused form of emotional care in which the sexual stimulation and arousal is a poor and sad substitute for absent parental emotional care.

In the Hansel-and-Gretel syndrome both children need to be treated as equal victims of emotional deprivation and abuse by adults with the sexual relationship as a secondary attempt to survive. The only important differences which always need to be addressed are the gender-specific differences of male and female sexual experiences and sexual roles within the sexual interaction of the Hansel-and-Gretel syndrome (see Confusion on different levels of dependency, 3.1).

The Hansel-and-Gretel syndrome of emotionally deprived and lost children may still create a girl who shows symptoms of sexualisation and victim behaviour and a boy who may grow up to become a sex offender and a sexual abuser. Although we find in the Hansel-and-Gretel syndrome a much greater mutual dependency for care and comfort and a greater equality in relating, both children learn in the long term that relating emotionally is identical to relating in sexual ways. This emotio-sexual confusion is translated in girls into sexualised victim behaviour and greater vulnerability for further abuse, and in boys into sexualised abuser-behaviour with a danger of sexual abuse in other relationships. Emotionally deprived and physically abused children often have very low frustration tolerance and underdeveloped coping mechanism. Direct forms of sexual activities can be the only way of achieving tension relief. Children of the Hansel-and-Gretel syndrome are deprived of emotional care and often have a very low frustration tolerance. They may have no other means to feel good and to achieve tension relief other than direct forms of mutual sexual stimulation. In the Hansel-and-Gretel syndrome we come nearest to an understanding of child sexual abuse as syndrome of addiction for both the child and the abuser. (See The individual process, Chapter 2.)

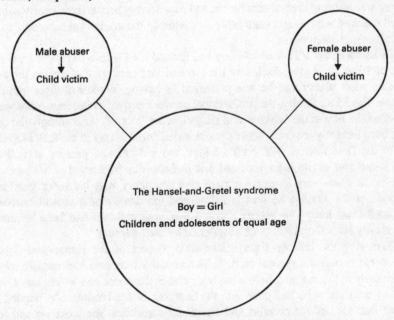

Figure 14.1 Adult abusers and the Hansel-and-Gretel syndrome

Adolescent boys in the Hansel-and-Gretel syndrome must not be treated like adult abusers and girls must not be seen like other child victims abused by parenting figures. Although the relationship can look like an adult–child abuse the issue of responsibility and structural dependency needs to be addressed differently. Both children need to take equally the appropriate responsibility for their inappropriate sexual relationship. Girls need to take their share of responsibility in order to be able to deal with any sexualised behaviour resulting from the emotio-sexual confusions. It is also important to avoid inappropriate scapegoating of brothers as solely responsible for the sexual acts even if they have seemed to be more active in the abuse.

The difference became very clear in one family in which a 12-year-old girl had sexual relationships with two brothers aged 13 and 19. The older brother took very much the father role in a chaotic household in which he was the authority figure. Both brothers had previously been sexually abused by their own father. The later abuse of the younger sister by the older brother took place in the context of violence. He forced the younger sister into sexual abuse in a way which was indistinguishable from sexual abuse by the father. The girl had no sense of control and she was terrified and confused about what happened to her.

In contrast the abuse by the younger brother carried no violence and the sexual act was a much more mutual interaction. The girl had a very different relationship to this younger brother. She talked with fear, anger and confusion about the older brother, but with much more warmth and fondness about the younger brother. There was a strong mutual attachment and dependency between the nearly-same-aged children who sought each other's comfort in the mutual sexual stimulation of full sexual intercourse.

In another case a 15-year-old boy had abused his 13-year-old sister from the age of 10 to 12. At the disclosure the professional network had treated the boy like an adult abuser and he was portrayed as having forced his sister into the abuse. The foster family, the professional network and the children unanimously labelled the boy as the 'abuser' and the girl as the 'victim'. Accordingly the boy had been instantly removed while the girl was allowed to stay in the foster family.

In the first session with both siblings, the girl showed passive sexualised behaviour and victim behaviour and said that she was frightened of her brother. The brother was very aggressive, explosive and angry with his sister. For long periods of the session he was brooding and the danger of a violent outburst radiated from him. The history showed that both children had been severely physically abused and had been abandoned by their parents.

Exploring the brother–sister relationship as part of the Hansel-and-Gretel syndrome revealed a typical picture. The sexual intercourse had usually taken place early in the morning before anybody else in the house had woken up. It was in fact the sister who had gone into the bedroom of her brother. She wanted to come into his bed for comfort and emotional care when she woke up and felt lonely and frightened. This relationship then turned into a sexual relationship which was as much initiated by the sister as by the brother. Once it had started the brother took a typical active male role and the sister a passive role in the sexual interaction itself.

The wish of both children for parental emotional care showed how much the sexual relationship was a desperate attempt to get mutual emotional parenting and to receive distorted closeness and comfort from each other. It was crucial to understand that despite the stereotyped behaviour of both children both had been equally involved. After the first session the girl told the foster parents at home that she felt she had been as active as her brother and was as much responsible as he was, and she wanted to apologise to him for accusing him of being an abuser. It was then that she disclosed that she had been the one who kept going into the brother's bedroom when he was still asleep. The mistaken labelling of this Hansel-and-Gretel syndrome as adult–child sexual abuse was the result of the confusion in the professional network that once the sexual interaction itself had started the boy indeed became more active and did not allow the sexual interaction to stop until he had found tension relief in ejaculation whilst the girl had behaved passively.

The therapeutic problem in the Hansel-and-Gretel syndrome lies in the mutual desexualisation of emotional relationships of both children. Therapy needs to include the re-introduction of modesty for both children and both need to find non-sexualised ways for tension relief under stress. In the Hansel-and-Gretel syndrome both children need equal emotional parenting and the boy still needs as much real external parenting as the girl. Therapy needs to include shared sessions where the sibling relationship can be re-examined and separate individual or group sessions where each child can develop a separate sense of autonomy, privacy and relating and where they can deal with the different gender-specific problems of the girl's female and the boy's male sexual identity. (See Aims and steps in the Primary Therapeutic Intervention, 6.2; Concurrent forms of therapy, 7.1; The need for behaviour modification, 7.3.4.)

14.3 Child and adolescent sex offenders who are sexually abused themselves

Child and adolescent sex offenders can be part of kinships of sexual abuse where many family members have been sexually abused and have in turn become abusers. Adolescent sex offenders who have been sexually abused themselves are a separate group who do not fit in either category of victims or abusers. They are both. Child and adolescent sex offenders who are abused themselves are neither 'mad' nor 'bad'. They are both. They are irresponsible and they have psychological problems. Both aspects need to be addressed separately but in an interlocking Primary Therapeutic Intervention (see The Primary Therapeutic Intervention, Chapter 6).

Adolescent sex offenders who have been sexually abused themselves need to take full responsibility on the level of their current psycho-sexual development for the abuse they themselves have committed. To send adolescent sex offenders to therapy without age-appropriate legal responsibility-taking for their own abusive behaviour can lead to non-therapeutic therapy. Conducting therapy only gives the adolescent the message that he has become an offender not because he is 'bad' and irresponsible but because he is entirely 'mad'. He is in fact considered so disturbed that people think he cannot even take age-appropriate responsibility for the badness he has committed for which anybody else who is not 'mad' would have to own up legally. Therapy alone can lead to the exact opposite of the wanted effect. It decreases the adolescent's sense of self-control and responsibility and increases low self-esteem and the stigma of being 'mad'. The message that the offender is totally 'mad' and not also 'bad' leads to an increased risk of re-offence. To deal with sexually abused adolescent sex offenders like adult offenders is equally inappropriate and can carry a similar risk of creating re-offenders. (See From mad to bad, Chapter 1.)

We need to employ a complementary approach which fully integrates legal and therapeutic aspects of abusing and being abused. A 14-year-old very disturbed boy who had been abused himself had sexually abused a pre-school girl in the neighbourhood. He had tried to penetrate her and was referred for assessment and therapy. In close co-operation between police, prosecution service and mental-health workers the boy had to make a statement and was fined a small sum of money which he had to earn himself. This gave the boy a sense of control over the process of responsibility-taking and reparation for his offence.

The second and even more therapeutically effective ruling of the court was for the boy to meet the abused child and her parents in an apology session. This was obviously a major task for the abuser which took several months of therapeutic preparation. After careful planning the apology session became a highly therapeutic event for the boy and the girl and her family. Legal and statutory actions had been taken in the context of a Primary Therapeutic Intervention in which the legal process itself became highly therapeutic. After the abuser work and the apology session, issues of the boy's own sexual abuse could be addressed in subsequent therapy.

The abuser aspect needs to be addressed first before aspects of children's own abuse can be considered in concurrent individual and family therapy. If we do victim work before abuser work the victim aspect becomes exploited as an excuse for the refusal to own up to the abuser behaviour. The complementary legal and therapeutic process enables sexual-abusing children who have been abused themselves to deal with their own confusion as sexual abusers and as victims of sexual abuse.

14.4 Children of incest

To acknowledge children of incest is still very much taboo. We have not yet learned to consider that adolescent pregnancy can be the result of child sexual abuse in the family. Girls say that they do not know who made them pregnant. They say that they have been at a party and that they got drunk and met a man and that they had slept with him, but that they do not know who he was. Then we find behind this story that it was in fact not somewhere at a party, that the girl was not at all drunk and that she did not get pregnant by somebody she did not know but by her own father, brother or other relative and at home in her own bed. Pregnancy and abortion counselling for girls who have become pregnant through child sexual abuse obviously needs to be conducted with the greatest care.

Once children of incest are born, the vexed question is whether, when and how these children should learn about their biological father. This question becomes even more urgent in the growing children's rights movement and in cases of adoption where children are later entitled to learn about their biological origins. The question therefore needs to be considered from the separate perspectives of children's rights and mental health (see Legal abuse and psychological damage, 1.1).

Children have the right to know where they come from. Children also have the right to grow up in a protective environment which takes account of structural dependence and immaturity and which safeguards the child's psychological development and emotional well-being. From a developmental point of view it seems quite inappropriate to confront a young and immature child with the confusing concept that the man who the child knows as 'grandad' is also the father. Children's right to grow up under psychological protection of their mental well-being does hold beyond adolescence until early adulthood.

Two examples may illustrate one possible way of handling the situation. I am fully aware that the issues involved are complex and that I may neglect important aspects. A 3-year-old boy was adopted by young parents who knew that their adoptive son was the result of father–daughter incest. The parents approached me for some counselling about how, when and what to say to the child about his biological origins. They wanted to tell the child about the adoption as soon as they felt he was able to understand and they did not know whether they should also tell the child that he was the product of incest. I suggested that they did not tell the boy of his biological origin of incest before adulthood and certainly not before late adolescence.

A child may very well learn about adoption already in childhood without confusion and mental damage. Adoption as alternative parenting is related to the parenting role of parents which even relatively young children can understand. To make sense of the notion of incest requires the mastery of the concept of adult sexual relationship and intergenerational boundaries. Children are much more able to accept that adoptive parents stand for the biological parents who are unable to look after the child. They can hardly understand that a grandfather is at the very same time also a father. He then becomes neither and the child loses both. (See From mad to bad, Chapter 1; Confusion of different levels of dependency, 3.1.)

In a second case a 13-year-old girl who lived in a children's home had only her grandfather as sole attachment figure and as the only family relationship in her life. Her mother had abandoned her and had left her in the children's home. There was no contact between the child and the mother. At the age of 13 the girl wanted to find out who her father was. She wanted to meet him and had the hope that she could live with him. It was known to social services that the grandfather was also her father and some colleagues in social services felt that the child had the right to know this fact.

I agreed with the right of the adolescent girl to know who her father was if that was known. As mental-health professional however I had to add the complementary right of the child for protection of her mental health and psychological development. The child's right to know her father, needed to be weighed against the fact that the very moment when she would learn that her grandfather was in fact her father, she would not only still not gain a father, but would also lose her grandfather as the only important relationship in her life. This element, which was especialy poignant in this case, holds for all cases of children of incest. By learning that their grandfather is also their father they lose both father and grandfather because they need to be able to rely on the clear structural differentiation between parent and grandparent.

The second mental-health consideration concerns the protection of the child's own psycho-sexual development. To tell a 13-year-old girl, who in her adolescent curiosity wants to know who her father is, about her origin of incest will throw this girl most likely into deep confusions about her own personal and sexual identity. Biological, physiological and psychological changes in adolescents are, in themselves, already deeply confusing and require considerable degrees of adaptation. It is crucial that children of incest have the chance to establish some adult identity and especially some adult sexual identity first before they learn of their origins of incest.

My recommendation was that both rights – the child's right to grow up under the protection of her mental health and psychosexual development and her legal right to know her origins – needed to be weighed in the light of crucial developmental factors. I suggested that the 13-year-old girl should be told at this point that her father was unknown, but that she should be told the full background as a young adult. At that stage she could even be told that her origins had in fact been known before, but that it had been regarded as in the best interest of her personal and psycho-sexual development not to tell her before she could deal with the sexual aspects as a fully grown-up woman.

14.5 The problem of the single father

It is very difficult to decide how to proceed in cases of sexual abuse by single fathers who are the only carer and possibly the only attachment figure in the child's life. Fathers as single parents have paternal and maternal functions and there seem to be two different relationship patterns between sexually abusing single fathers and their children. One group of strongly 'maternal' fathers had after separation and divorce chosen to sacrifice a more typical male career for the task of child rearing. These fathers had a great emotional investment in their children. The other group was living with the abused child because the wife or female partner had left them. The child had stayed behind as pseudo-partner for the father and looked after the father as much as the father looked after the child.

In single-father families we often find a strong mutual emotional dependence between father and child. The father is often the only attachment figure for the child as much as the child is the only confidant for the father. Children often pity single fathers and are very protective of them. Often they feel that they help and support the father through the abuse in the belief that otherwise he would be unable to cope. In one case a girl was frightened that her father would become severely depressed and suicidal without the abuse. Another girl told how she felt that her father, who looked after her and her two siblings, would be unable to cope and would collapse. The open sacrifice and the accepted victim role of the child did not make the abuse less frightening and less disturbing for the child.

Sexually abused children of single fathers are frightened of losing the only parent they have. The common emotional partner role for the abused child has the effect that children in single-father families can be very loyal to the abuser despite great suffering through the abuse. To these children, protection from sexual abuse and safety from the abuser often also mean the loss of the only parenting figure and the only emotional relationship and attachment in their life that matters. Loneliness, guilt feelings and desperation after separation from the father as abuser can be very marked in sexually abused children in single-father families. Mutual emotional dependency between abusing father and child often leads to increased denial and strong collusions against therapy. This problem is especially marked with adolescent daughters who have assumed a close pseudo-partner role.

A girl in individual therapy hinted at sexual abuse and displayed serious symptoms of self-mutilation and self-harming behaviour. The attempt to proceed from a second-line suspicion and partial disclosure to a full disclosure was unsuccessful. Although the relationship with the father included damaging sexual abuse she was so frightened of losing him and felt so protective of him that she did not want to disclose openly in therapy although she also talked about suicidal thoughts and feelings. Whenever she came close to a full disclosure and whenever the abuse was taken up by the therapist, she totally withdrew. It was a very difficult balancing act for the therapist to communicate to the girl that he understood the child's predicament. When he began to conduct denial work and raised the issue of sexual abuse explicitly the girl became very angry and hostile. At the same time she asked the therapist indirectly for protection from the abuse but she never dared to disclose. She talked excessively about her fear of losing her father whom she did not want to lose because she had nobody else. (See The individual process, Chapter 2; Dealing with primary denial, 10.6.)

Denial work in single-father families needs to address the predicament of the single-parent family first before dealing with the abuse itself. Child protective and therapeutic actions need to take into account the fact that children will often only disclose sexual abuse by single fathers when they have found another parental figure they can trust and confide in. Any relationship in the wider family or in the social environment of the child which could assume a parenting function needs to be actively fostered although relatives need to be chosen carefully. Another way to help children to disclose is to involve fathers in treatment for general parental problems and to encourage them to find other adult relationships. Both approaches to sexual abuse in single-father families require great patience. We need to be especially reminded that the disclosure of child sexual abuse often takes time and that panic and premature actions may make us feel good as professionals but do not help the child. (See The professional network, Chapter 5; Crisis of disclosure – crisis of professionals and family crisis, 8.1; Placement with relatives, 10.4.)

In fully acknowledged cases of sexual abuse in single-father families it is important to keep the father involved in treatment right from the beginning. The impulse of professionals to separate the child from the father, not just for protection from further abuse, but to wipe him out as the central, emotional attachment figure for the child, is a great temptation and a seemingly easy but often very damaging solution. The child is usually placed with foster parents and no contact is allowed to the father. An early responsibility session with the father and the child should be followed by intensive treatment of the father–child dyad in concurrent family sessions and group treatment or individual therapy. (See Confusion on different levels of dependency, 3.1; The primary therapeutic intervention, Chapter 6; Concurrent forms of therapy, 7.1.)

When we follow a Primary Therapeutic Intervention in single-father families we often need to place the child with mature and experienced foster parents who are able to give the child the space to work on the attachment to the father as parenting figure despite the abuse. But even experienced foster parents need continuing support to deal with the intensity of the dynamic of the father–child dyad. (See Placement with foster parents, 10.3; Working with foster parents, 12.17.)

14.6 Munchausen-syndrome-by-proxy in sexually abused mothers

I have seen some mothers who were very concerned and who made allegations that their children had been sexually abused. They were extremely protective and came forward immediately and firmly with clear allegations of child sexual abuse. Yet a close and careful assessment of the facts and circumstances did not seem to support the allegations. None of these cases were part of conflicts of separation or divorce. In each case, it turned out later, that the mothers themselves had been sexually abused as children. The allegations were part of a Munchausen-syndrome-by-proxy in which the mothers projected their own experience of sexual abuse on to their children. Under false allegations they sought help for their child instead of themselves.

There seemed to be a clinical pattern to the sexual-abuse form of the Munchausen-syndrome-by-proxy. It includes a referral in great urgency and a seemingly clear-cut situation of child sexual abuse. The close assessment of the circumstances of the alleged sexual abuse, the nature of the abuse and the circumstances of the alleged abuser increasingly diffuse the allegation. Over several weeks and months of treatment mothers increasingly contradicted themselves and described rather unlikely events and situations. In one case a mother asked in an acute crisis for help for her child whom she said had been sexually abused by her husband. She alleged having seen her husband sexually interfering with her 2-year-old daughter in the bathroom whilst bathing her. The mother was seemingly instantly protective. Several days after the alleged abuse she left home, taking the child without telling her husband in advance. She left only a short note to her husband to whom she had not mentioned any of her suspicions. She made urgent phone calls to several therapeutic clinics to ask for support but she did not want the police or social services to be involved.

Under close examination the situation in which she had seen her husband abusing her child became confused and contradictory but the mother insisted that she was absolutely sure that she had seen her husband sexually abusing her daughter. Having left home she became increasingly distressed, wanting with great urgency that her husband admit to the abuse, and she became more and more disturbed herself. There was a quality of distressed concern in this mother which indicated that she was not only acting as mother but that the alledged sexual abuse had triggered something in herself as a person in her own right. She distanced herself firmly from her husband and at the same time she did not want anything to be disclosed outside the family. She wanted to return home and live with him again immediately after his admission that he was a sexual abuser. She desperately wanted his admission but at the same time she did not want any real help for herself or for the child.

Contradictions, stories and actions which do not seem to fit, and increasingly changing and confusing accounts, seem to be typical of allegations of sexual abuse in the Munchausen-syndrome-by-proxy where mothers knowingly or unconsciously use false disclosures as their own personal cry for help for themselves, which they subsequently cannot accept and need to avoid. In sexually abused mothers the allegation can be triggered by a situation similar to that in which they themselves had been sexually abused. Or the allegation is made at a time when the child is the same age at which the mother was abused. In another case a mother alleged that an uncle had interfered with her daughter. The mother developed a permanently changing story of sexual abuse of her daughter which increasingly included other people and other situations, making it more and more clear that she was projecting her own problems and anxieties on to the child.

It seems that in the Munchausen-syndrome-by-proxy, mothers know at some level that they are projecting their own experience and anxieties on to the child because the allegations have such a different quality to those where both mothers and children have truly been sexually abused. In Munchausen-syndrome-by-proxy, mothers can persist with their alleged perception of a specific situation with an acute sense of personal urgency and despair. This is contrary to cases where mothers of sexually abused children have really been abused themselves. In these cases the reality of the repetition of sexual abuse in their own child usually becomes, soon after disclosure, very frightening to the mother, who then may withdraw from any contact, falling back into secondary secrecy and denial (see Sexually abused mothers of sexually abused children, 14.7).

The urgency and the strength of the allegations, which at times seem so obviously non-fitting with reality, the discrepancy between the demand for help and the non-involvement of police or child protective agencies and the active avoidance of real help form an important pattern of the Munchausen-syndrome-by-proxy in child sexual abuse. The demand for action for the child is accompanied by a difficult to describe, indirect but strong appeal for personal help which characterises these cases. On the other hand personal sexual abuse is fiercely denied and mothers evade effective help for themselves if the sexual abuse of the child is not believed. This makes the management of the Munchhausen-syndrome-by-proxy in child sexual abuse extremely difficult.

Any odd and not quite fitting allegation of child sexual abuse by mothers should raise the possibility of a Munchausen-syndrome-by proxy in which the parent projects her own childhood abuse on to her non-abused child. A highly attractive, highly paranoid woman accused her husband of child sexual abuse in a classic case of Munchausen-syndrome-by-proxy. The thorough assessment over several months revealed without doubt that no sexual abuse had taken place. Nevertheless the mother insisted on her allegation throughout and threatened to leave treatment. She continued her attempts to convince child protective services and therapists that her daughter had been sexually abused by her husband. She went to great lengths in this process to her own detriment and the detriment of the family. As in other forms of Munchausen-syndrome-by-proxy the case could not be contained in therapy and the mother went on accusing her husband until the family finally broke up.

14.7 Sexually abused mothers of sexually abused children

In many cases of child sexual abuse mothers and fathers have been sexually abused themselves. Engaging families in treatment where the mother has been sexually abused herself adds another dimension of complexity. Sexually abused mothers can be very ambivalent about their wish to find help for their children. On one hand they may want urgent help for the sexually abused child and this request for help can become very acute in a crisis. Yet when the crisis decreases we often see a wish to withdraw from treatment. I certainly lost two cases of sexually abused children where mothers had been sexually abused themselves when I was unable to deal both with the child's and the mother's sexual abuse at the same time.

Sexually abused mothers come easily into a vicious circle of avoidance. They cannot deal as mothers with the abuse of the child because it reminds them of their own abuse and they cannot deal as women in their own right with their victimisation because they have to face the fact that similar suffering has been inflicted on their child. The role as mother of a sexually abused child and the role as woman who has been sexually abused in her own right must not be confused and it is important to keep the mother's and the child's abuse separate.

Sometimes mothers disclose their own abuse during the treatment of sexually abused children. In severe and traumatic cases of maternal abuse the disclosure and the open acknowledgement of sexual abuse of their own children drive these mothers into a terrible predicament. They may desperately want help for their child but at the same time they are unable to face the abuse of their child because it provokes so much covered trauma and unfinished issues of their own abuse.

The anxiety in facing their own abuse is often compounded by severe guilt feelings about the failure to protect their child from exactly the same trauma the mother has suffered and wanted to avoid for her child. In a defensive reaction sexually abused mothers often take flight from treatment or show increased hostility towards the abused child.

Increased and unexplained open maternal hostility towards a sexually abused child should always lead to the suspicion of sexual abuse in the mother herself, when her own experience prevents her from becoming protective and from being able to face the sexual abuse of the child. Guilt feelings, low self-esteem and hostility towards the child make for a very different dynamic in sexually abused mothers of sexually abused children than in sexually abused mothers who seek help in a Munchausen-syndrome-by-proxy (see Munchausen-syndrome-by-proxy in sexually abused mothers, 14.6).

After seeking help in the initial crisis of disclosure, sexually abused mothers of sexually abused children often threaten to leave therapy and withdraw again. They feel too frightened about facing their own abuse as women or their guilt feelings as mothers and just want to forget. In the process they also sabotage the treatment of the sexually abused child.

Initial treatment needs to concentrate seemingly entirely on the sexual abuse of the child and not on the mother's abuse, but the mother's abuse needs to be constantly addressed indirectly in the abuse of the child as long as it is impossible openly and directly to talk about the mother's own experiences. The most helpful techniques are indirect approaches which deal with the mother's own sexual abuse through the child as 'Third Person' until the mother can cope with direct work on her own sexual abuse. (See Proof and belief, admission and owning up, 1.5; The individual process in context, 2.4; Explicit therapeutic permission to disclose, 8.5.)

When the mother becomes frightened to talk about sexual abuse or when she is frightened or angry with me as a man, I would say, not to her but to the child, 'I think you are very frightened of me today and you are an expert in showing me a lovely poker face and you may feel very angry and may not want to come back next time because I am such a horrible man.' Talking to children therefore has two functions. One function is to talk about their own sexual abuse. The second function is to use the communication with the child as 'The Story of the Third Person' and as indirect message to the mother that we understand her anxieties about talking of her own abuse. Implicitly addressing in the communication to the child all possible anxieties which may prevent the mother from facing herself or her own abuse often helps mothers to face their own anxieties.

I also use indirect techniques and 'The Story of the Third Person' when I have strong suspicions of maternal sexual abuse which has not yet been disclosed.

Using the child as the 'Third Person' for telling the story about possible maternal sexual abuse often produces an instant and visible relief in the mother. I would usually make the remark about the child's 'poker face' in a humorous way. I would then turn to the mother and say, 'Are you good at having a poker face and are you good at bottling up?', only to turn back to the child instantly when the mother shows any signs of distress. I would immediately comment indirectly on these signs of distress in the mother by talking to the child about fears which abused children have, addressing in fact the fears of the mother. In one case the mother was extremely ambivalent towards men. She was very drawn to men but was also extremely frightened. I was very aware of being a man when I talked to her and her sexually abused daughter and I suggested to the 3-year-old child how horrible men were and how much little girls were sometimes frightened of them. I did this although this child was in fact frightened of men very little. It was my way of addressing the mother's anxiety about me as a man in the context of the history of her own sexual abuse.

Sometimes I have been able to link the abuse of the mother and of the child by making the mother into 'the expert' on sexual abuse. I have said things like, 'You obviously know how it feels to be sexually abused and you have come through it, how do you think we should talk to your child?' We still need to address the mother's own anxiety but we can link her anxiety to the child's own abuse in a way which helps mothers to feel competent and able to help their children. The positive connotation of the mother's own abuse as positive parental skill to help the child can be extremely successful in mothers who are able to cope with their anxiety.

Another way to begin to address the mother's own abuse would be if the mother's GP or a health visitor or community nurse would see the mother regularly for some other medical reason and would use the contact to begin talking to the mother about her own abuse in the context of a normalised and less anxiety-provoking medical context until the mother is ready for more specific help for her own abuse. The initial contact can also be made by social workers or other professionals who have regular contact with the mother for reasons other than the abuse. Such arrangement always needs close co-operation between the professional who is in contact with the mother and the professional who deals with the family and the abused child. Once the maternal sexual abuse is truly in the open it can be brought back into the work on the child's abuse in sessions with mother and child. (See The interprofessional process, 5.1; Concurrent forms of therapy, 7.1; The Primary Therapeutic Intervention, Chapter 6.)

14.8 Family-of-origin work for sexually abused adults

Many sexually abused adults and certainly sexually abused parents of sexually abused children need to do some family-of-origin work on their own abuse. Family-of-origin work for sexually abused adults can be done indirectly in individual work or directly in family sessions. (See Sexually abused profes-sionals, 11.2; Sexually abused mothers of sexually abused children, 14.7.)

1 Indirect work

In young adults where the abuser is still alive and available, indirect family-of-origin work can serve as preparation for a direct confrontation with the abuser. In young sexually abused adults, guided fantasy, psycho-drama and role play can be helpful to prepare a family meeting. In family-meetings-by-proxy hypothetical anticipatory problem-solving questioning can be extremely helpful. We can ask the adult, 'If your parents were sitting here hearing you making the allegations of sexual abuse, who would believe you first?' We can continue on the hypothetical 'as if' level covering the initial steps of the Primary Therapeutic Intervention. (See Aims and steps in the Primary Therapeutic Intervention, 6.2; Family-session-by-proxy, 9.13; The use of different family therapy techniques, 12.10.)

2 Direct family-of-origin work

Nearly without exception, sexually abused adults who have not disclosed in childhood say things like, 'I wish I could once ask my father whether he was aware of what he did to me and I wish I could ask my mother why she did not listen to me and stop the abuse.' There is a great urge even in later adulthood directly to confront the abuser in family-of-origin. This relates to the need for sexually abused people to be allowed for once to call abuse abuse and by so doing creating the abuse as an individual and family reality. If the abuser is still alive, family-of-origin work as reality-creating responsibility session can be highly therapeutic. (See Child sexual abuse as syndrome of secrecy, 2.1; The family process, Chapter 3.)

The family-of-origin session can take the form of a confrontation session or reconciliation session. Very often there is a great urge to confront the abuser, but in most cases a reconciliation session should be attempted. A reconciliation session requires previous therapeutic work to confront the abuser indirectly in therapy before a family-of-origin session as responsibility session can be successful. Confrontation work does not only bear the danger of a general deterioration in the relationship between the abused adult and her or his own parents. Confrontation sessions with abusers who are too old and frail to cope with the confrontation do often induce renewed guilt feelings in the abused adult without leading to a therapeutic solution.

We need to keep in mind that abused young adults are often dismissed by their parents as mad or as liars. Parental denial and accusation can reactivate very traumatic previous rejections and scapegoating in the abused adult, and such a family-of-origin session can be devastating even if the abused adult thought he could cope with denial and rejection. It is therefore necessary to prepare any family-of-origin session very carefully. We need to consider whether the abuser is still healthy and fit enough to be able to handle a disclosure in adulthood. Any abused adult needs to go through role play or family-sessions-by-proxy with hypothetical anticipatory problem-solving questioning in order to be prepared for possible allegations of lying and fantasising by the abuser and other family members. If abused adults are unable to bear the possibly renewed scapegoating by their own parents, further individual preparatory and therapeutic work needs to be done before a family-of-origin session can be considered.

References

Alexander, P.C. (1985) A systems theory conceptualization of incest. *Family Process, 24*: 79–88.

Baker, A.W. (1983) Report on reader survey: child sexual abuse. Magazine *"19"*, May 1983.

Baker, A.W. and Duncan, S.P. (1985) Child sexual abuse – a study of prevalence in Great Britain. *Child Abuse & Neglect, 9*: 4.

Bastiaans, J. (1957) *Psychosomatische gevolgen van Onderdrukking en Verzet.* Noord-Hollandische Uitgevers Maatschappij, Amsterdam.

Beezley Mrazek, P. (1981a) Group psychotherapy with sexually abused children. In Beezley Mrazek, P. and Kempe, C.H. (Eds) *Sexually Abused Children and Their Families.* Pergamon Press, Oxford.

Beezley Mrazek, P. (1981b) Definition and recognition of sexual child abuse: historical and cultural perspectives. In Beezley Mrazek, P. and Kempe, C.H. (Eds) *Sexually Abused Children and Their Families.* Pergamon Press, Oxford.

Berliner, L. and Stevens, D. (1982) Clinical issues in child sexual abuse. In Conte, J.R. and Shore, D. (Eds) *Social Work and Sexual Abuse.* Haworth, New York.

Bion, W.R. (1961) *Experiences in Groups and Other Papers.* Tavistock Publications, London; republished Routledge, 1989.

Bowden, P. (1983) Madness or badness? *British Journal of Hospital Medicine,* December 1983, 388–94.

Eist, H.I., Mandel, A. (1968) Family treatment of ongoing incest behaviour. *Family Process, 7*: 216–32.

Finkelhor, D. (1979) *Sexually Victimized Children.* Free Press, New York.

Finkelhor, D. (1980) Risk factors in the sexual victimization of children. *Child Abuse & Neglect, 4*: 265–73.

Finkelhor, D. (1984) *Child Sexual Abuse: New Theory and Research.* Free Press, New York.

Freud, A. (1981) A psychoanalyst's view of sexual abuse by parents. In Beezley Mrazek P. and Kempe, C.H. (Eds) *Sexually Abused Children and Their Families.* Pergamon Press, Oxford.

Furniss, T. (1983a) Mutual influence and interlocking professional–family process in the treatment of child sexual abuse and incest. *Child Abuse & Neglect, 7*: 207–23.

Furniss, T. (1983b) Family process in the treatment of intra-familial child sexual abuse. *Journal of Family Therapy, 5*: 263–78.

Furniss, T. (1984a) Conflict-avoiding and conflict-regulating patterns in incest and child sexual abuse. *Acta Paedopsychiatrica, 50*: 299–313.

Furniss, T. (1984b) Organizing a therapeutic approach to intra–familial child sexual abuse. *Journal of Adolescence, 7*: 309–17.

Furniss, T. (1988) Klinischer Verlauf in der Intervention von Sexueller Kindes-misshandlung, unpublished manuscript.

Furniss, T., Bentovim, A. and Kinston, W. (1983) Clinical process recording in focal family therapy. *Journal of Marital and Family Therapy*, 9(2): 147–70.

Furniss T., Bingley-Miller, L. and Bentovim, A. (1984) Therapeutic approach to child sexual abuse. *Archives of Disease in Childhood*, 59: 865–70.

Furniss, T., Bingley-Miller, L. and Van Elburg, A. (1988) Goal-oriented group treatment for sexually abused adolescent girls. *British Journal of Psychiatry*, 152: 97–106.

Gabriel, R.M. (1985) Anatomically correct dolls in the diagnosis of sexual abuse of children. *Journal of the Melanie Klein Society*, 3(2): 40–50.

Giarretto, H. (1982) *Integrated Treatment of Child Sexual Abuse: A Treatment and Training Manual.* Science and Behavior Books, Palo Alto.

Glaser, D. and Collins, C. (1985) The response of young, non-sexually abused children to anatomically correct rag dolls. Paper given to Association for Child Psychology and Psychiatry, London, 19 November 1986.

Glaser, D., Furniss, T. and Bingley, L. (1984) Focal family therapy: the assessment stage. *Journal of Family Therapy*, 6: 265–74.

Goodwin, J. (1982) *Sexual Abuse: Incest Victims and Their Families*, John Wright – PSG, Boston.

Goodwin, J. McCarty, T. and Di Vasto, P. (1981) Prior incest mothers of abused children. *Child Abuse & Neglect*, 5: 87–95.

Groth, A.N. (1979) *Men Who Rape: The Psychology of the Offender*. Plenum, New York.

Groth, A.N. (1982) The incest offender. In S. Sgroi (Ed.) *Handbook of Clinical Intervention in Child Sexual Abuse*. Lexington Books, Lexington, Mass.

Groth, N.A. and Burgess A.W. (1979) Sexual traumas in the life histories of rapists and child molesters. *Victimology*, 4: 10–16.

Gutheil, T.G. and Avery, N.C. (1977) Multiple overt incest as family defence against loss. *Family Process*, 16: 105–16.

Heap, K. (1985) *The Practice of Social Work with Groups – A Systematic Approach*, National Institute, Social Services Library, 49, Allen and Unwin, London.

Hobbs, C. and Wynne, J.M. (1986) Buggery in childhood – a common syndrome of child abuse. *The Lancet*, 4 October 1986, 792–6.

Hobbs, C. and Wynne, J.M. (1987) Child sexual abuse – an increasing rate of diagnosis. *The Lancet*, October 1987, 837–41.

Jones, D.P.H. (1986) Individual psychotherapy for the sexually abused child. *Child Abuse & Neglect*, 10: 377–85.

Jones, D.P.H. and McGraw, J.M. (1987) Reliable and fictitious accounts of sexual abuse of children. *Journal of Interpersonal Violence*, 2: 25–45.

Jones, D.P.H. and McQuiston, M. (1986) *Interviewing the Sexually Abused Child*. Vol. 6 of a Series, 2nd edition. The C. Henry Kempe National Center for the Prevention and Treatment of Child Abuse and Neglect, Denver, Colorado.

Kinston, W. and Bentovim, A. (1981) Constructing a focal formulation and hypothesis in family therapy. *Australian Journal of Family Therapy*, 4(1) 37–50.

Kroth, J.A. (1979) *Child Sexual Abuse: Analysis of a Family Therapy Approach*. C.C. Thomas, Springfield.

Lustig, N., Dresser, J.W., Spellman, S.W. and Murray, T.B. (1966) Incest: a family group survival pattern. *Archives of Family Psychiatry*, 14: 31–40.

Macarthy, B. (1983) Therapeutic Problems in Working with Victims of Incest. Paper given to Royal College of Psychiatrists' Annual Conference.

Machotka, P., Pittman, F.S. and Flomenhaft, K. (1967) Incest as a family affair. *Family Process*, 6: 98–116.

Meiselman, K.C. (1978) *Incest: A Psychological Study of Causes and Effects with Treatment Recommendations*. Jossey-Bass, San Francisco.

Minuchin, S. (1974) *Families and Family Therapy*. Harvard University Press, Cambridge, Mass.

Mrazek, P., Lynch, M. and Bentovim, A. (1983) Recognition of child sexual abuse in the United Kingdom. *Child Abuse & Neglect*, 7: 147–54.

Oppenheimer, R., Howells, K., Palmer, R.L. and Chaloner, D.A. (1985) Adverse sexual experience in childhood and clinical eating disorders: a preliminary description. *Journal of Psychiatric Research*, *19*(2): 357–61.

Pincus, L. and Dare, C. (1978) *Secrets in the Family*. Faber and Faber, London.

Roberts, J. (1986) Fostering the sexually abused child. *Adoption and Fostering*, *10*(1): 8–11.

Rosenfeld, A.A. (1979) Endogamic incest and the victim-perpetrator model. *American Journal of Diseases of Children*, *133*: 406–10.

Rosenfeld, A.A., Nadelson, C.C., Kreiger, M. and Blackman, J.H. (1977) Incest and sexual abuse of children. *Journal of the American Academy of Child Psychiatry*, *16*: 327–39.

Russell, D.E.H. (1983) The incidence and prevalence of intrafamilial and extrafamilial sexual abuse of female children. *Child Abuse & Neglect*, 7: 133–46.

Schechter, M.D. and Roberge, L. (1976) Sexual exploitation. In Helfer, R.E. and Kempe, C.H. (Eds) *Child Abuse and Neglect: The Family and the Community*. Ballinger, Cambridge, Mass.

Selvini-Palazzoli, M., Cecchin, G., Prata, G. and Boscolo, L. (1978) *Paradox and Counterparadox*. Jason Aronson, New York.

Serrano, A.C., Zucker M.B., Howe, D.D. and Reposa, R.E. (1979) Ecology of abusive and non-abusive families. *Journal of the American Academy of Child Psychiatry*, *79*: 67–75.

Sgroi, S. (1982) *Handbook of Clinical Intervention in Child Sexual Abuse*. Lexington Books, Lexington, Mass.

Summit, R.C. (1983) The child sexual abuse accommodation syndrome. *Child Abuse & Neglect*, 7: 177–93.

Wild, N.J. and Wynne, J.M. (1986) Child sex rings. *British Medical Journal*, *293*: 183–5.

Index

facilitation 144, 148–9, 286–7; group
identity in 147–8; group structure
142–4; issues for boys in 150–2;
methods and techniques 145–7;
protection groups 140–2; setting up
285–7; for sex-ring children 329–30;
social skills in 147; splitting of
facilitators in 144, 148, 286–7
group work (parents); and sex-rings
329–30
guilt (abuser) 9–10, 11, 34
guilt (child) 29–30
Gutheil, T.G. 114

handover meeting 206, 230–3; in
fostering 316
Hansel-and-Gretel syndrome 333–7
Heimann, Paula 81
Hobbs, C. 22
homosexual abuse of boys 150–1

incest, children of 338–40
identification (psychic): of abused
colleagues 257; professional 80–3, 85
individuation, in group work 149
institutional conflicts: -by-proxy 87–8,
92, 101–4 passim; structural 87, 104;
see also splitting: in the professional
network
institutional responsibility 101–2
intergenerational perspective 14–15
interpretation: in group work 146, 148; in
therapy 42–4 passim, 157
interprofessional problems 255–77;
abused professionals 256–8; case
conferences 267–71; communicating
about abuse 255–6; 'expertise' 260–1;
hierarchies in consultations 263–4;
interprofessional support 258–60;
practical consultation problems 262–3;
preparing court reports 264–7;
scapegoating 271–3; statutory
hierarchies 272–5; see also
interprofessional process, professional
network
interprofessional process 80–113;
communication 301; mirroring
processes 80–2, 90–1, 101, 258, 259,
267–8; pre-intervention meeting and
191; preparation for disclosure 200–1;
respecting boundaries in 104–5;
secondary traumatisation in 16, 17; see

also Anonymous Diagnostic
Interprofessional Consultation,
interprofessional problems, Open
Diagnostic Interprofessional
Consultation, professional issues,
professional network
intervention: basic types of 60–79; choice
of type 64–5; need for consistency in
65; police 97–9; premature 100, 292;
see also non-intervention,
pre-intervention meeting, Primary
Child Protective Intervention, Primary
Punitive Intervention, Primary
Therapeutic Intervention

Jones, D.P.H. 182, 204, 205

Kempe, Henry 172

legal interviewing (child) 40, 204–5; and
permission to disclose 202–3
legal process 3–8, 87, 95–9 passim, 104,
106, 108–10; abuser therapy and
160–1, 167; abusers and the 234; child
privacy and 133; court-ordered therapy
313–16; court reports 264–7; family
process and 115; relapse and 305–6;
see also legal interviewing
loyalty (to abuser) 30–1, 49, 151, 326,
329–30
Lustig, N. 114
lying (child): and denial 24–5; under
threat 24

Machotka, P. 114
McQuiston, M. 182, 204, 205
Mandel, A. 114
masturbation, compulsive 34, 151
mirroring processes see interprofessional
process: mirroring processes
mothers 61, 284; abused, of abused
children 344–6; and child protection
97; –daughter relationships 48–9, 127,
234–5; denial work 304; and disclosure
206, 216–18 passim, 225; extrafamilial
abuse and 325; foster 318; helping
protective 301–3; mother–child dyad
120–1, 125, 129, 237, 304; non-belief
of 19–20, 234–5, 303–4, premature
involvement of 173; resistance to
treatment 66; role of non-abusing 48–9;
role in the therapeutic process 63–4; in